WEST VIRGINIANS IN THE AMERICAN REVOLUTION

Compiled by

Ross B. Johnston

Southern Historical Press, Inc.
Greenville, South Carolina

This volume was reproduced from
Excerpted copies of W.V. History
Vol. 1 (October 1939) –
Vol. 10 (October 1947)

All rights reserved. No part of this publication may be reproduced, stored in a retrieval system, transmitted in any form, posted on to the web in any form or by any means without the prior written permission of the publisher.

Please direct all correspondence and orders to:

www.southernhistoricalpress.com
or
SOUTHERN HISTORICAL PRESS, Inc.
PO BOX 1267
375 West Broad Street
Greenville, SC   29601
southernhistoricalpress@gmail.com

Originally published: West Virginia 1939-1947
Reprinted by:
Southern Historical Press, Inc.
Greenville, SC
ISBN #0-89308-990-7
All rights Reserved.
Printed in the United States of America

West Virginians in the American Revolution

The following pages of this and subsequent issues of this magazine will carry an alphabetical check list of Revolutionary soldiers who at one time or other lived in what is now West Virginia. This material has been assembled and edited by Ross B. Johnston. In the next few years, the Department of Archives and History hopes to publish this list in one volume, properly indexed. The public is invited to send in corrections as the material appears and to submit names of other Revolutionary soldiers whose authentic records qualify them to be listed among the other West Virginians who were with Washington's army.

This list of more than thirteen hundred sketches of Revolutionary soldiers from what is now West Virginia is offered with the full understanding that it represents only part of those who properly belong in this group. There are, for example, large lists of names, such as the roster of George Rogers Clark's forces of men, whose residences were uncertain, although many of the frontiersmen who joined Clark at Point Pleasant and Parkersburg on his western expedition lived west of the mountains.

The sources of this material are notes from the files of the Pension Office at Washington, from the pension applications in West Virginia counties, and from the minute books of the older West Virginia counties, copied by W. P. A. workers on the project sponsored by the West Virginia Commission on Historic and Scenic Markers; from notes of the Daughters of the American Revolution, Sons of the American Revolution, Sons of the Revolution, and other patriotic societies; and from a large miscellaneous group of published and private sources. It was found necessary to condense many extended notes in order to save space. Doubtless this omitted some points of interest, but in most instances the omissions were repetitions of facts common to many other cases.

(Note: Numbers and letters appearing with many names are references to files of Pension Bureau, War Department, Washington, D. C.)

ADAMS, JONATHAN
Service—New Jersey   Va. No. 6000   No. W-5596

Aged 61, 1818. Enlisted in New Jersey, 1778, in Fourth Troop, Fourth Jersey Regiment, Captain Plunkett, and in 1781 re-enlisted in Pennsylvania under Captain Herd in Colonel Bland's command. Was at siege of Yorktown. Remained in service until 1782.

Applied for pension, Harrison County, Va., June 15, 1818. Certificate was issued, 1819. Pension was suspended and new application was made in 1826. Among comrades was George Crislep. Married at Trenton, New Jersey, in fall of 1791. Wife, named Margaret, aged 52 in 1824; children, Tabitha, 14, Edie, 13, Irena, 12. Soldier died April 21, 1835.

Widow applied for and received pension. Widow also received bounty land warrant for 160 acres.

ADDISON, RICHARD
Service—Virginia   Va. No. 18301   No. S-37651

Served three years under Captain Peter Brown, 11th Virginia Regiment, Colonel Daniel Morgan. Resided in Hampshire County and enlisted in Berkeley County in the fall of 1776. Was at Monmouth, Blueford's Defeat and Yorktown.

Applied for pension in Hampshire County, Va., May 27, 1818. Certificate was issued October 12, 1821. Wife, named Priscilla, aged 64 in 1820. Among his comrades were Benjamin Smith, Patrick McCarty and George Calmus.

AITKEN, JAMES
Enlisted in Captain Shepherd's company of riflemen in June, 1776.

AKERD, ANDREW
Service—Virginia   Va. No. 23925   No. S-19178

Born in Philadelphia, Pa., September 15, 1757. Claimed six months service as private under Captain James Berry and Lieutenant Stokes, Colonel Edmund, General Wayne and General Muhlenberg. Enlisted in Frederick County, Va., April 2, 1779 and served until 1781. Residence before the Revolution was in Philadelphia. Applied for pension March 3, 1834, Mason County, Va. Certificate issued April 21, 1834.

ALDRIDGE, BENJAMIN
Enlisted in Captain Stephenson's company of riflemen in June, 1775.

ALDERSON, THOMAS
Service—Virginia   Va. No. 16447   No. S-8020
Born in Burks County, Pa., then moved to Shenandoah and Rockingham County, Va. He enlisted in Rockingham in September, 1780, and served six months in the Virginia Line. Among officers named are Captain Jeremiah Ragan, Captain Coger, Major Lockhard, Colonel Lewis, Colonel Vance, Colonel Harrison, General Stevens, General Mechingburg (Muhlenberg ?), and General Washington. Applied for pension, Monroe County, Va., October 16, 1832. Certificate issued, 1833. Among comrades named was Alexander Freeman.

ALESHIRE, JOHN C. (or Aleshite or Aleshete.)
Service—Virginia   Va. No. 23827   No. S-17816
Enlisted September 9, 1777, in Virginia. Served nine months as a private under Captain Rowsch, Captain Prince, Captain Denton, and Colonel Bowman. Was at siege of Yorktown. Applied for pension August 27, 1832, Page County, Va. Certificate issued, April 9, 1834, and claims paid to March 4, 1839. Among his comrades were David McIntarff, Henry Aleshite, Abraham Strickler, and Daniel Stover.

ALEXANDER, JAMES
Born 1750, died 1814. Served in the Revolution as a corporal in the First Artillery Regiment, Virginia Continental troops. Buried in Green Hill Cemetery, Union, Monroe County.
First permanent settler at Union, Monroe County, 1772-1774. Tavern keeper, 1797; judge, 1784; and sheriff in 1799. He was a leader in the formation of Monroe County from Greenbrier in 1799. After the first Monroe County Court was organized, it met at his home until the courthouse was built.

ALLEN, EBENEZER
Enlisted in Captain Stephenson's company of riflemen in 1775.

ALLEN, SAMUEL
Service—Virginia   Va. No. 2677   No. S-6484
Enlisted August 15, 1780, in Augusta County, Va. Served eighteen months as a private under Captain Bell, 6th Regiment, commanded by Colonel Blewford and Colonel Campbell. Was at Guilford, Eutaw Springs, Ninety-six and Augusta Fort.
Applied for pension October 17, 1820, Monroe County, Va., aged 72, and filed other applications February 16, 1829, and August, 1832. Certificate was issued December 13, 1832, later suspended, but payment was resumed October 21, 1835.

ALLEN, WILLIAM
Service—Virginia   No. W-25344
Born October 3, 1749, Albemarle County, later Amherst County, Va. Enlisted June 16, 1779, Amherst County, and served as private two years in Thomas Taylor's Company, Virginia Convention Guards. Married December 16, 1807.

Applied for pension September 25, 1832, Nelson County. Died March 6, 1838, Nelson Courthouse. Widow, Dolly, applied for pension, May 31, 1854, Kanawha County, Va. Residence Putnam County. Pension allowed. In 1862, lived at Coals Mouth; in 1866, aged 80, resided Kanawha County.

Names and dates of birth of children: Barbara L., December 14, 1808; George W., March 26, 1810; Jesse J., July 16, 1813; William H., June 14, 1816; Landon C., June 6, 1819; Sally B., May 9, 1822; James M., July 8, 1825; Elizabeth M., April 14, 1828; Andrew Jackson, June 10, 1831.

Soldier's sons, William and Landon, were with mother when she applied for pension. James Allen resided in Kanawha in 1855. In 1851, John Allen, who was apparently another son, lived in Nelson County, Ky. In 1854, John Hansford, justice of the peace for Kanawha County, Alva Hansford, and Victoria F. Hansford are mentioned. No family relationship shown.

ANDERSON, JACOB
Service—Virginia   Va. No. 12551   War Dept. No. 12507   No. 37675

Enlisted in Berkeley County, Va. Served six years in company of Captain W. T. Darke, 8th Virginia Regiment, under Colonel Bowman. Saw action at Brandywine, Germantown, and Monmouth. Wounded three times in action. Applied for pension, 1818, in Berkeley County. Died in 1834.

ANDERSON, JAMES (alias Asher Crockett)
Service—Virginia   Va. No. 12762   No. W-2533

Born September, 1760, Hampshire County, Va. Died January 16, 1846, Wayne County. Enlisted, 1776, Hampshire County, and served three years in the Virginia Line, in command under Captain Fitzpatrick and Colonel Hite. Mentions General Washington, Baron DeRall, General Lafayette, and others.

Married September 11, 1800, Montgomery County, Va., to Sarah Blankinship. He was married as Asher Crockett, the name which he assumed when he ran away from his master in Hampshire County to join the army in 1776.

Pension application, Cabell and Wayne Counties, January 1, 1836. Widow applied for pension July 7, 1851; September 10, 1853. Pension granted December 13, 1853. September 10, 1874, children claimed unpaid pension due parents. Widow died September 9, 1862, at Wayne Courthouse. Names of children: Andrew Crockett, and Elizabeth Kelley and Charlotte Miller, both widows. Among witnesses named were William Ratcliff, John Brown, John Frazies, and Spurlock Allen.

ANDERSON, PETER
Service—Virginia   No. R-199

Claimed to have been drafted in April, 1776, or 1777, and served five months under Captain Derrick Hogland; then saw other service on the frontier in Indian warfare under Captain William Scott, Colonel Williamson, Colonel Shepherd, Timothy Downing, and Samuel Tilton. Claim supported by F. L. Prentiss. Knew Sam Brady, Benjamin Biggs, and John

Mills. Pension application of December 17, 1832, Wood County, Va., refused. Had lived on Buffalo Creek since 1772.

ANDERSON, WILLIAM
Enlisted in 1775 in Captain Stephenson's company, and re-enlisted in Captain Shepherd's company in June, 1776. Was captured November 16, 1776, in the taking of Fort Washington. Is believed to have joined the British Army, with the advice of his officers, to save his life.

ANGEL, JOHN
Born in Baltimore, Md., and lived in Shepherdstown on Angel Hill, bearing the name of his family. Enlisted by Henry Bedinger December 3, 1782. Must have had previous service as he was at the battle of Eutaw Springs. He was also a survivor of St. Clair's defeat in 1791.

ARBOGAST, ADAM
Service—Virginia   Va. No. 6603   No. S-8037
Enlisted in Augusta County, Va., now Pendleton County, W. Va., summer of 1776, 1777, 1778, and served six months as Indian spy and soldier under Captain McCoy, Lieutenant Gwin, and Colonel Hugart, Virginia line. Applied for pension November 6, 1832, Pendleton County, Va., aged 72. Certificate issued March 5, 1833.

He mentions George Burner, Jacob Warwick, George Hull, Eli B. Wilson, and John Simmons in his pension application, and Warwick and Burner testify in his behalf. His application mentions service at Bush's Fort, West's Fort, Lowther's Fort, Coon's Fort, Nutter's Fort and other border outposts, and also at points in the Greenbrier Valley.

ARBUCKLE, MATHEW (Captain)
Born, 1742. Outstanding as a frontiersman from early life. Explored the Kanawha Valley in 1765. Chosen captain of company of scouts and acted as guide to General Lewis' army on way to Point Pleasant, 1774. In 1776, commanded Fort Randolph, Point Pleasant. Remained there three years during which time Chief Cornstalk was killed. Captain Arbuckle was an able officer, trusted by General Hand, commanding officer of Fort Pitt and the western borders. Arbuckle was killed on his way home from Staunton to Greenbrier (1781), by a falling tree during a storm. His son, of the same name, was a general in the regular army.

ARBUCKLE, WILLIAM
Testified in Mason County, Va., November 19, 1833, aged 81, that he volunteered about April, 1777, in Augusta County, Va., to serve against the Indians, under Captain Mathew Arbuckle, Lieutenant Andrew Wallis, and Ensign James Mouitt. Served in garrison at Point Pleasant. Mentions among other officers, Captain Stuart, Colonel Wood, General Clark, and General Hand. Samuel Price and Theophilus McCoy testified for him. Pension was rejected.

Born in Botetourt County, Va., 1752. Lived in Augusta County until he entered service. Later moved to Greenbrier and then to Mason County, Va.

ARCHER, STEPHEN
Service—Navy—Pennsylvania—Virginia   No. W-11133

Enlisted in Greene County, Pa., 1776, and served as marine, 1782-1783. In battles of Trenton, Princeton, and Yorktown, served under General Washington, Colonel Bowser, Captain Mullins, Alexander, Trimble, and Lieutenant Johnson. Mullins and Alexander were in command of Frigate Delaware on which Archer was stationed, and most of its crew were captured and died in prison following capture of Philadelphia. Lieutenant Richard Johnston testified for Archer; also Moses Sine, Jesse Wright, and Isaac Shriver. On June 12, 1822 or 1823, Archer married Mary, daughter of William and Margaret Lign, who was born August 21, 1800, York County, Pa. Their children were Elizabeth, aged 35, and Mary, aged 20. (Note some confusion as to dates.) Archer died May 12, 1824. Grave on Day's Run, Monongalia County. (May have been married twice.)

Applied for pension May 25, 1818, Greene County, Pa., at age of 75. Pension granted, and later tranferred to Monongalia County. Widow applied for pension February 27, 1855, and made application for bounty land, April 6, 1855. Widow seems to have married man named Rice, April 24, 1835.

ARGABRIGHT, JACOB (Argubrite, Argabrite)
Service—Virginia   Va. No. 16786   No. S-12907

Born, Lancaster County, Pa., about 1760, and as a boy moved to Rockingham County, Va. There enlisted in May, 1778, under Captain Cravens, and served nine months at Fort Westfall, and Fort Haddan in Tygarts Valley, and at Fort Lawrence and Fort McIntosh. In 1780, enlisted in cavalry from Berkeley County under Captain Sullivan. Saw service at Cowpens and at the Siege of Yorktown. Among other officers named were Colonel Frieze, Captain Croker, Colonel Darke, Colonel Crawford, Major Noll, Colonel Gibson, and General McIntosh. He saw the body of Lieutenant Park after he had been killed by the Indians.

Applied for pension in Monroe County, October 15, 1832. Certificate issued September 25, 1833, 22 months, which was soon after suspended but later resumed. Among those supporting his claim were Rev. William Adair, Henry Alexander, and John Hutchinson.

ARNETT (ARNOT), HENRY
Service—New Jersey—New York   Va. No. 6180   No. S-8030

Born in Orange County, N. Y., 1761; was in Sussex County, N. J., 1772; and in Monroe County, Va., 1832. Enlistments between 1776 and 1782, of ten months, under Captain Wessner and Major Logan in Colonel Nichol's regiment, New Jersey. Was on marches through New Jersey and New York under Captain Gordon, Major Logan, and Colonel Wisenfelt. Discharged at Albany. Only 14 years old when he saw his first service. Made application for pension, Monroe County, Va., August 22, 1832. Certificate granted, February 25, 1833. James Christy and Samuel Clark supported his claim. Applicant mentions Colonel John Hutchinson, Colonel Richard Shanklin, Colonel Andrew Burne, Henry Alexander, Isaac Corrothers, and William Erskine.

ASH, ADAM

Born in Germany in 1744, or in Holland: died May 1, 1819. Enlisted in 1776 in Captain Parker's company of Chester County, Pa., militia, and, in 1781, in Captain George Ensol's company, Bedford County, Pa., militia. Probably married in Germany to Catherine Yost. Resided in Harrison County, Va., after the Revolution. The children were Adam, Jr., Glovers Gap; John, Tyler County; Peter, Harrison County.

ASHBY, JOHN (Major)

Captain in the Third Virginia Regiment, March 18, 1776; wounded at Germantown, October 14, 1777; resigned October 30, 1777; major of Virginia militia, 1780-1781.

On April 13, 1838, by executive order of the State of Virginia, additional land bounty was given the heirs of John Ashby for his services as a Captain in the Continental Line, Revolutionary War. His name remains in Mineral County, W. Va., at Fort Ashby, where he was particularly active.

Following notes concern his heirs: Dolly Ashby died before her father. She had married Robert Jones and left the following children: Gabriel, Polly, Betsy, William A., Francis, Robert, Harriett, and Juliet Jones. Since the death of Ashby, the following children died before 1840: Martha, who married John Withers, Marshall, Thomas, Turner, Samuel (who left Maria, Henry, Jameson, Kitty, Clarkson, Martha, and Caroline); John (who left William, Elizabeth, Mary T., Lucy S., Susan, and Roberta); Nimrod, (who left Rebecca, Edwin, Albert, Nimrod, Mary, Amanda, Jane, Samuel, Adeline, and John); Elizabeth, (married John Tutt, since dead) whose children are: Mary Ann, Martha, Betsy, John, Dolly, Virginia, and Juliet Tutt.

ASHCRAFT (ASHCROFT), JOHN

Service—Pennsylvania   Va. No. 2131   No. S-6537

Enlisted in spring of 1781 and served 12 months as private in company of Captains Ashcraft, Cline, and Sutton under General Clark. Applied for pension July 28, 1832, in Harrison County. Certificate issued November 19, 1832. Aged 95 in 1832.

ASHCRAFT, URIAH

Service—Pennsylvania—Virginia   No. R-278

Born in Lancaster County, Pa., 1762. Enlisted in Fayette County, Pa., 1778. Service under Captain Sutton, Hayden, Ritchie, Bowers, George Jackson, Martin, Bradford, Haymond, Colonel John McClellan, and General Wayne, and others. Applied for pension, Harrison County, Va., October 12, 1833. Mentions Francis Goodwin and Daniel Morris. Letters filed by C. Nutter and Benjamin Copeland. Claim refused on ground of insufficient service.

ATHEY, JAMES

Application for pension dated in Wood County, Va. Soldier claimed to have enlisted February 10, 1778, as private in Captain Stephen Ashby's Company, under Colonel John Neville and Colonel James Wood's

Virginia Regiment, and to have served until February 16, 1779. Athey resided in Virginia in 1834 and stated that he had rendered no service in the Revolution. Claim was therefore rejected in letter of March 26, 1835, as was that of Spencer Sharp.

ATHY, THOMAS
Service—Virginia   No. S-37689

Made application for pension, Hampshire County, Va., August 18, 1818, at age of 72. Had two years service under Captain William Patterson, 16th Virginia Regiment, Continental Establishment. Honorably discharged at Middleton, N. J. Certificate issued March 6, 1819. He married Senna Ann Wilder in Fairfax County, Va., to whom two sons, Elisha and Benjamin, were born.

ATKINS, HEZEKIAH

Born September 20, 1759, Goochland County, Va. Enlisted from Montgomery County, Va., and served under Captain Thomas Burke and Captain George Faris. William Lucas of Logan County testified that Atkins served at Lucas Fort, Montgomery County, for three months. Also guarded baggage train in North Carolina. Applied for pension January 26, 1835, and died soon after. His widow, May Atkins, also made applications for pensions in 1852 and 1854, but apparently without success.

ATKINS, JOHN

Born 1755, Henry County, Va. Later moved to Montgomery County, then to Cabell, and then to Fayette County. Enlisted under Captain David Harrison in Henry County, marched to North Carolina, was stationed at Augurn's Mills, and was discharged in 1779, Salisbury, N. C. Re-enlisted under Captain Thomas Henderson, marched to Guilford Courthouse, and later joined General Green. Guarded prisoners after surrender at Yorktown, and was discharged there. Pension refused. Sufficient service not established.

ATKINSON, RICHARD THOMAS
Service—Virginia   Va. No. 18101   No. S-37691

Enlisted under name of Richard Thomas in order to disguise the fact that he had been a British soldier. Entered service June, 1776, Martinsburg, Berkeley County. Enlistment also shown from June 4, 1778, to March 20, 1779, under Lieutenant Pendleton and Captain Long, Fifth Maryland Regiment, Colonel Stephenson, General Stephens, General Putnam and General Washington. Was at surrender of Fort Washington on York Island. Fellow soldier prisoners were John Keene, William Boyd, Daniel Heartley, Patrick Howeringham, Sergeant David Gray, and Thomas Rogers. Later escaped. Was at Brandywine and Germantown. His claims supported by Nathaniel Pendleton, living in Dutchess County, N. Y., November 10, 1819.

Applied for pension April 20, 1818, and June 26, 1820, Monongalia County. He was 75 years old. Wife's age, 77. One child living, Margaret, aged 30. The applicant was stated to have died June 11, 1828.

AVIS, ROBERT
Service—Virginia   Va. No. 20425   No. S-38509

Enlisted, Berkeley County, March 6, 1776, and June, 1777. Served as private 18 months under Captain Darke, Virginia line regiment, commanded by Colonel Muhlenberg. Had service in the north and then with the southern Continental armies. Received honorable discharge in North Carolina.

Applied for pension April 20, 1829, Jefferson County. Certificate issued March 26, 1832. Died prior to September 22, 1834. Refers to four daughters. Mentions Richard Duffield, Philip Engle, Lewis Romans, William Adams, and William Phelan.

BAILEY, ISHAM
Service—Virginia   Va. No. 16687   No. S-12965

Enlisted 1777, Albemarle County, Va., under Captain London Jones and Lieutenant James Woods. Stationed along seaboard watching British shipping, with First Virginia Regiment. Re-enlisted and served under Captain Harris, Leaks, Thomas, and Wharton, and Colonel Matthews and General Nelson. For a time was with General Lafayette at Jamestown.

Applied for pension May 11, 1833, Kanawha County, Va. Certificate issued September 16, 1833. Died January 4, 1835. Reference to his son, Isham Bailey, Jr.

BAILEY, JOHN
Indication that he was drafted in Albemarle County, Va., in 1777, under Captain Landon (or London) Jones and Lieutenant James Wood, and attached to the First Virginia Regiment under General Nelson. Later drafted under Captain John Harris and Lieutenant Ralph Thomas. Third draft under Captain Mark Leake and Lieutenant John Wharton. Total service about five months. Resided in Kanawha County, 1833.

BAILEY, RICHARD
The first settlement at Beaver Pond, where Bluefield now stands, is believed to have been made by Richard Bailey, who is supposed to have had service in the Revolutionary War. He settled there in 1780, following the earlier settlement of Mitchell Clay at Clover Bottom. When the Indians broke up the Clover Bottom settlement in 1783, Bailey held his ground and helped build the Bailey-Davidson Fort as protection against the Indians.

BAILEY, WILLIAM
Service—Virginia   Va. No. 16688 and 25422   No. W-5777

Enlisted Albemarle County, Va., 1776, and served two years under Captain Walker, 9th Virginia Regiment. Was at Brunswick and Saratoga. Received discharge at White Horse, fifteen miles from Philadelphia. Applied for pension, Kanawha County, Va., May 14, 1833. Aged 79. Certificate granted September 16, 1833. Died February 28, 1837.

Married Sarah Sprouse, May, 1795, Albemarle County. Wife died July 17, 1851. Children's names: Nancy, 1798, married Mathew Philips; Betsy, 1802, married David Graham; Sally, 1803, died at age of two; Samuel,

1805, Putnam County; James, 1806, Kanawha County; William, 1808, Putnam County; John, 1810, died 1861, Kanawha County; Lucinda, 1812, no children; Martha, 1814, married Joseph Lanham (or Lanum); Reuben, 1817. Nancy Bailey Philips died, Warren County, Ky., about 1838, leaving seven children. Oldest, named James B. Betsy Graham, lived in Buckingham, Nelson, or Albemarle counties. John had three children: Mary, Elizabeth, and Martha Jane. Martha Lanham lived in Putnam County, Va. John, Pleasant, and Loving Lanham also mentioned. In Kanawha County, May 3, 1853, Nancy Hill, aged 76, formerly of Albemarle County, testified she was present at marriage of Sarah Sprouse and William Bailey, May, 1795, by Reverend Irving.

BAKER, ANTHONY
Service—Virginia   Va. No. 16690   No. S-12957

Born about 1761, Shenandoah County, Va. Enlisted April, 1780-81, Hampshire County, now Hardy County, Va. Served six months under Captain Richardson, Major Stubblefield, Colonel Stephens, and General Green in the Virginia line. Applied for pension May 23, 1833, Hardy County. Certificate issued September 16, 1833. Comrades named: William Heath, Jacob Hutton, Jacob Fisher, James Miles, Jacob Harness, John Yoacum, and George Jacob Neff.

BAKER (BECKER), GEORGE

Born, Lancaster County, Pa., February 6, 1762. Died in Monongalia County, Va., June 27, 1844. Took oath of allegiance July 18, 1778. Enlisted as private, Major Moore's Company, First Pennsylvania Regiment, 1780. His father, Peter Becker, who came to America on ship "Loyal Judith," about 1740, settled in Lancaster County, and was also in Revolution.

George settled on Cheat Neck, Monongalia County, after the Revolution. Married Elizabeth Norris whose father, William Norris, had patented land there in 1772. Five generations of the family are buried in the Baker graveyard.

BAKER, SOLOMON
Service—Tennessee. Indian Spy   No. 28449   No. 438

Born in Berkeley County, Va., 1763. Enlisted March, 1781, in company under Captain Baird. Applied for pension October 27, 1833, in Lewis County and Nicholas County. Claim supported by James Posey and Peter Bonnett. Pension refused on account of age of applicant.

BALEY, JOSEPH
Service—Pennsylvania   Va. No. 23711   No. S-17833

Born 1761. Enlisted in Bedford County, Pa., in command of Captain Fisher, Lieutenant Anderson, and Colonel Piper. Applied for pension July 12, 1835, Harrison County, Va. Certificate issued March 24, 1836, but later suspended.

BALLARD, PHILIP
Service—Virginia   Va. No. 23272   No. S-9094

Born in Albemarle or Orange County, Va., about 1757. Enlisted in Albemarle or Orange County and served two years as private under

Captain Spencer, Virginia Line, in commands of Colonel Taliaferro, Lieutenant Colonel Stevens, and Major Tom Marshall. Applied for pension August 21, 1832, Logan County. Certificate issued December 24, 1833, in favor of Mary Ballard, widow, since applicant had died April 13, 1833. Land bounty warrant for 100 acres also granted March 12, 1833.

BALLARD, WILLIAM

Grave of William Ballard is on the Cummings farm near Wikel Post Office, Monroe County. He died near the Shumate home on Indian Creek, September, 1799. He served in the Virginia militia in the Revolution with other brothers and was in the battle of Yorktown, October 19, 1781.

BANNOY, BENJAMIN

Shortly after the Revolution, Benjamin Bannoy, who had been a soldier in the Revolutionary Army, made a settlement near Meadowville, Barbour County.

BARGER, JOHN

Enlisted in Captain Shepherd's company in June, 1776. Was drafted into another unit in August of the same year.

BARNES, THOMAS

Born December 6, 1750; died October 19, 1836. Was a Revolutionary War sergeant in Captain Abner Crump's Company, First Virginia Regiment, commanded by Colonel George Gibson, October, 1777. (See payroll, War Department, Washington.) His name was on list of those receiving certificates for balance of pay, dated July 15, 1783, services prior to January, 1782. Graves of family moved from Barnsville to the Fairmont Cemetery. (Name sometimes spelled Barns, but the Revolutionary War records carry the old English spelling of the name as Barnes.)

BARNETT, ISAAC   No. R-532

Made application for pension in Nicholas and Lewis counties. Unfavorable reports made by Colonel Gideon C. Camden, Colonel Asa Squires, and P. B. Byrne, who believed that his age would not have permitted service in the Revolution. His claim, with 27 others, rejected in letter dated November 16, 1835, to Weedon Hoffman, Weston, Va.

West Virginians in the American Revolution

This is the second article in a series which contains an alphabetical check list of Revolutionary soldiers who at one time or another lived in what is now West Virginia. The series will continue for several numbers. This material has been assembled and edited by Ross B. Johnston. In the next few years, the Department of Archives and History hopes to publish this list in one volume, properly indexed. The public is invited to send in corrections as the material appears and to submit names of other Revolutionary soldiers whose authentic records qualify them to be listed among the other West Virginians who were with Washington's army.

This list of more than thirteen hundred sketches of Revolutionary soldiers from what is now West Virginia is offered with the full understanding that it represents only part of those who properly belong in this group. There are, for example, large lists of names, such as the roster of George Rogers Clark's forces of men, whose residences were uncertain, although many of the frontiersmen who joined Clark at Point Pleasant and Parkersburg on his western expedition lived west of the mountains.

The sources of this material are notes from the files of the Pension Office at Washington, from the pension applications in West Virginia counties, and from the minute books of the older West Virginia counties, copied by W. P. A. workers on the project sponsored by the West Virginia Commission on Historic and Scenic Markers; from notes of the Daughters of the American Revolution, Sons of the American Revolution, Sons of the Revolution, and other patriotic societies; and from a large miscellaneous group of published and private sources. It was found necessary to condense many extended notes in order to save space. Doubtless this omitted some points of interest, but in most instances the omissions were repetitions of facts common to many other cases.

(Note: Numbers and letters appearing with many names are references to files of Pension Bureau, War Department, Washington, D. C.)

BARNET, JOSEPH
Service—Pennsylvania   Va. No. 2129   No. S-6583
Enlisted, 1779, Franklin County, Pennsylvania, and served one year as private in company under Captain Campbell and Captain McKinney, Pennsylvania Regiment, Colonel James Young. Served in defense of the frontiers. Applied for pension, August 21, 1832, Harrison County, Virginia, aged 71. Certificate issued, November 9, 1832. Among supporting statements were those of Hamilton Gass and A. C. Holden.

Was in battle with the Indians at Clear Field beyond the Allegheny Mountains in which Captain Dunlap, Joseph Skinner, Joseph Martin, and a Mr. Murphy were killed.

BARRET, HENRY
Enlisted in Captain Stephenson's company in 1775.

BARRETT, SAMUEL
Service—Virginia   Va. No. 12129   No. S-6590
Enlisted, Shenandoah County, Va., 1776 or 1777, and served two years under Captain Alexander, Calimen, Catlett, Second Regiment Virginia Line, under Colonel Shotwood (Spottswood), General Wolford, and General Wayne. Applied for pension in Wood County, Virginia, August 20, 1832. Certificate issued, March 25, 1833. Among supporting claims were those of Patrick Board and John Stephenson, sheriff, Wood County.

BAYLOR, ROBERT (Captain)
Served in the Revolution as a captain. After its close, lived in Shepherdstown, and, in 1795, was in the Virginia Assembly. He went west later and settled in Logan County, Kentucky.

BEALL, (BELL), ISAAC (Major)
Captain in the Fourth Virginia, February 10, 1776; major, February 21, 1777; resigned June 19, 1778.
Warrant was issued May 19, 1823, in favor of Isaac Beall or Bell, as a major in the Fourth Virginia, Continental Line, Revolutionary Army. He died about June 1, 1779 (or 1797), and his will is recorded in the state of Maryland where he owned land. His widow, Margery, was dead in 1823, and so were three children, Nancy, Alexander, and Isaac. The only heir living was Mazy or Mary Beall Vance, wife of Robert Vance.

BEALL, SAMUEL B. (Lieutenant)
Service—Virginia   Va. No. 10497   No. S-37740
In Harrison County, May 18, 1818, Samuel B. Beall, aged 55, made application for pension. He enlisted August 1, 1781, as a second lieuten-

ant in Captain Reville's Company, First (or Fourth) Regiment of the Maryland line, and retired January 1, 1783. Was at the siege of Yorktown. He was granted 200 acres of land on April 14, 1818, for his Revolutionary services. Children were Benjamin, 17; Asa or Azra, 12; Samuel, 9; Sarah, 14.

BEATTY, THOMAS

Enlisted in Captain Shepherd's company. Was taken prisoner at Fort Washington on November 16, 1776, and died, or was killed, while a captive, February 15, 1777.

BEAUMONT, SAMUEL   No. S-37736

On August 25, 1836, Samuel Beaumont, in Kanawha County, petitioned that he be transferred from the Ohio pension rolls. His pension application, June, 1818, Washington County, Ohio, gives his age as 63. He enlisted in Saybrook, Connecticut, April, 1776, and served until February 8, 1781, under Captain John Hart, and Colonel Samuel Webbs, in the Continental Line. He was in the battles of Flat Bush, Turtle Bay, Harlem Heights, White Plains, and Elizabeth Town. In August, 1821, he filed a schedule of his property in Ross County, Ohio. He mentions his mother, aged 84, and a daughter, whose name was not given.

BEDINGER, DANIEL (Lieutenant)

By executive order of the state of Virginia, February 5, 1810, additional land grants were made to Daniel Bedinger for sixteen months' service more than the six-year period. Following order was issued in Jefferson County, June 12, 1839:

"Order certified that Daniel Bedinger, Lieutenant in the Revolutionary War, died in the county of Jefferson, Virginia, in the year 1817 (or 1818), leaving the following children:

Daniel, Sr. (since died without children, but was of age and made a will); Margaret Foster (who is since dead, leaving two children, Thomas M. Foster and Margaret Ann Morrison); Elizabeth Washington (wife of John T. A. Washington)—the said Elizabeth is dead, her husband surviving her, and the following children: Lawrence B. Washington (since dead, childless and intestate), Daniel B. Washington, Sally, Benjamin Franklin, Georgianna, Mary, Thornton, Susan, and George Washington; Ellen (dead, childless, without will); Mary Brian (dead, leaving two children, John L. Brian and Sarah Brian); Virginia Lucas (dead, leaving William, Sally, Daniel B., and Virginia); Susan P.; Cornwall (Conwall); Henrietta, wife of Edmund Lee; Henry Bedinger, Jr., and Sally Bedinger, widow of Daniel Bedinger.

Lieutenant Bedinger was born near York, Pennsylvania, in 1761. While an infant, his father moved to Shepherdstown, Jefferson County, Virginia. In June, 1776, he enlisted in Captain Shepherd's company of riflemen. He was an expert marksman, says tradition, and fired his rifle twenty-seven times at the British as they stormed the hill in the attack on Fort Washington. Heitman's *Historic Register* lists him as a first lieutenant in November, 1776, apparently dating from the time he was captured with the garrison when the fort surrendered. He was confined in the old Sugar

House Prison in New York, in which so many Revolutionary heroes lost their health, if not their lives, and also on a prison ship, but was exchanged after two months. Heitman says that he was also captured in the battle of Brandywine, September 11, 1777, and that he did not appear to have rejoined his regiment after his release.

BEDINGER, DANIEL (Ensign)
Enlisted as an ensign in the Fourth Virginia Regiment, May 7, 1782, and served until the close of the Revolution.

BEDINGER, GEORGE MICHAEL (Major)
Volunteered in Captain Hugh Stephenson's company of riflemen in 1775 and served as captain from July, 1775 to 1781. Major of a militia regiment at the battle of Blue Licks, August 19, 1782; major of the levies in 1791; major of infantry United States Army, March 11, 1792; assigned to Third Sub-Legion, September 14, 1792; resigned, February 28, 1793.

Born in 1756 and educated in Shepherdstown. After the Revolution, went to Kentucky and served in Congress from that state. Died, December 7, 1843.

BEDINGER, HENRY (Major)
Born, October 16, 1753, in York County, Pennsylvania. Resided in Shepherdstown during the Revolution. Died, May 14, 1843.

Enlisted in July, 1776, in Captain Hugh Stephenson's company and served as a private and sergeant; second lieutenant of Shepherd's Virginia rifle company, July 25, 1776; second lieutenant, Eleventh Virginia, November 13, 1776; taken prisoner at Fort Washington, November 16, 1776; held prisoner "four years, wanting sixteen days"; promoted, first lieutenant, while prisoner, September 23, 1777; transferred to Seventh Virginia, September 14, 1778; transferred to Third Virginia, February 12, 1781; made captain, May 21, 1781, and served to end of the Revolution. He was advanced to the rank of major during the Indian wars under General St. Clair in 1792. His heirs received unpaid claims of pension as a captain in the Revolutionary War in Berkeley County, Virginia, with a captain's land bounty.

Bedinger married Rachel Strode, December 22, 1784, in Berkeley County. She was born October 19, 1762. Their children were Nancy (married Colonel James Strode Swearingen, who was to lead the detachment of troops which established Fort Dearborn, the foundation of Chicago), January 7, 1786; Betty, March 9, 1787; Sarah, May 25, 1792; Elizabeth (married Braxton Davenport), March 25, 1793; Maria, July 10, 1794; Eleanor Strode, May 23, 1796.

BELL, RICHARD
Service—Virginia   Va. No. 23112   No. S-8064
Made application for pension, Harrison County, Virginia, August, 1834. Certificate issued, November 7, 1834. Unfavorable report, March 16, 1835. Dropped from roll, December 30, 1844. Mentions Manley Carder.

BENNETT, ABRAHAM
Born March 23, 1745, near Philadelphia, Pennsylvania, the son of Isaac

and Mary Bennett; came to Harrison County, Virginia, in 1796, and died in 1824. He was married to Catherine Roberts in 1775 or 1776. She was born December 24, 1754, the daughter of William and Elizabeth Siddons Roberts, and died in Harrison County, Virginia, in 1836. Their children were: Mary, Elizabeth, Abraham, Jane, Isaac, Jacob, Catherine, and five others.

He enlisted as a private in the second company of Philadelphia County militia under Captain Abram Wentz in the Sixth Battalion of Pennsylvania Volunteers under Colonel Antis (Antise). A marker near Dola, Harrison County, indicates where he made his first home in western Virginia.

BENNETT, WILLIAM
Service—New York   Va. No. 12520   No. S-5276

Enlistment, June 1, 1777, to 1781, Saratoga District, New York. Private two years under Captain McCracken, First Regiment, New York, Colonel Vanstoke, Colonel Vandyke, Major Graham, Peter Tice, General Gates, and General Washington. Was at Fort Edward, New York, Salem, Stillwater on the Hudson, Johnstown, Schenectady, Albany, and Valley Forge. Born in Rhode Island; date uncertain. Date of death, probably February 20, 1843 (date on pension office papers). Applied for pension, October 17, 1832, Tyler County, Virginia. Certificate issued May 6, 1833.

BENSON, LEVIN
Service—Virginia   Va. No. 16371   No. R-777

Enlisted, 1776, Augusta County, Virginia, and served until 1779. Private two years under Captain Laughridge, Second Virginia, Colonel Charles Lewis, Colonel Walter, and General Andrew Lewis, apparently in broken terms of enlistment. Applied for pension, August 27, 1832, Greenbrier County. Certificate issued August 2, 1833. Widow, Jane, applied for pension, November 7, 1844, Knox County, Illinois. Refers to minor children, Elsone and Jane Benson. Other persons named were Sam Price, Jacob Price, Joseph Ranes, and Zachariah Sterner. In Greenbrier County in 1835, the widow and son, William, established proof of claim on Levin Benson's estate.

BENTLEY, WILLIAM (Sergeant)

Enlisted, 1777, Jefferson County, Virginia. Previously resided in Frederick County, Maryland. Served as sergeant, 13th Virginia Regiment, under Captain James Russell and Colonel William Russell. Died, 1803. Wife's name, Margaret. Daughter, Prudence Bentley Collins Thornburg.

BERKHAMMER, HENRY

Affidavit in Harrison County shows Berkhammer enlisted as regular soldier in Philadelphia under Captain Church, and served upwards of four years. He was in battles of Germantown, Wood Bridge, Strawberry Hill, Trenton, Fox Chase, and was discharged at the "Trab" or "Trap," near Philadelphia. He fought under General Muhlenberg, under command of Captain John Smith. (Name is signed in German.)

BERRY, JOHN
Service—Continental Line and New Jersey   Va. No. 15811   No. S-37757
  Enlisted, March 12, 1777, Monmouth County, New Jersey. Private three years in company of Captain John Burris, Continental Line, Colonel David Furman. Was at Long Island, Germantown, White Plains, and Elizabethtown. Applied for pension, Hardy County, Virginia, February 11, 1818, aged 66. Died August 6, 1845, or 1847.
  Names of supporting persons: George Berry, Thomas Henry Berry, Benjamin Paw, March French, Lary McLony, Sissely Barrows, or Berry. Benjamin Berry testified that he served with John Berry. Sarah McCloud was the only heir. Certificate issued, November 17, 1818. Notification sent to John Hopewell, Moorefield, Virginia, September 30, 1820. Land bounty claim rejected.

BERRY, HENRY
Service—Virginia   Va. No. 23943   No. S-5794
  Enlisted, Louden County, Virginia, and served nine months, Captain Francis Russell and Captain Cleaveland, Virginia Line, Colonel Alexander. Was at Yorktown during its siege and capture, and later guarded prisoners at Leesburg and Noland's Ferry.
  Pension application, February 7, 1834, Hampshire County, Virginia, aged 90. Certificate issued, April 28, 1834. Died May 22, 1836. Bounty land claim also allowed. Married Elizabeth Watkins (spinster), Louden County, Virginia, May 22, 1793. Marriage bond signed by William Berry and Benjamin Cockrill. Widow born in Louden County, and applied for pension, April 26, 1841, aged 81. In support of their claims appeared Jeremiah Miller and George Short.

BERTRUG (BERTING), PETER
Service—Virginia   Va. No. 23021   No. S-18309
  Born in Fairfax County, Virginia, February 15, 1750. Enlisted, July, 1777, Augusta County, Virginia, and served two years under Captain John Hopkins, Captain Smith, Major McClanahan, Colonel Skillern, and Colonel John Dickinson. Applied for pension, October, 1833, Tyler County, Virginia, or Monongalia County, Virginia. Certificate issued, October 26, 1833. Isaac Horner and George Betruck supported his claim.
  In pension application in Tyler County, he describes the outward march of the Augusta troops, under Captain Hopkins, which was part of the regiment under Major McClanahan and Colonel Dickinson. They rendezvoused at Staunton and marched to Warm Springs, Bath County, thence to Jackson's River, and across Allegheny Mountain to Camp Union (Lewisburg). There they joined Skillern's forces from Botetourt, and crossed Sewell Mountain to the Great Kanawha. They halted, for several weeks, four miles below the falls, and then descended the river to Point Pleasant.

BESSLEY, ISAAC
Service—Virginia   No. R-710
  Born, Louden County, Virginia, 1753. Enlisted, March, 1778, Monongalia County, Virginia, and served as private under Captain Evans, Mor-

gan, Cochran, Springer, Colonel Gibson, General Clark, and General McIntosh, Virginia Militia. Applied for pension, Lewis County, Virginia, November 20, 1833.

Supporting affidavits by James Turner and James Tuttle. Statements told how Indians placed bells on horses to trap white settlers. Two children of John Haythorn killed by Indians in 1780 on Dunkard Creek. James Coon was also killed. Affidavit of John Runnion describes Indian hostilities about Fort Lawrence.

VAN BIBBER, JOHN AND PETER (Captains)

John and Peter Van Bibber were of Dutch ancestry and lived in Pennsylvania and Maryland before coming to the Greenbrier Valley, Botetourt County, about 1771. John made an early exploration of Kentucky, passing down the Ohio and the Mississippi to New Orleans. In 1773, he was one of the surveyors who explored the Great Kanawha, and left his name on a cliff below Kanawha Falls, still known as "Van Bibber's Rock." Both brothers took part in the Point Pleasant campaign in 1774, where a third brother, Isaac, was killed.

Both served as captains of militia. Peter had a blockhouse on Wolf Creek, which was an important frontier outpost. John wrote from Fort Greenbrier near Lowell, Summers County, in 1777. About 1781, the two brothers moved into the Kanawha Valley. Peter died at Point Pleasant in 1796 and John in 1821. Peter's sons, Matthias and Jacob, were noted in border warfare, and his daughter married a son of Daniel Boone.

BIBB, THOMAS
Service—Virginia   Va. No. 26329   No. S-9100

Enlisted, June, 1780, and served seven months. Pension certificate issued August 13, 1834. Married in Louisa County, Virginia, April 14, 1834. Other records missing.

BIGGS, BENJAMIN (General)

Born in Maryland, 1754. Family first removed to the Glades, then to the site of Uniontown, and finally, in 1774, to Short Creek, Ohio County. First military service was under Dunmore in 1774. In 1776, Biggs was commissioned first lieutenant of the Thirteenth Virginia Regiment, and in 1778 was made a captain. In February, 1781, he was transferred to the Seventh Virginia, and served on the western frontier until the close of the Revolution. During the Indian wars, he held important offices under Virginia; first colonel, and in 1793 was made brigadier-general of militia. He also was a member of the State Legislature and a Justice of the Peace. He died at his home in West Liberty, December 2, 1823.

BIGGS, JOSEPH (Ensign)

Records in Brooke County, Virginia, show that Biggs had been an invalid pensioner since 1796 on account of wounds received from Indians while commanding a detachment of rangers as ensign at a blockhouse on the west side of the Ohio River opposite Wheeling. He asked transfer to Ohio and lived for a time in Belmont County, Ohio. He died February 1, 1833.

In Marshall County, Virginia, October 12, 1840, Mary Biggs, his widow, made declaration, aged 70, that she had married him, January 14, 1794. Henry Baker, Belmont County, Ohio, declared that Mary Biggs, once Mary Daily, had married Biggs in 1794, the same day as the marriage of his sister.

BIGLER, JOSEPH

Born about 1752 in Bucks County, Pennsylvania, later moving to Hagerstown, Maryland. Enlisted, July 28, 1776, in Captain George P. Keeport's Company, First German Battalion, Continental Troops, under Colonel Nicholas Husacker. Came to Harrison County, Virginia, and settled on West Fork River. Died, September, 1829. Wife was Hannah (Booker) Bigler. They had ten children. Pension was granted while living in Harrison County.

BILLS, JOHN E.
Service—Virginia   Va. No. 23569   No. W-25243

Born in Hampshire County, Virginia, 1763. Enlisted there, fall of 1779, and served fifteen months under Lieutenant Fee and Captain Berry, Thirteenth Virginia Line, Colonel Enoch. Applied for pension, Hardy County, Virginia, December 17, 1833. Certificate issued February 25, 1834. Died July 9, 1852. Bounty land warrant also issued. Married to Mary Reel by Reverend Valentine Powers in Hardy County. Recorded there. Soldier's widow applied for pension, May 16, 1853. Supporting claims by Jacob and Daniel Kitterman, or Ketterman, John K. Prince, Robert Triplett, T. Louderman, and John Cavanan. Reference to Captain Enoch, an uncle of Bills, Joseph Berry, Lieutenant Hornback, or Hollenback, Colonel Holmes, and Colonel James Marshall.

BLACK, GEORGE   Va. No. S-6659

Born, January, 1760, Bucks County, Pennsylvania. While living in Shepherdstown, Berkeley County, Virginia, enlisted January, 1776, as private in Captain Mitchell's and Joseph Swearingen's companies, Colonel James Wood's Twelfth Virginia Regiment. Was in battle of Brandywine and there received wound in hip which fractured bone. He was taken prisoner, released, and again joined army in 1778. But, as an invalid, was sent to Philadelphia where he did garrison duty until January, 1779, when discharged by Colonel Nicola. Allowed pension from January 1, 1786, owing to wound disability. Later moved to Frederick County, Virginia.

BLACKHEAD, ANTHONY

Enlisted from Berkeley County, Virginia, in Captain Shepherd's company, in 1776. Killed in a skirmish near Fort Washington, November 15, 1776.

BLACKSHIRE, EBENEZER
Service—Delaware   Va. No. 906   No. S-45995, B.L.W. 349-100

Had apparently sought pension in early days, but according to letter of September 6, 1826, to Thomas Haymond, his claim had been refused, owing to having too much property. Applied for pension, July 25, 1828, Monongalia County, and was admitted to the pension lists. Joseph Sapp was among supporting affiants.

BLAIR, JOHN NEAL
Service—Virginia   Va. No. 4748   No. S-27779

Enlisted, 1775, Augusta County, Virginia. Served as a private under Captain Michael Bowser, or Bowyer, in Colonel Woods's Twelfth Virginia Regiment. Was in battles of Trenton, Brandywine, Germantown, Monmouth, siege of Amboy, and capture of Stony Point. Discharge, signed by Colonel Russell, at Stony Point, New York, in 1778, was placed in hands of Captain Jacob Lockheart to procure for him his back pay and land, but he got neither, and the discharge was not returned. Pension application made in Greenbrier County, June 23, 1818, aged 76. Pension certificate issued, December 1, 1818.

BLAIR, WILLIAM

William Blair, aged 50, a former pensioner, January 1, 1788, appeared before the Randolph County court, and declared that on the tenth day of October, 1774, in the militia service of the Colony of Virginia, under the command of Colonel Charles Lewis and in Lieutenant Lewis's company, he received a wound in his left shoulder that rendered him unable to labor for his living. Request for aid was approved by the Court to the Governor.

BLAKE, THOMAS
Service—Virginia   Va. No. 12699   No. S-6657

Enlisted as a substitute for John Blake in the fall of 1777 in the county of Augusta. Served under Lieutenant Captain Jacob Warwick, reconnoitering from Clover Lick to Tygart's Valley River. Drafted in 1778 and stationed at William Warnicks during the winter. In January, 1781, served under Captain William Kincaid, Colonel Sam Matthews, and General Muhlenberg, but was in no battles.

Applied for pension, November 23, 1832, aged 72 years. Certificate issued but was dropped March 9, 1835. Noted that service was in defense against Indians and Tory invasion, and was ruled to be non-regular army service, personal protection, and not authorized military service. Pension application of widow, Mary, likewise refused.

BLAND, (BLAN), JESSE
Service—Virginia   Va. No. 7003   No. S-8073

Born in Prince William County, Virginia, 1756. Enlisted in Greenbrier County, 1776, and served three years as a private under Captain Arbuckle, Thirteenth Virginia Regiment Continental Line. Applied for pension, Kanawha and Monroe counties, October 18, 1832. Certificate issued February 21, 1833. Death about April 15, 1842. Among supporting claims was that of M. Dunbar.

BLECHYNDEN, CHARLES
Service—Virginia   Va. No. 12608   No. S-6656

Enlistment, Rockingham County, Virginia, August, 1778 to 1781, in four enlistment periods, totaling twelve months, under Captain Davis, Messer, Harrison, in armies of General Washington and General Lafayette. Was at siege and capture of Cornwallis at Yorktown. Applied for pension, March 7, 1833, Pendleton County, aged 75, and certificate was issued, May 11, 1833.

BLIZZARD, BURTON
Service—Virginia   Va. No. 23374   No. W-20720
Enlisted in Rockingham County, September, 1777, and served under Captain Dan Smith and Lieutenant Keister in the Virginia line.

Married, December, 1780, to Sarah Kuster (or Keister). Soldier applied for pension, December 4, 1833, aged 73, in Pendleton County. Certificate issued July 10, 1834. Widow applied for pension May 6, 1839, and certificate was issued, July 2, 1841. Soldier died, March 17, 1837. Among supporting claims were those of William McCoy, Thomas Hoover, James Johnson, Frederick Kuster, John Davis, and Mary Swadley.

BLODGETT, ABISHA
Born in Stafford, Tolland County, Connecticut, November 25, 1763. Resided in Connecticut until 1788, then in New York and Pennsylvania, and last thirty years of his life were spent in Ohio County.

Enlisted, July, 1781, and remained in service through 1785 and 1788. Only eighteen months was during the Revolution. Served under Captain Sill of the Eighth company, Fifth Connecticut Regiment, Colonel Sherman and Harper. Applied for pension, December 2, 1833, Ohio County, Virginia, and certificate was issued, February 5, 1834.

BLOSS, VALENTINE
Service—Virginia   Va. No. 23370   No. S-9102
Born, 1754 or 1757, Augusta County. Died September 4, 1850, Cabell County. Enlisted in Augusta County, and served eight months as private under Captain John Hopkins, and Captain William Noll, Virginia regiment commanded by Colonel Smith.

Applied for pension, October 28, 1833, Cabell County. Certificate issued December, 1833. Letters of E. Bloss, a son, are on file. General Elisha McComas and John Samuels made supporting affidavits.

BLUE, PETER
Service—Virginia   Va. No. 15408   No. R-965
Enlistment, May 1, 1781, to November 1, 1781, Hampshire County in company of Captain Anderson, Virginia militia.

Married, January, 1787, in Hampshire County by Rev. Job Parker, Baptist, to Susannah Keltch. Soldier died, July 25, 1844. Soldier's widow applied for pension, August 1, 1856, aged 89, in Circleville, Fayette County, Ohio. She had one son, John, aged 56. Supporting claim also made by Sarah Carder.

BLUNT (or BLOUNT), NAT or NATHANIEL
Enlisted, 1778 and 1779, and served one year under Captain Anderson, Fifth Virginia Regiment, Colonel Ball, Continental Establishment. Hon-

orably discharged at Middlebrook, New Jersey. Applied for pension, August 21, 1821, Botetourt County, or Berkeley County, Virginia. Certificate issued, April 11, 1823. Supporting claims made by David Louden, Captain James Doswell, and Roger Mallory.

BOARD, PATRICK (or PATERICK)
Service—Virginia   Va. No. 12918   No. W. 5854, B.L.Wt. 47617

Born Pirson Hollow, Pennsylvania, June 12, 1750. Died November 6, 1839. Enlisted, Berkeley County, 1777, and served as private under Captain Darke, Second Virginia Regiment, under Colonel Wayne, General Wayne, and General Washington, at Long Island, Chestnut Hill, and Yorktown.

Applied for pension, October 15, 1832, Wood County. Certificate issued, then suspended, but later restored to his widow. She applied for pension, July 27, 1846, Jackson County, Virginia, aged 79 years in 1850. Bounty land warrant also granted. Soldier and Mary Heezer married, May or June, 1789-90, Washington County, Maryland. Had large family but names omitted. Claim supported by Samuel Barrett, J. M. Stead, David Hopkins, Charles Rector, William Sheppard, Thomas Cane, William Bonnett, David Seaman, and Ann Seaman.

BOCK, MICHAEL
Service—Virginia   Va. No. 12774   No. S-6679

Born near Frederick Town, Maryland, 1757, and removed to Monongalia County with his parents in 1769. Enlisted in Monongalia County, May, 1776, and served twenty months under Captain Brinkman, Whetzel, and Sinclair. Applied for pension, April 3, 1833, Harrison County, Virginia, and certificate issued May 22, 1833, but it may have been suspended later.

BOGGS, FRANCIS
Service—Virginia   Va. No. 30291   No. S-985

Born in Chester County, Pennsylvania, 1754. Enlisted, Greenbrier County, March 1, 1776, under Captain Arbuckle and Zera Combs. Applied for pension, October 4, 1833, Nicholas County, but claim was rejected. Among his comrades were John Given and William Boggs. His record shows service of nine months at Point Pleasant and vicinity in 1774.

BOGGS, JOHN (Captain)

Born on the Susquehanna in 1736, taken as a child to Berkeley County, and in 1768 came out to the Youghiogheny. In 1771, he was at Beeson's Fort (now Uniontown, Pennsylvania), and three years later made an improvement on Chartier's Creek three miles west of Catfish Camp. He was there when the siege of Wheeling occurred.

In 1781, while living on Buffalo Creek, his oldest son was captured. In August of the same year, he built a cabin three miles below Wheeling, and in the spring of the next year took his family to Fort Henry for safety. Captain Boggs was sent for reinforcements when the siege of 1782 took place but returned just after the besiegers had departed. He had expected to go to Kentucky, which he visited in 1776, but the Revolution held him on the Ohio frontier. In 1778, he was out with McIntosh in command of a company and for many years was a militia captain. He died in Pickaway County, Ohio, February, 1824.

BOLENER, ADAM
Service—Virginia   Va. No. 23414   No. S-12267

Born October, 1765, Bucks County, near Reading, Pennsylvania. Enlistment, September, 1781, and April, 1782, Winchester, Frederick County, Virginia. Served six months as private under Captain Taylor, Virginia Regiment commanded by Colonel Canaday. His duties were guarding prisoners.

Applied for pension, October 16, 1832, Hardy County, Virginia. Certificate issued January 17, 1834. Died, September, 1840. Supporting claims made by Diana Lambert, John Mullin, and Mary Jenkins.

West Virginians in the American Revolution

This is the third article in a series which contains an alphabetical check list of Revolutionary soldiers who at one time or another lived in what is now West Virginia. The series will continue for several numbers. This material has been assembled and edited by Ross B. Johnston. In the next few years, the Department of Archives and History hopes to publish this list in one volume, properly indexed. The public is invited to send in corrections as the material appears and to submit names of other Revolutionary soldiers whose authentic records qualify them to be listed among the other West Virginians who were with Washington's army.

This list of more than thirteen hundred sketches of Revolutionary soldiers from what is now West Virginia is offered with the full understanding that it represents only part of those who properly belong in this group. There are, for example, large lists of names, such as the roster of George Rogers Clark's forces of men, whose residences were uncertain, although many of the frontiersmen who joined Clark at Point Pleasant and Parkersburg on his western expedition lived west of the mountains.

The sources of this material are notes from the files of the Pension Office at Washington, from the pension applications in West Virginia counties, and from the minute books of the older West Virginia counties, copied by W. P. A. workers on the project sponsored by the West Virginia Commission on Historic and Scenic Markers; from notes of the Daughters of the American Revolution, Sons of the American Revolution, Sons of the Revolution, and other patriotic societies; and from a large miscellaneous group of published and private sources. It was found necessary to condense many extended notes in order to save space. Doubtless this omitted some points of interest, but in most instances the omissions were repetitions of facts common to many other cases.

(Note: Numbers and letters appearing with many names are references to files of Pension Bureau, War Department, Washington, D. C.)

BOND, JOHN (Sergeant)
Service—Maryland   Va. No. 18800   No. S-39199
Enlistment, April, 1782, to April, 1783, Baltimore, Maryland. Residence, Calvert County. Served one year as sergeant under Captains Hamilton and Bruce, Fourth Maryland Regiment, Major Lansdale, and Colonel Josiah Hall. Applied for pension, Hampshire County, Virginia, October 22, 1818, aged 56. Certificate issued, November 4, 1822.

BOND, RICHARD
Bond was born in Cecil County, Maryland, October 4, 1728, died on Lost Creek, January 14, 1809, and is believed to have had service in the Revolution. He was the son of Samuel Bond, born in England, January 1, 1692; died, April 10, 1783. He was married about 1726 to Ann Sharples, who was born June 23, 1708, and died in Cumberland County, New Jersey, on August 22, 1786.

BONNELL, JOHN
Bonnell appeared before the Harrison County court, May 19, 1818, and again in June, 1820, and said he was born in 1761; that he enlisted in Captain Machen's company, New York Artillery, under command of Colonel John Lamb or Calb; that he served from March, 1782, until his discharge at end of the war at West Point. Affidavit of Elijah Price attached. Had wife, aged 48, son, Charles, aged 12, and daughter, Margaret, aged 3, in 1820.

BONNER, JACOB (Joseph?)
Grave of Jacob Bonner, declared to have been a soldier in the Revolutionary War, is in Maple Grove Cemetery, Marion County.
Enlisted in Pennsylvania and served three years under Captains Nelson, Grant, and Davis, in Virginia State troops, and in the Pennsylvania Line, under Colonel Butler, General Wayne, and Lord Stirling. Served at Brandywine and Germantown. When he went to Philadelphia to get his depreciated pay, he was so long detained that he sold his pay for three guineas, and gave up his discharge. Applied for pension, May 27, 1818, Monongalia County, aged 66. Certificate issued, January 7, 1819. Wife, aged 60, in 1820; name not given. Names of children: Peggy (her children were Nancy and John), and Ruth.

BONNETT, JACOB
Service—Virginia   Va. No. 16461   No. S-8080
Born on Cedar Creek, Frederick County, Virginia, 1761. Enlisted in March, 1780, and served six months in the Virginia militia on the western borders under Captain Coburn, Major Lowther, and Colonel Crockett

as an Indian spy in Tyler and Brooke counties. Applied for pension, August 6, 1832, Lewis County. Certificate issued, August 26, 1833, but was later suspended as being too young for service. Bonnett died, about 1847, leaving following children: Martha, wife of Samuel Horner; Delilah, wife of Abraham Hess; Eliza, wife of Fleming Sprouse; Lucinda, wife of Jesse Butcher; Samuel, who died leaving children; Gracie West, dead, leaving children; Elizabeth Alkire, dead, leaving children.

Jacob Bonnett had four brothers: Samuel, Peter, John, and a twin, Lewis Bonnett. All the above are declared to have been Revolutionary soldiers. John was killed by the Indians and hidden in a cave on the Kanawha in 1783.

BONNETT, LEWIS
Service—Virginia   Va. No. 16242   No. S-5294

Born in Hardy County, 1761 or 1762. Enlisted, March, 1779 or 1780, and served until 1783 as Indian spy under Captains Coburn, Robinson, Jackson, Westfall, Major Lowther, Colonels Wilson, Gibson, Crockett, Duval, and General Clark. Applied for pension, July 5, 1833, Lewis County, or February 5, 1833, Lewis or Marshall County (both dates given). Certificate issued, 1833, then suspended as not having been in regular service. Mentions a brother, Peter Bonnett, Jacob Abbott, and Philip Cox. John, a brother, killed by Indians, 1783.

BONNETT, PETER
Service—Virginia   Va. No. 16241   No. S-5293

Born in Hardy County, 1764. Served from March, 1779, to 1783, total of about two years and six months, under Captain Coburn, Major Lowther, and Colonel Wilson with Ninth Virginia Regiment, along the Ohio River. Enlisted in Harrison County. Applied for pension, February 5, 1833, Lewis County, and certificate was issued July 19, 1833, but later suspended. Mentions a brother, Lewis Bonnett, Jacob Abbott, and Philip Cox. Evidence of Sam Bonnett, a brother, William Powers, Nicholas Carpenter, and Henry Flesher also submitted.

BONNIFIELD, SAMUEL
Service—Virginia   No. R-1007

Born, Prince George County, Maryland, April 11, 1750. Enlisted, Culpeper County, Virginia, and served 1778-1782 in company of minutemen of Gloucester, Virginia, under Captains Philip, Billups, and Slaughter. For a time was engaged in the manufacture of salt for Washington's army. He was also in the Battle of Point Pleasant, 1774, and had two companions, Thomas Gorman, or Gordon, and William Flanigan, killed.

Resided in Prince George County, Maryland, Culpeper County, Virginia, Hampshire County, and Randolph County, Virginia. Married Dorcas James, of near Piedmont, Mineral County. Applied for pension in Randolph County, November 5, 1833. Among comrades supporting his claim were John Long, James Long, James Parsons, and Henry M. Smith. Bonnifield was a French Huguenot who came to America by way of Scotland. The name is believed to have been originally spelled Bonnifant.

BOONE, (BOON), JOHN
Service—Pennsylvania   Va. No. 23161   No. R-1017

Born, York County, Pennsylvania, eight miles from York. Was 18 or 19 years old when he went with his uncle, Daniel Boone, to Kentucky, returning next year, 1774, to York, making the year of his birth about 1755. Died July 17, 1835. Enlisted, 1778, York County, Pennsylvania, under Captain Spangler, served upwards of two years, then marched under the command of General Gates with Maryland and Delaware troops to North Carolina to join Baron De Kalb's command. Was in several actions, including the defeat of Gates at Camden. From there he fled to Henry County, Virginia, where he remained at the Washington Iron Works for several years, then came to Monroe County (or Greenbrier County), where he made his home. No discharge was received, owing to dispersal of Gates' army.

Married Elizabeth Alford by published bans, 1787-88, Augusta County, Virginia. Wife died February 15, 1841. Children were John, Nancy, Henry, Sally, and Francis. Supporting claims by Peggy Alford and John Alford. Applied for pension, August 20, 1833, in Monroe County. Certificate issued, November 21, 1833.

Previous to the passage of the joint resolution of August 23, 1842, no widow whose husband was living on June 7, 1832, was entitled to a pension under the act of July 7, 1838. John Boone died after 1832, and his widow died prior to the resolution of 1842. (This note is from old letter book, mentioning three other widows.) NOTE: See affidavit of Henry Boone in 1847 before the Greenbrier County Court in interest of heirs of Elizabeth Boon.

BOOTH, JAMES (Captain)

Booth lived near Coon's Fort, Marion County. He was an officer of unusual ability, well educated for his time, and an outstanding leader in the early settlements of the Upper Monongahela Valley. He organized a company of militia which guarded the frontier against Indians, and he remained the chief protector of this region until his death at the hands of the Indians, June 16, 1778. Grave marked in cemetery on Booth's Creek.

BORER, CHARLES
Service—Virginia   Va. No. 16644   No. S-8082

Enlisted, October 1, 1777, Hampshire County, Virginia, and served nine months under Captain James Parsons, Colonels Shepherd, Gibson, Harrison, and General Hand and General Hamilton. Engaged in the Indian campaigns on the Ohio River. Applied for pension, Pendleton County, Virginia, May 8, 1833, and certificate was issued September 11, 1833. Statement of David Reed included in this record.

A note shows that his certificate of discharge, dated December 20, 1782, and signed by James Neville, Lieutenant, Hampshire County, has been removed from the regular pension office case, and may be found in the safe of the Chief of the O. W. and W. Div.

BOWMAN, MARSHALL
Service—North Carolina   Va. No. 23134   No. S-16651
(transferred to Missouri)

Born, October 13, 1760, Amherst County, Virginia. Moved to North

Carolina when 16 years old. After the Revolution returned to Amherst, and four or five years later came to Kanawha County.

Enlisted, October, 1779, and in 1781 re-enlisted, from Burke County, North Carolina. Served nine months as a private under Captain Clark in General Green's army. Was at Wilmington, Delaware, with General McDowell's army when Cornwallis surrendered at Yorktown. Applied for pension, October 20, 1833, Kanawha County, Virginia. Certificate issued, November 15, 1833. Claims supported by David Harbour and Charles Jones. Moved to Missouri to be with his children.

BOWMAN, SAMUEL
Service—Continental New York   Va. No. 19160   No. W-27663

Born in County Down, Ireland, and came with his father, Robert or John Bowman, to New York two or three years before the Revolution. Lived in Albany, then came to Ohio County, Virginia, where he had lived for forty years when he made a pension application, October 6, 1823. Served three years as a private in the Revolution, under Captain Swarthout, Colonel Lamb, Second New York Regiment. Certificate was issued, January 14, 1824, which was suspended in 1834, but in 1838, Bowman's claim was affirmed. He died, February 20, 1840, before he had been restored to the rolls. Evidence submitted that his discharge papers had been stolen. His widow, Dorothy Bowman, applied May 11, 1840, in Marshall County, Virginia, for a pension. The widow, by direct act of Congress, August 26, 1842, was authorized to collect all arrearages from time Bowman was dropped from roll on March 4, 1834, until his death, February 20, 1840.

Long list of persons submitted statements in favor of the Bowmans, including Nancy Mills, Robert Mills, Robert Bowman, Thomas Shannon, Lemuel B. Kimball, Nathaniel Price, Jacob Burley, Mary Burley, and Sam Howard.

BOYD, JAMES
Service—Maryland and Pennsylvania   Va. No. 31488   No. R-1086

Born in Chester County, Pennsylvania, October 3, 1759. Died April 13, 1846. Enlisted, Chester County, Pennsylvania, November, 1776, and served one year as private under Captains Dobson and Williams, Continental Line, Seventh Maryland Regiment. Was at Germantown, Monmouth, Trenton, Brandywine, and King's Bridge.

Applied for pension, February 27, 1829, Monroe County, Virginia. Certificate issued, July 20, 1838. Widow, Flora, applied for pension, 1846, Monroe County, Virginia, but claims were rejected. Supporting claims made by James Dunlap, Isabel Alexander, John Francis, John Raine, James Hanly, and Alexander Dunlap.

BOYD, PATRICK
Service—Virginia   Va. No. 16634   No. W-5846

Born in England, about 1759; died, Monroe County, Virginia, March 1, 1835. Enlisted, Augusta County, Virginia, September, 1777, October, 1781, and served as a private under Ensign Kirk, Captains Smith and Bell,

WEST VIRGINIANS IN THE REVOLUTION   29

Colonels Grayson, Moffitt, and Howyer. Was in battle of Guilford Courthouse.

Married Ann McDowell, April 20, 1787, in Greenbrier County, Virginia, with the Rev. John McCue as minister. Soldier applied for pension, September 17, 1832, Monroe County, and certificate was issued, September 10, 1833. Widow applied for pension April 19, 1841, Monroe County, aged 74, and received certificates. Name of Samuel Alton among those supporting claims.

Boyd enlisted under Ensign Robert Kirk, Augusta County, in the company of Captain Smith, Captain Bell, and Colonel Grayson. Marched to Valley Forge, thence to West Point, and to Middle Brooke of Bond Brook, New Jersey. Was sick in camp during battle of Monmouth. Hired a substitute to continue his service. Refused a lieutenant's commission, and got his discharge from his general at Ellensburg, but lost it. Colonel Gamble of Staunton got him warrant for land. In 1781, volunteered under Captain Thomas Smith, rendezvoused at Waynesboro under Colonel Moffitt, and marched to North Carolina where he was in battle of Guilford Courthouse. Again volunteered, and under Colonel Bowyer marched to Charlottesville, Richmond, and Williamsburg, and was discharged at Hickory Nut Church, 1781.

BOYER, PETER
Service—Pennsylvania   Va. No. 990   No. R-1098

Enlisted, Pennsylvania, 1779, and served as a matross under Captain Turnbull, Second Pennsylvania Artillery Regiment, under Colonel Proctor. Applied for pension, August 17, 1829, Fayette County, Virginia.

Married, August 16, 1793, Augusta County, Virginia; wife's name Catharine. Moved to Cass County, Indiana, in 1839. Died October 10, 1850.

BOYLE, WILLIAM
Enlisted in Captain Shepherd's company in 1776. Was taken prisoner at Fort Washington and died in captivity, February 28, 1777.

BRADSHAW, JOHN
Service—Virginia   Va. No. 12977   No. S-6738

Applied for pension September 4, 1832, and May 7, 1833, Pocahontas County, and received certificate for two-years' service as an Indian spy, June 21, 1833. Died in December, 1834. His claims were supported by Rev. John Blain, William McCord, John Slaven, and John Tallman. Slaven served with Bradshaw.

Bradshaw entered the service as an Indian spy, May, 1776, and served in 1777, 1778, and 1779. Stationed near Cook's Fort, Monroe County, and was accompanied by James Ellis and the late Colonel Samuel Estell of Kentucky. He was drafted in 1780 in company under Captain Thomas Hicklin and Colonel Samuel Vance, and was again drafted in 1781 under Hicklin, Lieutenant Joseph Given, and Ensign Thomas Wright, in regiment under Colonel Sampson Mathews. He was in several engagements and was at the siege of Yorktown and the surrender of Cornwallis. He guarded prisoners on their way to Winchester and was there discharged.

BRADY, CHRISTOPHER (Lieutenant)
Enlisted in Captain Stephenson's rifle company in 1775. On July 23, 1776, enlisted as second lieutenant in the company of his brother, William, in Stephenson's Rifle Regiment. Just before the battle at Fort Washington, he was taken ill and died, November 14, 1776.

BRADY, JAMES
Recruited by Captain Henry Bedinger in 1782. Born in Langford County, Ireland. Lived in Berkeley County during the Revolution.

BRADY, SAMUEL (Captain)
Born in Pennsylvania in 1756. Enlisted in 1775 and served at Boston, Princeton, Brandywine, Monmouth, and on the western borders. He was first lieutenant of Captain Doyle's independent Pennsylvania rifle company, July 17, 1776, attached to the Eighth Pennsylvania Regiment. In November, 1776, he was appointed captain-lieutenant to rank from July 17, 1776; he was made captain, August 2, 1779; transferred to the Third Pennsylvania, January 17, 1781, and served to the end of the war.

His father and brother were killed by the Indians and he became famous as a scout in western Pennsylvania and the northwestern counties of Virginia. He commanded the scouts for General "Mad Anthony" Wayne in 1792. He married Drusilla Swearingen and lived near Wellsburg, Brooke County, Virginia, and later near West Liberty. Here he died, December 25, 1795, and his grave is near his old home.

BRADY, WILLIAM (Captain)
The Journal of Congress, September 6, 1776, says that the "State of Virginia, on the 23rd of July last, appointed William Brady, captain; William Pyle, first lieutenant; and Christopher Brady, second lieutenant, in the battalion to be commanded by Col. Hugh Stephenson (Stevenson). Amos Thompson was to be chaplain of said battalion. It is resolved that the commissions be granted them accordingly." Brady was made captain of the Eleventh Virginia, January 1, 1777, to rank from July 23, 1776. He resigned March 11, 1778.

BRAKE, ABRAHAM
Service—Virginia   No. R-1147
Served in the company, commanded by Captain Bernion, under Ensign Harrison and Lieutenant Stump. Applied for pension, Moorefield, Hardy County. Information incomplete but report of Federal Special Agent indicates that Brake had moved to Harrison County.

BRAKE, JACOB (Lieutenant)
He was a lieutenant in Captain George Jackson's company of spies or rangers in 1778, according to McWhorter's History. He is also mentioned in a letter from the Commission of Pensions to Mrs. Chester M. Cunningham, 510 Stanley Ave., Clarksburg, October 19, 1922.

His mother was killed during an Indian raid in 1758, and perhaps during the same raid, Jacob, a lad of 11 years, was captured by the Indians and adopted into the tribe. He remained a captive almost eleven years. He married Mary Slaughter. His death was in 1831.

WEST VIRGINIANS IN THE REVOLUTION

BRAKE, JOHN
Service—Virginia　　　Va. No. 23559　　　No. S-15762
Claimed service as an Indian spy for twelve months under Captain J. Harriss, Colonel Vanmeter, and Major Ruddle. Applied for pension, Harrison County, July 8, 1834. Certificate was issued, but he was later stricken from the pension rolls.

BRAND, JAMES
The grave of James Brand, soldier in the Revolution, who died in 1836, is in the Burnt Meeting House Cemetery, Grant District, Monongalia County.

BRAND, JOHN
The grave of John Brand, Revolutionary soldier, who died in 1834, is in the Burnt Meeting House Cemetery, Grant District, Monongalia County.

BRAXTER (BAXTER?), WILLIAM (Lieutenant)
Service—Virginia　　　Va. No. 12099 and 8354　　　No. S-6591
Born, Baltimore County, Maryland, April 18, 1756. Enlisted in Virginia and served 13 months as private, sergeant, and lieutenant under Captain Isaac Cox, Lieutenant David Steel, and Ensign George Cox, Continental Establishment, Thirteenth Virginia Regiment, under Colonel Gibson. Stationed at Holliday's Cove on the Ohio River with Colonel Williamson's militia. Applied for pension, August 7, 1832, Brooke County, Virginia. Certificate issued, March 22, 1833. Supporting claims filed by Philip Doddridge, Captain George Cox, and the Rev. Edward Smith.

BRIAN, DANIEL
Service—Maryland　　　Va. No. 6802　　　No. S-39246
Served as private three years under Captain Morris, Colonel Gomby's Regiment of Maryland troops. Was at Brandywine, Germantown, and Staten Island. Enlisted at Frederick County, Maryland, 1777-1779. Applied for pension, April 18, 1818, Jefferson County, Virginia, aged 64. Certificate issued February 11, 1819.

BREEDIN, JOHN (Sergeant)
Lived near Harpers Ferry, Jefferson County. Served as a sergeant under General George Rogers Clark in the Illinois country.

BREEDIN, RICHARD
Served as private under George Rogers Clark on the expedition against Vincennes and Kaskaskia.

West Virginians in the American Revolution

This is the fourth article in a series which contains an alphabetical check list of Revolutionary soldiers who at one time or another lived in what is now West Virginia. The series will continue for several numbers. This material has been assembled and edited by Ross B. Johnston. In the next few years, the Department of Archives and History hopes to publish this list in one volume, properly indexed. The public is invited to send in corrections as the material appears and to submit names of other Revolutionary soldiers whose authentic records qualify them to be listed among the other West Virginians who were with Washington's army.

This list of more than thirteen hundred sketches of Revolutionary soldiers from what is now West Virginia is offered with the full understanding that it represents only part of those who properly belong in this group. There are, for example, large lists of names, such as the roster of George Rogers Clark's forces of men, whose residences were uncertain, although many of the frontiersmen who joined Clark at Point Pleasant and Parkersburg on his western expedition lived west of the mountains.

The sources of this material are notes from the files of the Pension Office at Washington, from the pension applications in West Virginia counties, and from the minute books of the older West Virginia counties, copied by W. P. A. workers on the project sponsored by the West Virginia Commission on Historic and Scenic Markers; from notes of the Daughters of the American Revolution, Sons of the American Revolution, Sons of the Revolution, and other patriotic societies; and from a large miscellaneous group of published and private sources. It was found necessary to condense many extended notes in order to save space. Doubtless this omitted some points of interest, but in most instances the omissions were repetitions of facts common to many other cases.

(Note: Numbers and letters appearing with many names are references to files of Pension Bureau, War Department, Washington, D. C.)

BRICKELL, GEORGE (Sergeant)
Service—Pennsylvania   Pa. No. 31320   No. S-5302

Born, York County, Pennsylvania, October 16, 1760. At age of five, was adopted by Robert Ross, Redstone, Westmoreland County, Pennsylvania. Ross was drafted in 1776, and Brickell served as his substitute under Daniel Cannon in 1777. Served another term as a volunteer in 1781 under Captain Benjamin Whaley.

Applied for pension, December 29, 1837, Birmingham Burrough, Allegheny County, Pennsylvania. Supporting affidavits from Robert Bruce, R. A. Bausman, Sam Murphy, and Colonel James Paull. Held commission of sergeant from Captain Sample. (Note that this record does not show residence in western Virginia but is included because it was filed in the Virginia group.)

BRINKER, HENRY
Service—Virginia   Va. No. 12558   No. S-5305

Enlisted in Virginia, 1781. Guarded English prisoners taken with General Burgoyne. While in Winchester under Captain Frost, was an express rider for General Lafayette. Stationed at Fredericksburg several weeks with volunteers under Colonel Thomas. Served two months with cavalry under Captain Gill and two months as lieutenant with Colonel Smith.

Applied for pension, September 24, 1832, Springfield, Hampshire County, Virginia. Certificate issued, May 9, 1833. Supporting affidavits by John J. Jacob and John Brady.

BRINKLEY, WILLIAM

On January 26, 1819, William Brinkley, aged sixty-one, resident of Greenbrier County, Virginia, appeared before its court and declared that he enlisted, Shenandoah County, Virginia, in company of Captain Jonathan Clark, in 1776, in Eighth Virginia Rifle Regiment under Colonel Muhlenberg, and that after two years he was honorably discharged in Suffolk County, Virginia.

BRISCOE, JOHN (Surgeon)

Settled near Shepherdstown in 1733; was active in organizing the militia during the Revolution and at one time acted as a surgeon of a company. He was born, March, 1717, and died, December 7, 1788. He married Elizabeth McMillan, a daughter of Captain John McMillan, who commanded a company of Berkeley County militia during the Revolution.

BRISCOE, REUBEN (Captain)
In April, 1778, was appointed captain of the Fourth Company of riflemen under Colonel Daniel Morgan.

BRITTON, JOSEPH
Service—Virginia   Va. No. 6258   No. S-8087
Britton, in statement in Harrison County, says he enlisted, Winchester, Virginia, in 1779-1781, under Captain J. Chapman, Virginia Regiment, under Colonel Crockett, Colonel Gibson, and General George Rogers Clark, and that he continued in service for two years. He was first marched to Albemarle County to guard prisoners, thence to Frederick Town, thence to Pittsburgh, and then to the Falls of the Ohio, where he was discharged. Was with party when Indians fired upon them, killing Captains Chapman and Tipton. Applied for pension, Harrison County, August 21, 1832. Certificate was issued, February 27, 1833, later discontinued, but was resumed in 1835.

BROADUS, WILLIAM (Lieutenant)
Service—Virginia   Va. No. 12757   No. W-8396 and B.L.Wt.-1875
Served from December 7, 1778, to February, 1781, in First Virginia Regiment, as a lieutenant under Colonel Gibson. Enlisted in Jefferson County where he applied for pension. Died October 7, 1830, or September, 1832. Married, February 18, 1805, in Hanover County, Virginia, by Rev. J. D. Blair. Name of wife given as Martha, who died, February 21, 1863, Harpers Ferry, Jefferson County, but widow is also referred to as Sara Ann Broaddus. Other heirs were Maria E. and Lavina. After much dispute, the heirs seem to have been given amount claimed, including bounty lands.

BROOKOVER, JOHN
Service—Virginia and Maryland   Va. No. 16376   No. S-5300
Born in Maryland, about 1760. Enlisted at Carroll Manor, Maryland, at age of eighteen to escape a hard taskmaster, and served eighteen months as a private under Captain Francis Smith and Colonel Aulk, or Alcott, of the Virginia Line. Applied for pension, Wood County, October 4, 1832, and certificate was issued, August 3, 1833. Supporting affidavits by John Pugh, David Uhl, John Marshall, Noah Ogden, David Watts, Nancy Carter Easter, Sergeant Ezekiel Carter, Amos Brown, and Josiah Smith. Suspended, December 13, 1834, and nothing to show resumption.

BROOKS, WILLIAM
Service—Virginia   Va. No. 12980 and 15458   No. R-1259
Born, February 3, 1752, Fauquier County, Virginia, and died, January 24, 1841. Enlisted in Culpeper County, Virginia, and shows following service: October, 1777, Culpeper County under Captain Richard Waugh, Colonels James Baxter and Hankiah Harmon, and Lieutenant Bazett Noe; February, 1781, Botetourt County, Captain James Woods, Colonel James Crockett; November 1, 1781, Captain Thomas Hamilton, Lieutenant William Slaughter, Ensign Robert Bush, and Colonel Charles Dabney.

WEST VIRGINIANS IN THE REVOLUTION

Applied for pension, Fayette County, Virginia, September 25, 1832. Pension granted. Married, September 5, 1769, to Nancy Brooks. His widow applied for pension, August 29, 1843, but pension certificate was not granted owing to failure to produce sufficient proof of claim.

BROWN, ADAM

The grave of Adam Brown, Revolutionary soldier, who died in 1820, is near Price, on Jake's Run, Monongalia County.

BROWN, EDWARD
Service—Virginia   No. 1292

Applied for pension, Lewis County, Virginia, June 29, 1834. He stated that he had lived in Lewis County for forty-three years, had previously lived in Harrison County, and before that time had been in Hardy County. He had enlisted in 1781 and was aged seventy or seventy-one in 1834. Special Federal Agent Singleton ruled that he had not had sufficient service to be granted a pension.

BROWN, GEORGE

Private in Captain Shepherd's rifle company. Taken captive at Fort Washington in 1776 but was exchanged.

BROWN, JAMES
Service—Virginia   Va. No. 12650   No. S-6718

Born, 1756, Cumberland County, Pennsylvania. Resided in Hampshire County, now Hardy County, when Revolution began, and resided in Lewis County, in 1832, where he applied for pension. Certificate issued, May 16, 1833, but was later dropped. Enlisted, March, 1776, and served two years under Ensign Baldwin Parsons, Lieutenant Cunningham, Captain James Parsons, Captain Isaac Parsons, Colonel Gibson, and General McIntosh. Was an Indian Spy under Captain Tanner and Colonel Lowther. Held three discharges, from Summerel, Parsons, and Stump. Supporting papers from John Brown, a brother, and Mark Smith.

BROWN, JAMES

Member of Captain Shepherd's rifle company. Taken prisoner at the capture of Fort Washington in 1776 and was exchanged. Bought the Glove Tavern, once known as Entler's Hotel, Shepherdstown, from Daniel Bedinger. Married Eleanor Rutherford of Flowing Springs, daughter of Robert Rutherford and wife, Mary Daubigny Howe, widow of Lord George Howe, killed at Ticonderoga in 1758.

BROWN, JOHN (Sergeant)
Service—Virginia   Va. No. 12189   No. R-1277

Born, August 25, 1763, and died February 10, 1843. Enlisted, Leeds Town, Westmoreland County, Virginia, 1779-1781, and served as private two years in company of Captain John Mazarott, Captain Christopher Roan, Fifth Virginia Regiment, Continental Line, Colonel Thomas Marshall and General Wayne. Was in campaigns about Petersburg, Hillsboro,

Camden, and Yorktown. Applied for pension, October 18, 1818, Hampshire County, Virginia; certificate issued May 17, 1819.

Married, November, 1792, to Ann Murphy. Widow applied for pension, October 5, 1843. Widow born about September 10, 1765. Following are children's names: Elizabeth Brown, born 1800; William and Margaret (twins), 1803; Peggy, 1805; Corbin, 1793; James F., 1804; Elizabeth Hansbrough, 1799; Tanney McClough Brown, (date uncertain).

Brown was a private in Marshall's artillery, receiving discharge from Colonel P. Kump, and his statement shows that he did the work of a sergeant during the same period. He received pension as a sergeant. He resided in Hampshire County in 1819, in Wheeling, Ohio County, in March, 1837, and in Pickaway County, Ohio, in August, 1837, and in 1839. Supporting affidavit by William Sandy.

BROWN, JOHN (Ensign)
Service—Virginia   Va. No. 12649   No. S-6720

Enlisted, Hampshire County, Virginia, March 1, 1781, and served as private and ensign under Captain M. Stump, Colonel William Darke, General Weeden, and General Muhlenberg. Applied for pension, August 7, 1832, Lewis County. Certificate issued, May 16, 1833, but was later dropped from the rolls.

BROWN, OLIVER (Captain-Lieutenant)
Service—Continental, Massachusetts   No. 6213 and 32409   No. S-8088

Born at Lexington, Massachusetts, in 1752; died, February 17, 1846, and is buried at Wellsburg, Brooke County, West Virginia. The epitaph on his tombstone reads: "He stood in front of the first cannon fired by the British on the Americans in the affray at Lexington; witnessed the 'Tea Party' in Boston Harbor; was at the Battle of Bunker Hill; commissioned by Congress, January 16, 1776; commanded the volunteer party which carried off the leaden statue of King George from the Battery of New York and made it into bullets for the American army; bore a conspicuous part in command of the artillery at the battles of White Plains, Harbor Heights, Princeton, Trenton, Germantown, and Monmouth."

Enlisted in corps of artillery commanded by Colonel Richard Gridley as lieutenant, June to December, 1775; received commission as lieutenant in regiment of artillery commanded by General Henry Knox, signed by John Hancock, president of Congress, dated December 13, 1775; on January 1, 1777, was commissioned captain-lieutenant of regiment of artillery commanded by Colonel Henry Crain. Resigned last commission, April 30, 1779.

Applied for pension, May 23, 1818, Wellsburg, Brooke County, Virginia. Name of wife, Abigail; daughter, Elizabeth, aged twenty, 1818. Pension granted, February 1, 1819, and increased, December 25, 1845. Died, February 17, 1846.

BROWN, SAMUEL

Private in Captain Shepherd's rifle company. Was taken prisoner in 1776, was exchanged, and was killed September 26, 1777.

WEST VIRGINIANS IN THE REVOLUTION 37

BROWN, THOMAS
Service—Virginia Va. No. 2581 No. S-6769
Born, September 7, 1760, Prince William County, Virginia. Enlisted, 1780, at Dumfries, Prince William County, and served as a private in company of Captain John Britt, under Colonel Lucas, General Stevens, and General Green in the Virginia Line. Engaged on marches and guard duty in Virginia, and North and South Carolina. Applied for pension, Preston County, Virginia, August 14, 1832, and certificate was granted, December 1, 1833.

BROWN, WILLIAM
William Brown, a private in the Revolution, was born in Cecil County, Maryland, October 11, 1752, and died in Brooke County, Virginia, July 3, 1832. Before the Revolution, he lived in Delaware. He was married to Patience Marvel in 1773. He is buried at West Liberty.

BROWNLEE, JOHN
Service—Pennsylvania No. S-39238
Enlisted, 1776, Washington County, Pennsylvania, with Captain James Carnaghen's and Captain Joseph Irvings' (Irvens') companies in the battalion of riflemen in the regiment, commanded by Colonel Samuel Mills. Colonel Mills was taken prisoner in the battle of Lewistown and his command reduced to thirty-five men, so it was consolidated with another commanded by Colonel Ball (later by Colonel Walter Stewart).
Continued to serve until receiving discharge, January, 1778, signed by Colonel Walter Stewart, of the 18th Pennsylvania Regiment at Valley Forge. Served eighteen months and was in battles of Long Island, White Plains, the taking of the Hessians at Trenton, Princeton, Brandywine, and Germantown. Supporting claims by John Marshall. Applied for pension, June 20, 1818, Washington County, Pennsylvania. Had moved to Brooke County, Virginia, prior to September 4, 1827.

BRYAN, DANIEL
Native of Maryland, and served in the Maryland Line, but after the Revolution came to Jefferson County, Virginia, where he was pensioned and died in 1834.

BRYAN, TIMMONS
Private in Captain Shepherd's rifle company. May not have been captured with greater part of his company, as he was drafted into another rifle company in January, 1777.

BUCHANAN, ROBERT
Service—New Jersey Va. No. 16400 No. S-37806
Enlisted, Orange County, New York, May, 1777, and remained in service until May, 1780. Was in company of Captain Bunnel, or Burrel, and Colonel Spencer, Fourth Jersey Regiment. Was in a battle against the Indians in the state of New York and was also in several skirmishes. Received honorable discharge at Morristown, New Jersey.

Pension application, November 23, 1819, Greenbrier County, Virginia. Certificate received, January 26, 1820. Wife was aged sixty-nine or seventy in 1820.

BUCKLEY, JOHN

In the court minutes of Berkeley County, Virginia, December 23, 1788, it is recorded that Ann Watson, late the widow of John Buckley, a drummer in the Continental service, who was enlisted for five years and died in New Jersey, appeared in court and proved that she was the said widow, and that she had remained a widow until January, 1787.

BUFFINGTON, DAVID

Service—Virginia   Ohio No. 4008   No. W-4906

Born, Romney, Hampshire County, 1762. Resided in Hampshire County until 1822, then lived in Fairfield County, Ohio. Died, October 6, 1836.

Served one year and eleven months under Captain Kirkpatrick, Colonels Febecker, Gaskins, and Baron Von Steuben. Married, Hampshire County, March 2, 1784. Wife, Margaret, aged eighty-two, in 1845. Soldier applied for pension, Walnut Township, Fairfield County, Ohio, November 6, 1832. Certificate issued, 1833. Widow applied for pension, January 17, 1845. Military warrant, No. 2991, issued for 200 acres of land. Supporting affidavits by John Wiseman and John Hall.

Children of David and Margaret Buffington and dates of birth: Mary, May 11, 1786; Rebecca, September 6, 1788; John, November 18, 1790; Catherine, April 16, 1793; Susannah, August 14, 1794; Peter, February 22, 1797; Richard, November 21, 1802; Mary Ann, June 20, 1806; William, August 11, 1808.

BUMGARNER (BOMGARDNER), DAVID

Born, Shenandoah County, Virginia, May, 1758. Died, October 9, 1835. Enlisted in Shenandoah County, September, 1777, and served six months as a private under Lieutenant McCarty, Captain Rader, in Virginia Line, under Colonels Steel and Gibson, and General Hand.

Married Catherine Bunner, Shenandoah County, April 18, 1786, or 1787; Rev. John Comer as the minister, as recorded in that county. Applied for pension, August 27, 1832, and October 7, 1833, Jackson and Mason Counties, Virginia. Certificates issued, as well as later certificates to the widow. Supporting claims filed by A. Waggoner and Adam Whitzel.

BUNNEL, JOHN

Service—Continental   Va. No. 5995   No. W-6222

Enlisted in Virginia, March, 1782, and served fourteen months as a gunner under Captain Malchen in Colonel Lamb's artillery regiment. Applied for pension, Harrison County, Virginia, May 19, 1818. Certificate issued, July 28, 1819. Married, May 8, 1792, to Hannah Smith, who was forty-eight years old in 1820, and who applied for pension in Marion County, Virginia, August 3, 1844. Two children: Charles, 12; Margaret, 3. (Widow appears to have married a second time.) Supporting claims by Sarah Johnson and Elijah Price.

BURDIN, JOHN
Service—Delaware-New York   Va. No. 23968   No. S-12369

Born Sussex County, Delaware, 1752. Enlisted, Chester County, Pennsylvania, and Broadhill, Delaware, 1778 and 1779, and served as private one year under Lieutenant Harrad, Ensigns Hall and Sackett, Colonel Hall, and Colonel Selden. Applied for pension, August 28, 1832, Monongalia County, Virginia. Certificate issued, March 7, 1833; then suspended but restored in later years.

BURGESS, EDWARD
Service—Maryland   Va. No. 18784-18983   No. S-37813

Enlisted, Fayette County, Pennsylvania, June 1, 1778, and July 1, 1779. Had previously lived in Maryland. Served as private one year under Captain Thomas Bell, Maryland Line, Continental Establishment, under Colonel Moses Rawlings. Received honorable discharge at Fort Pitt, Pennsylvania.

Pension application, March 5, 1822, Fayette County, Pennsylvania. Certificate issued, May 29, 1823. Transferred to Morgantown, Virginia, July 25, 1825. Supporting claims by Uriah Springer.

BURKHAM, STEPHEN

Born, Berkeley County. In the autumn of 1768, his father's family moved to the Youghiogheny near Beeson's Fort. McIntosh's campaign was the first military campaign in which he engaged. In 1781, he went on Williamson's Moravian expedition, and the next year on Crawford's disastrous Sandusky campaign. He was likewise present at the siege of Wheeling in 1782. In 1845, he was living near Wheeling.

BURNER, ABRAHAM
Service—Virginia   Va. No. 898   No. W-24693

Born, Shenandoah County, Virginia, about 1753, son of Earhart Burner. Died, June 28, 1827. Enlisted, January, 1777, and February or March, 1778, and served two years as private under Captains Mathias Hite and Rinker, Eighth Virginia Regiment, Continental Establishment commanded by Colonel Bowman.

Married, Mary Magdalene Hull, June 5, 1780, Pendleton County, Virginia. They had seven sons and two daughters. Soldier applied for pension, October 25, 1819, Randolph County, Virginia. Certificate issued, November 27, 1819. Widow applied for pension, June 3, 1839, and certificate was issued February 20, 1840. She was born in Pendleton County, Virginia, about 1763 and died January 18, 1840, before the pension in her favor had been granted, so it was paid to four living children.

Among persons making supporting affidavits were Henry Burner, brother of the soldier, Adam Arbogast, and John Slaven.

BURNS, GEORGE
Service—Virginia   No. R-1483

Born, Louden County, Virginia, March 12, 1757. Moved to Rockingham in 1772 and to Randolph County in 1800. Substituted for John Parsons as a private of militia, April, 1778, for seven months, and for Adam Simmons, April, 1781, for six months. Served under Generals Hand, McIntosh, Campbell, Wayne, Lafayette, Baron Von Steuben, Colonels Dickinson, Skillern, Van Meter, Harrison, Waggoner, Stricker, Butler, Hugart, and Captains Cunningham, Joseph Berry, Smith, Ragan, and Long. Claim was rejected.

BURROWS, EZEKIEL
Service—Delaware   Va. No. 5219   No. S-39259

Enlisted in Delaware and served one year as a private in the Flying Camp regiment, Delaware Line, under Captain Perry and Colonel D. Hall. Applied for pension, April 28, 1818, Monongalia County, Virginia. Certificate issued, January 7, 1819.

BUSH, DENNIS (Sergeant)

Was sergeant in Captain Shepherd's rifle company. Was recruited by Henry Bedinger in Berkeley County, Virginia. Taken prisoner at Fort Washington but was exchanged.

BUSH, JACOB
Service—Virginia   Va. No. 16970   No. W-24685

Enlisted, 1778, in Captain Samuel Pringle's company of Indian spies from Buckhannon Fort. Scouted from the West Fork and Little Kanawha rivers to the Ohio River under Lieutenant Westfall. Also served under the militia regiment of Colonel Morgan. Substituted for his brother, John Bush, with Captain Jackson and Lieutenant William White. Joined army of General Clark and descended the Ohio River to the Falls. Frequently acted as hunter. Killed two deer on the north side of river and took the brains of one to General Clark who treated him to whisky. Alexander West, David M. Sleeth, John Talbott, George Butcher, and Adam Flesher supported his claim. Mentions William Powers. Born, 1756, Hampshire County, Virginia. Before the Revolution, lived in Monongalia County, now Lewis County.

Bush married Margaret Snarr, or Swan, in Augusta or Hardy County, 1782-1784, by publication of Reverend Mitchell. Witnesses were Adam Flesher, John Cutright, and Christianna McCune. Their children were: Henry, Peter, Jacob, John, George, Elizabeth (Stump), Margaret (Stump), Barbary (Fisher), Susannah (Simpson), and Michael (dead, leaving a widow, Mary, and a son, Adam).

Soldier applied for pension, November 7, 1832. Certificate was issued, October 18, 1833, but as soldier had died in the meantime, November 27, 1832, pension was issued in favor of his widow, Margaret. Soldier is buried in Gilmer County. Widow applied for pension, August 7, 1833, and it was issued. She died, July 28, 1847.

BUTCHER, PAULSER (PAULCERE)

Both Lewis and Gilmer counties claim the burial place of Paulser Butcher, but the evidence is in favor of the Butcher cemetery in Lewis County. He is believed to be buried there with his wife, Elizabeth Bush

Butcher, and an unbroken line of descendants for eight generations. Butcher, with six brothers, is believed to have served in the Revolution under Washington, and four of this number gave up their lives in the service.

BUTCHER, SAMUEL (Lieutenant)
Born, Louden County, Virginia, March 28, 1756. There he enlisted, October, 1780, and served as first lieutenant, under commission of Governor of Virginia. His officers included Captains Davis, Shores, and Noland, Colonels Alexander and Dabney, Majors Jacob Reed, Quarles, and Campbell, Generals Washington, Weedon, Wayne, and Lafayette. Applied for pension, Wood County, Virginia, November 12, 1833, but was rejected as having insufficient service. Died, 1847. Had lived in Fauquier, Hardy, Randolph, and Wood counties.

Supporting affidavits by James Cooper, Turner Boulware, and Susannah Lenard (Leonard or Leander). Abstract of his will is as follows: To my son, Thomas, 100 acres; also "six acres adjoining the mansion house, three acres of which was conveyed to me by Margaret Dawkins and three acres by William Hill"; mentions among other heirs, daughter, Susannah Vaughn, Eli, John and Peyton Burcher, Ury Reeder, Tasy Hammer, Ann Vaughan, Deborah Pribble, and Hannah Kincheloe. Atwell Vaughan, Susan Vaughan, and J. D. Riley were named executors.

BURCHNELL, JAMES
Resided in Lewis County, Virginia, in 1824, where he applied for pension. His claim was rejected after report of Special Federal Agent Singleton.

BUTT, ARCHIBALD
Service—Maryland and North Carolina   Va. No. 16439   No. S-39252

Enlisted, Prince George County, Maryland, 1777-1782. Served five years as private under Captain Benjamin Coleman, William Smith, (recruiting officer) in Second North Carolina Regiment Continental Establishment, under Colonel Clark. In action at Monmouth, Charleston, and Little York. Taken prisoner at Charleston by Cornwallis' army, held for four weeks in close confinement, until he escaped. Joined American army at Annapolis, Maryland, under General Mordecai Gist and continued in service until the surrender of Cornwallis at Yorktown.

Applied for pension, Greenbrier County, Virginia, November 24, 1819, aged fifty-five. Certificate was issued, November 28, 1819. Widow was aged sixty-nine, September 1, 1820. Their children were Nancy, 14; William, 11; John, 9; and Thomas 5 or 6.

BUTT, (BUTTS) BARUCH
Service—Maryland   No. S-39258

Enlistments, April 3, 1778, August 1, 1780, to November 15, 1783, from Prince George County, Maryland. Served under Captain Williams, Second Maryland Regiment, and Colonel Wolford, at Camden and Cowpens. Honorably discharged at Annapolis, Maryland, 1783. Certificate of service supported by Joe Couss, Lieutenant, Osburn Williams, Lieutenant, and R. Loorherman, Adjutant General. (Note: Although all service seems to be in Maryland, this claim is grouped with the Virginia claims. His name appears in one of the rifle companies enrolled by Colonel Daniel Morgan in 1777.)

BUTT, EDWARD J. ZACHARIAH

Before the Greenbrier County Court, Thomas Butt secured approval of an order to the War Department that it appears to the satisfaction of the court by competent testimony that the said Thomas is one of the legitimate heirs at law of Edward J. Z. Butt, who was killed in battle while in the service of the States during the Revolutionary War. (His name is in Captain Shepherd's rifle company in 1776. He appears to have been drafted into another company in 1777.)

BUTT, THOMAS
Service—Maryland   Mo. No. 4799   No. W-8252   B. L. Wt.-10982

Served as a musician under Captain Silburn Williams, Second Maryland Regiment, Continental Line, Colonel Wolford. Applied for pension, May 25, 1829, Greenbrier County, Virginia. Married, February 6, 1809, to Mary Taylor. Soldier died March 1, 1833. Widow, aged sixty-eight, applied for pension, November 29, 1854, Henry County, Illinois, later Missouri, and certificate was issued in her favor, December 16, 1854. Supporting claims by William Humphrey, Thomas D. Butt, Sarah Butt, Thomas Perry, and Peter Beyer.

BURNS, JAMES (Sergeant)
Service—Pennsylvania-Maryland   Va. No. 17783   No. S-39267

Enlisted, Pennsylvania and Maryland, and served three years under Colonel Mordecai Gist in Captain John Smith's company. He was afterwards sergeant in the Maryland Line. After his first enlistment, he served to the end of the war in Captain John Head's company of infantry, attached to Colonel Stephen Moyland's, or Moylen's, light dragoons of the Pennsylvania Line and was discharged by Colonel Richard Butler at Lancaster, Pennsylvania. He also mentions Major Archibald Anderson and Major General Lincoln. He was wounded in the leg at Camden, South Carolina, where his captain was taken prisoner.

Applications for pension made in Brooke and Ohio counties, 1818 and 1820. At that time his wife was dead, and he was living with a granddaughter and her husband. A supporting claim is made by J. J. Bough.

BYRES, JACOB

Born in Chester County, Pennsylvania. Lived in Shepherdstown during the Revolution. Was enlisted for Captain Bedinger's company by Captain Cherry, December 3, 1782.

BYRNES (BYRNS), JOHN (Sergeant)
Service—Pennsylvania, Maryland, Continental   Va. No. 3482   No. W-6224

Enlisted, Hagerstown, Maryland, in 1775, as a private in the Virginia Line, and later as a sergeant in the Pennsylvania Line, under Captains Kersley, Skin, and Busher, Sixth Virginia Regiment, and Eleventh Pennsylvania Regiment, Colonels Hendricks, Hand, and Hulby.

Born in 1750 and died, November 7, 1836. Applied for pension, Harrison County, Virginia, April 13, 1818. Certificate issued, October 8, 1818. Married, Esther Cavalier, in Harrison County, Virginia, March 12, 1792. She applied for pension, June 23, 1847, and received certificate. Supporting claims by Rebecca Cavalier, William L. Richardson, and Elizabeth Wadsworth Byrnes, a daughter-in-law.

BYRNES, THOMAS

Born in Langford County, Ireland. Recruited by Henry Bedinger from Berkeley County, Virginia, in 1782.

CABBAGE, CONRAD

Enlisted for Captain Shepherd's rifle company, August 6, 1776, by Henry Bedinger. Taken prisoner at Fort Washington, November 16, 1776, and died in prison, January 7, 1777.

CAIN, JOHN (Sergeant)
Service—Virginia   Va. No. 16903   No. S-17873

Claimed service for twenty-two months as a private and sergeant with the Virginia troops in pension application in 1832. Certificate was issued October 12, 1833, but it was dropped in 1835, and not reinstated. Mrs. Catharine Lowther, July 19, 1834, gave her own birth as October 27, 1766, and the birth of her brother, John Cain, as February 26, 1769.

West Virginians in the American Revolution

Assembled and Edited by ROSS B. JOHNSTON

The sources of this material are from the files of the Pension Office at Washington, from various county records, from notes of patriotic societies, principally the Daughters of the American Revolution, Sons of the American Revolution, Sons of the Revolution, and from a large miscellaneous group of published and private sources. Corrections and additions to this list will receive the careful attention of the editor.

CALDWELL, JOHN
Service—Virginia   No. S-9146

Born in Ireland, January 22, 1753. While still a boy, his parents emigrated to America and first settled near Baltimore. In 1773, Caldwell removed to near Wheeling, and for several years was engaged in the Indian wars. In 1774, he was with Dunmore. In October, 1776, he was one of a party from Grave Creek Fort that went down the Ohio to rescue the wounded and bury the dead of Robert Patterson's party, coming from Kentucky. The next year, Caldwell was a volunteer under Captain Samuel Mason. At first stationed at Fort Shepherd, he was at Fort Henry during the siege.

Caldwell, while out scouting, ran up a hill to escape an ambuscade, tripped and fell, and was wedged between two trees. Seeing an Indian pursuing him, he wrenched himself loose with great effort, just as the Indian threw his tomahawk, which missed its aim. Caldwell escaped to Shepherd's Fort, six miles up the creek. In 1778 and 1779, he was a volunteer guard at Fort Henry, Wheeling, and in the latter year went on Brodhead's expedition.

He also saw service for a time at Rail's Fort (probably Rice's Fort), on Buffalo Creek. He lived on Wheeling Creek, about fourteen miles above its mouth, until his death in 1840. His father resided on site of Washington, Pennsylvania. He applied for pension, Ohio County, Virginia, August 10, 1832, and certificate was issued in his favor. Later, however, he was dropped from the rolls. Although he was known to be a valued and brave Indian fighter, his services did not come under the act of June 7, 1832.

Supporting claims by Marcus W. Chaplin, William Hoskins (Harkins), John Mills, Joseph Alexander, Abraham McCullock, and Isaac Seffler (Suffern).

CALL, HUGH

Born, January 24, 1764. Enlisted, 1782, under Captain Tast. Applied for pension, February 11, 1835, Greenbrier County, but his case was suspended on ground of insufficient service.

CANAFAX, WILLIAM
Service—Virginia   Va. No. 23938   No. S-19233

Born, Cumberland County, Virginia, July 9, 1758. Served twelve months in the Revolution in the companies of Captains Chiles and Montgomery, Virginia Regiment commanded by Colonels Larreson and Clark, and General Muhlenberg. Resided in Campbell County, Virginia, at time of enlistment. Applied for pension, Monroe County, Virginia, January 15, 1834. Certificate issued, April 28, 1834. Supporting affidavits by Rev. Jacob Cook and Adam Mann.

CANFIELD, DANIEL
Service—New York   Va. No. 19974   No. W-9768

Born, February 10, 1757. Enlisted, New York and served nine months under Captain J. Rosencrantz, New York Regiment, Continental Establishment, commanded by Colonel Holmes and General Clinton. Fought at Fort Montgomery. Applied for pension, April 2, 1825, Randolph County, Virginia. Certificate issued, September 15, 1828. Died, October 31, 1832.

Married, Dutchess County, New York, by Elder Lawrence, Baptist minister. Wife's name, Elizabeth. Born, May 25, 1759. Names of children: Nathan, January 20, 1779, (died near Chillicothe, Ohio, 1813); Mary, November 12, 1781; Titus, August 28, 1784; Sarah, February 16, 1787; Zachariah, September 8, 1790; Daniel, August 17, 1791; Amos, January 14, 1794; Zedediah, September 20, 1796; Moses, October 6, 1798; Henry, January 18, 1801; Margaret, June 20, 1804. Widow applied for pension, August, 1841, Jennings County, Indiana. The family had also lived for a time in Ohio. Supporting affidavits submitted by Elisha Daikin, John Canfield, and Henry Martin.

CANTERBURY, JOHN
Service—Virginia   No. R-1667

Born in Prince William County, Virginia, 1759; resided in Montgomery County, 1778, and in Washington County, Virginia, in 1781.

His pension declaration in Monroe County, Virginia, shows a varied service against the Indians. For a time, he was at the station of Benjamin Logan in Kentucky; then he served with Captain Joseph Martin on the French Broad River with the forces under Colonel Sevier against the Cherokee Indians; he was next on a campaign on the Holston River under Colonel Campbell with General Marion's army against the British forces in the Carolinas.

His claims were supported by Rev. Jacob Cook, James Stodghill, Rev. Johnson Keeton, John Roach, Rev. Joseph Ellison, and Samuel Clark. Claim rejected, pending submission of further proof.

CARDER, WILLIAM
Service—Virginia   Va. No. 16395   No. S-17872

Born, Hampshire County, Virginia, 1760. Enlisted, March, 1780, Hampshire County, and later was in Monongalia County. Served two years as a private under Captain Isaac Parsons, Colonels William Lowther and Carpenter. Applied for pension, September 27, 1833, Lewis County, Virginia, and certificate was issued, but later suspended, and money returned. His service on the frontier was not ruled sufficient to justify pension. Supporting claims were made by John Brown and John Schoolcraft. Manly Carder mentioned, possibly his wife or daughter. Richard Bell was also named, relationship not shown. A stepdaughter was named Mrs. John Mitchell.

CAREY (CARY), MICHAEL
Service—Maryland   Va. No. 11319   No. S-40039

Served three years as private under Captain Beaty in the Seventh Maryland Regiment, under Colonel Gumby. Saw service at Camden, Hanging Rock, Eutaw Springs, and Cowpens. Enlisted near Baltimore, 1778 to 1783. Applied for pension, Harrison County, October 20, 1818, and certificate was issued, June 4, 1818. Wife was sixty-one years old in 1820. Two children are named: Nancy, 19; Peggy, 16.

CARNEY, THOMAS
Service—Virginia   No. 1711

Application of Thomas Carney for pension, filed July, 1834, Lewis County, Virginia, was refused on account of the inability of claimant to prove that he was old enough for such service. John Reger, John Mitchell, Henry Flesher, and Samuel Bonnett testified in his behalf.

CARPENTER, CHRISTOPHER
Satisfactory evidence was produced before the Harrison County Court, March 18, 1833, to prove that Nicholas Carpenter, of said county, was the son and sole surviving heir of Christopher Carpenter; and that said Christopher Carpenter enlisted in the Revolution about 1776 under Captain Henry Heth to serve during the war in the Virginia Line; and that he was marched to Pittsburgh and there served to the end of the war as an artificer; and that he was in service seven years under different commanders, attached to the Ninth Regiment.

CARPENTER, DAVID
Pension application was refused in report of U. S. District Attorney, made in July, 1834. In application in Lewis County, Virginia, David Carpenter was shown to have come to Harrison County in 1776. He declared in 1834 that he was seventy-two years old and had rendered service for three years and nine months. He was declared too young to have rendered such service.

Testimony was submitted which indicated that he did serve in the Indian wars in 1785. Among statements submitted were those from John Reger, Nicholas Carpenter, a cousin, Isaac Washburn, John Neeley, William Powers, and Waldo P. Goff.

CARPENTER, JESSE
Service—Virginia   Va. No. 16589   No. S-9309

Applied in Lewis County, Virginia, for pension, on grounds of two years' service in the Revolution, under Captain Turnk. Certificate issued in 1833, but was later dropped along with many others who had been investigated by District Attorney Singleton.

CARPENTER, JOHN (CARLINTON?)
Service—Virginia   Va. No. 12648   No. S-8160

Born, Botetourt County, Virginia, about 1764, and lived on Hackers Creek, Lewis County, August 7, 1832, where he applied for pension. Certificate issued, May 16, 1833, later dropped, and nothing to show reinstatement. Among comrades were Martin Life and James Brown. Statements filed by Sam Bonnett, Nicholas Carpenter, Isaac Washburn, and William Powers.

Carpenter enlisted in Captain John Bowles' Rifle Company, Virginia militia, 1780, and served under General Green at Guilford Courthouse. He was discharged from service and re-enlisted with Captain David May's Company, Virginia militia, and was with General Wayne under General Lafayette at Yorktown. Later he was a guard at Winchester, and was discharged by Lieutenant Wallace Aster. He enlisted again in 1781, and served with Captain John McCoy's men at West's Fort, Bush's Fort, and Neal's Station. He was discharged in 1782, re-enlisted, and served under Captain Peter Hull until 1783.

CARPENTER, BENJAMIN, JEREMIAH, and JOSEPH

Joseph Carpenter, commonly accepted as a veteran of the Revolutionary War, is buried on the west fork of the Little Kanawha River.

Jeremiah Carpenter is buried at Union Mills, Braxton County.

Benjamin Carpenter is buried at the mouth of Holly River, Braxton County.

CARPENTER, SAMUEL
Service—Virginia   Va. No. 11822   No. W-6631

Samuel Carpenter saw service in the Revolution at the battles of Guilford Courthouse and at the Siege of Yorktown. His father was John Carpenter. He married Margaret or Polly Blankenbeker, March 26, 1793. The officiating minister was William Carpenter and the marriage is recorded in Culpeper County, or Clark County, Virginia, although this record is also referred to as in Jackson County, Virginia. The soldier's widow applied for a pension, Madison County, Virginia, May 26, 1854. Statements submitted by Adam Wayland, Joseph Carpenter, and Sarah Carpenter, a cousin.

CURRENCE (CARRANCE), WILLIAM

Born in Pennsylvania. Moved to the Tygarts Valley, 1774. Claimed to have been seventy years old in 1834 and to have had service under Captains Friend, George Jackson, and Curtis, Colonel Lowther, and General Clark. Application for pension was rejected.

CARTE, WILLIAM
Service—Pennsylvania   Va. No. 6791   No. S-29281

Enlistment, Northampton County, Pennsylvania, from 1775 to 1778. Served three years as private under Captain Sam Craig, First Pennsylvania Regiment, Colonel James Chambers. Was at Battle of Brandywine. Applied for pension, November 25, 1818, Greenbrier County. Certificate issued, February 11, 1819.

Name of wife, Catharine, who was aged 69 in 1820. Soldier moved to Ohio and made his home with daughter, Rachel Johnson, two granddaughters, Hannah Johnson, 6, Catharine Johnson, 5, and another granddaughter, Nancy Cart, 12.

CARTER, JOHN
John Carter is listed on the payroll of Captain William Haymond's company of Monongalia County militia as in active service during the War of the Revolution in 1777 as a private.

CARTER, JOSEPH
Enlisted in Captain Stephenson's company in 1775. Was at Roxbury Camp, January 1, 1776. May have been a son of the Joseph Carter who came from Bucks County, Pennsylvania, in 1743 and settled east of Winchester.

CARTER, WILLIAM
Service—North Carolina and Virginia   Va. No. 12339   No. S-9133

Born in Albemarle County, Virginia, April 2, 1760, and resided there until after the Revolution. Later lived in North Carolina ten or twelve years, thence to Greenbrier County, Virginia, later Monroe County.

Enlisted, Albemarle County, September, 1778, and served ten months as private in company of Captain J. Grayson Henderson, North Carolina and Virginia Line, under Colonels Boyer, Gibson, and Cleveland. In campaigns in the Carolinas and Virginia. He re-enlisted in North Carolina in 1780. Applied for pension, Monroe County, February 18, 1833. Certificate was issued but was later suspended. Supporting claims by Rev. William Adair and Patrick Donnelly.

CASE, WILLIAM
Enlisted as a private in Captain Shepherd's company. Taken prisoner at Fort Washington in 1776, and died in captivity March 15, 1777.

CASEY (CAISEY), JOHN
Service—Virginia   Va. No. 19554 and 7005   No. W-29604

Native of Buckingham County, Virginia. Resided in Amelia County when the Revolution broke out. Enlisted in Virginia state troops at Ragland or Ragged Islands, on Chesapeake Bay, under Captain Armaugh, in detachment of which Lieutenant Dudley Biggs, Major John Nelson, and Colonel William Grass were officers. He was at Suffolk, Old Town, Williamsburg, Jamestown, Hampton, and near Portsmouth. Was camped near Petersburg when that town was entered by the British. At surrender at Yorktown, he was ill in a hospital at Hanover. After recovery, he joined his troops when they went from Hanover to Winchester to guard prisoners. He was discharged at Yorktown, March, 1782, by Lieutenant Diggs (Biggs?).

Warrant for 200 acres issued to Casey, November 19, 1874, by order of the Virginia council on the land office as a "private in the Continental line who served to the end of the war."

Casey applied for a pension, January 15, 1833, Kanawha County, Virginia. Certificate was issued, February 21, 1833, but was stricken from roll, 1835. No evidence that any effort was made to have name restored until time of his death in 1845. The soldier had married Jane Barley and Lucinda Morton, both of whom had died. In Jackson County, Ohio, May 26, 1831, he married a third time, the bride being Mary Cox, and Frederick Winfough, Justice of the Peace, the presiding official. The widow applied for a pension, July 27, 1878, while residing at Washington Courthouse, Fayette County, Ohio. She was still living in 1888, one of the two living wives of Revolutionary soldiers at that time.

CASEY, NICHOLAS
Service—Virginia   Va. No. 13130   No. S-9152
Born in Hampshire County, Virginia, November 25, 1749, and died there in 1833. In April, 1781, he enlisted as a private in the cavalry unit under Captain Daniel Richardson, Virginia militia, under First Lieutenant John Harness and Second Lieutenant Robert Cunningham. Was engaged in guard duty and scouting. Applied for pension, Preston County, November 13, 1832. Certificate was issued, May 14, 1833. Supporting affidavit filed by John Ryon.

CASNER, ADAM
Service—Pennsylvania   Va. No. 12550   No. S-9141
Born, Germany, 1747, and came with his father's family to America, 1764. Lived in Cumberland County, Pennsylvania, when the Revolution started. Moved to Brooke County, Virginia, in 1814.
Enlisted in the fall of 1776 and served nine months as a private under Captain Culbertson and Colonel Johnston of the Pennsylvania Line. Patton and Lacy commanded his troop. Soldier was twice discharged by Colonel Johnston, once by Colonel Buchanan, and once by Captain Poe. Was with Washington's army at Valley Forge. Applied for pension, August, 1832, Franklin County, Pennsylvania.

CATLETT, DAVID
Service—Virginia   Va. No. 23833   No. R-1808
Enlisted, Frederick County, Virginia, and served nine months as private under Captains Nicewander, Heiskell, and Calamese, in Regiment of the Virginia Line under Colonel Drake (Darke?). Also names Lieutenants Catlett and Elkins.
Applied for pension, Morgan County, Virginia, February 24, 1834, and died September 11, 1843. Certificate issued, March 12, 1834. Married, February, 1783. Widow, Ann Catlett, applied for pension, February 13, 1839, and died October 20, 1840. Her claim was rejected in statement outlining the pension acts. Supporting claims filed by Cormwell (Cromwell) Orrick and William Neely.

CAUL (CALL), THOMAS M. (Sergeant)
Service—Virginia   Va. No. 16893   No. S-18342
Born, October 1, 1763, Augusta County, Virginia. Served sixteen months as sergeant under Captain Buchanan, Lieutenant Blair, Ensign Crawford, Colonel Howard, Generals Washington, Gates, Green, and Morgan. Also names Ensign George Anderson, Lieutenant J. Walker,

Captains Renicker and Given, Colonels S. Mathews, Hugart, McCleary, and Buller, General Campbell, and General Lafayette. Applied for pension, July 21, 1833, and it was granted the same year. Supporting affidavits submitted by Thomas Byrne and J. M. Camp.

CHALFANT (CHALFIN), SOLOMON (Wagon-Master)
Service—Continental Virginia   Va. No. 2765   No. S-9166

Born about 1753 and died February 26, 1837. Enlisted, Back Creek, Berkeley County, Virginia, August, 1777, as private in Gabriel Long's Company in Colonel Rawling's Eleventh Virginia Regiment, Continental Line. He was engaged in the battle of Brandywine, and soon after was made wagon-master, in which capacity he served until 1780.

Applied for pension, August 27, 1832. Certificate issued, December 5, 1832, Monongalia County, Virginia. Soldier is buried, Olive Church, near Pentress, Monongalia County. Statement of Captain G. P. Cotton, U. S. A., 47 Montgomery Street, Jersey City, New Jersey, in the files mentions James Cotton and Nicholas Hagar as being connected with the family.

CHAMBERS, ROBERT (Sergeant)
Service—Virginia   Va. No. 4857 and 12591   No. S-8194

Served as sergeant two years under Captain Higgins and Lieutenants Curry and Cooper, Eighth Virginia Regiment, Major Stevenson. Enlisted, Augusta County, Virginia, August, 1777, and after broken periods of service was discharged, 1781. Applied for pension, April 22, 1818, and certificate was issued, December 18, 1818. Soldier was fifty-six years old in 1822. Second certificate was issued in 1833.

CHAMPE (CHAMP), JOHN (Sergeant Major)
Service—Continental Virginia   No. W-4153   B. L. Wt. 948-100

Phebe Champe, widow of Sergeant Major Champe, made application for pension, January, 1819, in Franklin County, Ohio, which was rejected. A second application was made, January 15, 1838, which was referred to a special committee and a certificate was issued, by special Act of Congress, July 25, 1838, giving the pension. Champe never applied for a pension. Warrant for 400 acres of bounty land was issued to John Champe's heirs, July 31, 1835.

The story of John Champe is one of the most interesting in the entire Revolutionary period. Sergeant Champe was not by law entitled to land from the United States. The application of his widow to the Sixteenth Congress was refused. Probably the bounty land which seems to have been received was granted by the State of Virginia as a member of Major (General) Henry Lee's Legion.

Champe was a corporal in the second troop, 1778, after enlisting, April 20, of that year. He was made a sergeant in 1779. As such, he was chosen and ordered by Major Lee and General Washington to go into British camp in the feigned character of a deserter to watch the movements of the enemy, and also to seize the person of Benedict Arnold, whose flight to the British after discovery of his plan to turn traitor to the patriot cause had been the sensation of the war. Champe got within the British lines and nearly succeeded in carrying out the plan to bring back Arnold to the American lines in order that he might be tried as a traitor. These facts are related at length in General Henry ("Light Horse Harry") Lee's Memoirs.

Champe enlisted from Louden County, Virginia. Later he removed to Hampshire County, Virginia, and, according to Pension Office Records, died near Morgantown, Monongalia County, where he was looking over some land. The following children are named: Eleanor, married Jacob Hartman; William, Mary, and John Champe, living in Ohio; Amelia, married William Keys; Susannah, married Daniel Wilfong; Nathaniel Champe was living in Ohio.

CHANDLER, THOMAS
Service—North Carolina   Va. No. 19918   No. S-39314

Served three years as a private under Captain Lylle, Tenth Regiment, Continental Establishment, under Colonel Thaxton, after enlistment in North Carolina. He took part in the battle which resulted in the defeat of General Gates' army. He later established a home in Cabell County, Virginia, where he applied for a pension, October 22, 1827, and certificate was issued April 21, 1828. At that time, soldier was sixty-five years old and his wife was sixty-four.

CHAPLINE, ABRAHAM (Captain)

Served as a captain in the Virginia State Line, and also under General George Rogers Clark. Received land grant in Kentucky near Harrodsburg on which he settled. Was son of Captain William Chapline and Ann Forman.

CHAPMAN, JACOB
Service—Virginia   Va. No. 23920   No. S-19237

Born, Staunton, Augusta County, Virginia, 1755. Enlisted, Greenbrier County, spring of 1778, and served fifteen months under Captains Armstrong, Arbuckle, and William Hamilton, under Colonels Hamilton and Stewart, guarding border settlements and forts. Applied for pension in Nicholas County, December 10, 1833. Certificate issued, 1835, dropped in 1835, but later restored for six-months service. Supporting claims made by Elverton Walker, George Rader, Michael Rader, and Jonathan Wilson.

CHENOWETH, JOHN
Service—Virginia   Va. No. 2011   No. W-18899

Born, November 15, 1755, Hampshire County, Virginia, son of William. Died, Randolph County, Virginia, June 16, 1831. Enlisted, Big Cacapon, Hampshire County, 1776 or 1777, and served two years under Captain Westfall, Virginia Line, Continental service, Colonel Muhlenberg. Was in the Battle of Brandywine. Married Mary Pugh, January 7, 1779. She was born in Hampshire County, January 27, 1762. Widow applied for pension, June 28, 1837, and certificate was issued May 7, 1838. Supporting claims filed by Barney Kern and Andrew Arnold.

CHERRY, WILLIAM (Captain)

Cherry entered the Revolutionary service, according to a letter to Colonel James Wood, commandant at Albemarle Barracks, March 26, 1780, from Moses Hunter, Quartermaster, in 1776 as a second lieutenant in Captain Isaac Beall's company Fourth Virginia; first lieutenant, August 17, 1776; captain, November 29, 1777; retired September 14, 1778, after serving with distinction.

By order of the State of Virginia, May 17, 1832, the heirs of William Cherry were allowed one year and six months service as a captain in the Continental Line in addition to previous allowance. This was in response for a request for additional land grants, in Clinton County, Ohio, October 25, 1831, made by Joseph Wisong and Elizabeth, his wife, late Elizabeth Patton, and formerly Mary Cherry; John and Richard Cherry (the said Elizabeth, John, Mary, and Richard being children of the late Captain William Cherry); and John Patton, a grandchild.

The will of Captain Cherry is filed in Berkeley County. It is not dated, but was proved in Jefferson County, February 13, 1805. Captain Cherry was the proprietor of one of the earliest and best known taverns in Jefferson County.

CHESNEY (CHESTNUT), BENJAMIN
Service—Continental Virginia   Va. No. 5479   No. S-39297

Served six years, according to certificate of General Henry Lee. Enlisted in March, 1775, and served under Captain Rudolph, Continental Establishment, in Legion commanded by Colonel (General) Henry Lee. Fought at Brandywine, Stony Point, Powles (Paulus?) Hook, Guilford Courthouse, and Eutaw Springs, in which last battle he was wounded by a shot through the leg. Claims for horse, saddle, bridle, final settlement, and depreciation ticket were not received, according to his statement.

Not entitled to pension under act of 1818, but later applications were made in Monongalia County, Virginia, which were probably allowed. He was granted land bounty, December 30, 1812, for his services. Soldier is buried on Guston Run, Cass District, Monongalia County.

CHEW, RICHARD

Richard Chew, applied for pension in Monongalia County, as a soldier of the Revolutionary War, but his claim was rejected.

CHIDESTER, HOLDRIDGE

Served in Captain Smither's troop, Sheldon's Regiment of Light Dragoons, New Jersey Line, Continental Army, as listed on Page 167 of "Officers and Men of New Jersey in the Revolution." He settled in the Booth's Creek section of Harrison County (now Marion County), prior to 1795 when his name appears on the Harrison County tithable lists. His children were: Abraham, married Catherine Radcliff, April, 1806; Ann, married James Wells, son of Phineas Wells, November 5, 1804; Massey, married Abraham Wells, son of Phineas Wells, December 2, 1801; Jane, married, 1808; Margaret, married, 1812.

CHIDESTER, OLRAGE

Olrage Chidester was a private in Captain Benjamin Site's company, Morgan Township, Washington County, Pennsylvania, Militia, during the Revolutionary War. He was born in Pennsylvania, 1756, and there enlisted in the Revolutionary Army. He married May Pence, September 9, 1793. He died in Morgan County, Virginia.

CHILCOTT, ELIHU
Service—Virginia   Va. No. 19353   No. W-6665

Enlisted, May 27, 1776, and served two years as a private in the company of Captains Croghan and Hite, in the Eighth Virginia and the Third Virginia Regiment under Muhlenberg, Weedon, and Reed. Saw service at White Plains, Brandywine, Germantown, and Monmouth.

He was born, 1757, and died May 25, 1831. He married Lydia Payne, 1788. He applied for pension, December 4, 1819, and his widow, aged seventy-eight in 1838, applied in that year for her pension. She was placed cn the pension rolls in 1841. Children of Elihu and Lydia Chilcott were: Ann, 17; Rachel, 20; Isaac, 14; Joel, 22; two older daughters, and a granddaughter, aged 5. Supporting claims were filed by Matthias Hite and Rachel Wilson.

CHRISTIAN, ROBERT
Service—Virginia   Va. No. 12549   No. S-9177

Born, Augusta County, Virginia, February 28, 1764, and was living in Kanawha County in 1841. In March, 1781, was placed on the muster roll of his county, and in April was placed in the Virginia Militia under Captain Francis Long and Major Robert McCleary. Marched to Rock Fish Gap to protect the Legislature which had been driven from Richmond and then from Charlottesville. Attached to General William Campbell's brigade. General Campbell occupied Richmond after Lord Cornwallis had evacuated that city, and pursued him to Williamsburg. Joined General Lafayette's army, and after skirmishes at Kent, Hot Water Mills, and other points, the British were chased to their ships at Jamestown. Colonel John Willis and then Colonel Samuel Lewis in turn commanded this unit. Took part in siege and capture of Yorktown, soon after which he was discharged by General Campbell.

Applied for pension, September 10, 1832, Kanawha County. Certificate was issued, May 9, 1833.

CLAPPER (CLOPPER OR CLEPPER), VALENTINE
Service—Maryland   Va. No. 10498   No. S-39325

Enlisted in Maryland, August 1, 1780, in Captain Price's company, Second Brigade of the Maryland Line, under Colonel John Stewart of the Second Regiment. Served in General Green's army until November 15, 1783, when he was discharged at Annapolis. Was wounded in the right knee at the Battle of Eutaw Springs. Supporting affidavit by John Henry or Haney. Soldier was aged seventy-two in 1818, and his wife seventy-two in 1820. Pension certificate issued in Harrison County, March 8, 1819.

CLARK, SAMUEL
Service—Virginia   Va. No. 3525   No. S-9188 and B. L. Wt. 20366

Born, Augusta County, Virginia, April 18, 1764, and died in Monroe County, January 27, 1857. Supporting affidavits filed by Berryman Jones, who was a comrade with Clark during the Battle of Jamestown under Captain Patrick Buchanan; in a border campaign against the Indians in the Tygarts Valley, under Captain John McKitrick; and also at the capture of Lord Cornwallis at Yorktown. Testimony submitted in his behalf also by Rev. James Christy and Michael Alexander. Pension granted and also 160 acres of bounty land.

Much detail of his service is found in the pension application, made in Monroe County, 1832. Entering service, September, 1780, Clark served three months in Captain Samuel McCutcheon's Company; three months in Captain James Trimble's company of Colonel Sampson Matthew's regiment. Was in a skirmish with the British near Portsmouth in Captain Patrick Buchanan's company of Colonel Thomas Huggard's regiment; was wounded in the head by a British sabre in the Battle of Jamestown and spent several months in a hospital. Served three months in the companies of Captain Francis Long and Captain John Campbell. Guarded prisoners at Winchester after the surrender of Cornwallis at Yorktown. His last service was the three months under Captain John McKitrick against the Indians in the Tygarts Valley.

He moved from Augusta County to Greenbrier County, in March, 1786, settling in the part that is now Monroe County. (Note: His application papers go into considerable detail and refer to a large number of Revolutionary officers.)

West Virginians in the American Revolution

Assembled and Edited by ROSS B. JOHNSTON

The sources of this material are from the files of the Pension Office at Washington, from various county records, from notes of patriotic societies, principally the Daughters of the American Revolution, Sons of the American Revolution, Sons of the Revolution, and from a large miscellaneous group of published and private sources. Corrections and additions to this list will receive the careful attention of the editor.

CLARKE, WILLIAM
Service—Virginia   Va. No. 12347   No. W-6683

Born, Hominy (or Harmony) Ridge, Pennsylvania, 1760. Enlisted in the Revolutionary Army, Hampshire County, in the spring of 1778. Died July 23, 1841, Lewis County, Virginia. Served twelve months as a private under Captain Kirkpatrick, Eighth Regiment of the Virginia Line under General Scott. Later served three months under Captain James Neal in the militia of Virginia and took part in the Siege of Yorktown. Mentions Lieutenant Adrian Fisher and Ensign Thomas Douthet. Supporting claims by William Peterson, Abner Abbott, and John Raines. On August 8, 1798, married Barbara, daughter of Jacob Helmick, Randolph County, the Rev. Robert Marshall being the minister.

Soldier applied for pension in Lewis County, 1833, and received certificate the same year. The widow applied for pension, June 11, 1851. Her age was seventy-two in 1854, at which time she appears to have been living in Upshur County. She died August 30, 1855.

CLAYTON, ELISHA
Service—New Jersey   Va. No. 12942   No. W-1145 and B.L.Wt.-26529

Enlisted, Monmouth County, New Jersey, and between 1776 and 1780 served two years under Captain J. Smook in Colonel Herd's New Jersey Regiment. Took part in the fighting at Long Island and Monmouth, and was captured and held prisoner in New York for nine months.

Married by Joseph Powell, October 15, 1793, Allegheny County, Maryland, to Elizabeth Little. Granted pension in Monongalia County, in 1833. Died March 31, 1845, and is buried at Baxter Cunningham's Cemetery, Marion County. The widow applied for a pension, March 5, 1846, in Marion County, which was granted. Bounty land warrants were also issued for 160 acres. Supporting claims were made by Elizabeth Dawson, daughter, and John Clayton, son, Sarah Cunningham, John D. Parker, and Milly Parker.

CLEGG, ALEXANDER

The grave of Alexander Clegg, a soldier in the Revolutionary Army, is in the cemetery at Olive Church, near Pentress, Monongalia County.

CLENDENIN, ALEXANDER

Alexander Clendenin served as private in Revolutionary Army. Born, 1754 and died, 1829. Buried in Mason County. Married Katherine Spencer. Children: George, wife, Margaret Lowe; Charles; John, wife, Sarah; Andrew, wife, Rebecca Edwards; Lucinda, husband, William Lewis; Julia, husband, Isaac Lemaster; Narcissus, died in infancy.

CLENDENIN, GEORGE (Colonel)

Colonel George Clendenin was an officer in the army of General Andrew Lewis in the Battle of Point Pleasant in 1774, and was an active figure in the Greenbrier and Great Kanawha valleys in pioneer days. He was County-Lieutenant of Greenbrier County and was influential in having Fort Lee built on the Great Kanawha at Charleston. He commanded it and became County-Lieutenant of Militia when Kanawha County was formed.

CLENDENIN, WILLIAM

William Clendenin, born 1758 and died 1828, was in the army of General Andrew Lewis which defeated the federated Indian tribes under Chief Cornstalk at Point Pleasant in 1774. He had an active military career during the Revolutionary and Indian War periods, and spent his declining years in Mason County.

CLINE, CONRAD

In June, 1818, Conrad Cline, a resident of Berkeley County, appeared before the Berkeley County court, and testified that he enlisted in the Continental service during the Revolutionary War in Pennsylvania near Reading, and continued in service until the Battle of Monmouth. In this engagement, he was attached to the Sixth Regiment under Colonel Harmar, and served the remainder of his enlistment under Captain Dungin in a regiment commanded by Colonel Hampden.

CLOAK, (GEORGE?) (Captain)

Captain Cloak (probably George Cloak who had a farm in Berkeley County, Virginia), commanded a company of Berkeley County militia during the Revolution.

COALTER (COLTER), SAMUEL (Lieutenant)

Service—Pennsylvania   Va. No. 19719   No. S-39352

Enlisted, Bucks (or Berks) County, Pennsylvania, January 2, 1776, and served as quartermaster sergeant in the Second and Third Pennsylvania Regiments of the Continental Line, and as lieutenant, after receiving his commission in 1777. Was wounded at Monmouth and unable to continue service as an officer. Again enlisted in 1778 or 1779 under Captain Irish as orderly sergeant. Marched to Virginia, and was there appointed superintendent of the State laboratory, where he served until 1783, when he was discharged by Colonel Davis.

Applied for pension, October 11, 1825, Botetourt County, Virginia. Wife's age, sixty, at that time. Pension granted, January 3, 1827. Supporting affidavits filed by David Jones, Douglas Ireby, Peter Bachelor, and Jacob Poitsel.

COBB (COBBS), FLEMING
Service—Virginia   Indian Wars (1793)   B.L.Wt. 83776
Cobb did not have a Revolutionary War record, but served under Captain William Clendenin, Captain Moses Mann, and Colonel George Clendenin in the Indian Wars, and had service with General Wayne. Married, January 10, 1796, to Sally Morris, by Reverend James Johnson, Baptist minister, Kanawha County, Virginia. Soldier died, January 10, 1846. Widow, aged eighty in 1855, received bounty land warrants of 160 acres under act of March, 1835.

COBURN, JONATHAN (Captain)
In pension application in Harrison County, Coburn stated that he entered the service of the United States in Monongalia County, Virginia, in the year 1777, as a captain in the Thirteenth Virginia Regulars under Colonel Thomas Gibson. He continued in service from August 2, 1777, to September 26, 1779, when he was discharged at Pittsburgh. He was in several skirmishes and engagements with the Indians. He was sixty-seven years old at the time he asked for a pension and was blind.

COCHRAN, JAMES (Ensign)
Service—Virginia   Va. No. 7545   No. W-6743
Enlisted, October, 1776, as ensign in company of Captain D. Scott, Thirteenth Virginia Regiment, commanded by Colonel Russell, at West Augusta (Morgantown). He is supposed to have resigned his commission, the acceptance being signed by General Edward Hand at Fort Pitt, September 11, 1777, but the documents have been removed from claim file and are locked up in the Revolutionary War Section.

Soldier married at Morgantown, July 20, 1777; wife's name Temperance, name of minister, George Martin. Soldier applied for pension in Harrison County, in 1818, and it was issued the next year. Soldier's widow, aged sixty-one in 1821, applied for pension, January 31, 1837, which was likewise granted.

COCHRAN, NATHANIEL
Nathaniel Cochran was born of Irish parents, not far from Philadelphia, February 28, 1757. He moved to near Hagerstown, Maryland, while a boy, went to Virginia at the age of eighteen, and in 1776 enlisted in a Virginia company to serve as a soldier on the frontier. He was attached to the company of Captain James Booth, crossed the mountains, and settled in what is now Marion County, West Virginia. He was wounded and captured by the Indians in 1778 at the time that Captain Booth was killed. He is buried in the Willow Tree Cemetery, Marion County.

COCHRAN, SIMON (Sergeant)
An order of the Virginia Council Chamber, December 31, 1806, says

that Simon Cochran, sergeant, is entitled to land bounty for three years service in the Continental Line, Revolutionary Army. Cochran, of the State of Kentucky, but at that time of Morgantown, Monongalia County, appointed John Fairfax of Virginia as his attorney to obtain the warrants for his service.

COGER, PETER
Service—Virginia   Va. No. 16648   No. S-10481

Born in Pennsylvania in 1753. In infancy came to Hawksbill, Shenandoah County, Virginia, and enlisted in the Revolutionary Army from Rockingham County. He served as a private in the company of Captain Ragan and Lieutenant Harrison in the regiment of Colonel Skillern, his service extending from 1777 to 1781. He was at Point Pleasant when Chief Cornstalk was killed. He applied for pension from Lewis County, Virginia, December 3, 1832, and in support of his claim are affidavits of John and Isaac Mace, Tunis McIlvane, and Robert Hamilton. He names a long list of Revolutionary officers with whom he had seen service.

COLE, JOHN

Applied for pension in Harrison County, but in 1834 it appears that John Cole resided in Baltimore County, Maryland. During the Revolutionary War he served on several short tours. Entire length of service uncertain. Claim was not allowed as he did not prove six months service in a regiment embodied in a military corps as was required by the pension laws.

COLE, JOSEPH

Drafted into the army in 1780 from Captain Davis' company of Berkeley County militia.

COLGATE, ASAPH
Service—Maryland   Va. No. 15900   No. S-39341 and W.L.Wt. 63230

Served three years as a private under Captain Samdall of the Fourth Maryland Regiment, commanded by Colonel Hall and General Smallwood. Took part in the battles of Camden and Ninety-Six. Enlisted at Baltimore, Maryland, 1780, and applied for pension, July 27, 1818, Monongalia County, Virginia. Wife's name was Rosanna. Pension granted and also bounty land of 100 acres.

COLLINS, CHARLES

Private in Captain Shepherd's company. From Berkeley County. Died in prison, January 19, 1777.

COLLINS, GEORGE
Service—Virginia   Va. No. 12647   No. S-8247

Served eighteen months in the infantry and six months in the cavalry under Captain Lewis and Colonel Morgan. Applied for pension in Lewis County. Certificate was issued, May 16, 1833.

WEST VIRGINIANS IN THE REVOLUTION 59

COLLINS, JAMES
Service—Pennsylvania   Va. No. 23780   No. S-17895

Born in Lancaster County, Pennsylvania, 1761. Moved with parents while an infant to Louden County, Virginia. At age of twelve moved to Fayette County where he lived until 1796. Moved to Monongalia County where he was living in 1833.

Enlisted at Brownsville, Pennsylvania, in the summer of 1777, and served from six to nine months under Captain Jacob Springer, Isaac Pearce, John Beeson, Lieutenant John Dent, Colonel Gibson, Colonel Crawford, Colonel John Evans, and General McIntosh. Supporting claims made by Joseph Shackleford and Noah Ridgeway. Pension application was issued, April 4, 1834.

COMER, AUGUSTINE
Service—Virginia   Va. No. 12550   No. W-18945

Enlisted, Shenandoah County, Virginia, Easter Monday, 1776, and served four and one-half years under Captain Langley, Twelfth Virginia Regiment, Continental Establishment, Colonel Neville, and General Scott. He took part in the fighting at Brandywine, Germantown, Monmouth, Stony Point, and Charleston, South Carolina. Pension application filed 1819 and issued same year. Claim supported by statements of Jacob Comer, John Comer, John Peters, Sally C. Peters, Elizabeth C. Miller, and Catherine C. Ball, of Logan County; Frederick Comer, Barbara Comer, and Michael Comer.

County court records of Shenandoah County show that Augustine Comer and Catherine (or Cortreen) Rush were lawfully married by "publishment given" April 23, 1782, or July 22, 1782. The widow, aged sixty in 1820, died April 11, 1841. Heirs filed claim in 1847 which was eventually paid.

COMMANS (CUMMINS), ROBERT
Service—Pennsylvania   Va. No. 3390   No. S-9259

Enlisted at Carlisle, Pennsylvania, February or March, 1777, and served seventeen months as a private under Captain Adams in the Pennsylvania Regiment under Colonel William Irwin or Irvine. From Carlisle, marched to New York, then went by water to Albany to Lake George and Ticonderoga, thence to St. Johns to Chambalee. At Three Rivers was under Colonel Irving and Lieutenant Colonel Hartley. Retreated under Colonel Hartley to a small lake in Canada, thence to Chambalee, to St. Johns, to Crown Point, and to Ticonderoga at which place the winter of 1776 was spent. In March, 1777, Captain Adams and three other members of his company were killed by the Indians.

Pension was applied for in 1832.

CONAWAY (Conway), JOHN SPANN

Born, October 16, 1762, Hampshire County, Virginia, the son of Thomas and Eleriah Conaway. Died, 1841, in Marion County, and is buried in the Katy Clelland cemetery.

Served from 1776 to 1782 as an Indian spy, enlisting in Bedford

County, Pennsylvania, under Captain McCall in Virginia and Pennsylvania detachments. He was married, 1780, near Bean's Cover, Bedford County, to Rachel Willison, who was born in Allegheny County, Maryland. Her parents were Jeremiah and Sarah Willison. Applied for pension in Harrison County, but soldier and wife died before claim was allowed. Supporting affidavits made by William McRae and Daniel Arnett, Harrison County, and Jonathan Mausley, Lewis County.

The Conaways settled in Marion County as early as 1819. Their children were as follows: Basil, born, 1781; died, April 29, 1854; married, first, Mary Crosby and moved to Perry County, Ohio; second wife, Sara, one daughter, Hannah. Charles, born, 1785; married his cousin, Elizabeth Conaway, daughter of Thomas Conaway. John, born, April 17, 1785; died, October 15, 1868; married Sarah Fleming, daughter of Alexander, son of Matthew Fleming, Sr.; John married Hannah Randall as his second wife. John was known as "Big" John. Jeremiah married Sarah Hunter. Nancy married a Crosby and moved to Ohio. Sarah married a Ruby and moved to Ohio. Rachel died young. Mary married Joab Fleming. Hester, born, September 10, 1810; died June 30, 1894; married George W. Clelland. A daughter, Rachel, was living at a recent date—a real granddaughter of a soldier of the Revolution. Byrum died young. William Willison, born 1805, died, June 8, 1851; married Thoda Hendrick. After his death, his widow married James Everly, born, 1793, died October 17, 1862. He was a soldier in the War of 1812, a private in James Hurry's company from Monongalia County.

CONAWAY (CONWAY), THOMAS (Lieutenant)

Born, March 1, 1755, Hampshire County, Virginia, the son of Thomas Conaway, Sr., and wife, Eleriah. Died February 14, 1824.

His pension application states that in 1776 he volunteered under Captain Higgins, Hampshire County, and marched to Beesontown, now Uniontown, and thence against the Indians on the Muskingum. He was out nine months before returning to Pittsburgh at Christmas. In 1779, he was drafted to take part in the expedition of General McIntosh during which Fort McIntosh was built. After his discharge he moved to Bedford County where he was ordered out in 1780 as an Indian spy under Captain McCall. Two companies under McCall, with another captain, were ambushed by the Indians and but sixteen men escaped. War Department records show that Conaway was a private in Captain John McGuire's company and was also designated as a lieutenant in Captain Thomas Bell's company of Colonel Grayson's Regiment, Continental troops. His enlistment date is given as April 5, 1777, later being transferred to the Regiment commanded by Colonel Nathaniel Gist.

On January 9, 1783, in Hampshire County, Virginia, Conaway married Sarah Dew (or Dhu), daughter of Samuel Dew, sheriff of Hampshire County, 1769, and wife, Joanna Park Dew. Their children were as follows: Jeremiah, born, 1785; died February 26, 1865; married Mary Brown; lived at Basnettsville, Marion County. Daniel, born April 28, 1789; died, October 17, 1884; married, first, Phoebe See, second, Maria

Straight; lived at Barracksville, Marion County. Samuel, married Eleanor Ice, of Ice's Ferry; buried in Adams graveyard, near Barracksville. "Little John" Conaway, born, February 14, 1805; died August 21, 1891; twice married, first to Esther Baker, 1826, and second to Millie Moore; buried in Hamilton Graveyard, near Rymer, Marion County. Eli, born, March 14, 1797; died June 13, 1851; married twice, first to Mary Baker, 1818, and second, to Parthena Ruffner; buried in Tyler County. Harvey, born, 1815; moved to Hughes River, Tyler County; buried at Alma. Polly, never married. Charles, no record. Sarah, married a Yost and moved to Ohio. Mary, married John Hoge, Allegheny County, Maryland. Elizabeth, married her cousin, Charles Conaway, son of John Conaway, and brother of Thomas Conaway, Jr.

CONGLETON, MOSES

Service—Pennsylvania Va. No. 5806 and 5466 No. W-4930—B.L.Wt. 26738

Born, October 4, 1763, Allen Township, Northampton or Northumberland County, Pennsylvania, the son of William and Mary Congleton. He died, November 6, 1838. With the consent of his parents, he enlisted at the age of thirteen as a musician in Captain John Hay's company of the Pennsylvania militia under Major James Boyd in Lieutenant Colonel John Liggett's regiment. The night of the battle of Trenton, he repaired the American camp fires in company with William Moffit while the American Army withdrew towards Princeton. He was taken to Crosswick and rejoined General Rytman's brigade, thence to Norristown where he remained until March, 1777, when he was discharged. He re-enlisted under Captain John Sriver, Major Boyd's Battalion, in Colonel Stephen Beallett's Regiment of Northampton County militia at Brandywine. After being attached to several other military units, he accompanied the troops under General Sullivan in 1779 in an expedition against the Six Nations. He was discharged by Colonel Nicholas Kearns, 1781, after more than two years service.

He moved to Brooke County, Virginia, in 1794 and there was granted a pension and also bounty land warrant for 160 acres. His wife, Mary Grimes, daughter of Thomas and Margaret Grimes, was born, September 20, 1763. They were married, May 18, 1788, Northampton County, Pennsylvania, and had the following children: Margaret, March 29, 1789; Mary, April 30, 1791; John, May 31, 1793; Marie (married Thomas Good), December, 1795; William and Juliana (twins), July 27, 1799; Thomas, January, 1801. The children of Marie Congleton and Thomas Good were: Thomas, Elizabeth, Robert, Juliana, and Emily. Supporting affidavits were filed by Nicholas Headington, Sam Henderson, Elizabeth Patton, Sam M. Carty, and Robert Doak.

CONLEY, JOHN

Applied for pension in Giles County, Virginia (now Mercer), in 1840 for service in Indian wars in 1792 under Captains Preston and Crockett. Claim rejected. Supporting claims by Captain John Crockett, Oliver Winn, John Trollinger, John Rutter, and David Johnston.

CONROD (CONRAD), JACOB
Service—Virginia   Va. No. 16531   No. S-39361

Enlisted in 1776 and served in the Revolutionary Army with the Ninth and Thirteenth Virginia Regiments in company of Captain Benjamin Harrison under Colonel Russell and Colonel John Gibson. Fought in the battles of Brandywine and Germantown, and was honorably discharged at Pittsburgh, July 25, 1783. Pension granted in 1820. Buried in Gilmer County on the right-hand prong of Dust Camp, about three miles from mouth of the stream.

CONWAY (Conaway), RICHARD
Service—Virginia   Indiana No. 19365   No. S-16731 and B.L.Wt. 26414

Born in Queen Anne County, Maryland, 1762. Served as a private one year under Captain Neal and Captain Simmerel, Virginia Militia, under Colonel Helms and Colonel Cresap, in troops enlisting in Hampshire County in 1782. Supporting claims filed by Reverend Hugh Carrol, Miles Conaway, and Thomas Stanford in Henry County, Indiana, in November, 1832. Pension granted and also bounty land warrants for 160 acres.

COOK, JOHN
The Greenbrier County court in 1847 certified to the War Department that the declaration of Mary Cook and a certificate from James E. Heath, first auditor of the state, showing the settlement of John Cook for services in the Revolutionary War had been approved by the court. James Cary and George W. Rank subscribed to it.

In the same court in 1853 it was shown that John Cook, a Revolutionary soldier, died on June 3, 1836, and that Mary Cook, the wife and widow, applied for a pension as a resident of Greenbrier County. It was further stated that said Mary Cook remained the widow of John Cook and that John Cook, Nancy Church, Thomas Cook, Malinda Thompson, Elizabeth Nicely, Sarah Campbell, Lewis Cook, Jesse Cook, Andrew Cook, and Eli Cook are the children of John and Mary Cook.

COOK, THOMAS
Fifer in Captain Shepherd's company. Died July 1, 1777, after imprisonment.

COOK, ZACHARIAH
Before the Greenbrier County court in 1832, Zachariah Cook made affidavit that Land Warrant No. 4144 had been lost or mislaid, and a renewal of his warrant was ordered. The Land Office of the State of Kentucky had certified that Cook was entitled to 100 acres for service as a soldier in the Virginia Continental Line for three years.

COOKE, JOHN
Service—Virginia   Va. No. 23208   No. W-1232—B.L.Wt. 11017

Born in London, England, 1754, and died in Logan County, Virginia, November 21, 1832. He was connected with Thomas Buford's company of Radford's Riflemen in Dunmore's War, and served in the Revolutionary Army, largely under General Daniel Morgan. He enlisted in Shenandoah

County, Virginia, in January, 1777, and served as a private in Captain Jonathan Langdon's, Abraham Hite's and George Werle's companies, in Colonel James Wood's Eighth and Twelfth Virginia regiment. He was in the battles of Monmouth and Stony Point. He was discharged, December 29, 1779.

He was married, June 28, 1813, in Monroe County, Virginia, to Ann Keatley. The marriage was proved by Polly Abbott and Francis Hendricks, residents of Monroe County. Pension was granted in 1832 and also bounty land warrant for 160 acres. He was the first permanent settler in Wyoming County. His grave is marked by D.A.R. and War Department.

COOKMAN, WILLIAM

In pension application, Lewis County, Virginia, July 4, 1734, Cookman stated that he was born in Northumberland County, Virginia, in 1760, and that he enlisted in 1781 in the company of Captain Kean and served two years and six months in the Revolutionary Army. His claim was not allowed.

COOKUS, MICHAEL

After serving in the Revolution, lived in Shepherdstown where he appears on the tax list in 1797.

COON, ANTHONY

Service—Virginia   Va. No. 7496   No. S-9213

Enlisted in Monongalia County, Virginia, February 28, 1776, in Captain David Scott's company of the Thirteenth Regiment of Virginia Regulars, Continental Establishment, commanded by Colonel John Gibson. After three years service he was discharged at Pittsburgh. His pension application mentions supporting affidavit of James Arnold and James Cochran. In the Harrison County court records, are also filed the supporting affidavit of John Dent, formerly a lieutenant in the Thirteenth Regiment, and James Scott, a soldier in the same military unit.

His application for pension, filed in Harrison County in 1818, gave his age as seventy-two. His wife was aged sixty-four in 1826. Their children were Nancy Petit, a widow with three children; Rebecca, aged seven; Lylas, aged five; and Hezekiah, aged two; two sons, Abraham and Samuel. Pension certificates were issued in 1819 and 1832, and, after suspension for a time, pay was resumed in 1835.

COOPER, BARNABAS

Service—Virginia   Va. No. 16438   No. S-9201

Served two years as private under Captain Elijah Martin, Virginia Line regiment, under Colonel Joseph Cabell and General George Rogers Clark. Served in Ohio, Kentucky, Illinois, and Virginia. He was honorably discharged, August 11, 1781. He enlisted in Amherst County, Virginia, and applied for pension, August 20, 1832, Fayette County, Virginia. His certificate was issued, August 9, 1833.

COPLIN, BENJAMIN
Service—Virginia   Va. No. 16692   No. S-10464

Born in Rockingham County, March 28, 1752, and settled in Harrison County, 1770. Enlisted in Harrison County and served two years as a private under Captain William Lowther, Jackson, and Carpenter, and saw frontier service at Nutters Fort, Powers Fort and forts on Simpson and Elk creeks. He applied for pension in Harrison County, June 18, 1833, and certificate was issued, September 16 of same year.

CORBIN, ANDERSON
Service—Virginia   Va. No. 2361   No. W-6739 and B.L.Wt. 26456

Born, King George County, Virginia, about 1752; moved to Culpeper, Hampshire, and Harrison counties; died in Harrison County March 1, 1845. Enlisted, Hampshire County, 1781 and served until 1782, under Captain Isaac Parsons, and Captain Thomas Anderson, Colonel Edmondson, and General Muhlenberg in Virginia line regiments. Received pension and bounty land warrant for 160 acres. Claims supported by Joshua Martin, John Cottrill, Josina Gawthrop, and David Coplin.

Soldier was married, May 18, 1789, to Elizabeth Harris who was born in 1773. The minister was Reverend John Sousborough. Children of Anderson and Elizabeth Corbin were: Mary, October 30, 1790; Sarah, March 11, 1793; Nancy, May 22, 1795; Francis, November 2, 1798; Henry B., March 20, 1800; Elizabeth, October 18, 1802; Josanna, May 22, 1805; Benjamin, October 18, 1807; Edith, April 1, 1810; Anderson, March 15, 1813; O. P., September 6, 1816; and A. L., August 11, 1818.

COREY (CUREY), SAMUEL
Service—New Jersey   Va. No. 16169 and 23681   No. S-9194

Born, January 9, 1763, Essex County, New Jersey. Enlisted November, 1777, under Captain Wood in the New Jersey militia regiment under Colonel Patter in General Stevenson's brigade. Served in campaigns through the Jerseys and New York. Applied for pension, January 28, 1833, Brooke County, Virginia, and certificate was issued July 13 of same year for eighteen months service.

CORNETT, JESSE
Service—Virginia   Va. No. 16072   No. S-9193

Born, Henrico County, Virginia, 1762, and enlisted in same county in the Revolutionary Army. Served two years under Captain Prosser in Virginia Regiment commanded by Colonel Marshall. Mentions other officers as William Mosby, Samuel Price, William Price, John Brice, Marsdale Southall, and Pleasants Innis. Supporting claims by Mosley Pullium, Obadiah Griffin, J. Mosby, and Benjamin Sheppard. Pension was granted in 1833, upon application from Harrison County, Virginia.

COSGROVE, WILLIAM, SR.
Service—Virginia   Va. No. 23921   No. S-19261

Applied for pension in Wood County, Virginia, December 17, 1833, claiming to have been born in Prince William County, Virgina, 1753, and to have served six months under Captain Rixy and Lieutenant Dearing,

Virginia Line, under Colonel Green, in guard duty during the Revolution on the Delaware River. Claim was supported by A. Samuels and William Cosgrove, Jr., his son. Certificate was issued, 1834, but pension was suspended, 1835.

COTTLE, DIDE

Before the Greenbrier County court, 1785, William Cottle produced sufficient proof that he was the heir at law of Dide Cottle, who had enlisted in the late war and who had been killed in that service. It was also certified that Elizabeth Cottle, mother of Dide Cottle, deceased, had proved to the same court that Dide had enlisted in the Continental Army in June, 1779, and that William Cottle, brother, is the lawful heir of said Dide Cottle.

COTTRILL, JOHN
Service—Virginia   Va. No. 19376   No. S-39597

Enlisted, 1779, at the age of sixteen, in Hampshire County for a term of two years in Captain William Johnson's company in a Virginia line regiment, probably the Seventh Virginia. Marched to Winchester, there joined the command of Colonel Elias Edmonds, thence to Fredericksburg, Bowling Green, Richmond, and other points. Then marched south, joined Colonel Washington's regiment of cavalry, and was at the battle of Cowpens, Eutaw Springs, and at the Pine Tree. Re-enlisted in Captain William McGuire's company of artillery in Colonel Harrison's regiment. Marched north and joined the army under General Putnam, was in the Battle of Mud Island Fort, then returned to Virginia, and was at the capture of the British army at Yorktown, having served three years and nine months.

Soldier applied for pension, Harrison County, January 17, 1825. Certificate was issued same year but was later dropped and there is no evidence found of its restoration. Soldier died July 9, 1850. Widow was aged fifty-two in 1825. Their children were John, seventeen, Polly, eighteen, Elisha, fourteen, Barbara, twelve, William, ten. Supporting affidavits filed by Richard Cottrill, Nancy Williams, Edmond Cain, Elias Cottrill, Joseph Morris, and Ann Williams.

COTTRILL (COTTERALL or COTTRELL), THOMAS
Service—Virginia   Va. No. 16588   No. S-8242

Born, Georges Creek, Pennsylvania, January 22, 1762. Enlisted, Monongalia County, February 18, 1779, and served as private under Captain Carpenter in the Virginia Line, Continental army. Applied for pension, Lewis County, 1833, and certificate was issued, but was dropped in 1835. Statements filed from Christopher Nutter, Rebecca Nutter, Henry Flesher, John Waggoner, Nicholas Carpenter, John Ragan, Sam Bonnet, and Colonel Copeland.

West Virginians in the American Revolution

Assembled and Edited by ROSS B. JOHNSTON

The sources of this material are from the files of the Pension Office at Washington, from various county records, from notes of patriotic societies, principally the Daughters of the American Revolution, Sons of the American Revolution, Sons of the Revolution, and from a large miscellaneous group of published and private sources. Corrections and additions to this list will receive the careful attention of the editor.

COURTNER (CURTNER OR CORTNER), ANTHONY (Sergeant)

Born, Lancaster County, Pennsylvania, 1740 and died, April 30, 1833, Greenbrier County, Virginia. Enlisted in Rockingham County, Virginia, 1776, and served twenty-one months as private and sergeant under Captains Slump, Skidmore, Lieutenants Bright, Keaton, and Generals Morgan, Wayne and Muhlenberg. Stationed at Westfall's Fort in the Tygarts Valley and on the Ohio River, collecting cattle for the army, and performing other duties.

December 6, 1777, in Augusta County, later in Pendleton County, Virginia, married Catherine Coonstump, born in 1759 and died January 22, 1844. Their children were Lewis, aged 56, David, aged 54, and Phoebe, aged 46, in 1846. Pension applied for and received. Supporting claims by Perryman Jones, James Dougherty, Mary Swadly, Jacob Stover, Phoebe Daugherty, George Hull, Mary Carlisle, John Rexroad, and J. Pross.

Before the Greenbrier County court, 1883, Catherine Courtner proved she was the widow of Anthony Courtner, who had been a Revolutionary War pensioner. In 1847, Phoebe Daugherty and Lewis and David Courtner were established as the only remaining children of Anthony and Catherine Courtner.

COX, ABRAHAM (Lieutenant)

Born January 1, 1752, died March 24, 1834. Wife Elizabeth, born, 1752, died, March 15, 1823. Buried in Old Cox Graveyard, east of Arnettsville, Grant District, Monongalia County, West Virginia. Old stones. Revolutionary War record—Lieutenant in Western Battallion, organized at Hagerstown, Maryland.

Children of Abraham and Elizabeth Cox: Moses Cox, born August 7, 1781, died September 27, 1861. Married Mrs. Charlotte McDermott Foster, as second wife, first being Jane Musgrave; Abraham Cox, Jr., married Hester Ann Burrows, daughter of Boaz, April 4, 1814; Susannah Cox, married October 22, 1806, Peter Hess, Jr.; Letitia Cox, married October 10, 1818, Lewis Smith; Isaac Cox, married July 24, 1821, Frances, daughter of John Fisher.

COX, ELIZABETH

The grave of Elizabeth Cox, who received a Revolutionary War pension, is on the Burdette farm at Ona on the Prichard School Road in Cabell County.

COX, GEORGE (Ensign)
Service—Virginia   Va. No. 16217   No. S. 9203

Born, Hampshire County, Virginia, about 1749. Enlisted in the spring of 1776 as an ensign in the company of Captain Isaac Cox, and Lieutenant Steel, Virginia Line, and served six months. Settled on the Ohio River in 1772 or 1773, and served in Dunmore's War. Married, February, 1775. Applied for pension in Brooke County, Virginia, April 29, 1833, which was granted, July 18, 1833, but apparently was suspended in 1835 and not resumed. Supporting claims by Captain Isaac Cox, a brother, Abraham Rogers, William Braxton, Jacob Walker, Reverend Jeremiah Browning, and James Miller.

COX, ISAAC (Sergeant)
Service—New Jersey   Va. No. 3126 and No. 4463   No. S. 9215

Born, Somerset County, New Jersey, June 25, 1743, and resided there when the Revolution began. He served three years as private and one year as sergeant under Captains Linsley and Smalley, and Major Stout and Colonel Frelinghuysen. While living on the line between Harrison and Lewis County, he was granted a pension in 1832, but in 1835 was dropped from the rolls and not resumed. He was the father of Philip Cox, aged 69 in 1832. Supporting claims made by James Brown and John Neasley.

COX, ISAAC (Colonel)

Cox's Fort or Station was on the Ohio above Wellsburg. The Cox family of Swedish descent first settled in Maryland, then Captain Reuben Cox removed to the South Branch of the Potomac where his sons, Gabriel, George, Isaac and Joseph were born. Between 1772 and 1773, the family removed to the Ohio Valley and settled near the Pennsylvania Line.

Colonel Isaac Cox was made captain of militia and in 1776 commanded the fort at Holliday's Cove. In 1777, he became lieutenant-colonel of Youghioughany County militia, with his brother, Gabriel, as major. On October 25, 1779, Isaac asked the county court for a passport to enable him to remove his family to Kentucky. There he settled at Cox's Station in what was later Nelson County. In 1781, he was a delegate from Jefferson County to the Virginia assembly and was a member of three of the Kentucky conventions which urged statehood for Kentucky. During the latter part of the Indian wars he was killed by the savages.

COX, JAMES

James Cox was born in Buckingham County, Virginia, 1755. He served in the Illinois expedition of 1778-1779 under Colonel Joseph Crockett. He came to Cabell County about 1803 and settled on Mud River near the Great Falls between Ohio and Blue Sulphur. He died in 1840, being the ancestor of various Cox, Hernford or Hereford, and DeFore families. He is buried on the Burdette farm, Cabell County, near Ona.

COX, JAMES
Service—Virginia   Va. No. 16881   No. R. 2412

Born, February 24, 1763, Fort Clusel, Montgomery County, Virginia. As an Indian spy and scout, enlisted when 15 or 16 years old under his father, Captain John Cox, and served four years in the commands under Major William Love and Colonel Cleaveland. Applied for pension, Grayson County, Virginia, 1832, but it was rejected. Soldier died April 17, 1841. On February 19, 1819, married Sally Fiedler, who was born in 1782. Supporting claims by Benjamin Phipp, Charles Cole and Henry Harding.

COX, PHILIP
Service—New Jersey   No. S. 18360

Born, Somerset County, New Jersey, 1763, and resided there during the Revolution. Enlisted, March, 1780, under Captains Dunn, Clark, and Hunt under Colonel Frelinguysen. Supporting claims made by John Neeley, and John and James Brown. Pension granted, 1832, while living on line between Harrison and Lewis Counties for two years service in New Jersey militia but name was dropped from the rolls in 1835.

CRAIK, JAMES (Surgeon)
James Craik, Mason County, Virginia, August 3, 1831, was granted a land bounty as the heir of James Craik who had served as a surgeon in the Continental line during the Revolution. Warrants were issued, No. 7127 and No. 7128-30.

CRAMER, THOMAS (Major)
Major Thomas Cramer, who served in the Revolutionary Army, is buried in the Cramer Cemetery, Winfield, Marion County.

CRAWFORD, JOHN (Sergeant)
Enlisted in Captain Stephenson's company in 1775. Reenlisted as a sergeant in Captain Shepherd's company in 1776. Taken prisoner and exchanged. In 1782, accompanied his father, Colonel William Crawford, against the western Indians. He escaped and returned home in June of that year after the failure of the expedition.

CRAWFORD, THOMAS
Bounty Land Warrant No. 8183 was issued July 28, 1835, in favor of Thomas Crawford, a resident of Berkeley County, Virginia, who had served as a private in the Continental Line during the Revolution.

CRAWFORD, VALENTINE
Served at Fort Crawford and under his brother, Colonel William Crawford, in the western Indian campaigns. Lived on the Bullskin in Berkeley County, Virginia.

CRAWFORD, WILLIAM (Colonel)
Born in Westmoreland County, Pennsylvania, in 1722. His father died in 1725, and his widow married Richard Stephenson, by whom she had five sons, John, Hugh, Richard, James, and Marquis. William married Hannah Vance in 1744. The Crawfords lived in Berkeley County on the

Bullskin on land taken up in 1747. He had four children; Sarah (Major William Harrison); Effie (William Connell); Ann, (Zachariah McCormick); John.

Crawford served under Washington in the Indian wars. He was lieutenant-colonel of the Fifth Virginia, February 13, 1776; colonel of the Seventh Virginia, August 14, 1776. Fought at Trenton, Princeton, Brandywine, and Germantown. Resigned March 22, 1777. Later served on the western frontiers of Virginia, led an expedition against the Indians, was captured, tortured, and burned at the stake in Wyandotte County, Ohio, June 11, 1782.

CRAWFORD, WILLIAM (Captain)
Served as second lieutenant, Fifth Pennsylvania battalion, January 8, 1776; first lieutenant, October 12, 1776; captured at Fort Washington, November 16, 1776; captain, May, 1777; exchanged December 18, 1780; did not reenter service. Died, 1828.

CRESAP, THOMAS (Colonel)
Colonel Thomas Cresap was born about 1705 and lived to the age of almost a hundred. He had three sons, Daniel, Thomas, Michael, and two daughters, Sarah and Elizabeth. Thomas was killed by the Indians. Daniel had one son, Michael, who commanded a company in Dunmore's War. On June 10, 1774, the Earl of Dunmore sent Michael a captain's commission in the militia of Hampshire County, although having residence in Maryland. He led a company to Boston, 1775, from Maryland. He was in bad health and died in New York, October 5, 1777. Daniel, son of Daniel, was a lieutenant in the company of riflemen which marched to Boston under his uncle, Michael, from Allegheny County, Maryland, in 1775. By a second wife, Colonel Thomas Cresap had seven sons: Thomas, Daniel, Joseph, Van, Robert, James, and Thomas (the first Thomas having died young).

CRIM, HARMON
Service—Virginia   Va. No. 16641   No. S. 8254
Applied for pension, Harrison County, Virginia, Nov. 20, 1832. Certificate was issued, September 11, 1833. He was born in Culpeper County and enlisted in the Revolutionary Army in Fauquier County under Captains Chinn and Holmes and Colonel Armchurch. He was at the siege and capture of Yorktown.

CRIM, PETER
Served in the Revolution and died at Smithfield, Jefferson County, Virginia, in 1846, at the age of 94.

CRISSWELL, RICHARD
Service—Virginia   Va. No. 23682 and 121708   No. S. 6779
Born, Baltimore, Maryland, and enlisted there as a private under Captain Christian Owens in the Maryland militia under Colonel Sacks. Fought at Brandywine and other points. Received pension in 1833 while living in Brooke County, Virginia. Mention made of Susannah Gossage.

CRITZER, LEONARD
Service—New Jersey   Va. No. 2128   No. S. 9251

Enlisted, March, 1776, and served nineteen months as a private in the Third Jersey Regiment under Captain Goonenkike and Cornelius Cartheart under Colonel Mehelum in various campaigns in New Jersey. Many other officers named. Received pension, Harrison County, Virginia, in 1832.

CROM (CRUM), ADAM
Born, October 15, 1756. Pension application, Lawrence County Kentucky, 1834, aged 77. Drafted in Burke County, North Carolina, 1776, under Captain Brown and Colonel Cooke and marched against the Cherokees. Also served under Colonel Love, Captain Ward, Captain McGavock and Major Montgomery. Was at King's Mountain. Pension allowed.

CROOKSHANKS, JOHN
Service—Virginia   Va. No. 4719   No. S. 39384

Enlisted as a private, 1776, Augusta County, Virginia, and was discharged at Camden, South Carolina, 1782. Served more than three years as a private under Captain John Sims, Captain Linn, Colonel Stephens, Tenth Virginia Regiment under Colonel Henry Lee, and General Green. Fought at Brandywine, Germantown, Georgetown and Guilford Courthouse, where he was wounded in the right leg below the knee. He was 66 years old and his wife 53 when pension application was made in 1818. Their children were: Elizabeth, 27, Catherine, 17, Hester, 12, Nancy, 6, Abraham, 17, William, 15, and George, 1. Certificate was issued in Greenbrier County, in 1819.

CROSTON (CROSSTON), GUSTAVUS
Service—Virginia   Va. No. 3886   No. S. 39379

Enlisted at Alexandria, Virginia, and served from 1778 to 1783 as a private in the company of Lieutenant Harper, Captain Thomas Hamilton, and Colonels Green and Bladford. Born, 1757, and died, August, 1841. Applied for pension, 1818, Hampshire County, Virginia. Supporting claims by Bryan Kerken, Thomas Lewis, and Hezekiah Emery. Pension certificate issued, October 24, 1818.

CROUSE, CHRISTIAN
Service—Pennsylvania   Va. No. 12338   No. S. 9243

Enlisted, York, Pennsylvania, and served as a private six months under Captain George Long in the Pennsylvania line under Colonel Swope. Pension application granted in Morgan County, Virginia, April 26, 1833. Supporting claims by Isaac Bosher, Peter Stotler, Tolbert Rochhold, Joshua Gains, and Jesse Crouse.

CRUTCHERS, JAMES
Service—Pennsylvania   Va. No. 2893   No. S. 39377

Enlisted, Philadelphia, Pennsylvania, and served three years and three months as private in the company of Captain Francis Proctor, Pennsylvania Line, under Colonel Thomas Proctor. Fought at Brandywine, Germantown, and in the Indian campaign under General Sullivan. Granted pensio in Jefferson County, Virginia, 1818. The soldier was aged 57 in 1820.

CRUTCHLEY (CUTCHLEY), BENJAMIN
Service—Maryland   Va. No. 10577   No. 39378

Enlisted January 10, 1777, Baltimore, Maryland, as a private in the company commanded by Captain Woodman or Goodman of the Fourth Maryland Regiment under Colonel Hall, attached to the division commanded by General Sullivan. He continued to serve until 1780 when he was discharged in the state of New Jersey by Colonel Hall. He was in the battles of Brandywine and Germantown. He applied for a pension in Wood County, which was granted in 1819. He was 76 years old in 1820.

CUMMINGS, JOHN
Service—Continental Md.   Va. No. 17704   No. S. 39400

Born, Maryland, 1760, and there enlisted under Captain Rudolph in the Continental Establishment, Maryland Line, and served fifteen months in Lieutenant-Colonel Lee's Legion. He was engaged on many scouting parties and skirmishes. Pension granted in Ohio County, Virginia, in 1820 but later suspended. Wife named Araminta, aged 59, and son, named Robert, aged 21, in 1820.

CUMMINGS, JOHN
Served as a private in Captain Shepherd's company. Died in prison, June 27, 1777.

CUNDIFF, JOHN (Sergeant)
Service—Virginia   Va. No. 23100   No. S. 8272

Born, 1759, Lancaster County, Virginia. Enlisted, Northumberland County, Virginia, 1775, and reenlisted in different periods until 1778. He was a private and sergeant eight and a half months under Captain William Docuning, Captain William Nutt, Captain Christopher, in the Virginia regiment under Colonel Thomas Gaskins, Colonel Edward Conaway, and Colonel Windowkiner. Other officers were Lieutenant Raleigh Colston, James McAndrews, and Ensign Gray Eskridge. Supporting affidavits by Major Isaac Welsh, John T. Hickman, John and Jacob Vandiver, and Nathaniel Kuykendall. Pension granted, 1833, in Hampshire County.

CUNNINGHAM, THOMAS
Service—Virginia   Va. No. 3291   No. W. 4166

Cunningham served fourteen months as a private in the Virginia militia detachment, commanded by Captain James Booth. His wife, Phoebe, was captured by the Indians in 1785 and their four children murdered. They were married, April, 1776. The soldier died, June, 1826. Widow received pension, April 22, 1840, and had previously been aided by special act of the Virginia legislature. The family had removed from Harrison to Ritchie County in 1807, settling on the south fork of Hughes River.

CUNNINGHAM, WALTER
Service—Virginia   Va. No. 5056   No. S. 9263

Enlisted, Shenandoah County, Virginia, 1776, and served six months under Captain Scott and Captain Rador in the Virginia line. Supporting affidavits filed by Gass Winters and Anthony Kuhn. Pension granted, Harrison County Virginia, February 2, 1833.

CUNNINGHAM, WILLIAM
Service—Virginia   No. Va. 6529   No. S. 8462 and B. L. Wt. 26387

Born Shenandoah County, Virginia, July 23, 1864. Resided in Harrison County in 1794, when he removed to Wood County. Enlisted, Shenandoah County, May, 1780, and served seven months as a private in the company under Captain Richardson, Higgins, and Martin Aul under Colonel Hetherson. Fought at Maches, Chester Gap, and Yorktown. For a time substituted for his father, John Cunningham, and later was a substitute for his uncle, Thomas Cunningham. He was granted pension in 1832. Supporting claims were filed by Walter Cunningham, Ezekiel Wilkinson, the Reverend Hamilton Gass, John Culp, and William McGee. Bounty land warrant of 160 acres was also received.

CUPP LEONARD
Service—Pennsylvania   Va. No. 13132   No. W. 4167

Born, Northampton County Pennsylvania, January 17, 1755, and died, August 17, 1834. Enlisted, Northampton County, in the fall of 1775, and served seven months under Captains Leekfret and Greenwood in the Pennsylvania Minute Men, commanded by Colonel Kiger. Saw service in Pennsylvania, Delaware, New Jersey, and in the Indian campaigns.

Married, June 21, 1772, in Northampton County. Wife's name Susannah. She died, April 3, 1841. Pension granted soldier in Preston County in 1833 but widow did not survive long enough to get pension. The ages of their children in 1854 were: Leonard, Jr., 77; John, 68; Christopher, 73; Susannah Cupp Johnston, 70; William, 60. Leonard, Jr., was a captain in the War of 1812. Supporting affidavits filed by Reverend David Trowbridge, Benjamin Shaw, Jacob Guseman, Samuel Trowbridge, John Feather, Mary Freighter Strahnin, and Joe Brown.

CUPPY, JOHN

Born, May 11, 1761, in New Jersey, and died in Montgomery County, Ohio, 1861, having rounded out a full century. He was of German parentage. While an infant, his father moved to the South Branch of the Potomac in Hampshire County. There John was drafted for McIntosh's expedition, his first military service. The next year he married. Soon afterward he took a tour of military duty during the Loyalist insurrection of 1781. About 1788, he removed to a farm near Wellsburg, now Brooke County, where he engaged in the spy service under Captain Sam Brady and became an expert rifleman and scout. He moved to Ohio in 1818.

CURTIS, JESSE

Applied for pension, 1834, aged 74, in Lewis County. Supporting affidavits filed by John Mitchell, William Powers and others. Claim not allowed.

CURTIS, JOHN
Service—Pennsylvania   Va. No. 23967   No. S. 12645

Born, Lancaster County, Pennsylvania, May 5, 1753, and there enlisted May 5, 1776, in the Revolutionary Army. Served nineteen months as a private under Captain Garner, Lieutenant James Jack and William Moore, Seventh Pennsylvania Regiment, commanded by Colonel John Gibson, Major Bartholomew Bull or Beal and Generals Washington and Irving. Fought at Chestnut Hill. Supporting affidavits of Alex Hill, Joseph Wood, Jesse Wheat, John Good, and John Wilson accompanied his pension application filed April 22, 1834, West Liberty, Ohio County. Pension certificate issued 1834, but suspended in 1835, then reissued in 1838 and later reduced in amount.

CUTRIGHT, BENJAMIN
The grave of Benjamin Cutright, who had service during the Revolutionary War, is in the Philadelphia Cemetery, Hampton, Upshur County.

CUTRIGHT, JOHN
Service—Virginia   Va. No. 12646   No. W. 6626 and B. L. Wt. 30692

Born, Hampshire County, Virginia, 1754, died March 8, 1850, and is buried in Philadelphia Cemetery, Hampton, Upshur County. Enlisted in Monongalia County, in 1778 and served thirteen months as a private under Captain James Booth and Captain Jackson. Cutright was married to Rebecca Truby by Reverend Isaac Edward, in Harrison County, Virginia, January 2, 1788 or 1790. Rebecca Cutright was 80 years old in 1857.

Pensions were granted to both soldier and widow in Lewis, now Upshur County, and also bounty land warrant for 160 acres. Supporting claims were filed in their behalf by Jacob Cozad, Alex West, David Sleeth, and Susannah Stalnaker.

DAILEY (DAILY), JOHN
Service—Virginia   Va. No. 17057   No. S. 39414 and B. L. Wt. 2419

Enlisted, Berkeley County, Virginia, March 5, 1781, and received an honorable discharge in South Carolina in 1783 after two years and six months service under Captain Shelton with the Virginia troops. Received pension in Hampshire County July 31, 1820; also bounty land warrant for 100 acres. Soldier aged 55 in 1818, died, May 7, 1830. In 1820, wife, Catherine, was aged 54, and their children as follows: Sarah, 22; Mary, 19; Eleanor, 9; John; Jacob. Sarah married a Chapman and Eleanor married a Sears. John, married and died young, leaving a widow with six young children.

DAMRON, OENEFERUS
Before the Cabell County court, September 23, 1822, Oeneferus Damron made oath that he had served in the Revolutionary War and knew Asher Crockett (James Anderson), and filed a schedule of his property. This was certified to the War Department and considered as an application for a pension.

DANDRIDGE, ALEXANDER SPOTSWOOD (Captain)

Born, August 1, 1753, Hanover County, Virginia; died in April, 1785, and is buried at Martinsburg, Berkeley County, West Virginia. He was the son of Captain Nathaniel West Dandridge and his wife, Dorothea Spotswood, the daughter of Governor Alexander Spotswood, whose expedition across the Blue Ridge was the first to recognize the rich region beyond the mountains.

He was made lieutenant of the Fourth Virginia Dragoons, June 13, 1776; captain of the Virginia Artillery Battallion, November 30, 1777; for a time he was one of Washington's aides. He resigned from the army on April 14, 1780. He had also been active on the western frontiers when he went to Kentucky with Henderson in 1775 when the Transylvania Company made the Boonesborough settlement.

He married, Ann, daughter of General Adam Stephen, and settled on a plantation in what is now Jefferson County, West Virginia, about eight miles from Martinsburg. At his death in 1785, there was one child, Adam Stephen, aged two years. His widow, died in 1834, aged 76 years.

DARBY (DARLY), SAMUEL

Made application in Preston County, Virginia, for pension as a Revolutionary soldier, but the claim was rejected, No. R. 13662.

DARKE, WILLIAM (General)

Son of Joseph Darke; born in Buck or Lancaster County, Pensylvania, in 1736 and at age of five, accompanied his parents to Jefferson County, Virginia, where they settled at Duffield's Station. Entered the Revolutionary Army as captain of the Eighth Virginia Regiment, February 9, 1776; major, January 4, 1777; wounded and taken prisoner at Germantown, October 14, 1777; exchanged, November 1, 1780; lieutenant-colonel Fourth Virginia, February 12, 1781, to rank from November 29, 1777. Retired, January 1, 1783.

With Brigadier General Adam Stephen, he represented Berkeley County, Virginia, in the Virginia Federal convention of 1788, and there voted for the ratification of the National Constitution. He commanded the right wing of St. Clair's army at "St. Clair's defeat" and helped save the remnants of the defeated American forces. He died, November 20, 1801, and is buried in Jefferson County, West Virginia. Darke County, Ohio, is named for him.

The Revolutionary War section of the Pension Office shows that bounty Land Warrant No. 598 was issued for 500 acres of land, August 5, 1789, for services during the Revolutionary War. He married Sarah Delega (or Deleyea) Defauze. Four children are mentioned: Joseph, John, and Samuel; and Mary, who first married Thomas Rutherford, Jr., and later a Mr. Manning.

When Darke was captured by the British at Germantown, he was placed on a prison ship. His wife travelled from Gerkeley County to Philadelphia by stage, dressed as a cabin boy, says tradition, and was smuggled on board the ship. Through her intercessions, he was afterward released and served in the army the balance of the war. He became a brigadier general during the Indian wars which followed the War for Independence.

DAUGHERTY, GEORGE
Service—Pennsylvania   Va. No. 19208   No. S. 39456

Enlisted, 1775, in Pennsylvania, in a company commanded by Captain Henry Miller, Fifth Regiment, Continental Establishment, under Colonel Magory. Was taken prisoner at Fort Washington, and carried to New York. Then exchanged and discharged. Reenlisted, 1777, in Pennsylvania, in company commanded by Captain Jacob Mays, Second Pennsylvania Regiment, under Colonel Walter Stewart, known as the "Irish Beauty." He fought at Brandywine, Germantown, and Monmouth.

This detachment was discharged near Elizabethtown, New York. Daugherty's discharge, signed by Colonel Stewart, was given to Major William Preston. Pension was granted to the soldier in Greenbrier County, Virginia, March 5, 1824. Applicant stated that he lived apart from his wife, aged 58. Eleven children were mentioned but the soldier only named his daughter, Mary, wife of Sam Wilson, with whom he was living.

DAVENPORT, ABRAHAM, JR. (Lieutenant)

Abraham Davenport, son of Abraham Davenport, Sr., and Mary Simms, was born, February 9, 1752, Maryland. He was a resident of Berkeley County, now Jefferson County, Virginia, at the time of the Revolution. He died, April 17, 1825.

He was married to Frances Williams, January 21, 1779, in Maryland. She was born in 1751. Their children were as follows: Eleanor, December 27, 1779; Mazie, December 3, 1782; Amelia, May 13, 1784; Thomas, November 14, 1786; William, August 22, 1789; Braxton, Jr., December 19, 1781; Rebecca, April 8, 1783; Ariel, August 22, 1795; Juliet, October 4, 1797.

Served as a sergeant and lieutenant. Entered the service in the spring of 1776 in Colonel Moses Rawlings' Regiment of Maryland Riflemen. The inscription on his monument in the Edge Hill Cemetery at Charles Town Jefferson County, states that it is "In Memory of Major Abram Davenport, a soldier of the Revolution and an upright magistrate."

DAVENPORT, ADRIAN

Served in the Revolution as a private in Captain Thomas Beall's company in Colonel Moses Rawlings' Virginia and Maryland Rifle Regiment. One of the four sons of Abraham Davenport, Sr., who fought in the War for Independence.

DAVENPORT, ANTHONY S.

Son of Abraham Davenport, Sr., who came from St. Marys or Charles County, Maryland, to Berkeley County, Virginia, in 1775 with his family, which included four sons who were to serve in the Revolution. He served in the Revolutionary Army as a private in a company of a Virginia regiment.

DAVENPORT, JOHN

He was a private in Captain Samuel J. Cabell's company of the Sixth Battalion of Continentals Sixth Virginia Regiment commanded by Lieutenant-Colonel James Hendricks, 1776, and corporal in Captain Mathew Jobett's company, Seventh Virginia Regiment, commanded by Colonel Alexander McClenachan.

He was born, December 14, 1753, Maryland, the son of Abram Davenport and Mary Simms and died January 19, 1815. He resided in Berkeley County, now Jefferson County, during the Revolution. He married Ellen Harris, October 1780, in Calvert County, Maryland. Their children are as follows: Mary, October, 1781; Benjamin, December, 1783; John, January, 1788; Rebecca, March, 1790; George, January, 1792; Adrian, March, 1794; Katherine, November, 1798; Nancy Simms, January, 1801; and Eleanor, October, 1803.

DAVIDSON, JOSIAH
Service—Virginia   Va. No. 2126   No. S. 8301

Served fifteen months as a private in the Virginia line under Colonel John Pierce and Johnson in 1781 and 1782. Applied for pension, 1834, which was first issued, but was later suspended. Soldier was 71 years old in 1834.

West Virginians in the American Revolution

Assembled and Edited by ROSS B. JOHNSTON

The sources of this material are from the files of the Pension Office at Washington, from various county records, from notes of patriotic societies, principally the Daughters of the American Revolution, Sons of the American Revolution, Sons of the Revolution, and from a large miscellaneous group of published and private sources. Corrections and additions to this list will receive the careful attention of the editor.

DAVIS, DANIEL
Service—Virginia   Va. No. 23111 and 27449   No. S. 8287
Born, Chester County, Pennsylvania, February 11, 1759, and died in 1838. He was a private under Captain John Henderson, Virginia militia, for fourteen months. He was stationed at Fort Randolph, Point Pleasant, where he mentions Captain Arbuckle, Colonel Dickinson, and Colonel Skillern, and at King's Fort and Tott's Fort. He lived in Wayne County, on Twelve Pole Creek, and was placed on the pension roll from Cabell County in 1833. Supporting claims were made by Burwell Spurlock, John Samuels, and Jacob Kinnison.

DAVIS, JACOB
Service—Virginia   Va. No. 23824   No. S. 17916
Born, Sussex County, New Jersey, 1760, moved with his parents to Louden County, Virginia, 1770, and filed pension application in Harrison County in 1834. Enlisted, September, 1776, under James Ratlekin, Cox, and Mason in the Virginia line under Colonel Shepherd and General Hand, and served eight months. Pension was granted. Supporting claims were made by John Nay and Joseph Tetrick.

DAVIS, JOHN
Service—New Jersey   Va. No. 16220   No. W. 8654
Born, Monmouth County, New Jersey, May 1, 1755. Died June, 1842, and is buried at the Broad Run Baptist Church, Lewis County. Enlisted in New Jersey and served two years as drum major under Captain Fleming and Dennis in New Jersey regiments commanded by Colonels Heart and Henderson, and General Foreman.
Married Margaret Kelso, August 21, 1814-15. Widow died, February 10, 1855, at age of 84, in Harrison County. Pensions granted to soldier and widow in Lewis and Harrison counties. Supporting claims filed by William Davis, a brother, Benjamin Shannon, Jesse Chapman, William Fleming, and Amos Woofter.

DAVIS, JOSEPH (Surgeon)
Surgeon of Colonel Daniel Morgan's Rifle regiment in 1777.

DAVIS, JOSEPH (Lieutenant)
Born, Charles County, Maryland, April, 1761, and died in Hardy County, Virginia, September 16, 1831. He resided in Hampshire County during the Revolution and there married Rebecca Dent.

He served as a lieutenant in Company No. 2 of Colonel Daniel Morgan's Eleventh and Fifteenth Virginia regiments, which were organized May 31, 1777, to November 30, 1778. He was given a land grant in Louden County, Virginia, and settled there soon after his marriage in 1791.

DAVIS, JOSEPH
Born, Dorchester County, Maryland, October 24, 1767, moved to Fauquier County, 1780, thence to Louden, Rockingham, Monongalia, and Harrison counties. Enlisted at the age of fifteen as personal servant to General Henry Lee and served seven months under Captains Jennins, Wells, Lieutenants Skinner, Randolph, and General Lee. Claim for pension rejected as he had not established military service.

DAVIS, SAMUEL
Service—Virginia   Va. No. 6530   No. W. 2534 and B.L.Wt. 26528

Born, Louden County, Virginia, April 28, 1762, and died September 10, 1847. Enlisted in Louden County and served as a private six months under Captain Frank Broy and Carnes in the Virginia line under Colonel Merriweather.

Lived in Louden County until 21, then moved to Frederick County, thence to Kentucky, then back to Louden County, and finally to Harrison County. He married Ruth Lewis, January 27, 1802, who was born in 1784. Their children were: John, James, William, Israel, Humphrey, Matilda, Davis Young, Garry (dead), and Joseph. The marriage was performed by Isaac Morris in Harrison County. Both soldier and widow received pensions. Bounty land warrant was also issued for 160 acres. Supporting claims were filed by Robert Parks, David Dilworth, John Middleton, and John Romine.

DAVIS, SAMUEL
Member of Captain Shepherd's rifle company in 1776. Taken prisoner at Fort Washington in 1776, and died or was killed on a prison ship, February 15, 1777.

DAVIS, SAMUEL BARKER
Service—Virginia   Va. No. 6285   No. W. 1728 and B.L.Wt. 34532

Enlisted under Captain James Renn July 1, 1775, Fairfax County, Virginia, and was engaged in the defense of the city of Alexandria from threatened attacks of Lord Dunmore then on the Potomac River. In Captain Thomas Pollard's company, marched through Alexandria, Georgetown, Frederick, York, Lancaster, and Reading to join the main army under General Washington on their retreat from the Battle of Germantown, October 4, 1777. Enlisted in Louden County, Virginia militia under Captain John Linton, July 13, 1781. Marched to Fredicksburg and Richmond to join army of General Lafayette. Attached to Muhlenberg's regiment, under Colonel Merryweather and Major Hardman, and discharged, September 26, 1781.

Born, Charles County, Maryland. Removed to Fairfax County, Virginia, 1769 or 1770, thence to Louden County, then Prince William County, and in 1787 moved to Hampshire County. On December 7, 1814, married Ann Bogle, who was born about 1794. The soldier, according to Mineral County records, had married Rebecca Bussey in 1778. Pension certificates were issued and also bounty land warrants for 160 acres. Supporting claims were filed by William Welsh and Elias Jones.

DAVIS, SPENCER
Service—Virginia   Va. No. 16932   No. W. 5261

At the outbreak of the Revolution, resided in Louden County, Virginia, and there enlisted December 1, 1780, and served nineteen months as a private under Captain Daniel Feagans, and Lieutenants John Rapee and Lucket Humphreys in the Virginia service under Colonel West and General Wordsworth. Other officers were Captain William Smith, Lieutenant George Taylor, and Colonel Wolcott of Connecticut. Saw service with the northern army and was discharged, April 10, 1782.

In Louden County, marriage bond is filed of Spencer Davis and Ann Wornall of Shelbourn Parish. Van Davis was guarantor with Spencer. The marriage took place, December 26, 1786.

Soldier applied for pension, in Hampshire County, which was granted, October 16, 1833. The pensioner, born, 1761, died, July 6, 1838. His widow, aged 79 in 1840, applied for a pension in Muskegon County, Ohio, in 1844. Supporting claims were filed by Enoch Furr, Minor Furr (cousin of Davis whose mother was a Furr), James Wornall, and Nancy Chamberlain.

DAVIS, THOMAS

By executive order of the State of Virginia, May 28, 1834, the heirs of Thomas Davis were allowed land bounty for services as a soldier in the Continental Line for three years. Warrant 12282 was issued. In Logan County, Virginia, it was certified that Thomas Davis, Revolutionary soldier, had died in 1825 intestate, leaving William, Henry, Sally (Hensley), Nancy (Evans), and Jane Davis as heirs.

DAVIS, WILLIAM
Service—Virginia   Va. No. 13133   No. S. 8277

Resided in Orange County, Virginia, at outbreak of Revolution, and there enlisted and served two years as private in the company of Captain Taylor, Second Virginia Regiment, Continental Line, commanded by Colonel Spottswood. Fought at Brandywine, Germantown, and at other points in Maryland, Virginia, Pennsylvania and New Jersey. Made application for pension in Orange County, Virginia, which was granted in 1833. Supporting claims by John Williams, Cudden Davis, and Francis Cowherd. (This soldier is grouped with Preston County, Virginia, men.)

DAVIS, WILLIAM
Service—Virginia   Va. No. 12784   No. W. 284 and B.L.Wt. 333

Enlisted in Virginia in company of Captain Madison Fields, Ninth Virginia Regiment, under Colonel Davis Gaskins and Generals Morgan and Wayne. Served four years and six months, seeing action at Bunker Hill and Yorktown. Married, March 25, 1819, Logan County, Kentucky, to Mary Taylor by Reuben Giddens, Justice of the Peace. Received pension and bounty lands in Kentucky.

DAVIS, WILLIAM
Service—Virginia   Va. No. 6326   No. W. 6973

Enlisted, Amherst County, Virginia, 1777, and served two years and eight months as private in company of Captains Penn, Cabell, Dillard, and Franklin, under Colonels Washington and Preston, and Generals Lee, Green, and Washington. Was at Jamestown, Halifax, Guilford Courthouse, and Yorktown. Soldier married Benedicta Milstead, January 1, 1787. Certificate of pension issued to soldier, 1834, Fayette County, Virginia. Soldier died, January 20, 1846, and widow also received pension. Supporting claims by Walter Sandridge, Robert Carter, Henry Payton, and Colonel Anderson.

DAVIS, WILLIAM
Enlisted under Captain Hugh Stephenson in 1775; reenlisted in Captain William Brady's rifle company from Berkeley County, Virginia, in June, 1776. Badly wounded near Fort Washington. Later served under Colonel Daniel Morgan.

DAVIS, WILLIAM
Service—New Jersey   Va. No. 16222   No. S. 5329

Born, Monmouth County, New Jersey, 1758. There enlisted in the Revolutionary Army, June, 1776, and served nineteen months under Lieutenant Derrick Longstreet, Captain Dennis Cowherd, and Colonel Henderson, New Jersey Regiment. He fought at Germantown and James Town. Applied for pension, Harrison County, which was granted in 1833. Supporting claims were made by his brother, John, Jesse Chapman, and James Fleming.

DAVIS, WILLIAM
Service—Virginia   Va. No. 23411   No. S. 10521

Applied for Revolutionary War pension in Lewis County, under act of 1832. Certificate was issued, June 17, 1834, for two years service, but this was suspended in 1835.

DEEM, ADAM
Service—Pennsylvania   Va. No. 23988   No. S. 10522

Born, Fayette County, Pennsylvania, 1761, the son of John Deem. Enlisted in Fayette County in 1777 and served six months under Captain Stokely, Eighth Regiment, Pennsylvania Line, under Colonels Brodhead, Gibson, and Bayard, and Major Finley, engaged in scouting and guard duty. Pension was issued to him in Wood County in 1834, but was dropped from the rolls in 1835, and there is no record of reinstatement.

DEEM, JACOB (Ensign)

Born, Frederick County, Maryland, in 1764. Lived in Westmoreland, now Fayette County, Pennsylvania, at outbreak of Revolution. There enlisted, May 1, 1781, as ensign under Captains Pigman and Felty, and Colonel Cook. His commission as ensign at age of 17 was signed by Governor Mifflin of Pennsylvania. Applied for pension in Wood County, Virginia, in 1834. His claims were supported by Thomas Pribble, Hiram Pribble, and Adam Deem, a brother. The claim was rejected.

DEHART, ABRAHAM
Service—Pennsylvania   Va. No. 6012   No. S. 39426

Enlisted as a private in 1775 in Bucks County, Pennsylvania, under Captain Rees, Third Pennsylvania Regiment, Continental Establishment, Colonel Craig commanding, and served seven years. He fought at Brandywine, Monmouth, Green Springs, and Yorktown. Pension was granted him, July 29, 1819, in Monroe County, Virginia. He was 65 years old in 1820.

DELANY (DELANEY), MARTIN
Service—Pennsylvania   Va. No. 6381   No. S. 39425 and W.L.Wt. 1056

Enlisted, Chester County, Pennsylvania, under Captain John Christy, Fifth Pennsylvania Regiment, Colonel Johnston, and served six years. He was discharged at Philadelphia August, 1793, after having had service at Shorthill, Couches (Canches) Bridge, Brandywine, Germantown, Jamestown, and Little York.

The soldier, born in 1751, died June 20, 1827, or 1837, near the mouth of Birch River, Braxton County. His wife, Hannah, was 60 years old in 1820. Pension was granted to Delany in Greenbrier County, February 4, 1819, and bounty land warrant for 100 acres was also issued.

DENT, JOHN (Lieutenant)
Service—Virginia   Va. No. 2491   No. W. 4663

Born, February 18, 1755, Louden County, Virginia, and died, September 20, 1840, Monongalia County, Virginia. Enlisted, Monongalia County, April, 1777, as a private under Captain David Scott, Thirteenth Virginia Regiment Continental troops, commanded by Colonel John Gibson, Lieutenant-Colonel R. Campbell, and Major Taylor. Under General Hand he had written orders to go as sergeant to a fort on the Ohio between the mouth of Big Beaver and Wheeling Creek and remain there for further orders. On his return to Fort Pitt, General Hand and all but the two companies of troops under Captain Scott and Captain Heath had left. He remained there as sergeant until commissioned ensign, Ninth Virginia, October 31, 1778, and lieutenant, April 6, 1779, and attached to Captain Jacob Sullivan's company under General McIntosh during the summer and fall. Colonel Gibson offered him the captaincy of a company of cavalry but he settled his accounts and resigned in November, 1780.

Pensions were granted to both the soldier and his widow in Monongalia County. Records of 1829 show that he sought land bounty warrant as a lieutenant in the Revolutionary War but it is not clear whether this was granted. His claims are approved by statements of Waitman Fleming, Dudley Evans, aged 76 (brother of Margaret Dent), George Deering, Moses Cox, Aaron Barker, and George D. Evans.

Lieutenant Dent married Margaret Evans in Monongalia County, in June, 1780, and the records of their marriage are on file. Margaret Dent was 78 years old in 1841. Their children are: Elizabeth, December 26, 1780; John, January 24, 1783; George, November 18, 1784; Dudley, March 1, 1787; Ann, May 3, 1789; Nimrod, June 8, 1792; Margaret (Higgs), April 1, 1794; Enoch, May 21, 1796; James, August 15, 1798; Marmaduke, February 25, 1801; Arnradey, April 3, 1803; Barnady, February 25, 1808.

DEPUE, HENRY

Application for pension, December, 1833, in Wood County, by Henry Depue for Revolutionary War services following enlistment in New Jersey, was rejected as it was believed that Depue could not have been old enough.

DEVERS, JAMES
Service—Virginia   Va. No. 23877   No. S. 17924

Born, North Carolina, October 26, 1754, and later removed to Maryland, to Frederick County, Virginia, and to Fairfax, Fauquier, Harrison and Monongalia counties. He enlisted in Fairfax County, in September, 1777, and served nearly twelve months in the company commanded by Captain Dennis Ramsey in Colonel Gilpin's regiment of Virginia troops. He was in the battle of Germantown, Cowpens, and Eutaw Springs, and was taken prisoner on board the ship Tempest, which ship was taken by the British under the command of Arnold and Phillips. At that time he was under command of Captain Charles Little. He was discharged from service in 1781 at Richmond. He had passport signed by Ensign James Demah, dated April 30, 1781, that he was a prisoner of war upon parole and that he had leave to return to Fairfax County. He received pension while living in Monongalia County, Virginia, in 1834. This pension was suspended but later resumed.

DEVERICKS, JOHN
Service—Virginia   Va. No. 4868   No. W. 7007

Born, Pendleton County, Virginia, 1763, and there enlisted in February, 1781, under Captains Quinn, Hicklin, and Prage in the Virginia militia. He died June 13, 1843. The Augusta County records show the marriage of Devericks at the home of John Peples to his daughter, Mary, April 24, 1787, with Reverend Samuel Shannon as the minister. The soldier received pension as did his widow, who was 83 years old in 1846. Supporting claims in their behalf were filed by Edward Stewart, Ensign Samuel Rullin, and Mary Hodge.

DEVIEZE (DEVIESE), ABRAHAM

Born, Philadelphia, Pennsylvania, 1746, later moved to Washington County, then to Wood, and to Lewis County, Virginia. Enlisted in the Revolutionary Army, August 1, 1777. Applied for pension in Wood County, November 29, 1833, with supporting affidavits from Peter Stallman and Benniah Depue, but claim was not allowed.

DEY, SAMUEL
Service—Virginia   Va. No. 12828   No. S. 6782

Born, January, 1744, Monmouth County, East New Jersey, and died in 1835. In Augusta County, Virginia, enlisted, 1779, and served nine months under Captain James Finley and Captain John McCreay in the Virginia militia under Colonel Sampson Matthews and General McIntosh. Substituted for Andrew Johnson who was a drafted militia man from Augusta County. Applied for pension in Greenbrier County, which was granted in 1833. Supporting claim made by James Gregory.

DINGES, PETER

In Mercer County is the grave of Peter Dinges, a soldier of the American Revolution, who participated in the Battle of Point Pleasant, October 10, 1744, and was also in Trigg's Battalion of Artillery in Lafayette's corps at the Battle of Yorktown, October 19, 1781.

DIXON, WILLIAM

Born, New Castle County, Delaware, 1760. Enlisted in the Revolutionary Army from Wilmington, Delaware, October 1, 1777, under Captain James. Applied for pension, December 31, 1833, in Wood County. Widow applied for pension, November 18, 1854, Ritchie County. Supporting claims by Allen Calhoun and Edmund Taylor. Claim rejected.

DOBBINS, JOHN
Service—Pennsylvania   Va. No. 16401   No. W. 3784

On June 6, 1819, before the Greenbrier County Court, John Dobbins, aged 72, declared that he enlisted in 1776 in Lancaster County, Pennsylvania, in the company of Captain James Taylor, Fourth Pennsylvania Regiment. He served his term of one year and reenlisted at Charlestown, Pennsylvania, in 1777 in the same company, but this time was with the Fifth Pennsylvania Regiment, commanded by Colonel Francis Johnston. He continued in service until 1783 with the wagon trains and was not in any battles. The soldier received pension in 1820 for six years service. He died April 11, 1833.

Sometime before 1794, the soldier married Elizabeth Keener, daughter of Samuel Keener. She was born about 1755 in Millersville, now Woodstock, Virginia, and moved with her parents to Whiteley Creek, Green County, Pennsylvania, fifteen miles north of Morgantown when she was ten years old but they may have lived for a time in Lancaster County before going so far west. John and Elizabeth Dobbins had one son, Samuel, born on Patterson Creek, Hampshire County, about 1786. The widow applied for pension which was granted in 1846. Her claims were supported by her brothers, John, who lived in Braxton County, Virginia, and George, who lived in Taylor County, Virginia, in 1845. They both stated that they had been born on Whiteley Creek, Pennsylvania, and that they had attended the wedding of their older sister, Elizabeth.

DODD, EZRA

The grave of Ezra Dodd, who was a soldier in the Revolutionary Army, is in the Maple Grove Cemetery, Marion County.

DONNALLY, ANDREW (Colonel)

Born, 1745, in the north of Ireland and emigrated to America about the middle of the eighteenth century and settled in Augusta County, Virginia, where he married, in 1766, Jane McCreery, daughter of John McCreery, who had settled in Augusta about 1744.

He built Donnally's Fort, a strong blockhouse, consisting of a double log house, two stories high, surrounded by pickets, in 1771 or 1772, about ten miles north of Lewisburg. He is said to have been lieutenant of Botetourt County, in 1775. In 1776, he was captain of militia, and when Greenbrier County was formed in 1777, he became lieutenant-colonel of that county. In May, 1778, he defended his fort against one of the strongest Indian attacks experienced in western Virginia. More than two hundred Indians are believed to have taken part in this attack, after an unsuccessful assault on Fort Randolph, Point Pleasant. The heroic exploit of John Prior (Pryor) and Phillip Hammond, disguised as Indians by Nonhelema, the sister of Chief Cornstalk (who was staying at Fort Randolph at that time) in running from Point Pleasant to the Greenbrier settlements just before the attack in time to give warning of the approaching savages, is one of the outstanding events of western border history.

Colonel Donnally later moved to the Kanawha Valley and there continued his activities in the development of that region just as he had done in the Greenbrier Valley. He died and is buried on the south side of the Kanawha at Charleston.

The children of Andrew and Jane Donnally were: Catherine B., born, 1768, died, 1858, married John Wilson, June 5, 1803; Polly or Mary, born 1767, married Reuben Slaughter; Charles, born, 1769, died very young; Jennie; Elizabeth, married Jacob Skyles; Sallie, married Henderson; Andrew, Jr., born, October 17, 1778, died, June 21, 1849, married Marjory Van Bibber, May 31, 1802; John, born, 1784.

DONNELLY, WILLIAM

Enlisted as a private in Captain Shepherd's company in 1776. Taken prisoner at Fort Washington in 1776, and died in captivity, January 10, 1777.

DORAN, ALEXANDER

Service-New Jersey   Va. No. 31165   No. S. 12784

Born, 1760, Manhen Township, Morris County, New Jersey, where he lived until 1781 when he moved to Virginia. Enlisted, 1776, as a private under Lieutenant Robert Hoggans, Captain Thomas Reardon and Major Francis Barber, Third New Jersey Regiment, commanded by Colonel Elias Drayton. Continued in service sixteen months and engaging in campaigns about Albany, against Quebec, and on the Hudson River. Received pension in Hampshire County, Virginia, July 22, 1837. Supporting affidavits filed by Robert Young, John Howe, James Smith, and Alexander Poston.

DORTON, HENRY
Service—Virginia   Va. No. 12570   No. S. 5362

Born, Bladensburg, Maryland, in 1748, resided in Prince George County, Maryland, for nine years after the Revolution, and then removed to Monongalia County, Virginia. Enlisted in the fall of 1777 at Redstone (now Brownsville), Pennsylvania, in the company of Captain Joseph Foard in the Virginia service under Colonel John Gibson, Generals Hand and McIntosh. Mentions Captains Foreman, Scott, and Lieutenants Dent and Cross. Pension received by Dorton in Monongalia County, in 1833. Soldier died, June 11, 1836. (Certificate of service from Captain Foard's company is in the safe in the chief's room of the old War and Navy Division, Washington.) Affidavit in favor of Dorton was filed by Matthew Gray.

DOTSON, RICHARD
Service—Virginia   Va. No. 16219   No. S. 5364

Born, Shenandoah (now Frederick) County, Virginia, October 23, 1752, and lived there twenty years. Resided, Green County, Pennsylvania, 1774, and after the Revolution lived in Shenandoah, Louden, Hampshire, Wood, and Tyler counties, in the latter of which he filed his pension application in 1833. It was issued to him, July 18, 1833.

Dotson was in service from 1774 to 1779 as an Indian spy under Captain Minor in the Virginia militia guarding and protecting the frontiers in Green County, Pennsylvania and Virginia. He had three tours of service of six months each. In one skirmish, one Indian was killed by John Hall, and John Nichols, one of Dotson's comrades, lost his life.

DOWBERMAN (DOUBERMAN or TOWBERMAN), HENRY
Service—Continental Pennsylvania   Va. No. 1192   No. S. 39453

Enlisted, January 9, 1776, Chester County, Pennsylvania, and served three years and eight months under Captains North and Christie, Fifth and Fourth Pennsylvania Regiments, under Colonels Johnson and Nicholas, and General Wayne. He took part in the battles of Brandywine, Germantown, Monmouth, and Ticonderoga. He was wounded and discharged from service, August 18, 1780. He received a pension in Pendleton County, Virginia, June 30, 1818, aged 65. Supporting claims had been filed by Caleb North and Lieutenant George North.

DUDLEY (DUDLY), SAMUEL
Service—Conn. Privateer   Va. No. 12734   No. S. 6806

Born, New London, Middlesex County, February 21, 1763, and there resided until 1796 when he moved to Monongalia County, Virginia. His grave is in Dudley Cemetery, near Farmington, Dunkard Hill Run, Marion County.

Dudley enlisted June, 1778, Saybrook, Connecticut, in company commanded by Captain Shipman Lays, and Ensign Doty Mead in Connecticut regiment, commanded by Colonels Selden, Bebee, and Wells. He served fifteen months, part of which service was on the Sloop Sally as a privateer, under command of Captain Seth Warner, and in the

Sloop Lively in 1781, commanded by Master Peck and Master Elisha Hunt. Pension was granted in Monongalia County, 1833.

DUFFIELD, ABRAHAM
Service—Virginia   Va. No. 23325   No. S. 9389

Born, Fauquier County, Virginia, 1763, and enlisted, March 10, 1782, Greenbrier County, Virginia. Served six months as a private under Captain Hull of the Virginia line, guarding the frontier. Made application for pension, supported by statements of David Hannah and John Cutliss, in Nicholas County, October 19, 1833. Certificate was issued but was later suspended. Among other officers mentioned are Ensign George Orison, Captains Arbuckle and Stewart, and Colonel Donnally, and Majors Grims and Hamilton.

West Virginians in the American Revolution

Assembled and Edited by ROSS B. JOHNSTON

The sources of this material are from the files of the Pension Office at Washington, from various county records, from notes of patriotic societies, principally the Daughters of the American Revolution, Sons of the American Revolution, Sons of the Revolution, and from a large miscellaneous group of published and private sources. Corrections and additions to this list will receive the careful attention of the editor.

DUKE, GEORGE
Enlisted in the Revolutionary Army and was killed at Brandywine.

DUKE, JAMES
Served in the Revolutionary War and afterwards lived near Charles Town, Jefferson County, Virginia.

DUKE, JOHN
Enlisted in the Revolution from Berkeley County, Virginia. Received a pension for his military services.

DUKE, MATHEW
Son of John Duke, born July 5, 1758. Probably served in the Revolutionary Army as a substitute for Daniel Hedricks. Died near Uvilla in 1820.

DUKE, FRANCIS (Deputy Commissary)
Born in Ireland, February 11, 1751, and emigrated with his family to Berkeley County, Virginia, where in 1773 he married Sarah, the eldest daughter of Colonel David Shepherd. Removed with the latter's family to Wheeling Creek, Ohio County. He was appointed by his father-in-law deputy commissary, and as such was stationed at Beech Bottom Fort. It was probably from there that he approached Fort Henry during the Indian attack of 1777, and was killed in attempting to enter the fort under fire. He left an infant son, John, and a posthumous son, Francis.

DUNBAR, JONATHAN
Service—Virginia   Va. No. 23923   No. S. 19286
Born, Lancaster County, Pennsylvania, April 15, 1762. Enlisted in the fall of 1780, Augusta County, Virginia, and served twelve months as a private under Captain Cravens, Colonel Thomas Huggard, Lieutenant-Colonel John McCreery, Colonel Vance, Major Wilson, Captain Thomas Smith, Captain John Dickey, Lieutenant Chas. Baskins and others. Fought at Guilford Courthouse, Hot Water, and Jamestown. Pension certificate

issued April 21, 1834, Nicholas County, Virginia. Supporting claims by R. Hamilton, Edmond Rion, and Samuel Clark.

DUNLAP, JOSEPH

Born, Bucks County, Pennsylvania, July 24, 1757, and enlisted, Huntington County, New Jersey, for Revolutionary War service. Served under Captains Hulix, Kerhart, Colonels Bevers, West, Major Grudendyke, and General Wayne. Lived in Berkeley County for a time and moved to Monongalia County in 1796. There he applied for pension, April 22, 1833, but claim was rejected.

DUVAL, DANIEL

Applied for pension in Monongalia County, Virginia, but the record is not complete. Wife was Marie Brook. File No. W. 5069.

DUVALL, JOHN PIERCE (County Lieutenant)

Prominent on the border both in civil and military affairs. In 1776, homesteaded on the headwaters of the West Fork River at what was known as the Indian House. Then he appears to have had residence at Clarksburg where he was appointed under legislative act of May, 1779, with James Neal and William Haymond as commissioners to adjust land claims on the western waters, certificates of title for which were issued March 7, 1781. He was a member of the state senate from Monongalia County, and later from Harrison County, from 1780 to 1792. When Harrison County was formed in 1784, he was chosen county lieutenant and was prominent during the Indian wars. He was an incorporator of Randolph Academy, and a leader in county affairs until his death.

EAGLE (EAGLES), WILLIAM

Service—Virginia   Va. No. 20137   No. S. 39480

Enlisted, Pendleton County, Virginia, December 24, 1776, under Captain Stead. He was with Washington's army during the terrible winter at Valley Forge. Later he was transferred to Captain Kirkpatrick's company of the Fourth Virginia which was commanded by Colonel James Wood and also by Colonel John Neville, who was a son-in-law of General Daniel Morgan. He was discharged, September 18, 1778, because of "inability," which tradition says was a broken arm, but he later rejoined the army and is believed to have been present at the surrender of Cornwallis at Yorktown.

His wife, Mary Ann, was aged 35 in 1830. They had a son, George Washington Eagle, aged 6 in 1820. Soldier received pension in 1830 and his widow applied for pension in 1853. Supporting claims made by Jeremiah O'Dell. The celebrated Eagle Rocks of the Smoke Hole section of the South Branch of West Virginia are named for this Revolutionary soldier. It is said that Eagle narrowly escaped death at one time while trying to capture some young eagles from the nest on top of its lofty crag.

EARL, JAMES

Before the Wood County Court, August 3, 1818, James Earl, aged 71, testified that he had enlisted as a private in the State of Pennsylvania in company commanded by Captain Chambers of the First Regiment, that he continued in service for one year, when he was discharged. Pension application was therefore forwarded to the War Department.

EASTER, JOHN
Service—Maryland   Va. No. 16925   No. S. 18389
Born, January 17, 1760, Washington County, Maryland, and there enlisted under Captains Billmire, Brewer, and Casner in regiment of Maryland troops commanded by Colonel Moses Rawlings. Served nine months in marches and on guard duty. Pension was granted soldier, October 16, 1833, Morgan County, Virginia. Supporting claims were made by John Shinard.

ECKARD, ANDREW
Application for pension was filed before the Mason County Court, March, 1834, by Andrew Eckard, aged 76, for services as a Revolutionary soldier. His claim was supported by Samuel Summerville and others.

EDWARDS, JOSEPH
Joseph Edwards, a private in the Revolutionary Army, was born in Jefferson County, 1736, and died there, October 1, 1828. He was married four times.
He enlisted for three years and served as a private in Captain Thomas Blackwell's Company, Tenth Virginia Regiment, which was commanded by Colonel William Russell and Colonel John Green. He re-enlisted, December 18, 1778, to serve until the end of the war. His name last appeared on company muster roll, dated at camp near Morristown, December, 1779.

ELLIOTT, BENJAMIN
Enlisted, 1776, under Captains Bush and Hughs in the Seventh Pennsylvania Regiment, under Colonel Hartley, and took part in the fighting at Paoli, Monmouth, Brandywine, White Plains, and Stony Point. Applied for pension, January 19, 1835, Jefferson County, Virginia, at age of 78. Supporting affidavits filed by Jesse Phelan, Thomas Strider, James B. Wagoner, William Gilpin, and James Guest. Record No. R. 3293.

ENGLE, MICHAEL
Enlisted in Captain Stephenson's company in 1775. Reenlisted in one of the rifle companies raised in Berkeley in 1776. Probably died on a prison ship. Brother of Philip Engle.

ENGLE, PHILIP
Was in General Gate's army at Camden and was a guard at Gate's headquarters during the battle of Camden. After the war, he married Mary Darke, a sister of William Darke.

ELLIS, JAMES
Born, October 15, 1756, Frederick County, Maryland. Some time before the Revolution, he removed to Washington County, Pennsylvania, where he volunteered in the militia and spent six months (1776) at

Holliday's Cove. At the close of this service he removed to Ohio County, Virginia, where in July, 1778, he was drafted into the militia under Colonel John Stephenson. The next year he served in Brodhead's Allegheny campaign. After the Indian wars, he settled in the Northwest Territory, living in Adams County, Ohio, in 1845.

ELLISON, JAMES
Service—Virginia Va. No. 12944 No. S. 6821

Born, Mansfield County, New Jersey, 1757; resided in Augusta County, Virginia, 1768; and in Monroe County, Virginia, from 1771 to 1835. Enlisted in Monroe County, 1776, and served twelve months as an Indian spy under Captain Henderson in the Virginia militia commanded by Colonel Lewis. Received pension, June 18, 1834, in Monroe County, which was suspended in 1835, and may not have been resumed. Supporting claims were made by Colonel John Hutchinson, Peter Larue, and William McDaniel.

ENOCH, HENRY

Settled at an early date in Hampshire County, at the forks of the Great Cacapon River, on the road westward from Winchester. Here a fort was erected, November, 1755, for the protection of the settlers after Braddock's defeat. Washington stopped here on his return from the Ohio in 1770. Henry Enoch signed several receipts at Fort Henry, and in 1777 was stationed for a time at Grave Creek Fort. A brother was living at that time in Anwell Township, Washington County, Pennsylvania, which was then a part of Virginia.

ENTLER, PHILIP

Philip Entler, who had services in the Revolution, was born in York County, Pennsylvania, 1740, and died in Berkeley County, Virginia, in 1793. See D. A. R. National 123447.

ERNST, MARTIN

A Hessian soldier who deserted at the battle of Princeton, and later served with the American Army. He received a pension until his death some time after 1830. Resided at Shepherdstown.

ETHELL, ANTHONY
Service—Virginia Va. No. 12877 No. S. 6825

Born, Loudoun County, Virginia, February, 1757, and there enlisted, September 1, 1775. He served sixteen months in company of Captains, Triplett, Feggans, Cannon, Darke, and Major Levin Powell, Colonels Grayson, Merryweather, and Hardiman. Certificate issued, June 6, 1833, Fauquier County, Virginia, Greenbrier County, Virginia. Supporting data submitted by John Kemper, James Puckett, Reuben Murry, and Robert Coombs. (Probably a brother of Henry Ethell.)

ETHEL (ETHELL), BENJAMIN (Corporal)
Service—Virginia Ky. No. 177 No. S. 35286

Enlisted, March 28, 1777, and served three years as a corporal in the company of Captain Nathaniel Mitchell, Sixteenth Virginia Regiment,

WEST VIRGINIANS IN THE REVOLUTION 91

Continental Establishment, commanded by Colonel Grayson under Lafayette, Stephens, and Scott. Fought at Monmouth and Stony Point. Application for pension was filed, August 31, 1818, Winchester, Kentucky, and Greenbrier County, Virginia. Pension was granted in 1820. Supporting data submitted by George Speak, James Rains, and Oliver Parker.

ETHELL, HENRY
  Born, Loudoun County, Virginia, 1764, and there enlisted in company of Captain Cannon under Colonels Merryweather, West, Mathews, and Risbey. Lived in Loudoun, Prince William, Fauquier, Greenbrier, and Monroe counties. Pension application, filed in Greenbrier County, 1833, rejected on account of having less than six months service, and amended declaration was presented in 1838 showing additional service. Supporting claims made by William T. Mann and Joseph Newton. (Probably a brother of Anthony Ethell.)

ESKRIDGE, GEORGE (Captain)
Service—Virginia   Va. No. 14725 and 31355   No. S. 8428
  In 1775, volunteered in the Light Dragoons under Captain P. P. Thornton after the expiration of Minute Man service under Captain Thomas Jones. Enlisted, Northumberland, Virginia, 1776, under Captain Edward Hill in the Fifteenth Virginia Regiment. Commissioned ensign, 1776, and promoted to lieutenant, January 1, 1777. Captain Hill was killed at Northumberland Courthouse by a rioter. Eskridge was commissioned captain, August 9, 1779. He resigned his commission to General Washington at White Plains. Pension certificates were issued in his favor in Hampshire County, Virginia, in 1818 and 1838.

EVANS, EDWARD
  Fought as a soldier in Braddock's Campaign and as such received land in 1772 through George Washington. Was also at Fort Augusta in 1765. Volunteered in the Revolution and served on the western frontiers.

EVANS, JOHN (Colonel)
Service—Virginia   Va. No. 12508   No. S. 8444
  Born, Fairfax County, Virginia, December 9, 1737; resided in Loudoun County at age of 13; removed to Monongalia County in 1769-1770, and died there May 1, 1834. His grave is in Oak Grove Cemetery, Morgantown.
  He served in Dunmore's War in 1774 as a lieutenant. He enlisted in the Revolutionary Army, April or May, 1778, and served as colonel until December 20, 1778, under Generals McIntosh and Washington in command of militia from the South Branch and Ohio Valley. Built forts at Beaver Creek and Tuscarawas, and was county lieutenant for Monongalia County for many years. Many of his records were destroyed by fire in the office of the county court, Morgantown, in February, 1796.
  Pension issued to him, Monongalia County, May 3, 1833. Supporting data submitted by Major John McFarland, Colonel Jas. Scott, Captain John Dent, (Thirteenth Virginia Regiment), Reverend Joseph Shackleford, and Zachariah Morgan.

EVANS (EVAN), THOMAS
Service—Virginia   Va. No. 23449   No. 16002

Born, Chester County, Pennsylvania, February 28, 1753, and there enlisted, 1777, under Captains Robinson and Gregory Davidson. Received pension in Harrison County, 1834, but was dropped from the rolls in 1835. Supporting data submitted by Gass Martin and John Goodwin.

EVERETT, JOHN
Service—Virginia   Va. No. 29624   No. S. 16786

Born, 1737, died 1834. Enlisted, September 28, 1775, Albermarle County, Virginia, and served as a private under Captain William Campbell, First Virginia Regiment, under Colonel Francis Taylor. Discharged, September 27, 1776. Stationed on James River and Chesapeake Bay. Applied for pension, July 28, 1834, at age of 81, in Cabell County, and received certificate the following year. Supporting data submitted by John Samuels, J. W. Rice, and John Merritt. Grave of Everett is in Cabell County, near U. S. 60, three hundred yards from the county poorhouse. (One reference indicates that pension application was filed in Berkeley or Jefferson County, Virginia.)

He was married twice; first to Sarah Tarlton, and then to Sarah Deadman. Among his children were Colonel John Everett, of Guyandotte; Nathan Everett, of Ona; Mrs. John Morris, of Teays Valley; and Mrs. Abie Reese.

EVERHART, GEORGE
Service—Pennsylvania (Sea)   No. 19013   No. S. 6826

Enlisted, Lancaster County, Pennsylvania, 1776. He served in the Flying Camp for six months under Captain Hambrite and Colonel Sutts. He next was a wagoner in Continental Service under Captain Bayard for six months; served two months in Pennsylvania militia under Captain Reem, and three months under Captain Brady. Then sailed on board the Monk to Cape Francis from which point he returned to Philadelphia, having served six months in the navy. Enlisted, 1782, on the Hyder Ally, a ship of war, commanded by Captain Barney, and was on board this vessel when General Monk was captured. While in the militia was in the battles of Long Island, Brandywine, and Germantown. On Long Island, he was commanded by General Sterling. General Irving commanded the militia at Brandywine, and General Sullivan was in command at Germantown. Pension was granted him in Berkeley County, in 1832. Supporting data submitted by William Gregory and William Good.

EVERLY, SIMEON
Service—Virginia   Va. No. 23255   No. S. 8446

Born, Cumberland County, Maryland, October 15, 1763. Enlisted, Monongalia County, Virginia, June 10, 1777, and served nine months as private and Indian spy under Captains Neal, Ferrell, and Colonels Martin and Clark. Received pension, December 11, 1833, Monongalia County, but was dropped from the rolls later.

FARENCE, HENRY
Service—Continental		Va. No. 7499		No. S. 39508

Enlisted in Frederick Town, Maryland, in 1776, and there received discharge, 1782, after six years service with the Maryland German Regiment, Continental Service, under Captain Boger (or Boyer) and Colonel Hausegger. Received pension in Harrison County, March 11, 1819. His wife was aged 50 in 1822 and their children's names and ages follow; Abner, 14; Nancy, 11; Peggy, 8; and Hannah, 6.

FARIS, WILLIAM

Born, County Down, Ireland, 1734; died, August 1, 1818, and is buried in the Old Stone Church Cemetery, Elm Grove, Ohio County. Enlisted, 1776, as a private in Captain Bentley's company, Colonel Marshall's Virginia Regiment, Berkeley County, Virginia.

In 1758, before leaving Ireland married Dorothy Johnston, who was born in 1735. Their children were: John, 1759; David, 1761; Adam, 1763; Mary Faris Yates, 1768; William, Jr., 1772. (William was a soldier in the War of 1812.)

West Virginians in the American Revolution

Assembled and Edited by ROSS B. JOHNSTON

The sources of this material are from the files of the Pension Office at Washington, from various county records, from notes of patriotic societies, principally the Daughters of the American Revolution, Sons of the American Revolution, Sons of the Revolution, and from a large miscellaneous group of published and private sources. Corrections and additions to this list will receive the careful attention of the editor.

FARNSLER, HENRY
Service—Pennsylvania   Va. No. 23568   No. S. 15829

Born, 1761, Germantown, Berks County, Pennsylvania. Removed to Pendleton County, thence to Shenandoah, thence to Randolph County, where he resided when he received Revolutionary War pension in 1834.

In 1778, at the age of sixteen years, he enlisted in the Revolutionary Army and was assigned to the Eighth Company, Sixth Battalion, Lancaster County, Pennsylvania militia, under Captains Dark, Seley, Spoon and Colonel Cross. He served to the end of the war, including the Yorktown campaign. He is sometimes referred to as a private of infantry, and sometimes as a drummer, but could have been both.

FERREL, JAMES S.
Service—Virginia   Ohio-Va. No. 31559   No. S. 7697

Born, Berkeley County, Virginia, April 24, 1763. Resided in Morgantown, Monongalia County, Virginia, at the time of enlistment. Remained there until 1827, when he removed to Ohio Township, Monroe County, Ohio. Resided in Tyler County, Virginia, 1838, with his son, John B. Ferrel.

At time of enlistment, May, 1779, he gave his age as a little upwards of sixteen years. He volunteered under Captains David Scott and Robert Ferrel (his father), Virginia militia, under command of Colonels Crawford, Darke, General McIntosh and General Clark in Indian scouting and border patrol. Supporting data filed by the Rev. Resin White and Robert Longwell. Pension certificate issued November 14, 1838, but it was later suspended. No record of reinstatement.

FIATT, WIPON

Wipon Fiatt filed application for pension, September 6, 1832. He was born in York County, Pennsylvania, and then moved to Shepherdstown, Virginia. There was drafted in company of Captain Morrow, Captain Josiah Swearingen, and Lieutenant Islow. He accompanied General McIntosh on the march to the Muskingum River, and was also at Yorktown.

WEST VIRGINIANS IN THE REVOLUTION 95

FINLEY, SAMUEL (Major)
Born, April 15, 1752. When the Revolution broke out, he was working in a Martinsburg store. He enlisted in 1775 as a sergeant in Captain Stephenson's company; first lieutenant of Stephenson's Maryland and Virginia Rifle Regiment, July 9, 1776; taken prisoner at King's Bridge or Fort Washington, November 16, 1776, at which time he commanded Captain Shepherd's company. He was held prisoner four years until November, 1780, when he was exchanged with Captain Henry Bedinger, Captain Nat. Pendleton and others. He was made captain of the Eleventh Virginia, December 20, 1776; was transferred to the Fourth Virginia, February 12, 1781; made major of the Seventh Virginia, September 11, 1782; transferred to the First Virginia, January, 1783, and served to the end of the war. (See statement in pension office from Brigadier-General James Wood of Virginia, Continental Line, August 1, 1807.)

Finley later moved to Chillicothe, Ohio. He commanded a troop of horse during the War of 1812, and died in Philadelphia, April 2, 1829.

FINK, JOHN
On February 8, 1782, a season unusually early for Indian activities, John Fink, a Revolutionary soldier who had just returned from the eastern front, was shot and killed by an Indian, about where the Upshur County courthouse in Buckhannon now stands.

FLANAGAN, EBENEZER
Born, Huntington County, New Jersey, May 5, 1755, and there enlisted, September, 1776. Mentions Generals Washington, Lafayette, Campbell, Wayne, Clinton, and Knox. In New Jersey, Colonels Rittenhouse, Taylor, Bennett, Furmans, Captains Philip Snook, William Haslett, Henry Lane, and Lambert. In Virginia, Colonels Nyswanger, Mathews, Hugart, Captains Bell, Patterson, and Campbell. Moved from New Jersey to Augusta, now Pendleton County, Virginia, in 1778, and to Randolph County, Virginia, 1796. Applied for pension, Randolph County, 1833, but claim was rejected.

FISHER, EBENEZER
Service—Massachusetts   Va. No. 1910   No. S. 8475
Born, Norfolk County, Massachusetts, January 31, 1754. There enlisted, 1775, under Captains Briggs and South in the Massachusetts Regiment commanded by Colonels Joseph Reid and Robinson. After moving from Massachusetts, the soldier lived in Maine, New Hampshire, and Ohio, and was living in Harrison County, Virginia, November 13, 1832, when he received pension certificate. Supporting data was filed for him by the Reverend John Davis and Stephen Dix.

FISHER, ISAAC
Service—Virginia   Va. No. 7040   No. S. 39524
Enlisted, Greenbrier County, Virginia, 1775, and served until 1778 under Captain Arbuckle, Twelfth Virginia Regiment, under Colonels John Hutchinson and Woods. Granted pension in Monroe County, Virginia, March 5, 1819. In 1820, the age of his wife was shown as 30, a daughter, 10, and a son, 3. Bounty land warrant for 100 acres was also received.

West Virginians in the American Revolution

Assembled and Edited by ROSS B. JOHNSTON

The sources of this material are from the files of the Pension Office at Washington from various county records, from notes of patriotic societies, principally the Daughters of the American Revolution, Sons of the American Revolution, Sons of the Revolution, and from a large miscellaneous group of published and private sources. Corrections and additions to this list will receive the careful attention of the editor.

FERGUSON, JOHN (Lieutenant)

Born, Prince George County, Maryland. Died, Monongalia County, 1796. Enlisted in 1775 as a second lieutenant in Prince George militia and served until 1776. Moved to Morgantown in 1788 and there had a tavern until his death. He married while still living in Prince George County, and the name of his widow, Barshaba or Bathsheba Ferguson, appears on the Monongalia tithable lists for many years after her husband's death in 1796. Her name was also sometimes shown as "Ardow." Their children were: Catherine, married Joseph Wilson, August 29, 1777, Prince George County, Maryland, and later removed to Monongalia; Rebecca, married William Wilson, October 1, 1777, Prince George County, Maryland, and later moved to Morgantown. Will probated in Monongalia County. Susannah, married Fauquier McCrae, April 21, 1781, Prince George County, Maryland, who moved to Morgantown and there operated a tavern; Lydia, married Zephaniah Beall, lived in Monongalia County; John; Margaret.

FERGUSON, SAMUEL (Captain)

Samuel Ferguson was a captain in the Revolutionary Army and served under General Green. He was one of the earliest settlers of Wayne County, and was the ancestor of many prominent citizens of that county.

FERRYMAN, STEPHEN
Service—Virginia   Va. No. 4740   No. S. 39515

Enlisted, Winchester, Frederick County, Virginia. Served four years in company of Captain Mayo, Continental Establishment, under Major-General John Smith, and General Green. Was in battles of Blueford's Defeat and Ninety-Six. Received pension, December 12, 1818, while a resident of Hampshire County, Virginia. His wife, Priscilla, was aged 70 in 1820, a daughter, Rebecca, was 17, and a son, Henry, was 10. Supporting data was filed by General John Smith.

FISHER, JACOB
Service—Virginia   Va. No. 16698   No. S. 15120

Born, October 29, 1758, Berks County, Pennsylvania. While living in Hampshire County, Virginia, in March, 1778, enlisted under Captain Moses

Hutton and Captain Dan Richardson in a Virginia regiment under General Hand. In 1781, he volunteered for service against the Indians. Received pension, September 16, 1833, while living in Hardy County. Supporting data filed in his case by William Heath, Isaac Hutton, Jacob Yoakum, Jacob Randall, and Isaac Vanmetre.

FISHER, JACOB
Service—Virginia   Va. No. 16652 and 21973   No. R. 3565

Enlisted, Rockingham and Hardy Counties, Virginia, at the age of 16 or 17, in the fall of 1778 and served until 1781, as a substitute for his father. Served three months under Captain Rice in regiment commanded by Colonel Noll and Major Guy Hamilton. Reenlisted under Lieutenant Cornelius King and served on the South Branch and in the vicinity of Clarksburg. Reenlisted under Captain James Stevison or Stinson and marched to Winchester to guard the British prisoners brought from Yorktown. He received a pension, September 11, 1833, while living in Nicholas County. In 1840, he was living with William Cutlip on Holly River, Braxton County. He died, October 15, 1846, and his widow, Catharine, died November 16, 1850. Additional information concerning the soldier was filed by James McMillion, Addison McLaughlin, William Radcliffe, and George Fisher, a brother.

FISHER, PETER
Born, Middletown, Pennsylvania, November 3, 1763. Enlisted at Shepherdstown, then Berkeley County, Virginia, 1781, and served under Captains McIntire and Bedinger and Colonel Darke. Took part in the siege and capture of Yorktown. Supporting data filed by Alex Jones, David Snively, John Quidley, George Bedinger, and Adam Fisher, a brother, of Point Pleasant. Applied for pension, May 18, 1835, Jefferson County, but claim was rejected owing to length of service. See File No. R. 14157. Died in 1844 and was buried with military honors.

FLAGG, JOSIAH
Served in the Revolution as third sergeant in Captain H. Stephenson's Company.

FLEEHARTY, STEPHEN
Service—Maryland   Va. No. 13411   No. S. 39529

Enlisted in Maryland in 1775 and served as a private eight years, in the company of Captain Stricker, First Maryland Regiment, under Colonel Smallwood. Fought at Long Island, White Plains, Trenton, Princeton, Germantown, Monmouth, Camden, Guilford Courthouse, Eutaw Springs, Cowpens and the Siege of Ninety-Six. The soldier received pension in Harrison County, July 7, 1819, at which time he was 73 years old.

FLEMING, BOAZ
In Woodlawn Cemetery, Fairmont, Marion County, is buried Boaz Fleming, a soldier of the Revolutionary War, an early settler and an active leader in the early life of the Monongahela Valley.

FLEMING, JAMES (Lieutenant)
Service—Maryland   Va. No. 6809   No. R. 3605

Enlisted, Frederick, Maryland, 1776, and served nine months as a lieutenant under Captain Michael Troutman, Maryland Line, under Colonels Thornton, Johnson and Baker in the Thirty-fourth Battalion of Provincial Troops. Was wounded in the leg at Piscataway.

In Harrison County, February 13, 1820, was married to Polly Whitehair. Received pension, May 6, 1833, and died May 14 of the same year. Widow applied for pension, September 30, 1853. Supporting data filed by Hamilton Gass and Thornberry Bailey.

FLESHER, ADAM
Service—Virginia   Va. No. 23022   No. S. 18403 and B.L.Wt. 47388

Born, July 29, 1764; died, November 4, 1854. Went out in 1781, and again in 1782 on scout duty at Buckhannon Fort, Richard's Fort and at other points on the West Fork in Lewis County, and continued to serve in later years as a ranger or Indian spy against the northwestern Indians. Pension granted in 1833, but it was later dropped on the grounds that most of his service was against the Indians and not in regularly established military units in the Revolution. Bounty land warrant for 160 acres was later issued.

Adam Flesher and Elizabeth Staats were married February 22, 1792, in Harrison County, by Joseph Cheuvront, a Methodist minister.

FLESHMAN, MOSES
Service—Virginia   Va. No. 7008   No. S. 8484

Enlisted, Culpeper County, Virginia, March, 1781, and served six months as private under Captain Mark Fink in detachment of the Virginia militia commanded by Colonel Harry Hill. Was engaged in campaigns in Virginia and North Carolina. Pension granted in Fayette County, February 21, 1833, at which time the soldier was 72 years old.

FLOYD, HENRY F.

Enlisted, Berkeley County, Virginia, 1776 and served until 1782 under Captain Holmes, in regiment commanded by Colonels Spottswood and Febiger. Took part in the actions at Brandywine, Germantown, Princeton, Monmouth, Hackinsack, Stony Point, Powles (Paulus?) Hook. Taken prisoner at Blueford's Defeat. Escaped from the British and returned to his home.

Received pension for six years in Monongalia County, March 24, 1820. Died, December 16, 1829. Wife, Elizabeth, aged 36, in 1820. Children and ages in 1820 were Catherine, 14; John, 10; Thomas, 8; Elizabeth, 6; Mary Ann 4; Malinda, 2. Supporting data filed by Benjamin Satterfield and Michael Floyd.

FLUHARTY, STEPHEN

Before the Harrison County court Stephen Fluharty stated that he enlisted in the year 1775 in the State of Maryland in the company commanded by Captain George Stricker of the First Maryland Regiment, commanded by Colonel Smallwood. He continued in service until the end

WEST VIRGINIANS IN THE REVOLUTION 99

of the war, being discharged at Annapolis in 1782. He was in the battles of Long Island, White Plains, Trenton, Princeton, Germantown, Monmouth, Camden, Guilford Courthouse, Eutaw Springs, Cowpens and at the Siege of Ninety-six.

FOLCK (FOLK), DANIEL
Service—Pennsylvania   Va. No. 23561   No. S. 15636

Enlisted, Bethlehem, Northampton County, Pennsylvania, in the spring of 1775, and served eighteen months under Captain Craig, Lieutenants Parks and Church, in the regiment commanded by Keethline and Taylor, Continental Line. Took part in the expedition against Canada. Received pension certificate in Jefferson County, February 25, 1834. Died in 1838.

FOLEY, ENOCH
In the Wood County court is filed the certificate of John Marshall, Major of Artillery, that Enoch Foley in Colonel Marshall's Regiment of artillery has been discharged after three years of faithful service. There is also filed statement signed by Enoch Foley, October 20, 1785, directing Isaac Van Meter to forward the land warrant that is due him as a soldier of artillery in the Virginia Line.

FORD, DABNEY
Service—Virginia   Va. No. 7498   No. S. 39531

Enlisted, Harrison County, 1778, for three years in the company commanded by Captain Thomas Porter in Colonel Taylor's Regiment of the Virginia Continental troops. He continued in service until discharged at Winchester, Virginia, in 1781, after taking part in the siege of Yorktown and the capture of Lord Cornwallis and his army. Pension was granted to him in Harrison County, March 11, 1819.

FORD, GEORGE
Born, Charles County, Maryland, son of William Ford, October 10, 1782. Enlisted as a private in the Fifth Maryland Regiment, May 13, 1778, and served until August 15, 1778. Probably had additional service also. Buried, near Grafton, on Lanty Ford's farm. Wife was Charity Colvert. or Calvert· She is buried in Fauquier County, Virginia. Soldier was related to William Ford, who was also a Revolutionary soldier, and the Warder, Woodyard, and Payne families of Taylor County and other sections of northern West Virginia.

FORD, WILLIAM
Service—Virginia   Va. No. 5832   No. S. 8506

Enlisted, Fauquier County, Virginia, in the fall of 1779; served six months in Captain William Jenning's Company; in 1780, one year in Captains Ellis Edmunds' and William Frost's Company, Colonel Frank Triplett and Colonel Elias Edmunds' Regiments; 1781, six months in Captain William Balis' company, Colonel Elias Edmunds' Regiment. Was at battle of Jamestown where he was wounded in the hip, and was at the surrender of Cornwallis. Discharged, December 23, 1781.

Pension issued in Monongalia County, 1833, dropped in 1835, and reinstated in 1839. Supporting data filed by Charles Shaw, George Ford,

James Woodyard, Elisha Ford, Henry Ford, Mary Woodyard, Natious Ford, James Warder, John Warder. Died, July 4, 1839. Names of children are as follows: Elisha married Nellie Warder, 1811; Elizabeth married Andrew Miller; Mary, married Lewis Woodyard, 1810; Lucy, married John Ford, 1810; Nancy, married James Williams; Sally, married Isaac Trader, 1829; Catherine, married Josiah Wilson, 1830; Anna, married Solomon Hustead; William; Cynthia.

FORD, JOHN (Sergeant)
Service—Maryland   Va. No. 19239   No. S. 39532

Enlisted, Montgomery County, Maryland, August 3, 1776, and served three years as sergeant under Captains Bell and Calderwood in Rawlings' Regiment and the Fourth Maryland Regiment, Continental Establishment, under Colonels Rawlings, Febecker, Brodhead, and Major Williams. Fought at Brandywine, Monmouth, Germantown, and Iron Hill. Received pension, April 19, 1824, while living in Monroe County, Virginia.

FOREMAN, WILLIAM (Captain)

In 1777, Foreman brought a company of Hampshire County militia to the Ohio Valley to take part in the projected expedition of General Hand against the Indians. He was caught in an Indian ambush in the Narrows between Fort Henry and the fort at Grave Creek, and was killed with his son and the greater part of his command.

FOSTER, JAMES
Service—Pennsylvania   No. S. 39536

Born, Ireland, 1757, and enlisted in Pennsylvania under Captain James Campbell in Pennsylvania militia commanded by Colonel Allison. Pension was issued to him in Berkeley County, April 1, 1833. Supporting data filed by Captain James Campbell, Captain John McClelland, Colonel Allison, and Sam Culbertson, all of whom seem to have been at Cumberland, Maryland, when he entered service.

FOSTER, JAMES
Service—Virginia   Va. No. 7182   No. S. 8503

Enlisted, Bedford County, Virginia, 1776, and served three years under Captain Lambert, in the Fourteenth Virginia Regiment, commanded by Colonel William Davis. Was at Germantown, Brandywine, Monmouth, and Stony Point. Received pension, aged 72, while living in Monroe County, March 5, 1819. His wife was aged 52 in 1820, and a son was aged 13.

FOSTER, JOHN
Service—Virginia   Va. No. 12097   No. S. 8504

Enlisted in Virginia, 1780, and served as private under Captain Lamb in the Tenth Regiment, Virginia Continental Line, under Colonels Gaskins, Posey, Baron Von Steuben, and General Wayne. Took part in the siege and capture of Yorktown, was in several skirmishes near Savannah, and received his discharge near Charleston, South Carolina, in 1783.

Applied for pension, Monroe County, 1829, and received the certificate, March 22, 1833. Also was issued land bounty warrant for 100 acres.

WEST VIRGINIANS IN THE REVOLUTION 101

FOSTER, PEREGRINE
Peregrine Foster was born in Brookfield, Massachusetts, 1759. As a soldier in the Revolution, he was present at the execution of Major Andre, the British spy. In 1782, he started practice of law in Providence, Rhode Island, but moved west in 1786 and settled in Monongalia County.

FOSTER, WILLIAM
Service—Virginia   Va. No. 19651   No. S. 39534
Enlisted in Virginia in 1777, and served as a private three years under Captains Grant and Kirk, Third Virginia Regiment, Continental Establishment, commanded by Colonel Guess and General Woodford. Took part in battles at Stony Point and Charleston, South Carolina. Was wounded and taken prisoner. Remained prisoner twenty-two months, was then exchanged, and honorably discharged. Received pension, aged 65, August 3, 1826, while living in Nicholas County.

FOWLER, JOSEPH (Shown as Joseph F.,)
Service—Virginia   Va. No. 6215   No. S. 39530 and B.L.Wt. 1370
Served six years and six months in Continental Establishment, from January, 1777, to July 26, 1783, when he received his discharge from Major Congham at Pittsburgh. Served under Captain David Steel, Captain Benjamin Biggs, Thirteenth Virginia Regiment, Colonel Gibson, and Colonel William Crawford. Received bounty land warrant for 100 acres, and also pension while living in Brooke County. Supporting data filed by William Baxter. Soldier died, January 24, 1840.

FOX, ANTHONY
Before the Harrison County court, Anthony Fox made affidavit that he had enlisted in Fauquier County, Virginia, under Captain Fleebecker. He was commanded by Colonel Lewis and Colonel Smith of the regular army until Fleebecker was promoted to the command of the regiment. He was engaged in the battle of Brandywine and in the capture of Cornwallis at Little York. After the fall of Yorktown, Fox was taken from the line and employed in driving a team under Wagonmaster Holliback until the end of the war. He was discharged by Colonel Fleebecker on James River near Richmond.

FOX, JAMES
Enlisted in Captain Shepherd's rifle company in 1776. Was captured in November and died on board a prison ship, April 1, 1777. The Fox family were in Berkeley County before the Revolution.

FOX, HENRY
Service—Virginia   Pa. Va. No. 18389   No. S. 41540
Enlisted, 1777, at Muddy Creek, Pennsylvania, for three years under Ensign John Mills and Captain Benjamin Biggs, in Thirteenth Virginia, commanded by Colonel John Gibson. Saw service at Fort Lawrence against the Shawnee Indians on Tuscarora River. Captured by Indians at end of two years, and held prisoner seven years until treaty signed by General Clark and General Butler at the mouth of the Miami River.

Pension application, September 25, 1821, at Washington County, Pennsylvania, later Virginia. Certificate issued December 5, 1821. Had wife and five children.

Much evidence is submitted by H. A. Muhlenberg, Member of Congress, in the case of Fox and comrades. More evidence for Fox is found in the papers of Michael Spatz. Jacob Graul served in the same company and at the same time as Spatz. Papers certified by Commodore Gillon. John Fox, Jacob Fleisher, and Michael Spatz served on board the Frigate South Carolina as marines, under Gillon. Muhlenberg says they were alive June 7, 1832, and had been placed on pension rolls in 1818. Adam Gramline (Grambling), served one year in a regiment of artillery commanded by Colonel Benjamin Flower of the Pennsylvania Line. He was also placed on the pension roll in 1818 and was still living June 7, 1832.

FRANK, HENRY
Service—New York   Va. No. 11249   No. S. 10700

Enlisted, November 1, 1778, in New York. Served three years as a dragoon in company of Captain Barth Van Heer, Light Dragoons, General Washington's Lifeguards. Discharge papers signed by Captain Van Heer, October 20, 1781, at Camp York. Wounded in Battle of Stony Point, and was also at siege of Yorktown. Pension application, January 12 and April 3, 1818, Jefferson County, Virginia. Certificate issued June 2, 1819. Supporting claims by Conrad Kreemer.

FRANK, VALENTINE
Served in the Revolution as a dragoon in Washington's Lifeguards. Died in Jefferson County in 1831.

FRITZ, VALENTINE
Enlisted in Captain Shepherd's rifle company in June, 1776. Enrolled in another rifle company, January 1, 1777.

FRYER, JAMES
Service—Virginia   Va. No. 12595   No. S. 6866

Enlistment, September, 1777, September, 1780, Point Pleasant, Greenbrier County, Virginia. Private two years under Captain McKee and Captain Andrew Wallace, Virginia Line, Colonel Blueford, General Gates, and General Green. Spent two years under Captain McKee at Point Pleasant. In 1780, enlisted for 18 months in Virginia Line of the Regular Continental Establishment. In Captain Andrew Wallace's company, marched to Staunton, then to Hillsboro, North Carolina, where was attached to Colonel Blueford's detachment. Joined General Gates at Charlotte. After arrival of General Green, who took command of the army, marched to the Cheraw Hills, thence to Virginia. After the battle at Guilford Courthouse, transferred to Captain Oldham and stationed at the iron works. At Rock River was attached to Colonel Campbell's command. At Camden, General Green was wounded. At Hughes Mill John Fryer lost all of his mates except one. Was at Siege of Ninety-Six, and also at Eutaw Springs where he lost his officers, Captain Oldham and Colonel Campbell. Was honorably discharged at Salisbury by Lieutenant Hurt.

Pension application, May 26, 1829, Greenbrier County, Virginia. Certificate issued, May 13, 1833. Died, July 30, 1839, leaving as heirs two grandchildren. Supporting claims offered by John Williams, Elias Perkins Charles Hyde, and Richard Williams.

FRIEND, JOSEPH (Captain)

Joseph Friend was a captain in the Revolution, and his memory is commemorated in Randolph County, West Virginia, by a tablet placed in 1926 by the John Hart Chapter, Daughters of the American Revolution. Friends' Fort was built by Joseph and Jonas Friend in 1772. Jonas was a sergeant in the French and Indian War, 1754-60 in Pendleton County, and was constable of that county, 1767. The will of Israel Friend, dated August 12, 1749, is filed in Frederick County, Virginia. In it he bequeathed land on Leading Creek to his sons, James, Jacob, and Charles.

FULK, DAVID
Service—Virginia   Va. No. 15166   No. S. 39554

Enlisted, Shepherdstown, Berkeley County, Virginia, 1775-76; 1778-79, and served two years as private under Captain Drake and Captain Crogan, Eighth Virginia Regiment, Colonel Muhlenberg. Fought at Trenton, Germantown, Long Island, and White Plains. Pension application, October 16, 1818, Pendleton County, Virginia, aged 70 years. Pension granted, September 30, 1819. Had three children, two daughters and a son, living in Kentucky and Pennsylvania. Claim supported by Adam Bible.

FURBEE, CALEB (Lieutenant)
Service—Delaware   Va. No. 23421   No. W. 740

Born, Kent County, Delaware, November 22, 1752. Died, April 15, 1837. Enlisted, 1775-1777, as private under Captain Sipple. Was commissioned by Governor Radnor of Delaware as lieutenant in 1776 in Captain Sipple's Company. Fort Clow, built by the Tory, Chaney Clow, on Chester River was captured by Furbee in 1777. He was also at Brandywine. Mentions many prominent officers.

Married, December, 1833, Green County, Pennsylvania, by Justice of Peace James Dye to Mary Lemasters. Soldier applied for pension, August 28, 1832, from Monongalia County, Virginia, and pension was granted, January 7, 1834. It was later suspended but resumed, 1838. Widow applied for pension, April 11, 1835, for Tyler County, Virginia. Her petition was granted and bounty land warrants were also issued. Among those supporting their claims were the Rev. Shackelford, Richard Harrison, Charles Simpkins, Ann Davis (sister of Furbee), John Davis (brother-in-law of Furbee), Dallas Lemasters (brother of Mary Lemasters Furbee), and Alex Tennant. Furbee settled in Monongalia County, 1796.

GASKINS, JESSE
Service—Virginia   Va. No. 5221   No. S. 39660

Enlistments, 1776, 1780, 1781. Served three years under Captains Hull and Butler, Fifteenth Virginia Regiment, Colonels Gaskins, Ball and General Simpler. Fought at Germantown, Stony Point and the Siege of Charleston, South Carolina. He was taken prisoner at Germantown, lodged in jail at Philadelphia, and then carried to New York on a prison ship. Exchanged after a month. Had written instrument from General Sumpter, a free pass home, and authorization to draw provisions on the way.

Applied for pension, May 26, 1818, Monongalia County, Virginia, aged 78. Wife, formerly Susanna Gaskins, aged 75 or 78 years. Pension certificate issued, January 7, 1819. Mentions children, Chloe, 22 years; three grandchildren, and a son 18 years old.

GASS, PATRICK
NOTE: On account of special interest, included with the list of Revolutionary services, although military service was entirely in later wars.
War of 1812 and others   No. 527-7460   Bounty Land Warrants 6320, etc.

Enlisted, 1799, at Carlisle, Pennsylvania, in Regular Army and joined the Tenth Pennsylvania Regiment, Colonel Thomas L. Moore. Discharged. Re-enlisted under Major Cass, was stationed at Harper's Ferry, then sent to Pittsburgh where Cass resigned. Then removed to Kaskaskia, Illinois. Accompanied Lewis and Clark on their expedition to the Pacific, and his "Journal of the Expedition" is one of the most interesting accounts of the expedition. In 1812, he enlisted in the Regular Army under General Bissell and served until 1815. Saw service on the Missouri, and elsewhere. Was in fighting at Fort Erie, Chippewa and in battle of Lundy's Lane. Lost his left eye in service and was discharged for total disability, June, 1815. Married in 1831. Wife died 1847, leaving family of six children. Applied for pension, December 23, 1851. Received three warrants for bounty lands.

GATES, HORATIO (Major-General)
Born at Malden, Essex County, England, 1728; entered the army while a youth; came to America; commanded the King's Independent Company in New York; stationed at Halifax, Nova Scotia, with the rank of major; joined Braddock's ill-fated expedition in 1755 and was shot through the body at disastrous defeat at the Battle of the Monongahela; recovered and served to the close of the French and Indian War; then settled on an estate called "Traveler's Rest" in Berkeley County.

Entered the American service at the beginning of the Revolution; brigadier-general and adjutant-general, Continental Army, June 17, 1775; major-general, Continental Army, May 16, 1776; defeated the British army under Burgoyne at Saratoga, New York, October 17, 1777; made President of the Board of War, November, 1777; served to the close of the war. Then lived on his estate in Berkeley County, until he removed to New York where he died, April 10, 1806.

Bounty Land Warrant 863-1100 was issued November 18, 1790, to Gates as a major-general for Revolutionary services. His brilliant victory over Burgoyne at Saratoga is in contrast to his defeat at Camden, North Carolina. He was twice retired but Congress later acquitted him of blame and reinstated him about the time the Revolution ended.

GEORGE, JOSEPH
Service—Virginia   Va. No. 23564 and No. 2986   No. W. 7515
Enlisted, Hampshire County, Virginia, 1781, and served six months

under Captain James Cunningham of Virginia troops. Other officers, Lieutenant Bullet and Ensign Bogart. Applied for pension, December 25, 1833, Hardy County, Virginia. Certificate issued February 28, 1834. Born, Richmond County, Virginia, 1757. Died June 23, 1837.

Married Margaret Arnold, December 28, 1784. She applied for pension, August 9, 1836. Widow's certificate granted, May 29, 1839. Supporting claims filed by John Crowse and Daniel Arnold. Other officers were Ensign Dan Ashby, Captain Stevenson, Colonel Darke, Major Reed.

GEORGE, REUBEN
Service—Virginia   Va. No. 7602   No. S. 39567

Enlisted, Culpeper County, Virginia, fall of 1777, to November, 1783. Served three years, Captain J. Billison and Captain Ward, Continental Establishment, Tenth Virginia Regiment, Colonel Stevens, and was at Germantown, Brandywine, and White Marsh. Pension application, December 4, 1818, Pendleton County, Virginia. Certificate issued, March 13, 1818. Wife's name Ailcy (Elsie?). Supporting claims filed by Daniel and Benjamin Calvin, John Saunder, David Johnson, and Gabriel Tutt.

GIBBS, LUMAN
Service—Vermont   Va. No. 16661   No. S. 13169

Born, South Farms, Litchfield County, Connecticut, 1765. Enlisted in Vermont, 1781, and served eight months in Vermont Line under Colonel Fletcher. Applied for pension, November 6, 1832, Mason County, Virginia. Certificate issued, September 11, 1832, and paid until September 4, 1841. Since Revolution resided in New York and Kentucky as well as in Mason County. Supporting claims made by Isaac Robinson and James McDermot.

GIBSON, NICHOLAS
Service—Virginia   Va. No. 23324   No. S. 8559

Served two years as private in the Virginia Line under Captain Skinner. Original application papers sent to Special Agent Shingleton, August 9, 1834. Pension was granted, October 31, 1833, but it was later suspended.

GILLINGWATER, JAMES
Service—Virginia   Va. No. 10613   No. S. 39570   B. L. Wt. 6410

Served as private under Captain Newell, Second Virginia Infantry, Colonel Haws and General Green. Enlisted in Amherst County, Virginia, in 1780. He had eighteen months service and was wounded in the heel and ankle at Guilford Courthouse, Hillsboro, North Carolina. Applied for pension, Cabell County, Virginia, November 3, 1818, aged 65, and pension was granted, May 15, 1819. Also received Bounty Land Warrant for 160 acres. Supporting claims filed by James Peters, James Evans, Elisha Gillingwater, a brother, and Armstead B. Howell.

GILMORE, DAVID

Enlisted in August, 1776, in Captain Shepherd's company. Was taken prisoner at Fort Washington and died, January 26, 1777.

West Virginians in the American Revolution

Assembled and Edited by ROSS B. JOHNSTON

The sources of this material are from the files of the Pension Office at Washington from various county records, from notes of patriotic societies, principally the Daughters of the American Revolution, Sons of the American Revolution, Sons of the Revolution, and from a large miscellaneous group of published and private sources. Corrections and additions to this list will receive the careful attention of the editor.

GALLEGHER, JOHN
Service—Maryland   Va. No. 1025   No. S. 39561

Enlisted in Maryland, July 8, 1777. Discharged at Annapolis, May 16, 1780. Private in Captain Andrew Hayne's Company, Sixth Maryland Regiment, commanded by Colonel Williams. Was at Brandywine, Germantown, and Monmouth.

Applied for pension, May 23, 1818, Brooke County, Virginia. Aged 63, May 28, 1821. Wife aged 50 but name not given. Names of children: Nancy, 18; Betsy, 16; Rachel, 9; Hetty, 8; William, 11; Caleb, 8.

GALLION, GILBERT
Service—Maryland   No. R. 3876

Born in Hartford County, Maryland, March 27, 1758. Enlisted, June, 1777, in company of Captain Patterson and Captain Rogers, Seventeenth Regiment, Maryland Line. Applied for pension, February 26, 1834, Harrison County, Virginia. Supporting claims by John Gawthrop and Sam H. Morris. Claim rejected.

GANDEE (GANDY), URIAH
Service—Pennsylvania Continental   No. R. 3890

Born in Philadelphia, Pennsylvania, 1753. Enlisted, May 1, 1776, under Captain Thomas Forrest. Names Colonel Proctor, Colonel Marshall, and Washington, Lafayette and Wayne. Was at Trenton, Princeton, Germantown, and Brandywine.

Applied for pension in Jackson County, November 18, 1835. Claim supported by John M. Kown and Philip Hall. Claim rejected in report which include following additional names: James Maze, Samuel Tanner, Charles Stewart, Bazel Wright, Zachariah Rhodes, Elijah Runion, and Thomas Hughes.

GANT, ERASMUS HORATIO (Cornet of Horse)
Service—Connecticut-Maryland   Va. No. 26260   No. S. 10727

Applied for pension, Berkeley County, Virginia, May 26, 1834. Claim supported by Theodore Middleton.

Named cornet of horse in troop of cavalry raised by aid of Maryland Assembly to defend bay shores, 1780. Lieutenant Philip Hill, Captain

James McCubbin Lingain. Statements show that this troop remained in service through 1782 and had at least two skirmishes with the British. Its activity was effective in suppressing disorder along the Eastern Shore as well as in discouraging British raiders.

GAPEN, STEPHEN
Service—Pennsylvania   Va. No. 2493   No. S. 8545
Enlisted, Fort Minor, Green County, Pennsylvania, 1777, 1781-82, and served 22 months under Captains John Minor, Pigman, Foreman and other units under General Hand. Refers to Foreman massacre and other border events. Mentions Lieutenant James Marshall, Washington County, Pennsylvania.
Applied for pension, August 27, 1832, Monongalia County, Pennsylvania, aged 71. Certificate issued, November 28, 1832. Died, December 26, 1838. Grave in Fort Martin Cemetery, Monongalia County. Among supporting persons were Albia Minor, Jonathan Morris, John Knotts, John Gapen, and George Garrison.

GARTNER, (GARTIN, GARTER, GARLEN) NATHANIEL
Service—Virginia   Va. No. 23974 and 303335   No. S. 10719
Born, Orange County, Virginia, 1759. Enlisted, January 1, 1777, Rockingham County, Virginia, and served nine months as an Indian spy on western frontiers. Applied for pension, February 17, 1834, Monroe County, Virginia. Certificate issued, May 7, 1834.
Statements show that from January to March, 1777, he served as a spy under Captain Robert Cravens and Lieutenant Trout, Rockingham County. Marched to Tygart's Valley. Then spent three months at Warrick's Fort. Pursued one band of Indians 40 or 50 miles. Returned home and later was sent back into the Tygart's Valley under Lieutenant John Rice. Later served at Nutter's Fort under Captain William Kincaid. Following capture of James Meek's family on Indian Creek, Monroe County, in 1781, spent some time at Lafferty's Fort, guarding settlements against Indians.

GILLILAN, JAMES (Ensign)
Service—Virginia   No. R. 4029
Born, Augusta County, Virginia, 1748. Enlisted Botetourt County, Virginia, 1777, 1782, 1783. Served as sergeant, and ensign two years and ten months, also as Indian spy, under Captains Hamilton, Renick, and Colonels Lewis and Donnally. Filed application for pension, December 17, 1833, Greenbrier County, Virginia. Says he acquired his farm by settlement rights between 1776 and 1783. Claim rejected. Supporting claims by the Reverend Alex Campbell, John Patton, Joseph McClintock, and Henry Hedreich.

GILPIN, WILLIAM
Service—Maryland   Va. No. 4149   No. S. 3957
Enlisted, Charles County, Maryland, 1777 to February 23, 1780. Served as private three years under Captain Joe Marbury, Third Maryland Regiment, Brigadier General Smallwood. Saw action at Long Island,

York Island, White Plains, and Brandywine. Received honorable discharge from Major Arch Anderson. Applied for pension, May 25, 1818, Jefferson County, Virginia. Certificate issued, November 6, 1818. Supporting claim by Ferdinand Fairfax. Died in 1835.

GODFREY, JOHN
Service—Virginia   No. R. 4083

Enlisted in Fauquier County, Virginia, September, 1776. Served three years and three months as sergeant in company of Captain Smith. Captains Ball, Taliafero, Ballard, Campbell, and Colonel Brook and Colonel Mountjoy. Among his comrades were George P. Smith and George Fisher.

Born in Fauquier County, 1746, removed to Hardy County, 1788, and lived there until 1832 when he moved to the home of his son-in-law, George Duvall, son of the distinguished Colonel John P. Duvall, in Lewis County. He lived in Hardy County during the Revolution. He went from his home to enlist but was told by Colonels Brook and Ashby, after a physician had examined him, that he was unsound and incapable of bearing arms. However, the records indicate that he saw service as stated above.

GLENN, JAMES (Lieutenant)

Born about 1764; ran away from his Berkeley County home at the age of fourteen and joined the army under General Greene. Served with Lieutenant Daniel Bedinger as a sharpshooter in the southern campaigns of 1779-1780. Was at the siege and capture of Yorktown. He was with St. Clair's army in the expedition against the Indians in the west in 1791, and rescued Lieutenant Raleigh Morgan on the day of the terrible defeat of St. Clair's army, November 4, 1781. He was sent by Darke to carry the news of the defeat to Washington. He died in 1827.

Glenn was married twice. His first wife was Jane Duke. They had three children, all of whom died young. His second wife was Ruth Burns, by whom he also had three children: Elizabeth, Mary, and Captain James W.

GOFF, JOB
Service—Rhode Island   Va. No. 6035   No. W. 1752

Born in Kent County, Rhode Island, 1760, removed to Birmingham County, Vermont, and came to Rensselaer County, New York, 1782, from thence to Harrison County, Virginia. Enlistment, 1777-1782, in Rhode Island, and served one year under Lieutenant Robert Cook, Ensign John Calvin, Captain Benedict Calvin, Major Isaac Johnson, and Colonel John Abbott. Guarded coast and intercepted and prevented landing of hostile ship.

Pension application, Harrison County, Virginia, August 21, 1832, Harrison County. Certificate issued, February 23, 1833. Died, December 8, 1845.

Married, December 8, 1785, by the Reverend James Guthrie, to Zerviah Waldo, daughter of John and Emma Waldo, who had been married, March 12, 1751. Soldier's wife born in 1760. She made application for pension, November 8, 1849. She received pension and also bounty land warrant of 160 acres. Among supporting claims were those of Hamilton Gass and Jedidiah Waldo.

GOFF, SALATHIEL

Born, 1748. Died, 1791. Buried beneath a large hickory tree on the farm of the later W. E. Cupp, St. George, Tucker County. Saw service as a Revolutionary soldier and personally knew General Washington. Was first president of the county court of Randolph County, and was active in the settlement of the Cheat River section. He had two brothers, John T., and James, who were likewise active in the early settlements along Cheat River.

GOOD, THOMAS

Service—Virginia   No. S. 38742

Enlisted for two years, February, 1776, in Christian County, Kentucky, and served under Captain Hopkins and Colonel Buckner of the Sixth Virginia Regiment, and also in militia companies. Was at the Siege of Yorktown and the surrender of Cornwallis. Received pension in Alabama. Virginia residence is uncertain.

GOOD, PETER

Enlisted in Captain Shepherd's Rifle Company in 1776. Was one of the prisoners from the garrison at Fort Washington, which was surrendered to the British in 1776, who met death on a prison ship, February 15, 1777.

GOODMAN, WILLIAM (Captain-Lieutenant)

Service—Continental Maryland and Virginia   No. S. 39600

Enlisted at Baltimore, Maryland, January, 1776. Entered service in a company of artillery, under Captain Nathaniel Smith, and served as a commissioned officer from January 1, 1776, until October following at the port of Baltimore. Then was appointed first lieutenant in First Regiment of U. S. Artillery under Colonel Charles Harrison in Captain William Waters' Company and served until the spring of 1777. Then became Captain-Lieutenant in Captain Drury Ragsdale's command, and served until August, 1779, then left the army. In the fall of 1780, assisted in raising a company of volunteer artillery and served as its captain-lieutenant under Captain Laban Guffingam until the surrender of Lord Cornwallis at Yorktown.

Applied for pension, aged 64, May 14, 1818, Berkeley County, Virginia. Certificate issued. Died, July 10, 1825. Wife's name Allanor (Eleanor?). Children were Delilah, 20; Otha, 14; Bela, 12; Elizabeth, over 3.

GOODNIGHT, CHRISTOPHER

Service—Pennsylvania   Va. No. 23566   No. W. 9458   B.L.Wt. 75005

Born, Germantown, Pennsylvania, 1762. Died, January 19, 1852. Enlisted, Pennsylvania, fall of 1777, and served six months under Captain Mathias Hensill. Other officers were Lieutenant John Kernsell, Colonel

Willis, Captain Grady, and Generals Washington, Wayne, and Morgan.

Applied for pension, January 24, 1834, Hardy County, Virginia. Certificate issued, February 23, 1834. Married in 1810. Widow, Diannah, aged 95 in 1857, applied for pension, June 6, 1854. Certificate issued to her, and also land grant for 160 acres. Supporting claims by Henry Jones and John Sites.

GOODWIN, FRANCIS

Born in Londonderry, Derry County, Ireland, 1761. Enlisted, March, 1777, Fayette County, Pennsylvania, as an Indian spy, company of Captains Connell, Cook, Evans, Morgan, Colonels Zackquill Morgan, and Morgan, and Generals Hand and McIntosh. Applied for pension, Harrison, County, Virginia, October 24, 1833. Claim rejected. Supporting affidavits by Uriah Ashcraft and John Goodwin.

GORDON, GEORGE

Service—Connecticut Continental   Va. No. 12162   No. S. 39599

Born, Volurton, Connecticut, 1749. Died September 1, 1823. Enlisted, at Roseberry, Massachusetts, in 1775 in company under Colonel John Douglas, and continued until December, 1775, when he became corporal under Captain Trawbridge and Colonel Huntington. He was captured in Battle of Long Island, August 27, 1776. Was taken on prison ship, Montor, with hands tied behind him, where he remained several months. He was then transferred or exchanged and returned home the last of 1776. Squire Cady and Anthony Bradford testified for him in Connecticut courts; John Wylie was also a witness.

He applied for a pension, May 9, 1818, Norwich, Connecticut. Certificate issued, June 23, 1819. He applied for a transfer of pension to Ohio County, Virginia, May 7, 1821.

GRAHAM, DUNCAN

Greenbrier County, Virginia, courts in 1786 show that Duncan (Grymes) Graham was recommended for a pension, having been discharged from the Continental Army for wounds. (There being no surgeon in this county to examine his wounds.)

Before the same court, 1791, Graham produced a certificate of his service signed by Brigadier General Hugar which was lost or misplaced in the clerk's office. Said Graham swore that he enlisted, February 10, 1775, in the Eighth Virginia Regiment, commanded by Colonel Muhlenberg, and also served with the South Carolina troops in Colonel Hugar's Regiment until discharged in November, 1782. In 1793, John Stuart swore in the Greenbrier County Court that the certificate showing Graham's service in the American Army in the late war had been lost or miscarried.

GRAHAM, THOMAS

Service—Pennsylvania   Va. No. 15050   No. S. 39620

Enlisted in Pennsylvania, March 1776, as private under Captain Patrick Anderson and Colonel Atley. Saw service at Long Island, where Colonel

Atley was captured and Lieutenant-Colonel Perry killed. He was also in the fighting at Fort Washington, where he was wounded in the right hand and so disabled that he was discharged at Philadelphia, 1777. Applied for pension, Brooke County, Virginia, May 23, 1818. Certificate was issued, September 30, 1819. His wife was aged 60 and a daughter, Mary, 34, in 1818.

GRASS, PETER
Service—Virginia   Va. No. 23194   No. S. 8599

Enlisted, 1777, Staunton, Augusta County, Virginia, under Captain Thomas Smith, Lieutenant Charles Barkins. Marched to Fort Union, now Lewisburg, where these troops were included in a detachment from Rockbridge, Augusta, and Rockingham Counties, under Colonel Adam Dickinson, George Skillilem and Major Samuel McDowell. Marched to Point Pleasant and was there when Cornstalk, his son, and Chief Red Hawk were killed by frontiersmen. He later saw service at Fort Clover Lick, on the West Fork of the Monongahela River, and elsewhere on western borders under Captain William Anderson and Captain William Kincaid. Later he served against the British on the James River guarding magazines, making a total service of thirteen months. He lost his discharge papers.

Applied for pension, Kanawha County, November 12, 1833, and certificate was issued November 24, 1833. Supporting claims by H. Mann and S. J. Spangling.

GREATHOUSE, John
Service—Pennsylvania   Va. No. 5998   No. S. 8630

Greathouse, aged about 60 years in 1832, made oath before Harrison County court, that he enlisted in Bedford County, Pennsylvania, 1777, in Captain Kilgore's Company of the Eighth Pennsylvania Regiment, afterwards commanded by Colonel Broadhead, that he served three years, was in the battles of Brandywine, Germantown and Paoli, and was discharged at Pittsburgh, March, 1780. Pension was granted. Soldier died September 25, 1838. Supporting claims made by Jacob Coplin and Christopher Nutter.

GREEN, SAMUEL
                                                No. R. 4275

Application made for pension while residing in Lewis County, Virginia, but claim was rejected.

GREEN, WILLIAM

Enlisted in 1775 in Captain Stephenson's Rifle Company. Appears to have joined the detachment while it was at Roxbury Camp, September 10.

GRAY, DAVID

Enlisted in Captain Stephenson's Company in 1775. After the war, he resided in Shepherdstown, and then may have moved to near Leetown, where he is buried. His wife was Elizabeth Craighill. His brother, John, enlisted in Shepherd's Company in June, 1776, and was killed, December 27, of the same year.

GREGORY, JAMES
Service—North Carolina, Virginia   Va. No. 23334   No. R. 4292

Born in Gloucestershire, England, May 14, 1752. Emigrated to Virginia at age of 18 and settled in Augusta County. Served in the Revolution under Captain Sam Wilson and Colonel Lewis after enlistment in Augusta County.

Married Eleanor (Ellinor) Dikes, September 1, 1788, with the Reverend John Alderson as minister. Soldier applied for pension, August 29, 1832. Soldier died, November 30, 1836. Widow applied for pension, April 22, 1843, in Greenbrier County. Apparently dropped from the rolls on the ground that patrol duty on the frontier settlements afforded no grounds for pensions. Supporting claims by John McElhennery, Joshua and John Doman, Thomas Creigh, George Witzell, Mark Goshen.

GRIFFE, HUGH

Executive order of the State of Virginia, December 16, 1809, allowed land bounty to Hugh Griffe for his services in the Continental Line as a private for three years of the Revolutionary War. Order was issued in Berkeley County, Virginia, in February, 1810, that Margaret Neill, wife of John Neill of Shepherdstown, formerly Margaret Griffe, be recognized as the heir of Hugh Griffe, deceased, who had been a soldier in the Revolutionary War, and who had enlisted in Shepherdstown in the company of William Darke. Bounty Land Warrant 5845 in Margaret Neill's favor was issued.

GRIFFIN, ELIJAH
Service—Virginia   No. R. 4307

Enlisted, Halifax County, Virginia, February, 1781. In Muhlenberg County, Virginia, February 15, 1836, aged 75. Griffin applied for pension for services under Captains Stamford, Long, Grimes, Fualcover, and Colonel Rogers in Siege of Yorktown and other points. Supporting claims by Wallace Wilson and Robert W. Fitts. Following record was filed: "This is to certify that Elijah Griffing, soldier of militia from Halifax County, is discharged of his *tower* of duties of three months." Dated, April 9, 1781, signed by Richard Lanier, Corporal. Claim rejected as having served less than six months.

GRIFFITH, ELISHA (Sergeant)
Service—Maryland   Va. No. 30326   No. S. 10199

Born, 1750, Frederick County, Maryland. Enlisted, December 25, 1776, Frederick Town, Maryland, and served more than twenty months as first sergeant under Captain Ralph Hillery, Lieutenant Thomas Kirk, and Colonel Charles Betty, Maryland Line Regiment. Statement also mentions Lieutenant Elisha Bell, Ensign Charles Busey, Joseph Madden, Lieutenant-Colonel William Betty, Brigadier-General Thomas Johnson.

Supporting claims were made by Thomas McKinley and Joseph Winters.

Pension application made, August 22, 1832, in Harrison County, where Griffith had moved after coming from Maryland to Kanawha County. Certificate issued, January 14, 1836, declared not entitled by Special Agent Singleton, but later reinstated.

GRIFFITHS, ABRAHAM
Service—Pennsylvania   Va. No. 4716   No. W. 7587

Enlisted, 1776, Berks County, Pennsylvania, and served until July, 1779, under Captain John Day or Doyle, First Pennsylvania Rifle Regiment, under Colonel Edward Hand. Saw action at Brandywine, Germantown, Trenton, Piscataway. Honorably discharged at West Point, New York.

Applied for pension, October 27, 1818, aged 66, and certificate was issued December 1, 1818. Died October, 1824. Married, Reading, Pennsylvania, July 24, 1781, to Anna Maria Boyer. Widow applied for pension, April 22, 1842, in Greenbrier County. She had three sons and one daughter. In 1818, she was 62 years old. Her petition was granted and certificate issued April 6, 1843.

GUINN (GWIN), ANDREW
Service—Virginia   Va. No. 13017   No. S. 37980

Served three years as private under Captain M. Bowser, Continental Establishment, Twelfth Virginia Regiment, Colonel J. Woods, after enlisting in Augusta County, Virginia, in June, 1776. Applied for pension, October 26, 1818, aged 60 or 70 years, in Hampshire County, Virginia. Certificate issued, July 15, 1819. Supporting claims by Edward Williams, Ensign in the Eighth Virginia Regiment.

GUSEMAN, ABRAHAM

Guseman, who enlisted in the opening years of the Revolution in a company organized in Berkeley County, Virginia, served seven years as a private. A statement by Mrs. Susannah Guseman Cobun says that her father, Abraham Guseman, "Who enlisted in the Revolutionary Army from Harpers Ferry, Virginia, when but 17 years of age, served his country faithfully for seven years, and was wounded three times. He carried a bullet through his life that he received in his first engagement. His second wound was a saber cut on the head during a cavalry charge. During his seventh year of service, he was so severely wounded that he was unfitted for further field duty. Therefore, he returned to Harpers Ferry, determined to still give everything possible in service for his country, so he spent his time mending the old 'flintlocks' and other equipment of the active soldiers." Guseman, who died in 1821, is buried in the Oak Grove Cemetery, Monongalia County.

GWINN, SAMUEL
Service—Virginia   Va. No. 23706   No. S. 17992

Born, Augusta County, Virginia, 1750, or 1752. Served on the western frontiers from 1771 to 1774, and later under Captains Landbridge and

Glass, and Colonel Andrew Lewis. He also mentions Lieutenant Thompson, Lieutenant Donnelly, Captain John Stewart, Colonel Charles Lewis. Pension certificate issued, 1834, but dropped in 1835 on statement that his service was not in organized army service. Application shows that he had moved with his wife and ten children to Monroe County, 1776-78.

HAAS, CHRISTIAN
Service—Pennsylvania   Va. No. 16070   No. S. 5478

Born in Strasburg, Germany. Enlisted in North Hampton County, Pennsylvania, 1775-1776. Served ten months under Captain Koontz, Pennsylvania Line, and Colonels Strout and Hickman. Other officers were Captains John Siefret, Strothers, Slaybash, Santee, and others on frontier and in eastern campaigns. Applied for pension in Hampshire County, Virginia, February 25, 1833. Certificate issued, June 26, 1833. Claim supported by John Jacob, George Eskridge, James Higgins, John Brady, John H. Maxwell, James Taylor.

HACKER, JOHN
Served as a matross with General George Rogers Clark in his campaign against Kaskaskia and Vincennes. Represented Harrison County in negotiations with the Indians in making treaty of Fort Greenville, Ohio, in 1795. Born near Winchester, Virginia. Married Margaret Sleeth, and raised a large family. Pioneer, magistrate, sheriff, 1799-1801. First settler on Hacker's Creek, Lewis County, between 1769 and 1773. Died, April 20, 1824.

Two daughters were victims of the Indians. The following children survived him: William Hacker, deceased; John Hacker, deceased; Margaret Hacker, deceased; Sarah Smith (formerly Hacker); Jonathan Hacker, Alexander Hacker, Absolom Hacker, Thomas Hacker, Elizabeth Hardman (late Hacker), Mary Ann Helmick.

HADDOCK, WILLIAM
Service—Virginia   Va. No. 6810   No. S. 8694

Born in Fauquier County, Virginia, 1758. Enlisted in Hampshire County, 1778, and served twenty months in the Virginia service during the Revolution under Captain Robert Cunningham, Colonel Gibson, and General McIntosh. Applied for pension, Harrison County, January 26, 1833, and certificate was issued, March 5, 1833. Dropped from the rolls, 1835.

HAGLE, JOHN
Service—Virginia   Va. No. 7007   No. S. 8669

Born in Schuykill County, Pennsylvania, 1750. Entered military service in West Augusta, later Randolph and Monongalia Counties, in 1774, and re-enlisted in 1776, in the militia under Captains Stuart, Skidmore, Lieutenant White, Colonel Lewis, Colonel Lowther and Colonel Duvall. Applied for pension, Lewis County, August 7, 1832. Certificate issued, February 19, 1833, but suspended, 1836. Supporting claims by George Bush and Adam Fisher.

HAINES, PETER

Peter Haines served as a private in Captain Abraham Shepherd's company of Rawlings' Regiment of Continental troops. His name is on payroll for the period from July 1, 1776, to January 1, 1779, which says, "Enlisted, July 10, 1776; made prisoner, November 16, 1776. Pay charged for 29 months, 20 days." This company was raised by Captain Hugh Stevenson and Henry Bedinger as ensign and Samuel Findley as second lieutenant. Stevenson marched the company from Morgan's Grove near Shepherdstown, July 17, 1775. It served as an independent company for one year, and then became a part of the Continental troops, July 10, 1776, at Bergin, New Jersey.

Applied for pension, April 21, 1818, Jefferson County. Certificate issued, September 21, 1819. Supporting affidavit by Captain Abraham Shepherd. Soldier was born about 1754 and died in 1844. His wife was 63 years old in 1820.

HALE, EDWARD

Born, about 1750, and was active in border affairs. He was a soldier in the Revolution in 1781 under Captain Shannon whose company operated in North Carolina. He married Patsy Perdue and spent the later years of his life on Wolf Creek in the New River Valley in Monroe County. Their children were Thomas, Isaac, Charles, Jesse, Isaiah, Daniel, Elias, William, Mary, and Phoebe.

HALEY, ANTHONY

Pension applications made in 1818 and in 1820 before the Harrison County Court, stating that Haley, aged 60 in 1820, had enlisted in the year, 1778, in Colonel Blueford's Regiment, Captain Catlett or Captain Howard's Company, Virginia Line, and that he served to the end of the war. He was in the battle of Hanging Rock. Pension certificate No. 16737. Supporting affidavit by Jemimi Norman. Haley's family, 1820, was as follows: Wife, aged 49, Betsy, 20; James, 17; Mary, 15; Miranda, 9; Gabriel, 4.

HALL, JOSEPH

Service—Virginia   Va. No. 7497   No. S. 37983

Enlisted, Augusta County, Virginia, in the spring of 1776, as a private in a company of regulars, commanded by David Stephenson and attached to the Eighth Regiment of the Virginia troops under General Muhlenberg. He continued in service about two years when the Eighth Regiment was consolidated with the Twelfth Regiment under Colonel Bowman, and remained with this unit two years longer.

Pension application, July 20, 1818, aged 67, Harrison County, Virginia. Certificate issued, March 11, 1819, and second statement filed June 22, 1820. Two heirs named, Sarah, 28, a daughter, and a grandson, aged 10.

HALL, WILLIAM

Service—Delaware   Va. No. 18703   No. W. 7639

Enlisted, in Delaware, 1777, and served one year as private and two years as sergeant in Captain Perry's Company. Although no papers of this unit are filed in Delaware office, service of the company is admitted. Applied for pension, Monongalia County, June 22, 1833, and certificate issued September 16, 1833. Soldier died, April, 1835. He had been born, January 21, 1753.

The record of marriage of William Hall (blacksmith), and Betsy Wasles or Maples, Sussex County, Delaware, March 11, 1779, by the Rev. Matthew Wilson, D.D., former pastor of the Presbyterian Church of Lewes (improperly called Lewistown) is on file. There were two Elizabeth Halls, the latter being Elizabeth Stevenson Hall, which leaves uncertainty in the records. Elizabeth Maples Hall, 80 years old in 1843, when she applied for a pension, died in 1845. She was born, January 26, 1763. Other members of the family included Jane Maple, born, 1782; Sarah Rex, born, 1793; Elizabeth Martin, born, 1800; Lemuel Hall, Jonathan Hall, born, 1785; John L. Hall; Manny Hall, born, 1787 and died 1793; and James, born 1789, and died, 1793. Supporting claims filed by Joseph Sapp, Henry Downs, John Downs, Jacob Hall, brother, Lydia Butcher.

HAMILTON, JOHN
Service—North Carolina   No. R. 4516

Born, Chester County, Pennsylvania, 1756. Served ten months in the North Carolina Militia under Captain John Griffith. Volunteered in the light infantry of the line under Captain Little for seven or eight months. First, Fourth and Seventh Regiments are mentioned. Colonel Thackston and General Sumpter were officers. Pension applied for October 30, 1834, Logan County, Virginia, but claim was rejected.

HAMMER, PALSER
Service—Virginia   Va. No. 6290   No. S. 6950

Served as a private nine months under Captains Life, Keoffer, Davis, and Lieutenants Koffer and Shaffer, Virginia and Pennsylvania Line, General Washington, and General Lafayette. Enlisted from Philadelphia in 1776-77, and from Augusta County, Virginia, 1778-81. Applied for pension, Pendleton County, February 6, 1833, and certificate was issued, February 27, of same year. Supporting claims filed by Zachariah Rexrode, Z. Dyer, and Michael Hoover.

HAMMER, PETER
Service—Pennsylvania   Va. No. 12361   No. W. 5699

Born, Bucks County, Pennsylvania, August 9, 1757. At age of six, moved to New Jersey. Resided there three years, then moved to York County, Pennsylvania. At age of 20, moved to Frederick County, Maryland, to Fayette County, Pennsylvania, thence to Allegheny County, Pennsylvania, to Fayette County again in 1810, and thence to Monongalia County, Virginia.

Claimed fifteen months service after enlisting in Bucks County, under Captains Michael Dowvell, Bailey, Mackey, and Stake in the First Pennsylvania Regiment under Colonel Thompson, Colonel Donelson, and

General Putnam. Marched through Pennsylvania, New Jersey, Delaware, and New York during his service. Certificate issued after memorial to President Andrew Jackson in his behalf by group of soldier comrades. Among comrades were John White, Jonathan Neely, and James McElhaney. Other persons named were Simon Shore, Samuel Swearingen, and Thomas Bogges. Pension application of 1832 granted in 1833, but was suspended, 1835.

Monongalia County court shows record of marriage of Peter Hammer to Sarah Pearce, September 17, 1812. Sarah Rice mentioned as his widow, November 29, 1853, which may indicate a second marriage as she was only 60 years old in 1854 when she applied for pension.

West Virginians in the American Revolution

Assembled and Edited by ROSS B. JOHNSTON

The sources of this material are from the files of the Pension Office at Washington from various county records, from notes of patriotic societies, principally the Daughters of the American Revolution, Sons of the American Revolution, Sons of the Revolution, and from a large miscellaneous group of published and private sources. Corrections and additions to this list will receive the careful attention of the editor.

HAMMOCK, MARTIN
Service—Virginia   No. R. 4529
   Born, Albemarle County, Virginia, in 1760. Served two or three years as private under Ensign Taylor, Captains Burrell, Hawkins, Colonel Taylor and Colonel Forentain. Pension application filed in Kanawha County rejected.

HAMPTION, HENRY (Captain)
   Before the Cabell County Court, September 24, 1832, Henry Hampton, a lieutenant or captain, made oath that he had been a soldier in the Revolutionary Army and that he was entitled to a pension.

HAMRICK, BENJAMIN
Service—Virginia   Va. No. 2579   No. S. 5472
   Born, Prince William County, Virginia, about 1757. Enlisted in Fauquier County, Virginia, in November, 1775, and served until 1781 in broken enlistments under Captains Chilton and Shelton, Third Virginia Regiment, Continental Establishment, Colonels Mercer, Stephen, Marshall, Generals Weedon, Muhlenberg, and Woodford. Saw service at Trenton, Princeton, Brandywine, Germantown, and Monmouth. He was at the defeat of Fordica's grenadiers. He applied for pension, September 7, 1832, Nicholas County, Virginia, and certificate was issued, December 1, of the same year.
   He was married in the fall of 1779 in Fauquier County, Virginia, to a sister of Joseph McMillian. Among supporting claimants were Benjamin Lemaster, Joel Hamrick, and Joseph McMillian, a brother-in-law.

HAMRICK, SIARS (Sergeant)
Service—Virginia   Va. No. 3762   No. S. 18009
   Born, April 4, 1753, Fauquier County, Virginia. Served as private and sergeant thirteen months under Captain James Scott of the Virginia Regiment, commanded by Colonel Churchill. Took part in the capture of a brig and tender at Hampton and in other actions under Captain Scott, Captain J. Children, Captain Elias Edmond, and Captain John Chum.
   Applied for pension, November 2, 1833, Hampshire County, Virginia. Certificate issued, April 4, 1834. Supporting statements were made by Isaac Welsh, William Welsh, Thomas Dye, Sr., Sam B. Davis, Jacob Doll, Thomas Jones, John Cundiff, Sr., and Henry Miller, Sr.

WEST VIRGINIANS IN THE REVOLUTION

HAND, CHRISTOPHER
Service—Virginia   Va. No. 12793   No. S. 6951
Born, Ireland, 1756 and came to America when he was fifteen years old. His home was in Augusta County when he enlisted in 1781, and served eight months as a sergeant in Colonel Moffitt's Regiment of the Virginia Line. He marched from the New River settlements to Richmond, and then to Charles City, James City and Williamsburg; proceeded into North Carolina where his command fought under General Green at Guilford Courthouse. He was discharged in the Carolinas in 1781, after which he worked for a time in the iron furnaces, and then made his home in Monroe County.

He made application for pension, December 30, 1832, Monroe County, and certificate was issued, May 24, 1833. Supporting affidavits filed by William Ellis and James Fincher.

HANGER, GEORGE
Service—Virginia   No. R. 4565
Born, Shenandoah County, Virginia, February 7, 1759. Enlisted, 1779-80, under Captain Thomas Smith, Captain Buchanan, Colonel Bowyers, and Colonel Matthews, and saw service at Jamestown and Yorktown. Applied for pension, June 23, 1834, Greenbrier County, Virginia. Supporting statements made by William Handley, Thomas Creigh, and George Vellar. Listed as not entitled to pension, owing to length of service.

HANDLEY, JOHN (Lieutenant)
Served as a lieutenant in the company of Captain John Vartress, Jefferson County, Virginia, under the command of General George Rogers Clark. He enlisted in Greenbrier County, Virginia, and was the son of William Handley. He was born, 1746, and died, January 18, 1811. He was married in 1768 to Mary Harrison and they had the following children: William, John, Margaret, Sarah, Nancy, James, and Alexander.

HANKS, THOMAS
Service—Virginia   No. R. 4571
Born, 1759, in Virginia and died in Logan County, Ohio, date unknown. Resided in Hampshire County, Virginia, until 1800, then moved to Ross County, Ohio, thence to Logan County, Ohio, where he had resided a few years prior to 1833, when he applied for a pension from that place.

He seems to have served three months in 1780 and two months or more in 1781 in the company of Captain Daniel Richardson and the company of Captain Isaac Parsons under Major Vincent Williams.

HANLON, JAMES
Enlisted in company commanded by Captain Shulty or Shoots of the Second Regiment of New Jersey Regulars in Continental Establishment in 1775, and served until his discharge at Fort George, Canada, November, 1776. Enlisted in the spring of 1777, Martinsburg, Berkeley County, in company commanded by Captain Well, Fourth Virginia Regiment of

U. S. Regulars, commanded by Colonel Lawson. Served three years until discharged at Petersburg, Virginia, 1780. He was in the battles of Germantown, Brandywine, Powells Hook (or Paulus Hook), and Stony Point.

Applied for pension, November 17, 1818, Harrison County, Virginia, and certificate was issued, May 4, 1819. Names one daughter, Sarah, aged 23, living in 1820. Died, January 3, 1829.

HANNA, JOSEPH
Service—Virginia   No. R. 4576

Enlisted in Botetourt, later Greenbrier County and served from 1779 to 1783 as an Indian spy and garrison guard in the company of Captains A. Hamilton and Renick, under Colonel Donnally and Colonel Lewis. Supporting affidavits by the Reverend W. G. Campbell, Elisha Callison, George R. Gillileen, Captain James Gillian. Pension claim rejected. Died, February 13, 1835.

HANNAH (HANNA), DAVID
Service—Virginia   No. R. 4573

Born, Berkeley County, February 2, 1760. Enlisted in Greenbrier County, September, 1776, and served under Captains Corbell, Arch Stewart, Colonel Donnally, Majors Hamilton and Grimes. Claims to have had six months service at Donley's Fort in 1781. He says that Captain Graham's house stood outside of the fort and was much exposed so he evidently refers to the fort on Wolf Creek, and not Donnally's Fort, in Greenbrier County northwest of Lewisburg.

Supporting claims filed by John Cutlip, John Duffield, John Patterson, Sam Gwinn, Robert Kelly, John Groves, John Duffy, and David Hanna, a nephew. He applied for pension, October 22, 1833, in Nicholas County, but claim was rejected or suspended.

HANNAN, THOMAS

Enlisted as a sailor under Captain Elliott or Aylett from Augusta County, in the Virginia fleet, June 14, 1776, in the county of Greenbrier. Marched to Alexandria and served twelve months until discharged near Williamsburg by Captain Elliott. After returning to Greenbrier County was drafted into the militia, August, 1781, under command of Captain John Lewis and Lieutenant Thomas Goodson. Marched from Botetourt County, to Williamsburg in company of riflemen under Colonel Samuel Lewis; thence to Yorktown, where they participated in its siege and capture. He was discharged after three months service in his second enlistment. Pension claim supported by David Harbison and James Shelton, who had married his daughter, Susan.

Hannan was born in Frederick County, 1757. After his discharge from the army, he lived in Botetourt County until 1791, when he moved to Mason County, formerly Kanawha. He married Elizabeth Henry in Botetourt County where his marriage is recorded. His will and pension application are recorded in Mason County, West Virginia.

WEST VIRGINIANS IN THE REVOLUTION

HANSBROUGH, JOHN
Service—Virginia   Va. No. 12564   No. W. 2614 B.L.Wt. 26531
Born, 1763, Amherst County. Lived there until after the Revolution, then in Culpeper, Frederick and Hampshire counties. Died August 9, 1844. Served nine months as private in the Virginia Line under Captain James Barnett, Lieutenants Lewis, Neville, Woodruff, and Colonels Pope and Dabney. Took part in siege and capture of Yorktown.
Applied for pension, Hampshire County, Virginia, January 29, 1833, and certificate was issued same year. Married, September 21, 1820, Culpeper County, Virginia, to Fanny Kabler. Widow applied for pension, September 24, 1853, and received certificate. Pension was later increased. Her age was 94 in 1869. Bounty land warrant for 160 acres also issued. Supporting affidavits submitted by John Jack and Isaac Kuykendall.

HANWAY, SAMUEL (Captain)
In spring of 1775, Hanway raised a company of seventy men in Amelia County, Virginia, to march against Lord Dunmore at Williamsburg. He later raised a company of minute men and was commissioned Lieutenant in Captain Lewellyn Jones' Company and marched to Norfolk. He was discharged in 1777 and then applied for naval service and was commissioned a Captain of Marines. He resigned his commission at Williamsburg after several months naval service.
He was born in Chester County, Pennsylvania, September 26, 1743. Moved from there to Charles City County, Virginia, 1768, thence to near Petersburg, Virginia, to engage in trade with the West Indies. He moved to Monongalia County, Virginia, in 1783, was commissioned surveyor of that county and served until June 27, 1831.
Among persons named in his pension application are Dudley Evans, John Evans, Jr.; Matthias Gray or Mathew Gay, William Haymond, the Reverend Ashby Pool, and the Reverend Joseph A. Shackelford. Hanway died in 1834 and is buried in Oak Grove Cemetery, Morgantown, Monongalia County.

HARBERT, EDWARD
Service—Virginia   Va. No. 23725   No. S. 15448
Born, Burlington County, New Jersey, May 10, 1762. Removed to Augusta, later Harrison County, Virginia, 1775. Served two years as Indian spy under Captain William Robinson from 1779 to 1782. Certificate issued, Harrison County, 1834, but was later dropped. Supporting claims by John Allen, Jacob Copeland, and Samuel Harbert. Captains Read and Gregory also named. This case was examined again by Colonel Godwin in 1851 and was still in dispute in 1872. (Papers in this case are filed with that of Samuel Harbert, No. 16646.)

HARBERT, JOHN   No. R. 4585
Applied for pension in Harrison County, July 21, 1834, making following statement in part: "I am 67 or 68 years old. I was stationed at Powers Fort and at Grundy's blockhouse as much as six months but can't say whether it was before or after the year 1783. Can't say how old I was at the time. Captain William Robinson was in command of

the station during my service. I lived with my father who had a settlement within eight miles of the fort." His claim was rejected.

HARBERT, SAMUEL
Service—Virginia   Va. No. 16646   No. S. 15447

Born in New Jersey, 1760. When five or six years old moved into Virginia, and was living near Winchester when eleven years old. Moved to Monongalia County and in three years moved to Harrison County, where he was living when he applied for a Revolutionary War pension, November 19, 1832. Died, February, 1847.

The Harbert family lived on the frontier of Harrison County and in 1778 the Indians entered their home, killing the father, one daughter, and several others. Samuel Harbert then became employed as an Indian spy under Captains Thomas, Read, and Robinson. Depositions of John Harbert and Josiah Davidson are filed in his behalf.

HARMON, THOMAS

Born, Augusta County, Virginia, 1750, and died, 1824. Enlisted in Revolutionary forces, from Augusta County and later lived in Greenbrier, Monroe and Kanawha counties. He married Nancy, daughter of William and Mary Walker, in Botetourt County, in 1774. Their children are as follows: Thomas, 1774; Henry, 1777; Sarah, 1779; Mary, 1782; Elizabeth, 1785; Aggie, Patsy, John, George.

HARNESS, JOHN (Captain)

Harness, a captain during the Revolution, was born in Pennsylvania in 1725 and died in Hampshire County, Virginia, now Hardy County, about three miles southwest of Moorefield. His service is established in Kercheval's history, and Professor Jacob's account of Captain Cresap's Company in which Harness is rated as a sharpshooter. Lewis' history gives another account, as does Maxwell's and Swishers' history. He married Eunice Prety in 1757.

HARLAN, SILAS (Major)

Born near Martinsburg, Berkeley County, Virginia, about 1750; was killed at the battle of the Blue Licks in Kentucky.

HARRIS, DAVID
Service—Virginia   Va. No. 12387   No. S. 38796

Served three years under Captain William Taylor in the Second Virginia Regiment, under Colonel Febiger. Was in action at Monmouth. Enlisted in Davidson County, Tennessee, August 11, 1780, and later made his home in Jackson County, Virginia. His wife's name was Ann and they had a son, aged 12. The soldier applied for a pension, June, 1818, aged 59. His wife was 54 years old in 1820. The pension certificate was issued, July 15, 1819.

HARRIS, SIMEON

Near Meadowville, Barbour County, lived the Reverend Simeon Harris, Revolutionary soldier, Indian fighter, and later a prominent minister of the Gospel.

WEST VIRGINIANS IN THE REVOLUTION 123

HARRISON, BATTAILLE (Lieutenant)

Commanded Captain William Brady's company of riflemen at the battle of Fort Washington or King's Bridge, November 16, 1776. He was killed. His first service was as a private in the company raised by Captain Hugh Stephenson in 1775.

HARRISON, DAVIS

According to pension application filed in Harrison County, 1818, Harrison enlisted in the regular army in Virginia in company commanded by Captain Stewart in Colonel Wadsworth's Regiment for one year, and continued in service until the end of the war. He was discharged at Chesterfield, Vermont, after eleven months service. He was in the battle of Powells (Paulus) Hook.

HARRISON, JAMES
Service—Virginia   Va. No. 20387   No. W. 548

James Harrison, who is supposed to have lived at one time in Mason County, Virginia, served from 1776 to 1777 in the Revolutionary Army, after enlistment in Botetourt County, but after 1834 he lived in Hawkins County, Tennessee, so his Mason County, Virginia, residence is uncertain. He was married to Mary Haunce, December 12, 1823 or 1832 by the Reverend Henry Holston, in Botetourt County, but apparently had had a previous marriage. He was born in 1755 and left four children when he died in 1842. Pensions were granted to the soldier and to his widow.

HARRISS, SIMEON
Service—Virginia   Va. No. 23575   No. S. 15871

Applied for pension, November 1, 1834, Randolph County, Virginia, for six months service under Colonel Drake against the Indians. Certificate was issued but he was later dropped from the rolls. Records show that Harriss moved into Randolph County shortly after the Revolution.

HARROW, JACOB
Service—Virginia   Va. No. 16096   No. S. 5480

Born, Frederick County, Virginia, 1755. At eighteen years of age, joined the pack horse service and came west of the Allegheny Mountains. He was to lead, drive, and care for the pack horses which transported provisions to Fort McIntosh. Enlisted in the Revolutionary Army in Frederick County, 1778, and served ten months under Lieutenant Sullivan, Captain Coulter of the Virginia Line, under Colonel John Evans and Zadoc Wright, doing guard and other duties. Other officers mentioned are Lieutenants George Shilling and Hezekiah Row. He applied for pension, Harrison County, June 17, 1833, and it was granted the same year. His claim was supported by Hamilton Gass and John Cather.

HART, EDWARD
Service—New Jersey   No. 796   No. W. 7628

Edward Hart, son of John Hart, signer of the Declaration of Independence, was born in Hopewell, New Jersey, on December 20, 1755. He married Nancy Ann Stout, 1777, and they had nine children. He died,

October 5, 1812, and his wife in 1844, aged 87. Their graves are in the Beverly Cemetery, Randolph County.

Hart served twelve months as a private in the Revolutionary Army, under Captains Guito, and Houton, New Jersey militia, under Colonel Gauton, Colonel Hunt and Lord Sterling. Pension was applied for and received. Supporting claims were made by Daniel Hart, a brother, Levi War, and Thomas Collett.

HARTMAN, JOHN
Service—Pennsylvania   Va. No. 42 and 4565   No. W. 7680

Born in Germany in 1757 and came to America in 1775. Married Christina Kellar, Berks County, Pennsylvania, March 15, 1779. Soldier died, November 30, 1842.

Enlisted, Berks County, Pennsylvania, and served six months as private under Captains Seanly, Wagoner, and Crowl, Pennsylvania Line, Colonels Erwin Yager and Bull. Applied for pension, November 12, 1832, Preston County, Virginia. Certificate issued May 4, 1833, suspended later but reinstated in 1835. Widow, born, March 15, 1760, applied for pension, September 18, 1846, and certificate was issued the same year. Supporting affidavits filed by Joseph Smith, Samuel Trowbridge, William Gable, Michael Hartman, and Andrew Chidester.

HARTZELL, JACOB
Service—Pennsylvania   Va. No. 13141   No. W. 14891 B. L. Wt. 26040

Born, September 27, 1751, Bedford County, Pennsylvania, died, March 24, 1839. Married in Somerset County, Pennsylvania, to Margaret Smith on December 14, 1814, by Justice of the Peace John McMillen.

Served six months as private after enlistment, Bedford County, Pennsylvania, November, 1776, May, 1777, under Captains Tizar and Peyton, Colonel Woods, and General Washington. Fought at Trenton and Princeton. See records of Levi Hopkins and Tadoc Casteel. Applied for pension, October 29, 1832, Preston County, but was dropped from rolls on ground that sufficient service had not been established. Widow applied for pension, May 9, 1853, at age of 55. After long dispute, District Attorney Singleton marked this case "entitled" and bounty land warrant for 160 acres was apparently made, but there is no record of pension matters having ever been satisfactorily settled. Supporting affidavits by the Reverend David Trowbridge, Samuel Trowbridge, Jacob Martin, Jacob Graves, William Rush, Bidwell Parnell, Sarah Matheny, and Huffman, Guseman, and Martin (first names uncertain).

HARVEY, JOHN C.

Before the Wood County court, June 3, 1818, John Harvey testified that he enlisted in the Revolutionary Army in the State of New York in the company commanded by Captain John Hall, Nineteenth New York Regiment, and that he continued in the service until 1779 (?) when he was discharged at West Point. He was in the battle in which Burgoyne's Army was defeated at Saratoga. He filed application for pension, and the court approved and forwarded his petition to the War Department.

HAUGHT, PETER
Service—Virginia   Va. No. 12923   No. S. 6981 and B. L. Wt. 71143

Enlisted in Monongalia County, Virginia, as a private and served twelve months under Captains Daugherty and Catt under Colonel John Evans and General McIntosh in Virginia detachment of troops. He was born, July 1, 1755; died February 12, 1835, and is buried in the Tennant Cemetery, three miles from Mooresville, Monongalia County. Haught married Sarah Jones, in 1825, Green County, Pennsylvania, with David Worley as the minister. Sarah Haught died, April 16, 1857. Their children were Frances, John, Jacob and Benjamin.

The soldier applied for pension in Monongalia County, in 1832, and received pension, but it was dropped later. There followed a long period of litigation, which at length resulted in arrearages being paid to the heirs of Peter Haught. Bounty land of 160 acres was also given to Haught. Particularly interesting are the statements of Samuel Minor, Joseph Tennant, and Captain John Lantz in his support. Other favorable affidavits were those of Solomon and Sarah Moore.

Joseph Tennant said: "My father, Richard Tennant, emigrated from Scotland with others in his 16th year to the colony of Virginia in 1755, and settled soon afterwards on the South Branch of the Potomac near Moorefield. He there became acquainted with the Haughts, who were Germans. He married the sister of Peter Haught in 1764 or 1765. Every man at that day learned the use of fire arms from necessity on account of the frequency of Indian atrocities, and were also taught a certain amount of military discipline. My father and Peter Haught, the latter not more than 16 or 18 years of age, were out in the Dunmore Campaign in 1774 under a Captain Summers in the division under General Lewis.

"In 1775, my father emigrated to Monongalia County and was so pleased with the country that he returned to the South Branch, and persuaded Peter, Tobias, and Henry Haught, brothers-in-law, to accompany him to Monongalia in 1776. Tobias and Henry, after the breaking out of the Revolutionary War, returned to the South Branch, enlisted in the Virginia State Line, and lost their lives in service. There was a requisition for men from 1778 to 1780 to serve against the Indians of the Northwest. My father and Peter Haught were among those who went out in 1780."

The above Richard Tennant died in 1822, aged 85.

HAWK, ISAAC (Ensign)
Service—Virginia   Va. No. 23104   No. S. 9571

Born, at Winchester, Frederick County, Virginia, August 13, 1759. At outbreak of Revolution resided in Hampshire County. In 1794, he moved to Bath County, now Pocahontas County, Virginia.

In Hampshire County, March 1, 1777, he enlisted for six months under Captain Moses Hutton, Lieutenant West Ward, and Ensign Andrew Heith. He marched from Cacapon across the Alleghenies to the Yough Glades, then to Fort Pitt, and thence to Wheeling where he was stationed under command of General Hand for the remainder of his service. He was fired upon by Indians and two companions, Jacob Ware and Jacob

Crow, were killed. He was discharged, September 1, 1777. October 8, 1782, he was commissioned Ensign in Captain George Bell's Company under Lieutenant-Colonel Joseph Neville's Regiment of militia and served until November 10, 1782, when he received discharge from Colonel Neville. He was with the detachment which guarded Colonel Neville and party who were making the final survey of the Mason and Dixon line marking the boundary between Virginia and Pennsylvania.

Supporting claims in his behalf filed by the Reverend George Brooks, John Gilliland, Philip and John Switzer, and Jacob Hawk.

HAWKINS, JEREMIAH
Service—Pennsylvania   Va. No. 19923   No. W. 8885 and B. L. Wt. 51753

Served as private, 1778 and 1779, under Captain Thomas Dawson, Pennsylvania Regiment, Continental Establishment, under Colonel Daniel Brodhead and Colonel John Lee Gibson. Married, Georgetown, Baum County, Pennsylvania, 1811. Soldier applied for pension, Brooke County, Virginia, March 27, 1828, and certificate was issued. Soldier born in 1754, died December 10, 1836. Nancy Hawkins, widow, applied for pension, Hancock County, August 19, 1853, and later filed subsequent petitions. Certification was granted in her behalf. She was 83 years old in 1856. Bounty land warrant for 160 acres was also granted. Supporting affidavits were filed by Joshua Whims, Caleb Whims, and Milt Thompson.

HAWKINS, WILLIAM
Service—Virginia   Va. No. 12950   No. S. 6960

Born, Rockbridge County, Virginia, June 30, 1764. Enlisted in the fall of 1778 and served six months under Captain Robinson and Captain Galloway, Virginia Regiment, under Colonel Skillern, Colonel Lewis, and Generals McIntosh and Morgan. Was at siege and capture of Yorktown. Applied for pension, Mason County, Virginia, February 4, 1833, and certificate was issued, June 18, 1833. Supporting affidavits submitted by Andrew Waggener and Isaac Newman.

HAYHURST, BENJAMIN

The grave of Benjamin Hayhurst, commonly accepted as having been a soldier in the Revolutionary Army, is found in the Hayhurst Cemetery, Monongah, Marion County.

HAYMOND, EDWARD
Service—Pennsylvania-Virginia   Va. No. 16925   No. S. 38009

Enlisted, August 26, 1776, in the Eighth Pennsylvania Regiment, in Captain John Wilson's Company, and marched up Allegheny River under Colonel McCoy against the Indians, then to Philadelphia. When Colonel Morgan's Rifle Regiment was formed, he joined and served one year. When his regiment was detached to Pittsburgh, he was ordered to join it, and served under Colonel Daniel Brodhead one year. Received his discharge from Lieutenant-Colonel Stephen Bayard of said regiment, which discharge he sold ten years later for $15. His claim was supported in Greene County, Pennsylvania, by Gideon Long and Jeremiah Long, who stated they had served with him. Application for pension, November

WEST VIRGINIANS IN THE REVOLUTION

23, 1818, Monongalia County, Virginia. Certificate was issued May 13, 1820.

HAYMOND, WILLIAM (Major)
William Haymond, born, 1740, died 1821, was an outstanding figure in the settlement of the Monongahela Valley. He was active in the French and Indian wars and attained the rank of major in the Revolution. He is buried in Maple Grove Cemetery, Marion County.

He was commissioned Captain of Monongalia County militia by Governor Patrick Henry, March 13, 1776; was in command of Prickett's Fort, Marion County, in 1777; selected, May, 1777, as one of the officials to administer oath to the male inhabitants of Monongalia County, over 16 years of age, renouncing allegiance to King George III, and swearing allegiance to the new government. He was commissioned major of militia by Governor Benjamin Harrison, November 12, 1781, with a detachment at Scott's Mills. He was sheriff of Monongalia County in 1783.

HAYNES (HANES), JACOB (Captain)
Served in the Revolutionary Army from the battle of Brandywine until the surrender of Cornwallis' Army at Yorktown. After the war, he had a tavern on the road to Alexandria.

HEATH, WILLIAM
Service—Virginia   Va. No. 16707   No. S. 10829

Born, 1758, Fort Pleasant, Hampshire County, Virginia. Enlisted in Hampshire County, 1778, and served until 1781, under Captain John Harness, Virginia Regiment, under Captain Dan Richardson and Colonel John Gibson. Applied for pension, May 21, 1833, which was issued the same year. Supporting claims were made by Dr. J. Richser, Peter Hutton, Jacob Yoakum, Isaac Van Meeter, and Jacob Hutton.

HEBB, WILLIAM
Service—Virginia, Cont.   Va. No. 17851   No. S. 38022

Enlisted, Westmoreland County, Virginia, March 17, 1777, in the Third Regiment of Light Dragoons, which formed the lifeguards of General George Washington, commander-in-chief of the American Army. He served as a private three years under Captain Thom and Colonel Bayless, and was in the battles of Germantown and Brandywine. He was honorably discharged by Lieutenant-Colonel William Washington at Bacon Bridge, South Carolina, March 19, 1780.

He applied for a pension, November 2, 1818, Preston County, Virginia, and pension certificate was issued, July 3, 1820. His wife was mentioned as being 63 years old in 1820; a son, Robert, was 20, and a second son, Reuben, 18 years old the same year. Supporting claims were filed by Henry Harriss, Charles Swan, and Robert Muse.

HECK, YOUST
Service—Pennsylvania   Va. No. 5216   No. S. 38019

Enlisted, January 1, 1778, Berks County, Pennsylvania, under Captain Crist, Thirteenth Pennsylvania Regiment, commanded by Colonel Walter Stewart. Fought at White Plains, Long Island, Iron Hill, Brandywine, and Germantown. Applied for pension, Monongalia County, May 27, 1818. Certificate issued, January 7, 1819. Wife, aged 50, and children as follows: Youst, 21; Sarah, 19; George, 17; Rachel, 15; David, 14; Elizabeth, 12. Pension was later discontinued and there is no evidence of reinstatement.

HEDGES, SILAS (Colonel)

Born, Frederick County, Virginia, December 2, 1736. About 1770, removed to the Redstone region, and in 1773 settled on Buffalo Creek, Brooke County, Virginia, where he died at the family homestead, May 17, 1811. He was a cousin of Colonel David Shepherd, whom he succeeded as colonel of militia when Shepherd became lieutenant of Ohio County in 1778.

Hedges was in Dunmore's War; was on the Committee of Safety in 1775; was at the siege of Wheeling, 1777; and aided in burying the dead after Foreman's defeat. He was active throughout the Indian wars in enlisting and drilling the militia. He resigned his office in 1789 because of old age. His wife was Margaret, sister of Derrick Hoagland. Two of their sons were prominent in border spy and ranging service.

HENDERSON, JAMES (Lieutenant)

Brother of Colonel John Henderson. James did militia duty at the frontier forts while his older brother was with the Continental Army. James received large grants of land in Greenbrier County, from his father's estate, and became a militia officer.

HENDERSON, JOHN (Captain)

He was born about 1737 in Augusta County, Virginia, the son of James Henderson who served in the French and Indian War. In 1765, he married Anne Givens, sister of Mrs. Andrew Lewis, and a little later removed to the Greenbrier Valley, where he made a home not far from Lewisburg. He was a private in the troops of his brother-in-law, General Andrew Lewis, in the Battle of Point Pleasant, October 10, 1774; then served as lieutenant under Captain Harbert, and became a captain of militia. He held the captaincy until December, 1776, when he resigned to become an officer in the company of Captain John or Daniel Gregory in Colonel Daniel Morgan's Eleventh and Fifteenth Virginia Regiments. He left the army in April, 1779, became a justice of peace, and died in Greenbrier County in 1787.

HENDERSON, SAMPSON

Service—Virginia   Va. No. 6994   No. W. 7339 and B. L. Wt. 39230

Enlisted, Fairfax County, Virginia, November, 1776, and served two years as private under Captain Thomas West, Tenth Virginia Regiment, Colonel Edward Stephens. Fought at Monmouth and Savannah, Georgia. He was wounded in the latter engagement. Henderson married Elizabeth Grace Henderson, July, 1812, Hampshire County, Virginia. He died, July, 1820. His widow married Stephen Fuller, 1825, and who died, January 22, 1854. Pension certificates were issued, and also bounty land warrants

WEST VIRGINIANS IN THE REVOLUTION

for 160 acres. Supporting affidavits to their pension claims were filed by Charles Broadwater, Jesse Fryer, and James Parsons.

HENRY, NICHOLAS
Service—Pennsylvania   Va. No. 415   No. S. 5505

Born in Lancaster County, Pennsylvania, November, 1758, and enlisted in that county under Captains Outerholt, Holderbaum, and Aulderbrook in the Flying Camp Regiment under Colonel Grumble or Grubble. Fought at White Plains and Chestnut Hill. He was a substitute for Henry Cleaver, volunteering because he was exempt from conscription into military service on account of his age and his occupation as an employee in a grist mill. He was granted a pension while living in Morgan County, Virginia, 1832. Supporting claims were made for him by Peter Caw, Matthias Rizer, and Samuel Abernathy.

HENSHAW, WILLIAM (Captain)

William Henshaw, George Scott, and Thomas Heitt were elected lieutenants of a company of volunteers raised in Berkeley County, Virginia, by Colonel Hugh Stevenson under a resolution of Congress to serve one year in the Continental Army. This company reached Boston in 1775. On October 4, 1776, the unit was at Bergen Point, opposite New York. On November 12, these troops were engaged in three successive days in severe skirmishing at King's Bridge. The officers were rendered supernumerary by the reduction of the Virginia regiments from 15 to 11 by resolution of Congress.

Henshaw, born, March 16, 1736, was the son of Nicholas Henshaw and wife, Rebecca Smith, Philadelphia. He died April 9, 1799. On January 30, 1768, he was married to Agnes Ann Anderson, born, 1745, the daughter of William Anderson and Rachel, his wife, of "Anderson Bottom," Hampshire County. She died July 21, 1806. Their children were: Levi, 1769-1843; first wife, Nancy Davidson; second, Ann McConnell; Hiram, 1771-1845; married Mary McConnell; Adam Stephen, married Mary McConnell; Jonathan Seamon, married Elizabeth Stafford; Washington, married three times, his third wife, "Widow Robinson," moved to Tennessee; William Slaughter, 1784-1836, captain in the Fifth Infantry, U. S. A., married Harriet Byron Lyle; Uriah, married Elizabeth McDonald; Nicholas, moved to Pennsylvania; Rachel, married Joseph Lemon; Rebecca, born 1780, married Major Lewis Moore in 1793 and lived in Kentucky; Rhumah, married Seth Duncan, Kentucky.

HENSON, WILLIAM
Service—Virginia   Va. No. 4747   No. W. 3416 and B. L. Wt. 6450

Enlisted, Botetourt County, Virginia, 1776, and served two years as a private in the Seventh Virginia Regiment, Captain Thomas Posey's company, commanded by Colonel Eli McClenachan. He was with Colonel Morgan at Piscataway Meeting House and at Somerset. He was honorably discharged at Valley Forge, and delivered discharge to Colonel George Hancock to draw his pay but it was never returned.

Soldier was born in 1755 and died, February 9, 1834. He married Sivilly Duckwyler, who was born in 1765, in Greenbrier County, March

3, 1785. Henson received pension certificate in 1819 and his widow got pension in 1842. Bounty land warrant for 160 acres was also received. Supporting affidavits were filed by Jacob Price and Christopher Hedrick.

HEREFORD, JOHN (Adjutant)
Service—Virginia   Va. No. 12831   No. W. 1425 and B. L. Wt. 28613

Born, Fairfax County, Virginia, February 3, 1758, and died, Mason County, May 13, 1846. His boyhood home was on the paternal estate of his great-grandfather on the Potomac River, who settled there after coming from Wales. Before he was sixteen years old, Hereford in 1774 was enrolled in a company in Leesburg that was being drilled in expectation of the coming war with England. In 1777, John enlisted as a sergeant in the Second Virginia Regiment under Lieutenant Gill, and marched under Marquis Calmus or Colms to Philadelphia where he was attached to Captain John Peyton Morrison's Company, and was in the Battle of Monmouth. In 1778-79, he enlisted for the war, obtained a substitute and received a discharge from Colonel Christian Febiger. He was then appointed commissary at Leesburg. When Cornwallis invaded Virginia, Hereford was adjutant of Colonel John Alexander's Regiment under Lafayette, and finally drove Cornwallis to Yorktown where he was captured. He continued as adjutant of Colonel Charles Dabney's Regiment and of Colonel West's Regiment under General Weedon.

Hereford first married Elizabeth Patterson, July 22, 1784, of Fairfax County, Virginia, the daughter of Irish parents. She was a first cousin of the beautiful, witty, and ambitious Elizabeth Patterson of Baltimore, who married Jerome Bonaparte, heir to the French throne. Their children were: Thomas Patterson, June 26, 1786; John Wesley, September 24, 1788; James Madison, June 12, 1790; William, May 26, 1794; James Henry, December 11, 1796.

Hereford's second wife was Sarah Maurey (or Mauzy), a descendant of Henry Maurey, a French Huguenot who fled to America from France in 1685 and settled in Fairfax County. They were married, April 8, 1804. Their children were: Warren Mercer, April 12, 1805; Robert, March 24, 1807; Elizabeth Ann, October 25, 1809; George Washington, June 27, 1811; Ann Elizabeth, November 24, 1814; Margaret Ann, September 19, 1817; Francis, December 14, 1818; Benjamin Franklin, January 24, 1820; Mary, April 23, 1823; Marquisette Lafayette, April 4, 1825; Ammon Barns, December 16, 1827 (named after Grandfather Barns).

Pensions were granted to the soldier and also to his widow in Mason County. There was also a land bounty grant of 160 acres. Supporting claims were made by Mrs. Jan McCabe, James Hamilton, Samuel Tillett, Elinor Tillett, a sister of Lieutenant Gill, Joseph Smith, Charles Clendenin, M. Stribling, Hugh Daigh, and Charles B. Waggoner. An interesting comment was the statement that Colonel Febiger, under whom Hereford served, had been in 39 military actions in Europe and in America.

HERIN, WILLIAM (Sergeant)
Service—Virginia   Va. No. 6806   No. S. 8704

Enlisted, Culpeper County, Virginia, in December, 1776, and served two years as private, corporal, and sergeant under Captain Benjamin Roberts in Virginia regiments commanded by Colonel George Rogers Clark and Major George Staughton. Also mentions Captain Mark Thomas, Lieutenant James Saunders, Colonel Crockett, and Ensign William Asher. Pension granted, Hampshire County, Virginia, in 1833. Supporting claims made by Peter Triplett and James Ballard. Soldier died in January, 1839, aged 76.

West Virginians in the American Revolution

Assembled and Edited by ROSS B. JOHNSTON

The sources of this material are from the files of the Pension Office at Washington from various county records, from notes of patriotic societies, principally the Daughters of the American Revolution, Sons of the American Revolution, Sons of the Revolution, and from a large miscellaneous group of published and private sources. Corrections and additions to this list will receive the careful attention of the editor.

HESS, HEZEKIAH
Service-Virginia   Va. No. 23095 and 27414   No. S. 8707

Born, Dutchess County, New York, October 9, 1756, brought to Hampshire County when seven months old, and removed to Lewis County, Virginia, in 1822. Died October 4, 1848. Enlisted in Hampshire, now Hardy County, Virginia, in June, 1776, as an Indian spy under Captains Payne, Dunnell and Stuart, Second Battalion of Artillery, under Colonels Hughart and Mathew.

Received pension certificate for two years' service in 1833, but pension was suspended, March 16, 1835, in Lewis County. Supporting claims filed by Abram Wetzel, Jacob Wymer, and Horner Smith. Children of Hess were as follows: Charity Hess Hacher (Hacker), Mary Hess Parson, Matilda Hess Slantey, Melissa, Nancy Hess Williams, and Abraham.

HEYSHAM, DAVID
Service—Virginia   Va. No. 23724   No. W. 3810 and B. L. Wt. 24995

Born, Lower Smithfield, Northampton County, Pennsylvania, March 14, 1762, and died, September 6, 1834, Tyler County, Virginia. Enlisted in Pennsylvania in 1778 and served two years as a private under Lieutenant Shoemaker of the Virginia Line, guarding and defending the western frontier.

In June, 1786, or 1787, married Elizabeth Bush, who was born in 1767. They were married by the Reverend Appleton. Pension certificates were issued in Tyler County to the soldier and his widow. Bounty land warrant for 160 acres was also issued. Supporting claims were made by the Reverend John W. Allen, W. Dalashanutt, Robert Govel, Thomas Heysham (nephew), Josiah Thomas, Jane Heysham (sister-in-law), William Martin, and J. G. Morgan.

HICKMAN, ADAM
Service—Virginia   Va. No. 8278   No. S. 38030

Enlisted, Berks County, Pennsylvania, 1775, and served as a private in the company of Captain George Nogle and Captain Neal in the Pennsylvania Line under Colonel Oulds or Colonel Utrey. Pension granted in

Harrison County, 1819, discontinued in 1820 as having too much property, but was reinstated when reviewed by Secretary of War, October 5, 1820. Died February 16, 1833.

HICKMAN, SOTHA

Service—Virginia   Va. No. 12527   No. S. 5516

Sotha Hickman, pioneer settler of Harrison County, was born June 10, 1748, on the Sugar Land bottom on the Potomac River near Rockville, Maryland, and died March 26, 1834, at his home on Elk Creek, Quiet Dell, Harrison County, where he had lived many years. He was a son of Arthur and Mary Hickman of English descent. His wife died in 1837.

Hickman served as a private fourteen months in the Revolutionary War under Captain William Lowther of the Virginia Line in checking Indian depredations on the western borders, residing at that time in Monongalia County. He was granted a pension in 1833. Supporting claims were filed for him by Isaac Richards, Joseph Davidson, A. C. Holden, and Josiah Peek.

HICKS, MORDECAI

Bounty Land Warrant No. 8118 was issued, August 14, 1834, in favor of Susanna Jarrett, Elizabeth Johnson, and Catherine Skaggs, heirs of Mordecai Hicks, who had served as a volunteer under General George Rogers Clark at the capture of the British posts in-the Northwest. These heirs, who were sisters, were living in Monroe County, Virginia, February 25, 1835.

HILL, RICHARD

Born, North Carolina, July, 1763. In Pocahontas County, February 18, 1832, made application for pension, stating that he came to Pocahontas County, in March after the surrender of Lord Cornwallis. Said he had volunteered for military service in the Carolinas, and that after settlement in Virginia in 1782 he served at Bucks Station under Captain Clendenin and Colonel Samuel Lewis. Supporting affidavits filed by Jacob Kinnison, Henry Casebolt, James Lewis, and the Reverend John S. Blair. Claim was rejected.

HILL, ROBERT

The grave of Robert Hill, who served in the Revolutionary War, and who died in 1822, is in Mount Union Cemetery, Union District, Monongalia County.

HINKLE, ISAAC (Captain)

Captain Isaac Hinkle, a soldier of ability, served in the Revolutionary War and in 1781, was named captain (vier) in the place of his brother-in-law, Andrew Johnson, who was given another command. (See Vol. 2, Augusta County Records, D. A. R. Record Building, Washington.) He married Mary Cunningham, December 13, 1781. He died in 1824 and is buried in Hinkle Gap in Pendleton County.

HITCHCOCK, WILLIAM

Before the Harrison County, Virginia, Court, William Hitchcock stated that he enlisted in 1780 in the Regular Army of the United States in Captain Henry Heath's, or Heth's, Company of the Ninth Virginia Regiment, commanded by Colonel John Gibson, on Continental Establishment. He continued in this service until 1781 when he was taken prisoner by the Indians and was badly wounded. He continued a prisoner four years and eight months before being set at liberty. No further record is available.

HITE, ABRAHAM (Captain)

Second Lieutenant, Twelfth Virginia, November 15, 1776; first lieutenant, January 8, 1777; captain-lieutenant, May, 1778; regimental paymaster, January 1, 1779; captain, April 4, 1779; taken prisoner at Charleston, May 12, 1780; prisoner on parole to end of war. Died in 1832.

HITE, GEORGE (Captain)

Born, October 28, 1761, Frederick County, Virginia. Enlisted in Berkeley County. Ensign, Eighth Virginia, September 10, 1780; transfererd to Third Continental Dragoons, August, 1782; lieutenant, October, 1782, later becoming a captain. He was wounded in the Revolution and was one of the original members of the Order of the Cincinnati. He was the first clerk of Jefferson County, and was succeeded by his son, Major Robert G. Hite. He died, December 16, 1816.

In Jefferson County, February 18, 1834, it was certified that Deborah Rutherford Hite was the widow of George Hite, deceased, and that the other heirs are: Frances M. Ransom, widow of James Ransom, Margaret L. Hite, Susan B. Flagg, wife of John F. Flagg, Sarah E. R. Beckwith, widow of R. B. Beckwith, deceased, and Mary E. Merritt, wife of Samuel Merritt.

George was the son of Jacob Hite by his second wife. Jacob was the son of Jost Hite, the colonist. Just before the Revolution, Jacob had moved to South Carolina, and there Jacob, his wife, and several children were married, and two daughters were taken captive by the Indians.

HITE, ISAAC (Lieutenant)

Ensign in Eighth Virginia, July 1, 1780; first lieutenant, July, 1781; retired January 1, 1783; died, November 30, 1836.

HITE, JOSEPH (Lieutenant)

Cadet in Eighth Virginia, February 21, 1778; lieutenant, February, 1779; resigned, January 8, 1780.

HITE, MATHIAS (Captain)

Service—Virginia   Va. Na. 5989   No. S. 38031

Before the Harrison County, Virginia, Court in 1818, Mathias Hite certified that he entered the service of the United States as a first lieutenant in the Eighth Virginia Regiment, and that after remaining in service for a year, he received his commission as captain which was filed in court. Pension was granted in 1819. Hite, born in 1750, died

January 9, 1823. First lieutenant, Eighth Virginia, January 23, 1776; captain, August 10, 1777; resigned, May 7, 1778.

HITE, WILLIAM (Ensign)
Ensign in Eighth Virginia, August, 1777; retired, July 1, 1778.

HIXON (HIXSON), JOHN
Enlisted, New Jersey, 1776, in the Flying Camp Regiment, under Captain John Anderson and General Sullivan. He also enlisted in Captain Ballard's Company of the Third Jersey Regiment, commanded by Colonel Dayton. He continued to serve until 1778 when he was discharged from service in Elizabeth Town, New Jersey. He was in the battles of Long Island, White Plains, and Monmouth. He applied for pension in Berkeley County, April 28, 1818. His claims were supported by affidavits of Joseph Rowe and James Richardson.

HOFFMAN, JOHN
Service—Virginia   Va. No. 23035   No. S. 8755

Born, Frederick County, Virginia, 1760, and resided in Jefferson County, Virginia, during the Revolution. He died in 1827. He was married to Mary Blake, May 9, 1790, in Berkeley County. They had one child, Mary.

He was a private in Captain John Marshall's Company, Seventh Virginia Regiment, commanded by Colonel Daniel Morgan in General Woodford's Brigade. His record includes the names of Captain Roberts and Colonel Francis Taylor. There is filed a statement by Major John Roberts, of Virginia, that he enlisted John Hoffman as a soldier in the regiment of guards of the Albemarle Barracks, and that Hoffman served faithfully until May, 1781, when he was discharged at Winchester by Colonel Francis Taylor. Hoffman was granted a pension in Ohio County, Virginia, in 1833. Pay was suspended in 1835 but was resumed in 1836.

HOLL (HULL), PETER, JR. (Colonel)
Served as an officer in the Revolution; captain of militia in 1781; lieutenant-colonel, 1788, and colonel of Virginia militia, 1793. He was a son of Peter Holl, Sr., of Holland descent, who arrived in Philadelphia, May 30, 1741, on the ship Francis and Ann from Rotterdam. He lived in Lancaster County, Pennsylvania, Rockingham and Highland sections of Augusta County. His will was probated at Staunton, February, 1776.

HOLBERT, AARON
Service—Virginia   Va. No. 16902   No. S. 18028

Certificate issued for pension, October 12, 1833, for service of one year and two days in military service during the Revolution. Claim later suspended.

HOLDER, JAMES
Service—Virginia   Va. No. 23047   No. 8736

Born, County of Kent, Delaware, 1762. Lived in the Tygarts Valley section of Randolph County when the Revolution began. Enlisted there and served nine months as a private under Captains Friend, Jackson, Mascawell, under General George Rogers Clark scouting and doing guard duty on the western frontier. Certificate of pension issued in Randolph County, in 1833, but it was suspended in 1835. Supporting claims by Valentine Stalnaker and William Currence.

HOLLAND, JACOB
Service—Continental Md.   Va. No. 21135   No. R. 5141

Served as corporal of dragoons for three years under Captains Simms and Howard, First and Fourth Maryland Regiment, under Colonel William Smallwood and Colonel Moylan. Fought at Long Island, Harlem Heights, White Plains, Brandywine, and Germantown. Enlisted, Unity, Montgomery County, Maryland, March 1, 1776, and was discharged in June, 1780, by Colonel Moylan.

Born, March, 1754, and died, September 17, 1838. Married, 1790, Montgomery County, Virginia, by the Reverend Reed. Wife's name, Mary, and their children as follows: Allen, Elizabeth, Daniel, William, Richard, Solomon, Isaac (deceased), and his two children, Alpheus and Eliza. The widow died, April 12, 1840. Pension was applied for in Monongalia County, Virginia, July 3, 1832, and granted, November 20, 1832.

HOLLIDAY, JAMES
Service—Pennsylvania   Va. No. 12951   No. S. 7026

Born in Ireland, came to America in 1773. Settled in Cumberland County, Pennsylvania, lived there until 31 years old, and then came to Ohio County, Virginia.

Enlisted, January, 1776, Cumberland County, Pennsylvania, as a private and served fifteen months under Captains A. Smith and Maxwell, Pennsylvania Line, under Colonel Ervine, Generals Thompson and Sullivan. Discharged, April 15, 1777. Pension granted in Ohio County June 18, 1833. Supporting affidavits filed by Robert Cummings, the Reverend George Robinson, and Samuel McKeehan.

HOOFMAN, CHRISTIAN
Service—Pennsylvania   Va. No. 16530   No. S. 38042

Enlisted, Easton, Northampton County, Pennsylvania, April 18, 1776, and served as a private three years under Captains Craig and Simpson, First Pennsylvania Regiment, Colonel Chambers and General Wayne. Saw service at Brandywine, Brunswick, Germantown, Trenton, and Monmouth.

Received pension in Pendleton County, Virginia, March 9, 1820. Names of children: Solomon, 15; George, 13; Laban, 10. Soldier was born in 1755 and died December 13, 1822. (This record is not identical with that of Christian Hofman, No. S. 39752.)

HOOK, WILLIAM
Born, 1759, in Gloucestershire, England. Resided in Hampshire County, Virginia, when the Revolution broke out. Died, January 30, 1837. En-

listed, September, 1781, and served ten months as a private under Captain John Neel in Virginia military units. Was at the siege and capture of Yorktown. The record of his marriage, August 13, 1782, to Mary McKee by the Reverend I. Riding is filed in the Hampshire County court. Pensions were granted in Hampshire County. Supporting claims were filed by James Smith and Elisha Gardner.

HOOVER, JACOB
Service—VIRGINIA   Va. No. 23373   No. S. 10842

Enlisted, September, 1779, Rockingham County, Virginia, and served six months under Captains Davis and Noll McCoy under Colonel Smith in activities against the Indians in the Monongahela Valley. Discharged, 1780. Applied for pension, at age of 82, November 6, 1833, Pendleton County, Virginia, and certificate was issued in 1834. Supporting claims by Thomas Hoover and Burton Blizzard. Lawrence Hoover, a brother, was killed by the Tories in 1780.

HOOVER, MICHAEL
Service—Virginia   Va. No. 4126   No. S. 5560

Enlisted, 1778, in Augusta, now Pendleton County, Virginia, and served as a private six months under Captain Davis and Ensign Evick in the Virginia militia in the Indian campaigns in western Virginia. Pension was granted in Pendleton County, January 11, 1833. Pensioner was 80 years old. Supporting claims filed by Palser Hammer and William McCoy.

HOOVER, THOMAS
Service—Virginia   Va. No. 16954   No. S. 18029

Enlisted, Augusta County, Virginia, September 1, 1778, and served as a private nine months under Captains Davis, Houston and Smith, Virginia Line, under Colonel Benjamin Harrison, Generals Campbell Lafayette and Wayne. Fought on the western borders in the Indian country and at Jamestown. Discharged in 1782. Pension granted, 1833, in Pendleton County, at which time soldier was 70 years old. Supporting claims filed by John and Frederick Hedrick, and Palser Hammer.

HOPKINS, LEVI
Service—Massachusetts   Va. No. 166211   No. W. 11330 and B. L. Wt. 26139

Born, March 31, 1753, Great Barrington, Berkshire County, Massachusetts; resided there until 1784, when he moved to Baltimore, Maryland; settled in Preston County, Virginia, in 1794. His death occurred, September 1, 1835.

In the fall of 1776, Hopkins enlisted in Massachusetts and served seven months as private under Captains King and Goetrich in Colonel Stark's Company under Colonel Baum and General Lincoln. Fought at White Plains and Bennington.

Soldier was married to Elizabeth Looper by the Reverend Painter in Allegheny County, Maryland, September 10, 1811. Pension was granted in Preston County, in 1833, but it was dropped in 1835, and there is no evidence of restoration. Supporting claims by John A. Wootring, Tevault Shafer, Thomas Rinehart, Solomon Heckert, Silas Fells, E. G. Piper, and Willam Wheeler. Bounty land grant of 160 acres was issued to the widow in 1855.

HORNBECK, BENJAMIN

In Randolph County, on the bank opposite the marker of Currence Fort is the grave of Benjamin Hornbeck, a soldier in the Revolutionary War, born in 1754 and died in 1827.

HOUSTON, PURNELL

Born, Sussex County, Delaware, February 1, 1758; died in 1835, and is buried in Mount Union Cemetery, Union District, Monongalia County, West Virginia.

Enlisted in Delaware, April, 1776, and served a little more than eight months under Captains Harrard and Chambers, Colonel Bland and General Caldwallander. Fought at Trenton and Princeton (on board a brig). Received pension in Monongalia County, May 14, 1833, which was later suspended, but was restored August 17, 1859, in favor of his heirs. Supporting claims by J. Evans and the Reverend Shackleford.

HOUT, JACOB

In the court of Berkeley County, Virginia, February 20, 1787, it was certified that Jacob Hout was a native of Virginia, and that he enlisted under Captain Kelly of Colonel Hartley's Regiment, and that he was wounded in the knee in the battle of Germantown. Dr. Graf was appointed to examine his wound and certify the same. The order was signed by Godwin Swift.

HOWARD, IGNATIUS

In the court of Greenbrier County, August, 1786, Sarah Howard, widow of Ignatius (Ignarations) Howard, who was a soldier under Captain Arbuckle in the State service and who died with smallpox on his return from the Point station in the year 1774, "remains a widow and has three children to maintain." It was ordered that pension for her be continued.

HOWELL, MICHAEL

Before the Randolph County Court, November 25, 1811, William Howell testified that Michael Howell had never received compensation in land for his services as a soldier under Colonel Murtenbridge in the Revolutionary War.

HUDSON, THOMAS
Service—Virginia   Va. No. 9980 and 5612   No. W. 7832

Enlisted, August, 1779, Augusta County, Virginia, and served two years as private under Captain Kinley in the Virginia Line under Colonel Crockett. Rendezvoused in Staunton, marched to Albemarle Barracks and wintered there. In spring marched to Fort Frederick, Maryland, remained there for short time, then returned to Albemarle, where remained until fall. Returned to Frederick Town and spent the winter there. In the spring of 1781, took up march for Kentucky. Was taken sick at Shepherdstown, Virginia; was sent to barracks in Winchester, and remained there as guard for prisoners.

Married, August 31, 1784, Shenandoah County, Virginia, to Dorothy Heltzley. Received pension in 1833, and 1843. Soldier was born in 1763 and died March 11, 1843.

HUFFMAN, HENRY
Service—Virginia   Va. No. 4125   No. S. 5580

Born, Rockingham County, Virginia, 1757. There enlisted, January 8, 1778, and served ten months as a private under Captain Cravens and Ensign George Mallow, Virginia militia, under Colonels Benjamin Harrison, Van Metre, and General McIntosh, in campaigns against the Indians. Pension was granted in Pendleton County, Virginia, January 11, 1833.

HUFFMAN (HOFFMAN), JOHN

Enlisted in the Revolutionary War from Morris County, in the New Jersey militia, and is buried at Meadowville, Barbour County, West Virginia. He was born, March 3, 1759, the son of Jacob and Catherine Huffman, and came to Barbour County from Loudon County, Virginia, in 1797. John and Elizabeth Huffman had the following children: Israel, 1790, married Anna Black; Daniel, served in War of 1812; Elizabeth, married Robert Johnson, September 19, 1817; Alexander, married Hannah Vannoy, December 18, 1817.

HUFFMAN (HOFFMAN), REUBEN
Service—Virginia   Va. No. 4720   No. W. 7827

Enlisted, Culpepper County, Virginia, March, 1777, and served three years as a private under Captain Angus Bucker, First Virginia Regiment, under Colonel George Gibson and General Muhlenberg. He was honorably discharged at Valley Forge in 1782. Soldier was born in 1754 and died in 1832. He was married in the fall of 1788, Madison County, Virginia. His wife, Catherine, was born, August 12, 1767, and died February 6, 1844. Their children were: Solomon, Philip, Thomas, and Eleanor Hoffman Goodrich.

Pension was granted to the soldier in Greenbrier County, Virginia, December 1, 1818, and pension was likewise granted the widow in later years. Supporting claims were filed by Paschal Early, Daniel Field, Joseph Huffman, Zachariah Cook, and Thomas Reynolds.

HUGHES, ELIAS (Captain)

Elias Hughes, son of Thomas Hughes, was born on the South Branch before 1755, and died in Utica, Ohio, 1840, said to have been the last survivor of the Battle of Point Pleasant in 1774. He received a Revolutionary War pension, August 23, 1832.

He enlisted at the outbreak of the Revolution under Colonel Benjamin Wilson, and later under Colonel William Lowther and Colonel George Jackson. He was a private 1775 to 1778, a captain of spies from 1778 to

1781, then continued service to the end of the war and for many years afterward as a border scout.

He filed his pension application in Ohio. He mentions Captain **James Booth** and says that he succeeded Captain Stephen Ratcliff as captain of spies in 1778. He mentions moving with his father before the Revolution to the Monongahela Valley above Clarksburg with several families among which were those of John Hacker, William Hacker, Samuel Pringle, William Ratcliff, and John Cutright. His claim for pension was supported by Captain William Powers, of Harrison County, by Jesse Lowther, son of Colonel William Lowther, and by General Thomas W. Wilson, son of Colonel Benjamin Wilson.

HUGHES, JONATHAN (Ensign)
Service—Virginia   Va. No. 26219   No. S. 9591

Born in Hampshire County, Virginia, March 25, 1753. Entered military service in June, 1774, Greenbrier County, Virginia, and had several periods of service until 1780 as private and ensign under Captain J. Cook, Virginia militia, Lieutenant Queerland Lewis, and Colonel Poston. Was under Captain Cook and Lieutenant William Gilliland in Greenbrier County until the spring of 1777, and under Captain Hamilton at Major Runion's Fort from June or July, 1777, to September; to the spring of 1778, was in Hampshire County. In October joined Captain Bell in Colonel Poston's Regiment and was an ensign from 1779 to 1780. His commission was signed by Governor Thomas Jefferson. After the Revolution, went to North and South Carolina, thence back to Greenbrier County, then to Harrison County, Virginia, and then to Jefferson County, Indiana. He received pension, April 12, 1834, in Harrison County, Virginia.

HUGHES, ROBERT
Service—Virginia   Va. No. 29654   No. R. 5355

Born, Prince William County, Virginia, August 18, 1760. Since the Revolution, resided in Greenbrier, Kanawha, and Fayette counties. Enlisted, July, 1777, in Prince William and Botetourt counties, Virginia, under Captains Brent, Culbertson, Uriah Springer in the Seventh Virginia Regiment under Colonel Jesse Ewell, John Gibson and Major J. Ewell. Applied for pension, October 13, 1833, Fayette County, Virginia. Supporting claims made by John Hill, William Riggs, William Sims, Thomas Hughes, Elizabeth (Hughes) Garret, J. Hansford, and the Reverend John Johnson. Claim rejected.

HUGHES, THOMAS (Lieutenant)

The claim of Thomas Hughes, filed in Jackson County, Virginia, for a pension as a soldier in the Revolutionary War was suspended. It was shown that he had performed valuable services in the Indian war period from 1784 to 1795 and that he had been a lieutenant of militia but he did not produce satisfactory evidence of sufficient service in the Revolution. His statement mentions Jesse and Elias Hughes, the famous border scouts. Their father and one brother had been killed by the Indians. The claims of Hughes were supported by affidavits of Alexander West, Adam Flesher, John Cutright, and William Powers.

HUGHES, JESSE

Although it is commonly believed that Jesse Hughes, the famous frontier scout and Indian fighter, served in the Revolutionary Army, no proof is available. He spent his most active years on Hackers Creek, Lewis County, but died and is buried at Ravenswood, Jackson County.

HULL, GEORGE
Service—Virginia   Va. No. 16657   Dept. of Interior S. 13317

George Hull, Sr., was born near Harrisonburg, Rockingham County, October 10, 1757, and died on Anthony's Creek, Greenbrier County, Virginia, in 1849. He enlisted at Crab Bottom, Augusta County, now on the edge of Pendleton County, West Virginia, and Highland County, Virginia, and fought in the battle of Jamestown and on the Yorktown Peninsula. He was three months under Captain John McCoy in 1777, three months under Captain McCoy again in 1780, and three months in 1781 under Captain Charles Cameron, and Colonels Huggart and McCreary. He was a member of Captain William James' Company of Pendleton County militia, September 6, 1794, as shown on muster rolls of that date. He received pension, 1833, in Greenbrier County. His claims were supported by John Slavin and Adam Arbogast.

HULDERMAN (HOLDERMAN), JOHN

Born, Frederick County, Maryland, August 2, 1768, and later lived in Monongalia and Harrison counties, Virginia. Enlisted, March, 1783, Martinsburg, Virginia, and served under Captain Jacob Koontz and Lieutenant Bowers. His claim for pension, filed in Harrison County in 1838 and supported by the Reverend Oliver Shurtleff and Henry Booher, was rejected.

HUMPHREY, JONATHAN
Service—Virginia   Va. No. 5055   No. S. 5583

Resided in Culpepper County, Virginia, at the outbreak of the Revolution, and there enlisted, in the fall of 1777, and served six months as a private under Captains Chapman and Francis Nalls in the Virginia Line under Adjutant Robert Pollard, Colonel Alcott, Baron Von Steuben, and Generals Washington and Lafayette. He removed from Culpepper to Harrison County, Virginia, in 1811 and there applied for pension which was granted in 1833. He was then aged 74. Supporting claims in his behalf were made by Colonel Mathias Winters, Dan Flenchalor, George Williams, Anderson Corbin, and Jacob Riffles.

HUMPHREY, ROBERT
Service—Pennsylvania   Va. No. 2137   No. S. 5582

Residing in Cumberland County, Pennsylvania, at outbreak of the Revolution. There he enlisted, spring of 1776, as a private and served two years under Captain J. Marshal in the Second Battalion of Pennsylvania Riflemen under Colonels Brodhead, Null and Stuart. He was in action at Germantown, Long Island, Princeton, Trenton, and Brandywine. He was granted pension, November 20, 1832, and was dead in 1835. (Filed with West Virginia material but residence in this state is uncertain.)

HUNT, JACOB
Service—Continental, Mass.　　　Va. No. 15020　　　No. W. 424

Born, September 7, 1754, and died January 18, 1847. Enlisted, Franklin County, Massachusetts, April, 1775, and served one year as a private under Captains Wilde and Gould, Massachusetts Line, Continental Establishment, under Colonel Grayton. In Bramtree Township, October 10, 1780, he was married to Hannah Littlefield, who was born, November 24, 1757. Their children were: Hannah, June 5, 1781; Jacob, January 1, 1785; Sally, February 25, 1787; Abner, August 8, 1791; John, June 10, 1799.

Pension granted soldier, 1819, while living in Lewis County, Virginia, later dropped, but was continued in 1821. Claim supported by Robert Millon, Micah White, James and David Shurcliffe. Widow was granted pension in 1849 while living in Summit County, Ohio.

HUNT, SAMUEL

Pension declaration was made in Monroe County that Samuel Hunt had Revolutionary War service in Captain Ernest Mend's Company of musketry in the Second Virginia Regiment. He lived in Cumberland at the time of the Revolution, but had lived in Monroe County for 22 years.

HUSBANDS, JAMES

Residing in Wilmington, Delaware, when Revolution started. There enlisted, served as a private until May, 1777, and then as a corporal until August, 1778, under Captain Ballen, Delaware Line, under Colonel David Hall. Fought at Brandywine, Germantown, and Monmouth, and then accompanied the Delaware troops under Colonel William Purgneal which took part in the battle at Camden and at other points in North and South Carolina in 1780. He was reported missing, August 10, 1780. He applied for pension, aged 60, in Berkeley County, Virginia, April 28, 1818.

HUSSTEAD, MOSES
Service—Virginia　　　Va. No. 23051　　　No. S. 9600

Born, Dutchess County, New York, May 15, 1748. Enlisted in Monongalia County, March, 1778, and served two years as a private soldier and Indian spy under Captain William Robinson. Pension was granted him in Harrison County, October 29, 1833, but was suspended in 1835.

HUTCHINSON, WILLIAM
Service—Virginia　　　　　　　　　　No. R. 5457

Born, Augusta County, Virginia, 1757. Enlisted in 1776 and served until 1782 in guarding the frontier settlements against Indians. Served under Captain John Henderson, Captain Archibald Wood, and Captain Gray. Stationed at Cook's Fort, Indian Creek, and Wood's Fort, Rich Creek, Monroe County, during most of this period. Often out as Indian spy with Philip Cavender and Nicholas Woodfin. Names the Reverend Jacob Cook, the Reverend Isaac Cook, Asa Ellison, John Ellison, James Ellison Richard Shanklin, James Houchins, Henry Alexander, and John Neely.

Pension was applied for by the soldier in Monroe County, in 1836, but the claim was rejected. A letter from J. L. Edwards to the Pension Office, Department of War, in rejecting this claim and also that of Thomas Steele, gives interesting light on this case and also of many others. Mr. Edwards says: "The claim of William Hutchinson was originally suspended because he had set forth service at variance with all historical facts touching the frontier service in Virginia during the War of the Revolution. He then, and now claims, an actual and continuous service of five or six years in the character of a volunteer in the companies commanded by Captains Wood and Hutchinson. When it is recollected that at that early date in western Virginia during a great part of the year, all the inhabitants were "forted" in order to avoid the dangers of an attack from the Indians, and that even while a part of the settlers were engaged in the clearing and cultivation of their fields, the residue was abroad, scouting and watching the movements of the common enemy, and to give the alarm in case of his approach, it will in some measure account for the error into which William Hutchinson has fallen.

"Every able bodied man was engaged in this manner for several years, but their service was not at that time considered as military, nor is it so regarded at the present. It is true, however, that there were at the period I speak of, regularly embodied corps authorized by the state for the protection of the frontier; and also a corps of spies and rangers were established. The service of the latter generally commenced in the spring, and terminated in the fall of the year. But the service of Mr. Hutchinson seems to have been performed in neither of these corps, as the militia did not serve for years successively, nor was either Captains Wood or Henderson in the regular service.

"It appears from the papers of Jacob Cook and John Ellison that Wood's and Cook's Fort were blockhouses built and owned by these two men for their own, and the safety of its neighboring settlers in times of danger. Having received grants of land from the Crown before the breaking out of the War as an inducement for them to settle upon the frontiers, this was a sort of domestic service to give permanency to their settlements and had no connection whatever with the military operations of the country."

HUTSON (HUDSON), JOHN

Before the Cabell County Court, September 24, 1832, John Hutson or Hudson made oath that he had served in the Revolutionary War and that he was entitled to a pension.

West Virginians in the American Revolution

Assembled and Edited by ROSS B. JOHNSTON

The sources of this material are from the files of the Pension Office at Washington from various county records, from notes of patriotic societies, principally the Daughters of the American Revolution, Sons of the American Revolution, Sons of the Revolution, and from a large miscellaneous group of published and private sources. Corrections and additions to this list will receive the careful attention of the editor.

HUTTON, MOSES (Colonel)

Born in 1734, probably in Philadelphia. Emigrated to Moorefield where he served in the Virginia militia, and later made a settlement in the Tygarts Valley which retains his name as Huttonsville. Among his children was Jonathan, born about June 3, 1769, in the South Branch, who married Mary Trautwein in May, 1790.

HYRE, JACOB

Service—Virginia   Va. No. 23039   No. 7856

Born Hampshire County, Virginia, May 25, 1757; died in Lewis County, Virginia, March 6, 1841, and is buried in Baptist Cemetery, Buckhannon. Enlisted May, 1778, in Hampshire County, and served as a private of militia and Indian spy seven months under Captains Cunningham, Skidmore, George Jackson, Jesse Berry, Lieutenant Bogard, Colonels Hopkins, Striker, Van Meter, Broadhead, and Generals McIntosh and Campbell. Married to Elizabeth Powers August, 1783, in Hardy County, by publication by Parson Powers. Received pension in Lewis County, 1833. Widow, aged 84, in 1845, received pension also. Supporting data filed in their case by John Brake, Robert Lowther, and William Clarke.

ICE, ADAM

In Monongalia County, 1837, Adam Ice filed application for pension. He stated that he had enlisted at the beginning of the Revolution under Colonel Zackquill Morgan. He gave his age as 77 at time of application. Claim was rejected owing to the apparent youth of claimant—about 16 years.

ICENER (ISNER), HENRY

Before the Randolph County Court, November 25, 1811, Henry Icener made oath that he never knew his father to receive any compensation for his services while a soldier under Colonel Armstrong. Pension application of Henry Isner, filed in Randolph County, March 23, 1835, was rejected.

ISNER, THOMAS

On November 1, 1834, Thomas Isner made application for a pension on the grounds of service as an Indian spy in the Revolution. His statement says that he was about 76 years old, and had been raised in Randolph County. He was a spy during the Revolution under Captain Benjamin Wilson. Went from the Tygarts Valley and was stationed at West's Fort for three months. Got no pay nor was he offered any. He was again employed by Captain Wilson for three months. Served on Roaring Creek in that county, with his headquarters at Wilson's Fort. His claim was rejected.

ISRAEL, ISAAC (Captain)

Captain Isaac Israel, who served in the Eighth Virginia Regiment, Continental Line, for three years, was formerly of Berkeley County, Virginia, and later of Green County, Pennsylvania.

JACK, JAMES

Service—Virginia   Tenn. East, No. 4100   No. S. 2644

Enlisted, Berkeley County, Virginia, March, 1777, and served six months under Captains John Van Metre, Swearingen, and Nichol, of the Virginia militia, commanded by Colonels Pendleton, Morrow, Dark, Morgan, and Generals Hand and McIntosh in campaigns against the Shawnee Indians. Applied for pension, aged 75, in Green County, Tennessee, and certificate was issued in 1833.

JACK, JAMES

Enlisted, November 25, 1777, to serve three years, and was a matross in Captain Richard Dorsey's company, First Virginia Artillery, Continental Line, commanded by Colonel Charles Harrison. He received one of the first pensions granted by the newly formed Federal Government, and after his death, the widow was granted the same. He was the grandfather of Mrs. Jesse E. Price, near Smithfield, Wetzel County.

JACKSON, EDWARD (Colonel)

Son of John Jackson and Elizabeth Cummins Jackson. John was born about 1719 in Londonderry, Ireland, moved to London, and in 1748 emigrated to America. He married Elizabeth Cummins in Maryland. The father died in Clarksburg in 1804, aged 84. The mother died in 1825, aged 101.

Edward Jackson was born March 1, 1759, at Moorefield and served in the Revolution. He first married Mary, daughter of David Haddon, October 13, 1783, in Randolph County. She was born May 15, 1764, in New Jersey. To her were born six children. She died April 17, 1796.

Jackson married again October 13, 1799. His second wife was Elizabeth Brake, daughter of John and Elizabeth Netherholt Brake. She was born January 11, 1772, and died August 19, 1835. There were nine children in this family.

Edward Jackson died December 25, 1828, at Jackson's Mill, Lewis County. He built the first mill at the spot which now has the State 4-H Camp for boys and girls. One of the six children of Edward and

Mary Jackson, his first wife, was Jonathan, who married Julia Beckwith Neale. One of their sons, Thomas J. "Stonewall" Jackson, achieved fame as a soldier in the Mexican War but won his way to the very pinnacle of the heights of military genius as a Confederate general during the War between the States.

JACKSON, EDWARD

Born in England in 1742 and died in Harrison County, Virginia, in 1820. Enlisted August 13, 1776, for three years, was transferred in August, 1778, to Captain Marquis Colmes' company, same regiment, and his name last appears on muster roll dated September 8, 1778, with notation "present." Served as a private in Captain John Willis' company, Second Virginia Regiment, commanded successively by Colonel Alex Spottswood and Colonel Christian Febeger.

JACKSON, GEORGE ((Colonel)

After participating in the Indian wars, Jackson served as a soldier during the Revolution. In 1781, he recruited a company to join General George Rogers Clark's expedition against the British in Detroit. The company built canoes, joined the expedition near Fort Pitt, now Pittsburgh, Pennsylvania, and proceeded down the Ohio River to the falls at the present site of Louisville, Kentucky. There the expedition was abandoned and the company returned home by river. Affidavits are filed by Alexander West and Christopher Nutter, who were members of Colonel Jackson's company. The affidavit of William Powers before the Harrison County Court further supports these statements and names Jackson as captain, William White as first lieutenant, Jacob Westfall as second lieutenant, and Hezekiah Davisson as ensign of this company. On August 23, 1787, Jackson qualified before the Harrison County Court as lieutenant colonel of Harrison County.

He married Elizabeth, daughter of Jacob Brake, at Moorefield, November 13, 1776. She was born February 22, 1757, and died March 22, 1812. They had eleven children, as follows: John George, Elizabeth, Catherine, Jacob, Sarah, Prudunce, George Washington, Edward Brake, Mary Webster, William Lowther, and Thomas Jefferson.

He married a second time, December 6, 1814. To this second wife, formerly Mrs. Nancy Richardson Adams, three children were born: Andrew Richardson, Susan Ann, and Sophia. Jackson died in Ohio in 1831, aged 74.

JACKSON, ISAAC

Service—Virginia   Va. No. 18753   No. S. 38072

Enlisted, Botetourt County, Virginia, and served three years as a private under Captain Roby Madison, Twelfth Virginia Regiment, Continental Establishment, commanded by Colonel Woods and General Scott. Fought at Brandywine, Monmouth, and Stony Point. Received pension, aged 78, in Mason County, Virginia, October 10, 1820.

JACKSON, JOHN

Served as a private in the Revolutionary Army and was the great-grandfather of General Thomas J. "Stonewall" Jackson, rated as the greatest military strategist of all time.

John Jackson was born in Londonderry, Ireland, between 1715 and 1719, moved to London, and in 1848 emigrated to America. He married Elizabeth Cummins of English descent in Cecil County, Maryland. They settled in what is now Hardy County, West Virginia, about 1750 and lived there for a time before establishing a home on the Buckhannon River. He died in Clarksburg in 1801-1804, aged 84. Elizabeth Cummins Jackson died at Clarksburg in 1825 at the age of 101.

JACOB, JOHN JEREMIAH (Lieutenant)
Service—Maryland   Va. No. 6801   Bo. W. 11930 and B. L. Wt. 1405

Served four years and three months as lieutenant and paymaster in the Sixth Maryland Regiment, under Colonel Shryock, General Washington, and General Gates, from the summer of 1776 until the fall of 1780. Was in action at Brandywine, Germantown, and Monmouth. Pension granted, Hampshire County, Virginia, 1819. His marriage to Susan J. McDavitt took place at the house of Joseph Cresap, July 4, 1821, with the Reverend Louis Fechtig of the M. E. Church as minister, and is recorded in Allegheny County, Maryland. Pension was also granted the widow and bounty land warrants were issued for two tracts of land.

JACOBS, DAVID

Native of Pennsylvania. Enlisted in the spring of 1777; served as a private in Captain James Black's company, Colonel Malcolm's regiment, and in Captain John Orr's company, Colonel Spencer's regiment, and in quarters seven miles from Morristown; was in the battle of Monmouth where he was wounded by a bayonet in his thigh; was in the battle of Paramus under Major Thomas Byles where Jacobs was taken prisoner and held in New York nine months; was exchanged, and joined his regiment at Stony Point; was transferred and served in Colonel Walter Finney's company, Colonel Richard Humpton's and Walter Stewart's Pennsylvania regiments; was in the battle of Eutaw Springs, was at the capture of Cornwallis, and was discharged in 1783.

During his service he lost the sight of one eye, and the other eye was later affected. He was granted pension, 1818, upon his application in Tyler County, aged 59. He died May 18, 1835. The soldier's wife, Elizabeth, was born October, 1788. Their children were: Jacob, born May 17, 1811; John, born May 22, 1813; and Prudence, born May 29, 1821.

JACOBS, SAMUEL

Before the Wood County Court June 2, 1818, Jacobs testified that he was 87 years old and that he enlisted in the Revolutionary Army under Captain Voss. He served for nine months until he received a wound which disabled his limb and rendered him unfit for military duty. He consequently received his discharge at Philadelphia. His claim for pension as a Revolutionary soldier was approved by the court and forwarded to the War Department.

JAMES, ISAAC
Service—Virginia   Va. No. 23823   No. S. 18053
  Born March 16, 1758, Northumberland County, Virginia, and in the same county enlisted August, 1781, in the company of Captain Kirkpatrick in a Virginia Continental regiment, commanded by Colonel Gaskins, and remained in service nine months. In Hampshire County, Virginia, the soldier applied for pension, which was granted April 9, 1834. Supporting statements were submitted in his behalf by William Welsh and R. Davis.

JARREL, SOLOMON
Service-Virginia   Va. No. 7459   No. S. 38076
  Enlisted, Orange County, Virginia, as a private and served three years under Captain Holt of the First Virginia Regiment, under Colonel Rigson and General Wayne. Fought at Stony Point and Monmouth. He was on the Virginia rolls from late in 1776 until 1779 or 1780. Pension was granted him in Monroe County, March 8, 1819.

JARVIS (JARVICE), FIELD
  Born Westmoreland County, Virginia, April 25, 1756. Resided in Bedford County, Virginia, in 1773 and enlisted in that county in 1776. Resided in Botetourt County, a part of which is now Monroe County, Virginia, in 1781. First service was guarding the lead mines of Wythe County, with the militia under Captain William Loftridge and Lieutenant Stephen Saunders. He was discharged by Colonel Ennis. He volunteered again in 1777 under Captain John Tolbert, Lieutenant Arthur Mosely, and Ensign Edmund Tate and marched to Richmond, Williamsburg and to Little York, then returned to Williamsburg at end of his enlistment and was discharged by Colonel Thompson Mason. In 1779 he was called on by Colonel James Calloway to guard prisoners taken at Tarleton's defeat by Colonel Washington and General Morgan. Pension was granted him in Monroe County, July 5, 1833. Supporting data submitted by Samuel Clark, Hugh Caperton, R. S. Shanklin, and John Holsapple.

JARVIS, JOHN
  Before both Harrison and Lewis County, Virginia, Courts, John Jarvis made application for pension as a Revolutionary soldier. He stated that he had enlisted in the Revolutionary Army under Captain Bennett Mathews, Baltimore County, Maryland, the commander of a rowing galley; that this galley made trips to Norfolk, Portsmouth, Hampton, and later three trips to Little York. He then secured a substitute, later re-enlisted on a French galley commanded by Captain Davy, and then made another trip with Captain Mathews. He enlisted on St. Patricks Day in company with William Miles, James Hughes, John Ellis, Edward Reed, Mitchell Wheeling, Thomas Munhews or Monhon, John, his brother, and John Stephenson.

JENKINS, JOHN
Service—Continental Va.   Ill.-Va., 19018   No. S. 36632 and B. L. Wt. 2174
  Enlisted, Hampshire County, Virginia, January, 1777, and served

until 1783. For a time was private under Captain Bedinger and James Gumm, Virginia Continental Line, and First Regiment of Light Dragoons, under Colonels James Posey and Anthony White, and General Wayne. Was at Camden, Guilford Courthouse, Geeche River, and at surprise of General Wayne at the Widow Gibbons. Discharged by Major John Swan at Ebenezer, Georgia, at end of war. At age of 65 applied for pension, which was granted in Hardy County, Virginia, July, 1823. Supporting data submitted by John Henis, Van C. Dawson, Drusilla Dawson, Leonard Bowers, Joseph A. Kee, and John Hopewell. Transferred to Illinois in 1839.

JENKINS, REUBEN

Born Westmoreland County, Virginia, 1759, and there enlisted in 1777 under Captains Sanford and Harper, Colonels Parker and Campbell, and Major Austin. Took part in the siege and capture of Yorktown and saw other service. Applied for pension November 30, 1833, Preston County, Virginia. Supporting claims presented by Thomas Hobbs and Moses Beavers. Claim was rejected.

JENNINGS, JOHN
Service—Virginia   Va. No. 31016   No. S. 13529

Born in England in 1753. At the outbreak of the Revolution resided in Berkeley County, Virginia, where he enlisted October, 1780, under Captain Hunter in the Virginia Line under Colonel Morgan. Participated in the siege of Yorktown and the capture of Lord Cornwallis. Removed to Fayette County, Pennsylvania, after the Revolution, and there applied for a pension which was granted March 14, 1837. He was transferred to Preston County, Virginia, in 1841. Supporting data submitted by Philip Langstreth, John Delany, and William Shinnsberger.

JOHNSON, ANDREW
Service—New Jersey-Penna.   Va. No. 23507   No. S. 15905

Born Germantown, Pennsylvania, in the fall of 1758; died March 4, 1846. Enlisted Buck County Pennsylvania, in the summer of 1776, and saw service under Captains Gibson, Stokes, Bentley, Ross, Cadwallader, Bulls, Smallwood, and Generals Washington and Smallwood. In 1791, saw service in the Indian wars under Captains Kerby, Slough and Hamilton, enlisting in this service from New Brunswick, New Jersey.

His wife was Elizabeth Green, who was captured by the Indians and held prisoner for years. The names of their children were: Rebecca Johnson Castle, Nancy Ann Johnson Small, Sarah, Isaac, and Jesse.

Pension was granted the soldier in 1834 while living in Preston County. Then his service was disputed and pay was suspended for 12 or 15 years, but was reinstated in 1846 through the efforts of William G. Brown. Supporting data was submitted by James Carroll, Philip Martin, Thomas Squires, Edmonson Moore, James Brown, John Miller, Henry Miller, John Mason, Robert Hawthorne, and W. G. Payne.

JOHNSON, BENJAMIN
Service—Maryland   Va. No. 26396   No. 27761

Enlisted, Charles County, Maryland, June 10, 1778, and served as private and fifer under Captain Winchester in the Third Maryland Regiment, commanded by Colonel Guess and General Smallwood. Took part in the Battle of Princeton.

Kanawha County has the record of the marriage, August 8, 1829, of Benjamin Johnson and Elizabeth Price (McGraw) by James Callahan and the Reverend Whitten, of Loop Creek, Fayette County. Soldier received pension in Fayette County in 1832, at age of 76. His widow, aged 75, applied for and received a pension December 5, 1878, and died January 22, 1881.

JOHNSON, BENJAMIN   No. 5564

Pension application of Benjamin Johnson was filed in Kanawha County, August 13, 1833, and was supported by statements of Andrew Donnally and George W. Summers. His claim, however, was rejected on the grounds: "First, that his alleged service in collecting beeves for the Army is not considered military service and is, of course, inadmissible; and secondly, that the last named term does not amount to six months."

JOHNSON, BENJAMIN (REBECCA)   No. 5562

Application of Rebecca Johnson, widow of Benjamin Johnson, for a pension as a widow of a Revolutionary soldier, was filed in Mason County, Virginia, May 26, 1858, at which time she was 88 years old. Benjamin and Rebecca Johnson had married February 15, 1794, and the soldier had died January 29, 1834. Supporting claims were made by William McCallister, William Bitgood, Alfred Brown, Thomas Summers, John Harmon, and Charles I. Amos. Although evidence was available that a Benjamin Johnson had seen service as an infantryman, and again as a sergeant of infantry, the claim was rejected awaiting further proof.

JOHNSON, GEORGE

Service—Virginia   Va. No. 4120   No. S. 38088

Enlisted, Martinsburg, Berkeley County, Virginia, February, 1776, and remained in service until 1781. Served as a private under Captains George Wayler and Griffin, Fourth Virginia Regiment, commanded by Colonel Neville. Took part in engagements at Germantown, Monmouth, Trenton, and Yorktown. Received pension, November 4, 1818, Jefferson County, Virginia, at which time he was 68 years old. Supporting data submitted by Major Abram Davenport.

JOHNSON, ROBERT

Born in New Jersey, 1744, son of Judith and Garrett Johnson; came with ten brothers and sisters to make his home east of Meadowville, Barbour County, about 1788, and died March 16, 1831. Garrett Johnson was the son of Rutger Janson or Johnson and Annetje Gerritt's, who lived in Somerset County, New Jersey. Robert Johnson lived in Hopewell, New Jersey, at the outbreak of the Revolution, saw service as a private in that war, and was discharged from service, March 19, 1781.

He married in Henterdox County, New Jersey, Mary Vannoy, born, 1749, and died, December 1, 1827. Their children were: Garrett, married

WEST VIRGINIANS IN THE REVOLUTION 151

Mary, daughter of James England; Isaac, married Hannah, daughter of James Poling; Benjamin; Francis (Frank), married Elizabeth England; Rachel, married Ebenezer Kelley; John, married Elizabeth, daughter of Peter Poland; William, married Catherine, daughter of Christopher Hovatter; Robert, married Elizabeth, daughter of John Hoffman; Rebecca, married William Hoff; Levi, married Rebecca, daughter of William McMillan.

JOHNSON, THOMAS
Served in Captain Drake's company. In 1781, he was with Colonel Drake's Berkeley and Hampshire regiment at the siege of Yorktown. He was living in Shepherdstown in 1781.

JOHNSON, THOMAS
Before the Greenbrier County Court in 1850, Mathew Mattics proved to the satisfaction of the court that Thomas Johnson, deceased, was the individual who was entitled to a pension from the United States Government under the Act of June 7, 1832.

JOHNSON, WILLIAM
Born on the Eastern Shore of Virginia, 1755, and enlisted in the Revolutionary Army in Augusta or Bath County, Virginia. He was on the tax books of Kanawha County in 1802, and died, December 22, 1805. His wife, Amy, was born between 1750 and 1760 and died December 23, 1837. Their children were: the Reverend John Johnson, born 1777, died 1861; married, June, 1802, Elizabeth Sims, died 1842; married, February 19, 1846, Mrs. Polly Peters Windsor; William Johnson, Jr., married, October 15, 1814, Nancy Ann Lewis; Polly, married, April 23, 1810, Benjamin Darlington; James, married, April 29, 1815, Elizabeth Miller; Nelson, married, 1813, Nancy Murphy; Amy, married, November 16, 1816, Turley Foster, of Nimrod; Elizabeth, married, March 12, 1822, Preysley Foster of Nimrod; Nancy, married, January 11, 1815, Peyton Foster of Nimrod.

JOHNSTON (JOHNSON), JOHN
Service—Virginia   Va. No. 16585   No. S. 8763
Born in Ireland in 1732. Enlisted in Berkeley County, Virginia, under Captain Lyle in the Virginia Line under command of Major Scott, Colonel Morrow, and General McIntosh, and took part in McIntosh's campaign and the Indian wars. Pension certificate was issued to the soldier in Morgan County, September 5, 1833. Supporting data was submitted by M. Pentony, W. Neely, and M. Roony.

JOHNSTON, RICHARD
Service—Virginia   Va. No. 12458   No. S. 38873
Resided before the Revolution in Pennsylvania and Virginia. Enlisted at Valley Forge, Pennsylvania, in 1777 and served until 1781 as a private under Captain Wells in the Fifteenth Pennsylvania Regiment, commanded by Colonels Russell and Wallace, and Generals Wayne, Lafayette, Wolford, and Washington. Saw service at Monmouth, Stony Point, and Charleston. Pension certificate issued July 9, 1819, Monongalia County, Virginia.

JOHNSTON, ROBERT

Enlisted, Lancaster County, Pennsylvania, in 1780 and served until 1783 as a private under Captain Turnbath, Twelfth Pennsylvania Regiment, under Colonel Proctor. Received pension, Frederick County, Virginia, June 30, 1819. (Residence in West Virginia is uncertain.)

JOHNSTONE (JOHNSTON or JOHNSON), PETER
Service—Pennsylvania   Certificate No. 938

Enlisted under Captain John Wilson, Lancaster County, Pennsylvania, in the Eighth Pennsylvania Regiment, in 1776 under Colonel Broadhead and Lieutenant Colonel Stephen Bayard. In pension application filed in Monongalia County, Virginia, he says that he got permission from his captain, 1777, to go to North Carolina where he remained until 1779; then rejoined his command which had returned to Fort Pitt after serving on the eastern battle front.

Continued to make his headquarters at Fort Pitt until his discharge in 1783 as a corporal. He served with Captain Sam Brady and Captain John Clark in the two companies that were given special duty there under Lieutenant Colonel Bayard. These men, apparently picked riflemen, some of whom had served with Colonel Daniel Morgan's Riflemen, ranged the frontier from Fort Pitt and Fort McIntosh to Fort Henry, Wheeling, and other points on the frontier. His oldest daughter, says family tradition, was born in a blockhouse, possibly at Fort Pitt.

Johnstone appeared in Harrison County, about 1788 and lived there until his death, September 6, 1840, aged 88. He had been a pensioner since 1829. He was first married to Eleanor (or Nelly) Peters. The marriage bonds of all five children: Mary (Hall), Margaret (Current), Abraham, John, and Robert, are filed at Clarksburg, his signature being "Johnstone" in every case. He was the ferryman on the Tygart Valley north of Grafton, was one of the commissioners who established Pruntytown, first county seat of Taylor County, and was High Sheriff of Harrison County, 1820-1822. His second wife was Susannah Armstrong, a widow.

JONES, BERRYMAN
Service—Virginia   Va. No. 16395   No. S. 5632

Born Amherst County, Virginia, 1757. Enlisted in 1781 in the Revolutionary Army in Augusta County, Virginia, under Captain Brown in unit commanded by Colonel Cameron. Served at Richmond and Jamestown. Then substituted for his brother, Valentine Jones, and marched to Carolina in pursuit of Cornwallis, through Charlottesville, Williamsburg, Salisbury, Catalia, Broad River, thence to Cowpens. Detailed to march back to Salisbury with prisoners. On next "tour" marched against the Indians in the Greenbrier and Monongahela Valleys under Captain John McKenzie. Took part in siege and capture of Yorktown, and later helped guard prisoners at Winchester.

Pension granted soldier for eighteen months service August 5, 1833, Greenbrier County, Virginia. Supporting data filed by Samuel Sams, Samuel Clark, Mark H. Goshen, and the Rev. John McElhenney.

JONES, HARRISON
Received a pension in Berkeley County, Virginia, as a private in the Virginia Line during the Revolution. Died after 1835.

JONES, HENRY
Service—Virginia   Va. No. 23581   No. W. 4249

Born December 7, 1751, King George County, Virginia. Died, February 6, 1838. Enlisted in the Revolution, August 20, 1775, in Fauquier County, and was honorably discharged July 10, 1781. Served seven months as a private under Captain Prickett or Pickett, Ensign Withers, and Lieutenant Marshall in Virginia Regiment commanded by Colonels Taliaferro and Stephens.

Pension granted soldier in Hardy County, February 28, 1834. Supporting data filed by William Harr and Christian Goodnight. Married, September 17, 1776. Wife's name was Rachel. Widow applied for pension, March 12, 1840, aged 82, and certificate was issued following year.

JONES, JAMES
Service—Virginia   Va. No. 1912   No. W. 17917

Born, Prince William County November 16, 1760, son of Peter and Elizabeth Jones; died, March 16, 1849. By publication, October 27, 1781, in Fauquier County, married Mary, daughter of William and Susanna Leach. She was born, August 10, 1763. Their children were: William, born, December 6, 1782; Samuel, born, March 2, 1784. Soldier enlisted, August 16, 1777, under Captain Elias Edmonds in the Second Virginia Artillery Regiment, commanded by Colonel Thomas Marshall. He served his full period of three years and left the service in August, 1780, receiving his discharge at Richmond. He was at Greenville, North Carolina, and at Hillsborough at the time of General Gates' defeat.

Soldier received pension, Monroe County, Virginia, 1832. Widow received pension, January 7, 1850, which was later suspended. Supporting data filed by Lieutenant Colonel Elias Edmonds. In his pension declaration in Monroe County he says that Chief Justice Marshall can prove his claim.

JONES, JACOB (Ensign)
Served as an ensign in the rangers of West Moreland County, Pennsylvania, and Monongalia County, Virginia. For a time was a member of Captain Nicholas Shinn's company. Pennsylvania archives show that he received payment for at least four expeditions and also "depreciation pay" as a Continental Army soldier in Pennsylvania. Other records indicate that he was considered a part of the military quota from Virginia and received depreciation pay also in Richmond for the War.

Born, 1732, in New Jersey and died in 1829, near Khottsville, now Taylor County. In Burlington County, New Jersey, September 28, 1763, married Dinah Staunton or Stanton, born at Egg Harbor, New Jersey. Their children were: Mary, 1764; John, 1766; Benjamin, 1768; Samuel, 1772; William, 1774; Jacob, Jr., 1775; Rebecca; Martha. Jacob and Dinah Jones migrated from New Jersey first to Loudon County, Virginia, and about 1769 came into the Monongahela Valley. In 1771, they settled on Dunkard Creek in West Augusta County, near the Mason and Dixon Line, north of Pentress, now in Monongalia County. Dinah Staunton Jones, who died in 1829 three weeks before her husband, was the daughter of John Staunton and Dinah Gale, who were married at Burlington, New Jersey, October 6, 1732.

There is also found among New Jersey wills that of Samuel Gale (also spelled Galee, Gaill, Geall, Gail, and Gaile) of Great Egg Harbor, Gloucester County, New Jersey, dated October, 1720, and proved, December 25, 1730, in which is mentioned his wife, Mary, and daughters Dinah and Sarah, evidently a continuation of the above line of descent.

West Virginians in the American Revolution

Assembled and Edited by ROSS B. JOHNSTON

The sources of this material are from the files of the Pension Office at Washington, from various county records, from notes of patriotic societies, principally the Daughters of the American Revolution, Sons of the American Revolution, Sons of the Revolution, and from a large miscellaneous group of published and private sources. Corrections and additions to this list will receive the careful attention of the editor.

JONES, JOHN

Statements filed in Kanawha County, Virginia, January 15, 1833, show that John Jones, a Revolutionary soldier, was born, February 2, 1756. In 1773, he and two others settled on the Great Kanawha and next spring were driven back to Muddy Creek, Greenbrier County, by the Indians. They built a fort there by order of Captain Mathew Arbuckle, and were subsequently in the battle of Point Pleasant. In the middle of September, 1776, he enlisted as a regular soldier under Captain Arbuckle, First Lieutenant Andrew Wallace, Second Lieutenant William Wood, and Ensign John Gallagher. Served at Point Pleasant to the close of 1777. The garrison there was reinforced by Botetourt men under Captain McKee, Lieutenants William and John Moore, and Ensign James Gilmer. An attack by the Indians on Fort Randolph there was repulsed, after which the savages set out against the Greenbrier settlements. Two bold and daring soldiers, dressed in Indian costume, made their way from Point Pleasant to warn the Greenbrier Valley settlers, particularly Fort Donnally, of the approaching Indians.

Jones was employed as an Indian scout in 1778 and 1779 over a distance of 60 to 70 miles west of the inhabited section of the country to watch the movements of the Indians. William and Leonard Morris and John Patterson were scouts with him. The statement of Jones also mentions William Arbuckle, who was then at Point Pleasant.

JONES, JOSHUA
 Service—Pennsylvania   Va. No. 2362   No. S. 5628
Born, Bucks County, Pennsylvania, August, 1760. Resided in Philadelphia County, Pennsylvania, in 1776, where he enlisted as a private under Captains Smith, Gray, Hart, Bloom, and Hines, Fourth Pennsylvania Regiment, under Colonel Butler and General Wayne. Served nearly eighteen months at various military stations. Pension certificate issued to him in Harrison County, Virginia, November 24, 1832, and continued to October 24, 1843, probably the date of his death.

JONES, RICHARD
Service—Continental Pennsylvania   Va. No. 5986   No. S. 38081

Enlisted, 1775, at York, Pennsylvania, in Captain Hops' company of the First Regiment of Guards, commanded by Colonel Barclay or Colonel Hartley. Took part in the battles of Brandywine, Germantown, and Paoli, and remained in service three years. Received pension in Harrison County, 1818, and died September 1, 1822. His wife was aged 75 in 1820. Two children, apparently grandchildren, Sally, 10, and Mary Beck, 15, are also named.

JONES, RICHARD LORD

Before the Cabell County court, June 26, 1827, Richard Lord Jones made affidavit that he had served as a Revolutionary soldier and that he was entitled to a pension.

JONES, SAMUEL Z. (Lieutenant)
Service—Pennsylvania   Va. No. 16896   No. S. 18474

Born, Gloucester County, New Jersey, January 30, 1759. Resided at the outbreak of the Revolution in Cumberland County, Pennsylvania. In 1782 or 1783 moved to Philadelphia, and came from Philadelphia to Virginia in 1811; resided in Lewis County, Virginia, in 1832, and died there, April 16, 1846. He is buried on the Albert Hardman farm near Mt. Hebron.

Enlisted, December, 1776; served seventeen months as a private, and eleven months as a lieutenant. Substituted for John Smith for two months. Commissioned as lieutenant in July, 1778, under Captain Dimsey and General Potter after the Wyoming massacre. Mentions the killing of Captain Sam Brady by the Indians. The Indians also killed the wife and son of John Smith and tomahawked and scalped the daughter, but she survived. Mentions the killing near Freeland's Fort of Captain Boone, James Watt, Green, Little, and others by the savages, including John McCarl and James Story. Jones received two wounds, one in the thigh and the other in the arm.

Received pension, Lewis County, Virginia, October 12, 1833, but in 1842 his pension seems to have been questioned and suspended. Supporting data submitted by David Sleeth, Salathiel Collins, and John Byrne. Members of his family were: Mrs. Hannah Jones McWhorter, Mrs. Mary Simms, Mrs. Elizabeth Powers, William Jones (dead), Samuel Jones (dead).

JONES, THOMAS
Service—Virginia   Va. No. 16466   No. W. 7901

Born, Amherst County, Virginia, 1748, and died August 26, 1839. Enlisted, Henrico County, Virginia, 1777 or 1778, and served two years as a private of cavalry under Captains Sam Scott and Dooling, Virginia Line, Continental Establishment, commanded by Major Taylor, on campaigns in North and South Carolina, and Georgia. Pension certificates issued to soldier and widow in Greenbrier County, 1818,

1833, and reissued in 1844. Supporting data submitted by Joseph and John Alderson. Marriage of Thomas Jones and Lavinia Thomas took place in Greenbrier County, Virginia, August 19, 1789, with the Reverend John Alderson officiating.

KEARNEY, EDWARD
Service—Delaware   Va. No. 12778   No. S. 15495

Born, Kent County, Delaware, May 10, 1753, and there enlisted in the Revolutionary Army, August 1, 1777 and was discharged from his last period of service in 1783. He served as a private eighteen months under Captains Raymond, Manliff, Combufoot, Snow, and Cornish in Delaware Line regiment, commanded by Colonel West. Was in the battle of Smyrna Landing.

The soldier was granted a pension in Ohio County, Virginia, May 22, 1833, which was dropped from the roll, July 4, 1835. Supporting data was filed by Reverend George Robinson, John Hawslet, and Mrs. Ann Biggs, a daughter. Captains William Clark and Curry are mentioned in connection with an appeal of this case which was still before the Federal Government June 10, 1872, at which time a decision was rendered. See letter on file in case of Samuel Harbert, No. 16646. No evidence of restoration.

KEARN, MICHAEL

The grave of Michael Kearn, a veteran of the Revolutionary War, who died in 1778, is near the site of Kearn's Fort, Arch Street, Morgantown, Monongalia County.

KEARSLEY, JOHN

Volunteered in Captain William Morgan's company. In 1780, accompanied George M. Bedinger to South Carolina with supplies for the troops there. After the war, he resided in Shepherdstown.

KEISKELL, ADAM (Captain)

Adam Keiskell, of Hampshire County, was recommended for a captaincy in the militia of Frederick County, in April, 1779, and qualified later. He was one of General Daniel Morgan's company of sharpshooters who participated in the capture of Quebec when the French Army under General Montcalm surrendered to the forces of General Wolfe.

KEITER, GEORGE

George Keiter, who served as a soldier in the Revolutionary Army, was born in Hampshire County, in 1757, enlisted in the army there, and died on November 26, 1850.

KELLER, CONRAD

Before the Monroe County, Virginia, court, Conrad Keller testified that he enlisted in the Revolutionary Army in Shenandoah County, in the year 1776 or 1777, for three years, and that he served as a waiting man to General Muhlenberg. He was discharged by General Muhlenberg at the end of his enlistment period, was drafted into the Shenandoah County militia for two months in 1781 or 1782, marched to Winchester under Captain Downy, and was stationed for a time at Fort Frederick.

KELLER, GEORGE
Service—Virginia   Va. No. 12571   No. S. 5649

Born, Stovers Town, Shenandoah County, April 19, 1758. Enlisted at Staunton, Augusta County, Virginia, July, 1779, and served nearly two years as a private under Captains Christee, Thompson, Rankin, in commands of Colonels Mathews and Morgan. Took part in engagements at Cowpens, Jamestown, Portsmouth, and Yorktown. Pension certificate was issued to him in Monongalia County, Virginia, May 10, 1833, which was reduced in 1836. Supporting data filed in his behalf by Henry Whiteman, Francis Billingslea, and William Haymond. He also mentions Captains Evans, Triplett, Tait, and Colonels Howard, Williams, Lee, and Dudley.

KELLY, WILLIAM (Captain)

An official order of the executive department of the State of Virginia, November 15, 1838, declared that John Kelly, the heir of William Kelly, was allowed land bounty for the latter's services as a captain in the Continental Line for eight years and four months. Warrant No. 8669 was issued for 5777 acres of land.

He was second lieutenant of Shepherd's company of Virginia riflemen, July 9, 1776; taken prisoner at Fort Washington, November 16, 1776; captain of Hartley's Regiment, January 16, 1777. Captain Kelly died in Berkeley County, some time prior to September 9, 1777, as is shown by his will of that date, recorded in the Berkeley County courthouse under date of September 16, 1777. (This leaves unexplained the fact that he received bounty lands for services that extended to the close of the war.)

KERBY (KIRBY), WILLIAM
Service—Virginia   Va. No. 7091   No. W. 7998 and B. L. Wt. 17717

Enlisted, Hanover County, Virginia, 1779, and served eighteen months as a private under Captain Richardson and Stribling in Colonel Blueford's Regiment. Took part in the battles of Guilford Courthouse, Camden, the Siege of Ninety-Six, and Eutaw Springs.

Applied for pension, aged 69, Albemarle County, Virginia, which was issued, 1819. Died, August 17, 1848. Married before 1800 to Elizabeth McDaniels, born near Alta Vista in 1769. She received a widow's pension in 1851. In 1821, their children were: Nancy, 12; Martin, 10; Minor, 5. (Uncertain as to West Virginia residence.)

KERNEY (KEARNEY), JAMES

Enlisted in Captain Hugh Stephenson's company in 1775, and was

WEST VIRGINIANS IN THE REVOLUTION

elected one of its corporals. Reenlisted in one of the companies raised in Berkeley County, in 1776. He lived near Kearneysville which took its name from this family. He died in 1821.

KERNEY, JOHN (Captain)

By order of the State of Virginia, October 19, 1830, the heirs of John Kerney were allowed land bounty for service as a captain in the Virginia State Line under Colonel Joseph Crockett from 1778 to 1782. In Berkeley County, Virginia, November 30, 1830, it was certified that Captain Kerney had died intestate, leaving the following heirs: Robert, John, Jane, wife of James Blue; Elizabeth, wife of Henry Muier; Susan, wife of George St. Auben; Mehala, wife of Solomon Blue; James B., Elliott, and Thomas. Of these children, Robert, John, and James were dead, intestate; John and James B. without children; Robert left a widow, who married Thomas Patton; his children were: John, William, and Eldigert, and Eliza, wife of David Seibert. Elliott and James Kerney were living in White County, Illinois.

KESTER, JOSEPH
Service—Virginia   Va. No. 2133   No. S. 2690

Before the Harrison County court, Joseph Kester made two affidavits for pension as a Revolutionary soldier, showing he was born in Pennsylvania but that at the age of nine years his parents had moved to Brock's Gap, Virginia. He was aged 79 in 1832. He served nine months as a private under Captains Biddle and Huston in a Virginia regiment commanded by Major Hamilton, Colonels Nalls and Harris, as a substitute for his father, Conrad Kester. Pension was granted in Harrison County, in 1832 and 1835. Pensioner removed to Ohio in 1837.

KETTERMAN, DANIEL
Service—Virginia   Va. No. 23582   No. S. 15908

Born in Berks County, Pennsylvania, 1762. Enlisted, June 15, 1781, in Hampshire County, Virginia, under Captain James Cunningham and Tabb in Virginia regiment commanded by Colonels Darke and Dabney, and was engaged in guarding prisoners. On April 1, 1782, reenlisted as a substitute for Adam Harper for a period of three months, in unit commanded by Colonel DeFabough. Supporting data submitted by Jacob Ketterman and John Sites. Pension granted in Hardy County, February 28, 1836.

KEYS, JOHN

Enlisted in Captain Stephenson's company, was taken ill on the march to Boston, and left near Reading but rejoined his comrades later at Roxbury Camp. His home was at Keyes Ferry on the Shenandoah.

KEYS, WILLIAM
Service—Virginia   Va. No. 23788   No. S. 18070

Born, Prince William County, Virginia, there enlisted and served six months under Captains Valentine, Peyton and Hedge in Colonel Ewell's Virginia regiment. The soldier moved to Harrison County, Virginia, in 1819 and there applied for a pension which was granted April 4, 1834, after he had died. Supporting data was submitted in his case by William Harden and W. Copin.

KEYSER (KAYSER), JACOB (Sergeant)
Service—Continental, Maryland   Va. No. 12584   No. W. 7952

Enlisted, February 15, 1779, in Fredericktown, Maryland, in the company commanded by Captain Baltzer of the German battalion, commanded by Colonel Weltner. This unit was afterwards attached to General Guest's Brigade of the Maryland Line, and formed the Second Maryland Regiment, under command of Colonel Adams. He served in this unit until December, 1782, when he was discharged from service at Ponpon in South Carolina. He was in several engagements between Wyoming and Niagara in Pennsylvania. He afterwards served in the southern army and was at the capture of Cornwallis.

Keyser, born in 1738, was married, October 11, 1785, in Leesburgh, Virginia, to Pamela Thompson, born in 1764. Keyser died February 6, 1834, and his widow died November 5, 1844. The soldier received pension in Harrison County in 1819 which was discontinued in 1820. The widow received pension in 1839. There was a family of eight children, according to deposition of Ann Cunningham in 1838. A son, Joseph, aged 14, was mentioned in 1818. The names of S. P. Moore, Joseph Johnson, Jedediah Waldo, Samuel Washington, W. H. Rodgers, T. J. Tyson, A. W. Britton, and William Campbell are mentioned in declaration filed in Harrison County.

KIBLER, JOHN
Service—Maryland   No. 3949   No. W. 5014 and B.L.Wt. 30753

Enlisted, Hagerstown, Maryland, in 1779 and served three years as a private in the company of Captain Heyser, Maryland Regiment commanded by Colonel Housecker. Fought at Princeton, Trenton, Monmouth, Bordentown. Both soldier and widow received pension. Bounty land warrant for 160 acres was also granted.

Soldier's first wife was Mary Manford to whom he was married, April 9, 1781. His second wife was Mary Rife, whom he married in 1795-96. Their children's ages in 1820 were: John, 24; William, 22; Margaret, 19; Elizabeth, 17; George, 12; Nancy, 9; Mary Ann, 4. At that time soldier was aged 75 and his wife 46. (The West Virginia residence of this soldier is uncertain.)

KIDLINGER, MICHAEL

The grave of Michael Kidlinger, a soldier in the Revolutionary War, who died in 1778, is in the Price Memorial Cemetery near Oliver Church, Monongalia County.

KILBRETH, JOSEPH

Joseph Kilbreth made application for pension before the Harrison

County Court, May 20, 1818. He declared that he enlisted in New Orleans in the marine company commanded by Captain William Peebles of the United States Navy and served two years as a marine in the frigate *Boston* and the ship *Morris* of Philadelphia. He was discharged at Boston, Massachusetts. He re-enlisted there in the company under Captain Larned and served two years and a half until the close of the war. He was discharged from service in the State of New York. He was in the Battle of King's Bridge, New York, and in other engagements.

KINCAID, JOHN
Service—Virginia   Va. 23913   No. S. 19367

Born, March 10, 1760, Amherst County, Virginia. Enlisted, February, 1781, in Greenbrier County, Virginia, and served ten months as a private under Captain John Henderson, Captain Arch Woods and Major Andrew Hamilton against the Indians and Tories. His application for pension was granted in 1834. Supporting affidavits were filed by James Lickens, Joseph Skaggs, and John Patterson. (In some records, this man's case was confused with another Kincaid.)

KINCHELOE, DANIEL

The grave of Daniel Kincheloe, understood to have been a soldier in the Revolution, is on the slope across the road from the Wood County Infirmary. He came to Wood from Harrison County in 1796-97 and died there in 1834.

KINKEAD, THOMAS
Service—Virginia   Va. No. 4122   No. S. 5997

Enlisted, Augusta County, Virginia, 1780 and 1781, and served as a private nine months under Captains Tate, Guinn, and Brown in Colonel Campbell's militia regiment, under Colonel Washington, and Generals Morgan and Green. Fought at Cowpens, Guilford Courthouse, and James Town. Pension granted in Pendleton County, Virginia, 1833. Supporting data filed by Robert Thompson, Robert Gittington, Samuel Pullin, and William McCoy.

KINNISON, CHARLES and EDWARD

Charles and Edward Kinnison were in the Revolutionary Army from Culpeper County, Virginia. They lived near Capon Springs a few miles from Winchester. They also lived in Pocahontas County, Virginia, for a time.

KINNISON, JACOB

Before the Pocahontas County court in 1832 and again in 1833, Jacob Kinnison made application for pension as a soldier in the Revolutionary War. He was aged 75 in 1832. He volunteered under Captain Arbuckle in March, 1777, at which time he lived in the Little Levels of Greenbrier County. He was marched under Ensign John Williams to Point Pleasant where he served in the border defense ten months under Captain Arbuckle, Ensign Williams and Ensign James Gilmer. There he was discharged by General Hand, but before he left the "Point" remembers the coming of seven hundred soldiers under Colonel Dickinson and Colonel Skilleron.

In 1779, he entered service as an Indian spy on Elk, Greenbrier and Tygarts Valley rivers under command of Captain John Cook. His companion, John Bridger, was killed by the Indians the next spring. His claim was supported by George G. Brooke, John Gilleland, John Bradshaw, and Thomas Hill.

KIRBY, PATRICK

In April, 1778, the Berkeley County, Virginia, court ordered that aid be given the wife of Patrick Kirby, who had been a soldier in the Continental Army.

KITTLE, ABRAHAM

Born, 1735, probably in New Jersey. Wife's name, Mary. Settled in Randolph County as early as 1782. Served in the Continental Army in New Jersey. Died about 1816 and is buried in the Collett Cemetery four miles below Beverly. His children were: Jacob, born in New Jersey; Richard, Abraham, Jr., married a daughter of John Chenoweth first and then took as his second wife, Mary Scott; George, Daniel, a daughter who married Phineas Wells; a daughter who married Henry Petro; a daughter, Ingra, who married David Henderson; a daughter who married Abraham Teter.

Before the Randolph County court, November 25, 1811, Richard Kittle testified that he never knew his father, Abraham Kittle, to receive any land for his services under General Clark against the Indians.

KITTLE, JACOB

Service—Pennsylvania   Va. No. 16657   No. S. 13630

Born in Sussex County, New Jersey, 1757, son of Abraham and Mary Kittle. Enlisted in Northampton County, Pennsylvania, February 19, 1776, across the New Jersey line. Served fourteen months in Third Battalion of Pennsylvania Brigade under Captains Boyles, Conkle, Hoover, Shiner, and Colonels Cadwallader, Miller, Stroud, Major Baker, and General Lacey. Pension certificates were issued in Randolph County in 1833 and 1835. Supporting data submitted by Benjamin Dolbear, Arch Earl, William Martiny, Michael See, Isaac Baker, and the Reverend Collett and Rowan.

KNIGHT, CHRISTOPHER

The claim of Christopher Knight for a Revolutionary War pension, which was filed in Harrison County, was rejected.

KNIGHT, JAMES

On motion of James Knight, Jr., and Rebecca Williams, formerly Rebecca Knight, before the Greenbrier County court, 1832, it was certified to the Department of War that it had been established that they were the children and sole heirs of James Knight, Sr., who was a regularly enlisted soldier of the Revolutionary War.

KNIGHT, PETER
Service—Virginia   Va. No. 1909   No. S. 5660

Born, Stafford County, Virginia, April 5, 1760. Served six months as a private under Captain Phillips in the Virginia militia. Pension granted the soldier in Harrison County, November 13, 1832. Supporting data filed by John Latham and Christopher Knight.

KROSEN (KROESNER), ISAAC
Service—Virginia   No. S. 5663

Served eighteen months as a private soldier and sergeant in the Virginia Line under Captain Morgan and Colonel Campbell, after enlisting December, 1780. Was seen by another soldier, Henry Bedinger, in the spring of 1781 at Fredericksburg, Virginia, as he was marching south. After Cornwallis' surrender was stationed at Winchester to guard prisoners until discharged. Received pension in 1833, apparently in Berkeley County, Virginia.

KUMP (CUMP), HENRY
Service—Virginia   Va. No. 23579   No. S. 15792

Born, 1757. Enlisted in Hampshire County, and served as a private nine months in company of Captains Stump and James Parsons in the Virginia Line regiments under General Wayne. He served from 1781 to 1782. His first service was apparently a three months' "tour" as a substitute for George Sly. He was then drafted for three months and in January, 1782, enlisted under Captain James Eaton. He was granted a pension in Hampshire County in 1834. His claims were supported by affidavits of Elisha Gardner, Philip Kline, and Daniel Loy.

LAIDLEY, THOMAS (Captain)
Service—Pennsylvania Sea Service   Va. No. 23468   No. S. 15596

Born, Argyleshire, Scotland, January 1, 1756. Died, March 17, 1838. Married Sarah Osborne before emigrating to America in 1774. Lived for a time in Philadelphia, Mt. Holley, New Jersey, Morgantown, Monongalia County, and then moved to Cabell County, to be with his son, John Laidley.

In March, 1776, enlisted as a private in the First Independent Rifle Company of Pennsylvania, John Doyle, Captain, and Samuel Brady, Lieutenant. In March, 1777, enlisted under Captain William Lysle, commander of the boat *Resolution* of the Pennsylvania fleet under Commander John Hazelwood, then lying at Fort Mifflin in the Delaware, and served as a gunner. He then received commission as captain of the *Resolution*. Continued there until British captured Fort Mifflin and Red Banks, November 15, 1777. Served as hospital steward from that time until November, 1778, when he was discharged. Received pension,

1834, Cabell County. Supporting data filed by William Paine and Stephen Spurlock.

LANGFITT (LANGFITTE), FRANCIS
Service—Continental Pennsylvania   Va. No. 19665   No. S. 38131

Enlisted, 1777, in the Eleventh Virginia Regiment. In 1780, enlisted for a second term and served in the Fourth Virginia Regiment of Light Dragoons until honorably discharged at Colchester, Connecticut, May, 1782. Was under Captains Doris, Craigs, and Gray, and Lieutenant Colonel Walton Moyland. Received pension in Wood County, Virginia, 1826, at which time the soldier was 65 years years old, his wife, Emily, 65, and a daughter, Nancy Glasscock, 30. Supporting data was filed in their behalf by John Stone, Baily Rice, Mary Foley, John J. Johnson, and John T. Langfitt. He was in the actions at York Island, White Plains, Princeton, Germantown, Trenton, Brandywine, and Monmouth.

LARKIN, ANTHONY
Enlisted as a private in Captain Shepherd's company of riflemen, and was killed, September 15, 1776.

LARKINS, JAMES
Service—Virginia   Va. No. 6010   No. S. 38130

Enlisted in Augusta County, Virginia, and served two years as a private under Captain Bowser in the Twelfth Virginia Regiment commanded by Colonel Neville and General Scott. Was in battle of Germantown. Received pension at age of 66 in Monroe County, Virginia, July 29, 1819.

LATHAM, JOHN
Service—Virginia   Va. No. 2127   No. S. 8811

Enlisted, March, 1780-82, Stafford County, Virginia, in company of Captain Johnson in the regiment of Virginia regulars commanded by Colonel Ludamy. Other officers were Captains Montgomery, Fitzpatrick, Ballard and Colonel Haws. Pension granted in Harrison County, Virginia, 1832. Case investigated by U. S. Attorney Singleton in 1834, ordered suspended in 1835, with no indication of reinstatement. Supporting data filed by Peter Buser, John Curry, Michael Greathouse, and John Cathers.

LAWRENCE, WILLIAM
Service—Maryland   Va. No. 16289   No. S. 38128 and B. L. Wt. 1968

Enlisted, Frederick County, Maryland, 1778, and served four years as a fifer under Captain David Lynn in the Fourth and Seventh Maryland Regiment commanded by Colonel Gumbo and General Smallwood. Was engaged on guard duty. Applied for pension in Pendleton County, 1819, at which time soldier was 52 years old. Pension granted 1820, suspended in 1821, and restored in 1826. Bounty land warrant for 100 acres was also received. The soldier's wife, named Elizabeth, was 48 years old in 1820, and their children were: James or Jonas, 20; Margaret, 18; Rhuey, 14; Feliska, 12; Patsy, 9; Rebecca, 7; Sally, 5; Jacob, 2. Supporting data was filed in their behalf by Thomas Kinkead, John Dice, Oliver McCoy, James Johnson, Henry Hull, and General James Boggs.

LAZEAR, HYATT

Born in Frederick County, Virginia, 1744. Enlisted in the spring of 1776 in the Revolutionary Army under Captains Harrison, Biggs, Vance, Springer, Crockett, and Colonel Gibson, and Generals Broadhead, Hand, and McIntosh. His claim for pension, filed in Lewis County, Virgina, September 3, 1833, was supported by Martin Life and Jacob Schoolcraft, but was rejected. This is a particularly interesting example of the services which were not found to justify pensions.

LEACH, GEORGE

Service—Virginia   Va. No. 467   No. W. 27584 and B. L. Wt. 3764
(transferred to Ohio, 1837)

Enlisted, Fauquier County, Virginia, 1777, and served as a bombardier under Captain Edmonds in the Second Regiment of Virginia Artillery, commanded by Colonel Marshall. Took part in several campaigns in Virginia and North Carolina.

Born, 1757, and died February 20, 1838. Married Ann Bigbee December 29, 1785, in Fauquier County. She was born in 1765 and died July 22, 1856. The family moved from Wood County, to Jackson County, Ohio, in 1837. Their children and date of birth were: Fanny, December, 1786; Susannah, November, 1788; Willis, December, 1790; Louis, May, 1793; Thomas, February, 1797; Amelia, 1799; Mary, 1800; George, 1809.

Pension was granted the soldier in 1832. The widow also received a pension and bounty land warrant was received for 160 acres. Supporting data was filed by Bailey Rice, Thomas Leach, a brother, and James M. Quality.

LEACH, THOMAS

Service—Virginia   Va. No. 23037   No. S. 8837

Born, Prince William County, Virginia, 1764, the son of James Leach. While living in Fauquier County, Virginia, enlisted in the Virginia Line under Captains O'Bannion, Foley, Jennins, and Winn. Took part in several campaigns and was present at the siege and capture of Yorktown. Received pension in Wood County, October 29, 1833, which was suspended by Special Agent Singleton in 1834, but it seems to have been restored at Wheeling in 1838.

Supporting data filed by George Leach, a brother, James Leach, John Dawkins, Sr., and Samuel Butcher.

LEDLEE, JAMES

Service—Pennsylvania   No. 6224   No. S. 38133

Enlisted, July, 1775, and reenlisted, 1776, in First Pennsylvania Line

Regiment of Artillery under Captains Miller, Craig, and Rice, commanded by Colonels Harden and Proctor. Fought at Brandywine, Germantown, and Trenton. Was honorably discharged by Colonel Proctor at Valley Forge, February, 1778. Received pension in Brooke County, Virginia, February 1, 1819.

LEE, CHARLES (General)

Born at Dernhall, Cheshire, England, 1731; died at Philadelphia, October 2, 1782. A general in the American Revolutionary service. He was appointed major-general by the Continental Congress June 17, 1775; was captured by the British at his headquarters at Baskenridge, New Jersey, 4 miles from his army, December 13, 1776; and was exchanged May 6, 1778. He disobeyed the orders of General Washington at the battle of Monmouth in 1778, and was sentenced by a court martial to one year's suspension from military service. He was afterward dismissed altogether by Congress, January 10, 1780; died October 2, 1782.

Requested in his will that he might not be buried within a mile of any church or meeting house but it was ignored and he is buried at Christ Church. Soldier of fortune. Got baptism of fire as lieutenant under Braddock in 1755, 44th Regiment, on the Monongahela. Made a captain. Adopted into Mohawk Indian tribe and married daughter of a Seneca chief; wounded at Ticonderoga, 1758. Was at capture of Fort Niagara and Montreal in 1760. Fought in Poland and for Russia against Turkey. Returned to America in 1773, settled in Berkeley County, in 1775; made major-general, June 17, 1775. Success in the Carolinas. Opposed Washington as commander in chief. Challenged by Colonel John Laurens and wounded in the shoulder in a duel.

His home was at Leetown, Jefferson County, now West Virginia. The town is named for the Lee family. The old home of General Lee is still standing in much the same condition as when the General lived in it.

LEE, DANIEL

Enlisted in New York in 1776. Served seven years as a private under Captain Grimes in the First New York Regiment, under Colonels Posey, Van Scheck, and Generals Arnold and Washington. Fought at Monmouth. Received pension in Monongalia County, Virginia, February 2, 1819, at which time he was 61 years old.

LEE, DAVID

The statement of David Lee, December 23, 1834, before the Wood County Court, concerning pension as a Revolutionary soldier, stated that he was not a soldier during the War of the Revolution. He said that at the suggestion of William Mitchell he had applied for a pension for service rendered in the Indian wars in expectation that such service would be covered by a pension law that would be passed by Congress.

LEMASTERS, BENJAMIN
Service—Virginia   Va. No. 16923   No. S. 18490

Enlisted in Berkeley County, Virginia, in 1777, but was living at that time in Monongalia County. Served until 1780 as private and sergeant under Captain Lewis and Lieutenant Culk in Continental Establishment in the First Virginia Regiment of the line, commanded by Colonel Parker. Among other officers were Lieutenants Francis Miner, Holeman Minear, Majors Fleming, Ball, Green, and Smith, and General Washington and Lord Stirling. Fought at Monmouth, Princeton, Germantown, Brandywine and Fort Mifflin. Was wounded in the ankle in the battle of Princeton, and was carried on Major Fleming's horse to the hospital at Philadelphia.

Pension was granted to the soldier in Nicholas County, in 1833. Supporting data filed in his behalf by Andrew Friend, Peter McCune, Mary Wiggins, and Hamrick Given.

LEMON, JAMES (Ensign)
Was raised at Shepherdstown. About January 1, 1777, was commissioned ensign in Colonel Hartley's regiment of Pennsylvania troops, and was killed in the battle of Brandywine.

LEMON, JOHN (Captain)
Served in the Revolution and retired as a captain. Had a plantation in Berkeley County.

LESSLEY, JOHN
Service—Pennsylvania   Va. No. 14298   No. S. 38139

Native of Maryland. Before the Revolution lived in Delaware and Pennsylvania. Entered the Continental Army in 1775 soon after battle of Bunker Hill, under Captain Claggett of Bedford, Pennsylvania. Honorably discharged, Gravesend, New York, 1776. Enlisted, spring of 1777 in company commanded by Captain Archibald McAllister in Colonel Hartley's Pennsylvania Line Regiment, under General Anthony Wayne. Served three years in this unit. In 1820, soldier was 85 years old and his wife, Sarah, an invalid, aged 60. Pension granted in Berkeley County, Virginia, in 1819. Supporting data filed by Captain Archibald McAllister, Captain Benjamin Comers, and Judge White. Soldier died, 1832, in Michigan.

LEVICK (SEVICK), CALEB (Sergeant)
Warrant No. 6316 for 400 acres of land was issued May, 1819, to the heirs of Caleb Levick or Sevick for service as a sergeant in the Continental Line, Revolutionary War. Before the Jefferson County court, January 28, 1818, it was certified that Rachel Ayers, the widow of Alexander Ayers, was the widow of Caleb Levick, deceased, late of the Revolutionary Army; that Levick left the following children: Sarah, Mary, Elizabeth, wife of Elijah Rechart; John, Ann, Margaret, and that the widow and children all lived in Jefferson County, Virginia.

LEWIS, ABRAHAM
Service—Pennsylvania   No. 25845   No. R. 6307

Served four years and four months as a fifer under Captains Grub, and Byrd, Major A. Waggoner, and Colonel Stephenson. Took part in the battles of Iron Hill and Brandywine. Born, Chester County, Pennsylvania, in 1758, lived for a time in Delaware, and enlisted at New Castle, Pennsylvania. Application for pension, filed in 1833 in Randolph County, Virginia, was rejected.

LEWIS, ANDREW
Lived on the Bullskin in Jefferson County. Served as a private during the Revolution.

LEWIS, JACOB
Service—Virginia   Va. No. 16224   No. W. 8044

Born, Berkeley County, Virginia, April 15, 1755, died, June 20, 1840. There enlisted in 1775, and served as a private thirteen months under Captains Scott, Thurston, Buckels, Ambrose, Evans, in the Virginia Regiment commanded by Colonel Morrow and Lord Sterling. Married Mary Watson (nee Parker) in Tyler County, Virginia, December 17, 1816, the ceremony being performed by William Wells. Pension was granted in Tyler County in 1833, and widow later also received pension. Supporting data was submitted by the Reverend Thomas Jones, Benjamin Brewer, James Curtis, William Johnson, Ruth Davis, Richard Parker, Elizabeth Parker, and Ralph Gorell.

LEWIS, JOHN
Enlisted under Captain Shepherd in Berkeley County in 1776. Was drafted into another company in August of that year. Died in Jefferson County, Virginia, on Babb's Marsh in 1846, aged 104 years.

LEWIS, THOMAS
Thomas, third son of General Andrew Lewis, was born in 1756. He served in his brother John's company at the battle of Point Pleasant, probably as a volunteer since his name does not occur on the muster roll; however, his son stated that his father was in the battle. He also served at the battle of Guilford Courthouse in 1780.

About the year, 1785, he removed to Point Pleasant, and entered the Indian trade. In Ohio he was captured by the Indians, taken to their towns on the Maumee, and saved from torture and death by an Indian known as John Hollis, a boyhood friend, who had accompanied his father on a visit to Virginia thirteen years before. In 1789, Thomas Lewis, Jr., laid out the town of Point Pleasant, and was one of the magistrates of the newly erected Kanawha County, which he afterwards represented in the legislature. He was killed by a falling tree in November, 1800.

LIKENS, JACOB A.
Enlisted in the Revolution from Shepherdstown.

LILLY, WILLIAM

Born, Cambridgeshire, England, 1751. Enlisted, March 1, 1777, in Frederick County, Virginia, in company commanded by Captains Reynolds, Gilkinson, Handley, under Colonel Kennedy. Application for pension, filed in Nicholas County, Virginia, in 1833. Supporting data had been filed by Joseph and Paschal Backhouse, Bernard Hendricks, and Addison McLaughlin.

This claim was rejected with the following: David Hannah, John Wright, John Mollihan, Francis Boggs. At the same time, March 21, 1835, payment was ordered resumed on Jacob Fisher.

LINDSEY (LINDSAY or LINSEY), WALTER (Sergeant)
Service—Pennsylvania   Va. No. 5991   No. W. 8048

Enlisted, January 1776, Chester County, Pennsylvania, in company commanded by Captain Frederick Varnam (or Cannon) of the Fifth Regiment of the Pennsylvania Line, commanded by General Anthony Wayne. After serving a year, he was discharged. In Albany, he enlisted again in the same military unit and served until January, 1781, when he was discharged. He was in the battles of Brandywine, Germantown, and Monmouth.

In February, 1781, he married Mary, daughter of James McCullough, at the home of his brother-in-law, John Louden. They moved to Harrison County, Virginia, in 1785 or 1786. There pension was granted in 1819. Soldier was born in 1755 and his wife in 1764. Soldier died June 28, 1820. His widow applied for pension in 1839. Supporting data filed by Martha Blain, sister; Catherine Carpenter, sister; and Colonel William Martin.

LINTON, ISAAC
Service—Maryland   No. 12500   No. S. 5690

Born, Frederick County, Maryland, October, 1764, and there enlisted in August, 1777, in the Maryland militia under Captain Ralph Hillery. Other officers were Ensign Ralph Craigg, Lieutenant Joseph Madding, Colonels Butler and Burkett, and Chaplain Beally. Served fifteen months, being engaged on marches to Baltimore, Fredericktown, and elsewhere. Received pension, Wellsburg, Brooke County, 1832. Supporting data filed by Robert Marshall, Pascal Taylor, Thomas Bucey, and the Reverend Edward Smith.

LINTON, WILLIAM T. (Colonel)
Service—North Carolina   No. 5349   No. W. 8046

Born, January 8, 1758, Westmoreland County, Virginia. Enlisted, April 16, 1776, Surry County, North Carolina, under Captain William Barrett, Third North Carolina Regiment, Continental Establishment, under Colonel Sumner. Was in attack on Fort Moultrie, Sullivan's Island, marched north to join the northern army at Princeton, and fought at Brandywine, Germantown, and Monmouth. Served as captain, major, and colonel.

Wife, Mary Ann, was born December 6, 1769. Their children were Mary, John, Elizabeth, Margaret Haynes, Ann Thomas. They were married in Chester, South Carolina, April 5, 1793, by the Reverend William Martin, Reformed Presbyterian minister. Pensions were granted. (Although included in the Virginia pensions, residence in western Virginia is uncertain.)

LIPSCOMB, AMBROSE
Service—Virginia   Va. No. 16710   No. W. 8252

Born, 1762; died, May 18, 1841; enlisted, Frederick County, Virginia, March, 1781, and served seven months as a private under Captains Frost and Bell in the Virginia Line under Generals Lafayette and Washington. Took part in the siege and capture of Yorktown. Received pension, Randolph County, Virginia, 1833.

Married Winny Mardis, December, 1785, King George County, Virginia. She received widow's pension, 1846, at which time she was 78 years old. Their children were: Lucy, 1786; Richard, 1788; James, 1793; John, 1795; Margaret, 1796; Henry, 1798; Fielding, 1802; Eben, 1805. Supporting affidavits are on file in this case from John Taggart, John Long, and John White.

LITTERAL (LITTREL), RICHARD
Service—Continental Virginia   Va. No. 9848   No. W. 26220 and
                                                B. L. Wt. 521

Served three years as a private in company of Captain Stith, Third Virginia Regiment, Continental Line, under Colonel Baylor. Received pension, aged 58, Botetourt County, Virginia (probably in what is now Berkeley County, Virginia), in 1819, and widow received pension in Tennessee in 1853. Bounty land warrant also issued for 160 acres. Soldier's widow was formerly Jane Champe (nee Welch), widow of George Champe. Supporting witnesses in this case were Mary Darbin and Margaret Stacks.

LITTLE, GEORGE
Service—Pennsylvania   Va. No. 12629   No. R. 6382

Enlisted at Chester Town, Pennsylvania, September 18, 1778, and served eleven months as a fifer under Captains Thomas Laty and Orbison in the Pennsylvania Regiment, commanded by Colonel Bull. He fought at Brandywine and Germantown. Before the Revolution he had lived in Adams and York Counties, Pennsylvania. He was born in 1755 and died July 4, 1844. His wife's name was Elizabeth. Pension was granted to the soldier in Hampshire County, Virginia, May 8, 1833. Supporting data was filed by Marmus Murman and Branson Posten.

LIVELY, GODRILL (GOODWILL, GODESEL, COTREL, CARTEL)
Service—Continental Virginia   Va. No. 23101   No. R. 6389 and
                                                B. L. Wt. 4973

Born, Albemarle County, Virginia, 1760. Died December 3, 1838.

WEST VIRGINIANS IN THE REVOLUTION

Enlisted, 1780, and served two years as a private of infantry and cavalry under Captains West Luke, and Barrett in the Virginia Regiment of the Continental Line commanded by Colonel Armand. Served at various points in Virginia and Pennsylvania. Received land bounty warrant for 200 acres and also was granted pension in Monroe County, Virginia. Supporting statements were filed by John Hutchinson, John H. Vawter, and the Reverend John Cook. Bounty land statement was signed by Samuel Coleman and James Monroe.

Lively was married, October 24, 1790, to Sarah Maddy by the Reverend John Alderson, Greenbrier County, Virginia. Widow died August 19, 1839. Their children were: Jane Pact, 1791; Joseph, 1793; William, 1795; Judith McGhee, 1797; John (Cotral), 1799; James, 1802; Thomas, 1805; Hamphill, 1807; Madison, 1809; Mary, 1811; Sallie Smith, 1813; Wilson, 1815; Lorenzo, 1818; James Ellison, 1823; (a bound boy).

LOAR, JOHN
Enlisted in the Revolutionary Army from Sheperdstown.

LOAR, PHILIP
Enlisted in the Revolutionary Army from Shepherdstown.

LOGAN, WILLIAM
Enlisted under Captain Stephenson in 1775. Owned a farm in Berkeley County.

LOCH, JOHN (may appear on rolls as HOLE)
Service—Continental—French   No. R. 6396

Enlisted, Bucks County, Pennsylvania, 1782, and served from April to December in the French artillery under Captains Yunkin and Joshua Grove under Colonel D'Olcott and Count de Rochambeau. Applied for pension in Shenandoah County, Virginia, in 1832. Claim supported by Philip Hartman, but was rejected on grounds that the Act of June 7, 1832, did not cover service in the French troops which were cooperating with the American Army.

LOCKHART, AARON
Service—Pennsylvania   Va. No. 5975   No. S. 38146

Enlisted in 1776 or 1777 in Captain Lacy or Lacey's company of the Fourth Regiment of the Pennsylvania Line, and continued in the regular service for four years until discharged by General St. Clair. Married in 1793. Received pension in Harrison County, Virginia, 1819. Died in the fall of the same year.

LOCKHEART, WILLIAM (Ensign)
Service—Pennsylvania   No. R. 6400

Born in Chester County, Pennsylvania, 1759. Enlisted and served as an ensign under Captain Pitt in the Pennsylvania militia under command of Colonel Pierce. Applied for pension in Hampshire County, July

LOCKMAN, JOHN

Enlisted January 1, 1776, in Captain Church's company of riflemen of the Pennsylvania Line, commanded by General Butler. After twelve months was discharged at Staten Island by Captain Farmer. In Ohio County in 1820, he testified, at age of 67, that he had enlisted in Philadelphia County, Pennsylvania. He was wounded twice in the battle of White Plains, New York.

In Ohio County in 1855, Catharine Lockman stated she was the widow of John Lockman. She was 79 years old and had been married to him by the Reverend John Armstrong at Wheeling, April 9, 1821, and that her husband died at Wheeling, December 12, 1827. He had been wounded at the battle of Cowpens, South Carolina. Her maiden name was Catharine Eichner and she had been born in Wurtenberg, Germany. In Westmoreland County, Pennsylvania, 1905, John Isaac Lockman, aged 80, a resident of Arnold, testified that he was the only child of John and Catharine Lockman. His mother died, May 18, 1860. He made application for bounty land.

LONG, JOHN PHILLIP
Service—Pennsylvania   Va. No. 20310   No. S. 38147

Enlisted in New York in October, 1778, under Captains Van Hare and Christie in the company of Light Dragoons of the Fifth Regiment of Pennsylvania troops under Colonel Minghes and General Wayne. Evidently had more than three years service, according to evidence in his pension packet. Daniel Recknor of Allegheny County, Maryland, made affidavit that he served with Long under Captain Christie in the Fifth Pennsylvania Regiment. John Ignatious Effinger swore that he served under Captain Bartholomew in Van Heer's company of Light Dragoons of New York and that John Phillip Long served at the same time in the same company. Supporting data was also submitted by Conrad Keener. Pension was granted the soldier February 18, 1831, in Pendleton County, Virginia.

LOOFBOROUGH, JOHN WADE

Born in 1748 in New Jersey. Married Mary Hoff, 1767. Died Pickaway County, Ohio, 1814. Settled in Randolph County, prior to 1788. Believed to have been a Revolutionary soldier; see records of Middlesex County, New Jersey, "Officers and Men of New Jersey in the Revolution, Page 672." Children of Loofborough were: Sarah, married John Harbert, 1789; Jacob, married Mary Davis, 1792; Rebecca, married Elijah Barkley, 1795; Abigail, married Samuel Harbert, 1788; Mary, married Thomas Barkley, 1795.

LOVE, CHARLES

Charles Love was born in 1753 and died in 1824. He served from

May 25, 1776, as a private in Captain Thomas Berry's company, Eighth Virginia Regiment under Colonel Bowman in General Scott's Brigade. He was at Valley Forge where he was discharged March 5, 1778. Affidavits for him are filed by Bean Smallwood, in whose stead he served, and Michael Dean, of Pendleton County, Kentucky. His wife was Susannah. Their children were: Samuel Allen, Agnes Wolfe, William, Susannah Hampton, and Elizabeth Ann Shortridge. Pension was granted him in Kentucky as a Revolutionary soldier. Later he moved to Cabell County, Virginia, where he died, 1824.

LOVE, ROBERT
Service—North Carolina   Va. No. 23712   No. S. 18093

Born, Caswell County, North Carolina, December 17, 1762. Enlisted under Captain Donnel in November or December, 1780, in the Carolinas and served six months in the North Carolina Line under Colonel James Martin, and Generals Green, Morgan, and Rutherford. Received pension in Mason County, Virginia, March 24, 1834. Supporting data supplied by John and George Roush.

LOWTHER, WILLIAM (Colonel)

Born, December 22, 1743, Augusta County, Virginia, a son of Robert Lowther. Married Sudna, daughter of Thomas Hughes, Sr., in Hardy County, came in 1772 to Harrison County, died October 28, 1814, and is buried on the West Fork River one and a half miles below West Milford. His ancestors were English. Henry Lowther had three sons, Henry, George, and William, who were English miners. William had a son, Robert, who with his wife, Aquilla Ross Lowther, emigrated in 1740 to America. In 1772, they settled in Hackers Creek Valley, Harrison County, with their sons, Jonathan and William.

Jonathan was killed with Thomas Hughes, Sr., in May, 1788, by Indians within sight of Jane Lew on their way from Clarksburg to West's Fort to give alarm of an Indian invasion. William led a party of settlers who pursued the Indians into Ohio, surprised them near Chillicothe and killed thirteen of the savages. When 17 years old, William Lowther volunteered under David Scott in Indian service. In 1781, he joined General George Rogers Clark's expedition against Detroit as a major in Colonel Joseph Crockett's regiment at Fort Pitt, returned in 1783 and was soon promoted to the rank of colonel. In 1787, he was made colonel of the northwestern counties of Virginia and retained command of the region until the Wayne treaty with the Indians in 1795. He took a leading part in many border activities as long as Indians appeared on the eastern shores of the Ohio. He was sheriff of Harrison County, was also the first sheriff of Wood County, and was active in many civil capacities.

The children of William and Sudna Lowther were: Robert, 1765; Thomas, 1767; William, Jr., 1768; Jesse, 1773; Elias, 1776; and Sudna, who married Jacob Jackson December 15, 1796.

LUCAS, BASIL (Sergeant)
Service—Maryland   Va. No. 23736   No. S. 18097

Enlisted, January 17, 1776, and served as a sergeant under Captain Rezin Bell, Second Maryland Regiment, Continental Establishment, commanded by Colonel Thomas Price. Discharged in the State of New Jersey, January 10, 1780.

Married, February, 1786, Berkeley County, Virginia. Wife's name Elizabeth. Applied for pension, Berkeley County, September 12, 1831, which was granted. Soldier was born, 1757, and died, October 2, 1841. Among relatives named was G. Dural. Henry Brent of Winchester received pension certificate for Lucas in 1834.

LUCAS, EDWARD (Lieutenant)
Served as second lieutenant in Captain William Morgan's company late in 1776 or early in 1777.

LUCAS, JOB
Served with the Revolutionary forces in the southern campaign, died of smallpox while in service.

LUCAS, WILLIAM (Lieutenant)
Born near Shepherdstown, January 18, 1742. Was first lieutenant in Captain William Morgan's company. After the Revolution, he moved to Ohio where his son, Robert, became governor. He was the son of Edward Lucas, as were Edward and Job. Their father moved to near Shepherdstown before 1732. Four brothers were killed by Indians: Robert, Benjamin, David, and Isaac. William was wounded at Laurel Hill but survived to become a bitter enemy of the Indians and one of their most relentless opponents.

LUCAS, WILLIAM
Born, Pittsylvania County, Virginia, 1749. Called into service from Botetourt County. Later lived in Montgomery, and then in Logan County, Virginia. Served under Captains Burke, Trigg, Burns, Lucas, Brown, Colonels Preston, Shelby, and General Campbell at Lucas Fort, Wood's Fort, Farley's Fort, and other frontier outposts. Had two periods of service of three months each and two tours of eighteen months each between 1772 and 1781. Supporting data was submitted by the Reverend Richard Brooks, Parker Lucas, Hezekiah Adkins, James Johnson, Christian Snidow, and Thomas Farley. Mention is made of a son, John. Pension claim was rejected because agent stated that three declarations did not check.

LYNOTT (SYNOTT), THOMAS
Born in Fairfax County, Virginia. Enlisted under Captain Sprowl and served as a cabin boy on the ship *Hope*. Application for pension in Harrison County, Virginia, in 1832 was rejected on ground that his service was on a vessel not commissioned by the general or state govern-

ment, and as such was not under the Revolutionary pension laws. Supporting data was filed by Notley Shuttleworth, Jonas Adam, Stephen Dicks, and the Reverend Hamilton Gass.

West Virginians in the American Revolution

Assembled and Edited by ROSS B. JOHNSTON

The sources of this material are from the files of the Pension Office at Washington from various county records, from notes of patriotic societies, principally the Daughters of the American Revolution, Sons of the American Revolution, Sons of the Revolution, and from a large miscellaneous group of published and private sources. Corrections and additions to this list will receive the careful attention of the editor.

MACE, ISAAC
Service—Virginia   Va. No. 23036   No. S. 8995

Born, Augusta County, Virginia, July 16, 1755. Enlisted as a substitute for Abram Brake in 1781 and served under Captains Hopkins and Cunningham. Pension was granted in 1833 for two years service as a private in the Revolutionary Army, but Mace was dropped from the pension rolls in 1835.

MACE, JOHN
Service—Virginia   Va. No. 16649   No. S. 13847

Born, March 25, 1752, in Pennsylvania. Enlisted, May 1, 1777, in Hampshire County, Virginia, and served twenty-three months in the Virginia militia under Lieutenant Isaac Hinkle, Ensign Sam Skidmore, Captain John Skidmore, Colonel Joseph Darke, and Generals Campbell and Wayne. Took part in siege and capture of Yorktown. Supporting data submitted by Peter Coger and Isaac Mace. Pension granted in Lewis County, Virginia, 1833. On January 9, 1835, pensioned requested transfer to Gallia County, Ohio, but he was dropped from the rolls in August of that year.

MADDOX, MATTHEW
Service—Virginia   Va. No. 17802   No. S. 38181

Enlisted, Shenandoah County, Virginia, October, 1780, and served as a private two years under Captain Oldham in the Third Virginia Line Regiment, commanded by Colonel Campbell, Generals Green and Muhlenberg. Took part in the battles at Guilford Courthouse and Camden. He was living in Wood County, Virginia, in 1820, aged 68 years, and there in 1823 he received pension. At that time his wife was old and infirm. One son was mentioned. Soldier died, January 1, 1831.

MADERA, CHRISTIAN (Ensign)
Service—Continental Pennsylvania   Va. No. 15217   No. S. 38180

Born, Berks County, Pennsylvania, 1759; died, March 15, 1822, and is buried in East Grove Cemetery, Morgantown, Monongalia County. In the spring of 1776, enlisted and served two years as a private under Captains Nagle, Harris, and Wilson, First Pennsylvania Regiment, under Colonel James Chambers, Generals Hand and Wayne. Took part in the battles of Long Island, White Plains, Brandywine, the massacre of Paoli, Chestnut Hill, and Germantown. Another notation of service says that he served as an ensign in Captain Jacob Baldy's company in the battalion commanded by Lieutenant Colonel Joseph Hiezer, Berks County, Pennsylvania, from August 10, 1780, to September 9, 1780.

Madera was married to Ann Bierly in the German Reformed Church at Reading, Pennsylvania, February 23, 1779. She was 65 years old in 1820. Pension was granted Madera in 1820, later dropped, but was restored, February 16, 1821.

MADEIRA, NICHOLAS
Service—Pennsylvania   Va. No. 24081   No. R. 21708

Born, Reading, Pennsylvania, December 26, 1763. There enlisted in 1777 as a private of artillery and drummer and served two years and six months under Captains Kennedy, John Fasick, and Sebastian Miller in Seventh Pennsylvania Regiment commanded by Major Oment, Colonel Chambers, Generals Wayne and St. Clair. Fought at Brandywine and Yorktown. Supporting data was filed in his case in Monongalia County, where he applied for pension, October 22, 1832, by Matthew Gray, Nicholas B. Madeira, nephew; Michael Madeira, brother; Philip Nagle, and Rev. J. Shackleford, but claim was rejected.

Letters on file give details of Madeira's reply to the rejection of his claim. He described the union of the company under Captain John Fasick, which he had joined at Reading, Pennsylvania, with one of the regiments under Count Rochambeau. Madeira stated that at Yorktown he and twenty-four other men attended two field pieces. He describes the four regiments and corps of hussars under Rochambeau and gives an interesting description of their colorful uniforms.

In "Lee's Combattants, Francaise de la Guerre Americaine," served three other brothers, Michael, Casper, and Christian Madeira, in the same company. Nicholas Madeira was with Captain Sebastian Miller in 1778 in campaign against Indians and Tories. At Allentown, Miller's command was joined to another company, and both served under Major Cuners. While at Stony Point, they had to subsist on meat and apples as the officers heard that poison had been mixed in the flour, since treason had appeared in the camp.

MAIL, WILMORE
Service—Virginia   Va. No. 2522   No. S. 38171

Enlisted, Berkeley County, Virginia, 1776 or 1777, as a private under Lieutenant (later Captain) Robert White in company of the Twelfth Virginia Regiment Continental Establishment, under Captain Joseph Mitchell, Glass, Colonel James Wood, Generals Scott and Wolford. Fought at Monmouth and Stony Point. Moved to Hampshire County, in 1790.

Applied for pension, May 27, 1818, aged 70, while living in Hampshire County, which was granted for four years service the same year. In 1820, his wife, Priscilla, was aged 59, and a son, George, 16. His claim was supported by Captain Robert White, his former commanding officer.

In the file is a statement by John B. White in which he says that he, White, feels much interested in this case, as Mail had been one of his father's recruits and was with the elder White when he was wounded. A duplicate of Mail's original pension certificate was destroyed at Romney when the store of Samuel D. Brady, where he had placed this record in a safe, was burned in 1838 at which time Mail was still living.

MALCHER, JOHN

Enlisted in Captain Shepherd's company, July 15, 1776. Died in prison, February 10, 1777.

MALES, JOHN
Service—Maryland   Va. No. 7460   No. S. 38168

Enlisted in Hagerstown, Maryland, and served five years between 1777 and 1783 as a private in the company of Captain Stult in the Seventh Virginia Regiment Continental Establishment, commanded by General Smallwood. Fought at Brandywine, Germantown, Monmouth, Eutaw Springs, Guilford Courthouse, and Gates' Defeat. Certificate filed in this case by Captain Christian Orndorff, Sixth Maryland Regiment, dated October 12, 1818, says that Males received four wounds in his period of service. Pension was granted May 8, 1819, in Monroe County, Virginia. Pensioner died the following year.

MALICK, JOHN
Service—New Jersey   Va. No. 12580   No. S. 7177

Born, January 11, 1762, Bridgewater, Somerset County, Pennsylvania. Enlisted in New Jersey one month before the British captured New York and served eight months as a private under Captain Selon, New Jersey Regiment Continental Establishment, under Colonels Frelinghuysen, Taylor, and Hunt. Soldier also knew Lieutenant Richard Sane and Major Piat. Took part in battle of Springfield. Supporting data filed by Philip Fahs and Jacob Peppers. Pension granted in Hampshire County, Virginia, May 11, 1833.

MALLOW (MALLOWS), HENRY
Service—Virginia   Va. No. 4123   No. S. 45892

Born on the Mississippi River in 1759. His mother had been taken prisoner by the Indians and sold to the French in whose possession she was at the time of her son's birth on the Mississippi River.

Enlisted, Rockingham County, Virginia, April, 1778, and served six months under Ensign George Mallow, Lieutenant Herron, Captain Cravens, Virginia Militia commanded by Colonel Benjamin Harrison, Colonel Campbell and General McIntosh, in McIntosh's campaign and other border

WEST VIRGINIANS IN THE REVOLUTION

activities. Supporting data was filed in this case by Henry Huffman. Pension was granted January 11, 1833.

MALONE, HUGH
Service—Maryland   Va. No. 12735   No. S. 38167
Enlisted, White Mountain, Hartford County, Maryland, and served five years as a private under Captain Alexander Trueman in the Sixth Maryland Regiment, commanded by Colonel William Ford. He was in the battles at Fort Montgomery, Buttermilk Falls, Long Island, and at the siege and capture of Yorktown. He received pension while living in Hampshire County, Virginia, July 21, 1819.

MALONE, THOMAS
Service—Maryland   No. S. 38929
Enlisted, Frederick County, Maryland, and served from March 3, 1777, to August 16, 1780, as a private under Captain Kirby in the Seventh Maryland Regiment Continental Line, commanded by Colonel Smallwood. Was in the battles of Germantown, Brandywine, and at the massacre of Paoli. He was wounded on March 15, 1781, according to records of the Maryland auditor's office. He applied for pension in Monongalia County, January 25, 1820, died in November of that year, and pension certificate was issued December 20, 1821. In 1820, the age of his wife, Mary, was between 50 and 60. They had a son, John, living at that time.

MANGE, PETER
Enlisted under Stephenson in 1775. Died in Shepherdstown.

MARLAT (MORLATT), PETER
Service—New Jersey   S. 38177
Enlisted, Reading Town, New Jersey, June, 1778, and was discharged at Newark, New Jersey, March 5, 1779. Served as a private under Captain Henry Luce, Second New Jersey Regiment, commanded by Colonel J. Shreve. Took part in fighting at Long Island, Cucles Town on Staten Island, Mill Stone in the Jerseys, and Battle of Monmouth. Received pension, May 1, 1818, aged 58, Berkeley County, Virginia. At this date, his wife, Jane, was also 58 years old; a son, Jacob, 12; and a daughter, Elizabeth, 9 years old.

MARRATT (MERRITT), LAROSE (ROSEY)
Service—Virginia   Va. No. 7795   No. S. 38176
Born, 1749. Enlisted 1777, at Winchester, Virginia, and served three years as a private under Captain John McGuire, Sixteenth Virginia Regiment, commanded by Colonel Grayson. Took part in battles of Germantown, Brandywine, and Monmouth. Received pension in Mason County, September 28, 1820. Supporting affidavits filed by Abel Armstrong and Smith Thompson.

MARSHALL, BENJAMIN
Service—Virginia   Va. No. 23830   No. W. 4279
Born, Prince George County, Maryland, 1755; died March 29, 1834.

Enlisted, Hampshire County, Virginia, and served from 1780 to 1781 under Captain M. Stump Berry, in a Virginia regiment. Other officers were Lieutenants Sans, Johnson, and Simon Hornbeck. Received pension in 1834 in Hardy County, Virginia.

Married in Montgomery County, Maryland. Wife's name was Elizabeth. Ann Marshall, probably a sister, was present at the wedding. Widow, who was born in 1760, secured a pension in 1841. Supporting data was submitted by Elizabeth Bean, Thomas Marshall, Hezekiah Linthicum, and James Thompson.

MARKET, JONATHAN
Drafted from Captain Ambrose's Berkeley County militia, 1780.

MARSHEL (MARSHAL), JAMES (Colonel)
Born, Ireland, in 1753. Removed some time between 1776 and 1778 to what is now Washington County, Pennsylvania, and bought up large amounts of land in Cross Creek Township. Upon the organization of Washington County, was appointed (1781) county lieutenant, which office he held three years. He was sheriff, 1784 to 1789, member of the Legislature, and recorder of the land office. He later removed to Brooke County, Virginia, where he died in 1829.

MARTIN, CHARLES
One of the Minute Men. He commanded a fort on Crooked Run, Monongalia County, not far from Morgantown, 1773 to 1783. This fort was first built to defend the frontier against the Indians. When the Revolution broke out, it became an outpost against both British and Indians. It was attacked, June, 1779, and ten whites killed or captured. Martin was granted 400 acres of land in Monongalia County, in 1769.

MARTIN, DANIEL
Service—New Jersey   Va. No. 23839   No. R. 6938

Enlisted, 1777, and served in the New Jersey Line under Captain Holm and Colonel Ogden. Took part in the siege of Yorktown and the capture of Cornwallis. Wife's name was Elizabeth. Applied for pension in Preston County, Virginia, April 18, 1828, but it appears to have been rejected.

MARTIN, DANIEL
Service—New Jersey   Va. No. 744   No. W. 2401 and B.L.Wt. 4

Served as a private under Captain Holmes in the First Regiment of the New Jersey Line. Applied for pension, Preston County, September 19, 1828. In Preston County, September 23, 1841, was married to Eve Everly by William Glover, Esq. Widow applied for pension, April 27, 1853. She died December 4, 1882. Supporting data submitted by Jacob Martin, a son; John Miller, and Nathan Graham. Bounty land warrant also seems to have been issued for 160 acres. The names of Savilla and Margaret Lester are mentioned in connection with this land grant.

MARTIN, JOB
Service—Virginia   Va. No. 16924   No. S. 18496

In 1832 he testified before the Kanawha County Court that he had enlisted in Bedford County, Virginia, in 1776, under Captain Henry Ferrell in the Fifth Virginia Regiment of the Continental Line commanded by Colonel Josiah Parker. Colonel Scott was to have commanded the unit but had been made a general in charge of other troops. He thought the Adjutant was named Johnston, and First Lieutenant John Goggins, Second Lieutenant Thomas McGrunnels, and Ensign Robert Watkins, all of Bedford County, Virginia. Discharged, March, 1778, after two years service. He was marched from Bedford to "Hobbs Hole," then to Williamsburg, Suffolk, Kemp Landing, Wilmington, Delaware, and discharged at Williamsburg. Reenlisted, 1781, in same regiment under Captain William Lovely, commanded by Colonel Thomas Gaskins and Major John Willis at Cobham. Was at Yorktown at surrender of Cornwallis. Was discharged by Colonel Thomas Gaskins.

Had been born in Pennsylvania, April 11, 1753, and moved to Bedford County when 14 years old. Mentions Samuel Martin, a brother, who had his first discharge papers but moved to Tennessee where he died in 1812. Received pension in Kanawha County, in 1833.

MARTIN, SAMUEL
Service—Maryland   No. R. 6971

Born, Cecil County, Maryland, March 14, 1760. Resided in Maryland at outbreak of the Revolution, and remained there until 1779 when he moved to Pennsylvania; in Berkeley County, Virginia, 1785 to 1789; then in Greenbrier County until 1791; in Monroe County until 1835; after this date soldier lived in Fayette County.

Enlisted in Kent County, Maryland, 1777, under Captain David Crane of the Fourth Maryland Regiment, commanded by Colonels Morgan, Gillispie, Generals Stephens and Washington, Fought at Brandywine and Monmouth. Supporting data submitted by John and Henry Smith, William Radin, Samuel, Edward, and Andrew Quinn, Edward Williams, Levin Benson, William Young, Alex Quarrier, and Joel Shunberg. Pension application rejected from Monroe County in 1834. Statement from Maryland land office, July 11, 1839, says that David Crane was appointed a captain in the Thirteenth Battalion of Kent County, Maryland, militia, September 9, 1778. Martin's name is not on the muster roll of this company which, however, was very incomplete.

MARTIN, WILLIAM
Service—Virginia   Va. No. 5822   No. S. 5736

Enlisted in Hampshire County, Virginia, before March 17, 1779, and served three years in the company of Captain Benjamin Biggs of the Thirteenth Virginia Regiment, commanded by Colonel John Gibson, Generals Broadhead and Irvine. Mentions Captains Uriah Springer, Jacob Springer, Sam Brady and Lieutenant John Dent. Took part in activities at Fort Pitt, Fort McIntosh, Fort Henry and elsewhere. Was present at the burning of the old Keshockton Town on the Muskingum River.

After receiving his discharge, started home when he was fired upon by a party of Indians, and was struck by five balls, wounding him in both thighs, legs and one arm. One leg had to be amputated below the knee. Pension granted in Harrison County, February 19, 1833. Supporting data filed by Peter Johnstone (Johnson or Johnston) and Anderson Corbin.

MARTIN, WILLIAM (Colonel)
Service—Continental New Jersey Va. No. 23087 No. 9937 and B.L.Wt. 113541

Born, New Jersey, October 10, 1763; died August 25, 1851. Enlisted, Lebanon, New Jersey, in the spring of 1779. Served at West Point, Pittstown, Raritan's Landing, and Middlebrook. Was present at the storming of Stony Point. Among his officers were Captain McKnight, James Johnston, John Bray, Colonel Stewart, and General Wayne.

Upon enlistment at the age of 16 was attached to the commissary department, and was rated as Assistant Commisary when pensioned in Harrison County, November 5, 1833. His rate was increased from $480 per year to $600 per year in 1850. However, his widow did not receive the bounty land ordinarily given an officer, but received the 160 acres of a soldier.

He was married in Harrison County, February 23, 1815, to Jane Powers with Phineas Wells, Baptist minister, officiating. She was aged 59 when she applied for a widow's pension in 1853, at which time she gave her name as Jane Chidester. Supporting data was filed in this case by John Bray (Commisary), John Davis, John Wilson, Jr., Leonard Critzer, D. Kincheloe, George Davidson, and James Little.

MARTIN, WILLIAM
Service—Virginia Va. No. 12838 No. W. 5342 and B.L.Wt. 5080

Enlisted, Albemarle County, Virginia, 1775 or 1776, and served two years as a private under Captain Dewet of the Seventh Virginia Regiment. Married Patsy Key Davidson in Nelson County, Virginia, 1789, the Rev. Darnell officiating. Soldier received pension in 1832 and after his death in 1834, his widow received pension. She was aged 74 in 1844. Supporting data submitted by William Topling and Hannah Bridgewater. (No proof that soldier ever lived in West Virginia except that his pension was paid at the Wheeling agency.)

MARTIN, REUBEN

Born, Somerset County, New Jersey, in 1748. Lived in Essex County, New Jersey, and then settled at Wheeling, Virginia. He died near Mansfield, Ohio, 1851. He enlisted in Sussex County, June 1, 1777, in Colonel Edward Martin's Second Regiment of Sussex Militia, was in Battle of Brandywine, and was shot in the right leg at Germantown; was discharged, December 10, 1777. Reenlisted, May 10, 1778; discharged November 15, 1778. Served as a private in Captain Harbaugh's company, Colonel David Chamber's Regiment, June 1, 1778, until discharged, December 1, 1779. Was a private in the Hunterdon County Militia until December 3, 1780. He came to West Virginia with three brothers; his cabin at the site of New Martinsville was among the first.

MATHENGER, WILLIAM
Enlisted from Berkeley County. Wife given aid by court order in 1777.

MATHEWS, ISAAC
Enlisted, Fauquier County, Virginia, 1777, and served six months and twenty-one days, under Captains Blackwell, James Repshaw, Major Triplett, Colonel Picket, and Generals Wayne and Washington. Received pension in Preston County, in 1833. Supporting data was filed by Colonel John Fairfax and Benjamin Mathews, a brother.

MATHEWS, RICHARD
Service—Pennsylvania   No. 123679   No. R. 7028
Born, Cumberland County, Pennsylvania, February, 1753, where he resided until 1801 when he removed west of the Alleghenies. Enlisted, Chester County, Pennsylvania, February 14, 1776, and was discharged, February 19, 1777. He served with Captains Robinson, Moore, and Church; Colonels Hartley and Irvine; and General Sullivan. His company was attached to Colonel Anthony Wayne's Regiment of Pennsylvania troops in the expedition against Canada. He took part in the battle of Three Rivers, June 8, 1776, when the American Army was defeated.
Pension was issued to the soldier in Brooke County, Virginia, 1833. Soldier died March 6, 1836. His widow, Martha, died August 30, 1841, after which the only surviving child sought the pension claimed by her mother but was rejected. Supporting data was filed by Nicholas Headington and William Mahan.

MAXWELL, DAVID (Lieutenant)
Born, June 19, 1750, in Delaware. Entered the regular army of the United States as a lieutenant in Captain Skillington's company of Colonel Patterson's battalion of Delaware regulars, in 1776. Served at various times for a total length of eighteen months until his discharge from service at Morristown, New Jersey, April, 1777. He was reappointed a lieutenant in Captain Colwell's company of regulars, commissioned to repel the British along the Delaware. He took part in the Battle of Staten Island and White Plains.
Maxwell came to Harrison County in 1802, settled on a tract of 300 acres the next year, and built a home. He died there, January 20, 1820, and is buried in the cemetery on the late Guy D. Goff lands, ten miles from Clarksburg.

MAXWELL, THOMAS (Captain)
In Maxwell Gap, midway between the towns of Filbert and Elbert, Adkins District, McDowell County, Captain Thomas Maxwell, a hero of the Battle of King's Mountain, was killed by Indians. His small son was

wounded by the Indians, dying a few hours later, and was buried in the same grave with his father.

McCANDLESS, JOHN

Before the Greenbrier County Court in 1787, John McCandless made affidavit that he had served three years in the brigade commanded by Colonel Benjamin Templeton during the Revolutionary War.

McCANN (McCAN), PATRICK
Service—Pennsylvania   Va. No. 16894   No. S. 18502

Pension certificate was issued to this soldier for two years service in Virginia and Pennsylvania, October 15, 1853, but was dropped from rolls, March 16, 1835. The soldier was aged 75 in 1833. A letter from a descendant, James M. Kellogg, says that Patrick and Hannah McCann lived in Randolph County, 1850. They had one child, Mary, born, June 22, 1788.

McCARTNEY, HENRY

Enlisted under Captain Stephenson in 1775.

McCARTY, ANDREW
Service—Pennsylvania   Va. No. 6804   No. S. 38194

Enlisted in Pennsylvania in the spring of 1778 and served as a private two years under Captain Scott in the Second Pennsylvania Regiment, Continental Line, commanded by Colonel Stuart. Received pension in Jefferson County, Virginia, 1819, at which time he was 64 years old. Supporting data filed by James and Robert Fulton.

McCLEERY, WILLIAM (Colonel)

Born, Tyrone County, Ireland, 1741; died in Monongalia County, Virginia, 1821, and is buried in the Presbyterian Cemetery, Morgantown. He came to America, first settling in Maryland, then in Berkeley County, Virginia, and before the close of the Revolution moved to western Pennsylvania. In 1780, he was county clerk of old Monongalia County. From 1781, when Washington County, Pennsylvania was formed, to 1783 he was lieutenant of a company of Washington County rangers. Soon after 1783, he moved to Morgantown. He was given a colonel's commission and served under Colonel John Evans in defending the frontier from Indian attacks. His home on the southwest corner of High and Pleasant Streets, Morgantown, built about 1790, was standing in 1937.

His wife, Isabelle Stockton, was one of the white captives taken by the Indians when they captured Fort Neally, Berkeley County, in 1756. She was sold to a French family in Canada, released after several years imprisonment, and was wooed and won in a series of romantic incidents that are among the most fascinating of Virginia frontier stories.

McCLURE, DAVID (Colonel)

Served as lieutenant-colonel of Ohio County militia until his death which occurred about 1788. Was one of the most influential members of the Ohio Valley settlements in both civil and military affairs.

McCOLLOCH (McCULLOCH), ABRAHAM
Service-Virginia   No. S. 15534
    Born, 1761; died, May 5, 1839. Records missing from the files, except evidence that adverse decision had been appealed but confirmed. Refer to letter in case of Samuel Harbert, No. 16646. Names of his children are given as follows: Samuel, Elizabeth (Smith), Sarah, Ebenezer, Abraham, Rebecca (Wilson), James, William, Margaret (Morgan), John.

McCOLLOCH, JOHN, JR. (Major)
    Born, 1752, in Hardy County, Virginia. When twenty years of age, removed with his father's family to Short Creek, Ohio County. There the McCollochs became famous hunters. During the Revolution and Indian wars they served as scouts and spies. John was out under Brodhead in 1781, and under Williamson in 1782. In July of the latter year, he and his elder brother, Samuel, were scouting when they fell into an Indian ambush; Samuel was killed, and John had a hairbreadth escape from capture at the hands of the enemy.
    In 1792, John McColloch was captain and three years later major of the county militia. In 1793, he commanded an important exploring trip into the region beyond the Ohio. After the border wars were over, McColloch and his wife, formerly Mary Bukey, lived on their estate on Short Creek until John's death, April 6, 1821.

McCOLLOCH, SAMUEL (Major)
    One of the most widely known frontiersmen. Born in 1750, and came with his father's family from the South Branch of the Potomac, Hardy County, to the waters of Short Creek, Ohio County. He commanded Fort Van Meter on the lands of Abraham and John Van Meter, four miles south of West Liberty.
    In 1777, while bringing relief to Fort Henry during one of its two sieges by Indians, he escaped from the Indians only by leaping his horse over a precipice some two hundred feet high, one of the celebrated exploits of border history. In 1779, he was in the Virginia legislature as a representative of Ohio County, and was out with Brodhead on the latter's campaign. He was mortally wounded by the Indians near Fort Van Meter July 30, 1782.

McCOMAS, JOHN
Service—Virginia   Va. No. 28863   No. W. 18496
    Born, October 15, 1757; died March 31, 1837. Served as a private eleven months under Captain Cravens in detachment of Virginia troops under Colonel Matthew, after enlisting in Rockingham County, in 1778. On February 21, 1786, married Catherine Hatfield in Montgomery County, under Baptist ceremony. She was the daughter of Isaac Hatfield. Pension was granted in Cabell County, September 4, 1836, and widow likewise received pension.

McCONNELL, HUGH (Ensign)

Hugh McConnell was ensign in the Ohio County militia in 1778. His sister, Rebecca, was the wife of William Shepherd.

McCORD, ARTHUR

Enlisted under Captain Stephenson in 1775.

McCORMICK, MOSES

Drafted out of Captain Cloak's company of Berkeley County militia in 1780.

McCREERY, JOHN (Captain)

Born in the British Isles, son of James McCreery. He married Agnes Crawford of Darmack, Ireland, emigrated to America, and settled in Montgomery County, Virginia. He was made captain of the fort at Staunton in 1752, and his will is recorded there, 1769.

His children, listed below, were prominent in many parts of the frontier: Sarah, born in Ireland, married James Trimble, and lived in Virginia; Nancy, married James Huston; Betsy married Major George Wilson; Mary married Colonel John Lewis; Lieutenant Colonel John McCreery, married a Miss Estill; Captain Robert McCreery, married Polly McClanahan; Jane, married Colonel Andrew Donnally.

McCUE (McKEW), WILLIAM or WILLIAMS

Served in Captain Stephenson's company. Henry Bedinger stated that he took the first prisoner in the skirmish on Staten Island, April 7, 1776. Two days later, he lost his left hand when his rifle burst. He drew a pension. He died before 1833.

McCULLUM, DANIEL (Ensign)

Born, 1754; died, 1842. Was an ensign in the second company, first battalion, York County, Pennsylvania Associators. His battalion was incorporated with the force known as the "Flying Camp," in the year, 1776; served in the battle of Long Island, and was present at the surrender of Fort Washington in November following. He lived near Coopers Rock in Monongalia County.

McCUNE, PETER

Service—Virginia   Va. No. 7165   No. W. 7412

Born, 1748; died June 15, 1832. Enlisted, Pittsburgh, Pennsylvania, 1778, and served as a private three years under Captains Campbell and Lewis, Ninth Virginia Regiment Continental Line, commanded by Colonel Gibson. Married, January 13, 1781, at Ft. Richards, Monongalia County, Virginia, to Christiana McCune, with the Rev. Edwards officiating. Soldier received pension in Lewis County, in 1819, and widow, aged 72 in 1836, received pension also. They had ten children—four daughters and six sons. Supporting claims were filed for them by Adam Flesher and Elijah Runion.

West Virginians in the American Revolution

Assembled and Edited by ROSS B. JOHNSTON

The sources of this material are from the files of the Pension Office at Washington from various county records, from notes of patriotic societies, principally the Daughters of the American Revolution, Sons of the American Revolution, Sons of the Revolution, and from a large miscellaneous group of published and private sources. Corrections and additions to this list will receive the careful attention of the editor.

McCLAIN, DANIEL (Lieutenant)
Was lieutenant of the Ohio County militia and saw other Revolutionary War service about Wheeling. He was justice of the peace of that county early in 1777. He died some time before April, 1778, when his estate was administered.

McCREE, WILLIAM
Service—Pennsylvania　　　Va. No. 16208　　　No. S. 5754
Born in Ireland, 1756. Enlisted at Chambersburg, Pennsylvania, May or June, 1778, and served as a private for six months under Captain Hustead in the Pennsylvania Regiment Continental Line, commanded by Colonel Horton and General Morgan. Mentions Captains Smith and Russell, and Lieutenant Spears of the New Jersey Line, with whom he seems to have served in the Seventeenth or Eighteenth Regiment of New Jersey. Supporting data submitted by Benjamin Bruce, Charles Knotts, John Allen, W. P. Neff, Joshua Hawkins, and Abraham Hawkins. Pension granted in Harrison County, 1833, reduced in 1835, but apparently restored in 1836. He took part in the battles of Carlisle, Lancaster, Philadelphia, two skirmishes on the Delaware River, Monmouth, and Springfield, New Jersey.

McDADE, JAMES
Service—Virginia　　　Va. No. 7181　　　No. S. 38193
Born, 1749, and died July 30, 1833. Enlisted from Hampshire County, Virginia, Captain William Voss of the Twelfth Virginia Regiment under Colonel Wood in General Scott's Brigade. Took part in the engagements at Trenton, Brandywine, Germantown, Monmouth, Eutaw Springs and Camden. At Eutaw Springs received a bayonet thrust through the body and a sword wound on the wrist. At Camden he received a bullet wound in his ankle which rendered him unfit for service. Served three years. Substituted for Uriah Gandee for eighteen months. Received pension in Mason County.

His will, filed in Jackson County, mentions his wife, Margaret, and daughter, Sally Greathouse, and other children. They were probably Edward, Samuel, and Margaret.

McDANIEL, THOMAS
Service—North Carolina   Va. No. 18449   No. S. 38192

Born, 1752; died December 17, 1834. Enlisted, North Carolina, and served from 1776 to 1779 as a private under Captain Emmett in the Third North Carolina Regiment, Continental Line, under Colonels Patton and Summer and General Nash. Fought at Brandywine, Germantown, Monmouth, and Guilford Courthouse. Received pension in Monroe County, January 7, 1822. Wife is not named, but three children are mentioned, none of whom were at home in 1821.

McDANIELS, JOHN
John McDaniels, a soldier in the Revolutionary War, who died in 1778, is buried in the Price Memorial Cemetery near Olive Church, Mononalia County.

McDEAD, JOHN
Enlisted in Captain Stephenson's company in 1775.

McDONALD, ARCHIBALD
Service—Pennsylvania   No. S. 8889½

Enlisted, April, 1777, as a musician under Captain Finney, First Pennsylvania Regiment, Continental Line. Record is confused, but he seems to have received a pension in Virginia under the Act of 1828.

McDONALD, EDWARD (Captain)
Edward McDonald, who lived on the Clear Fork of Guyandotte, Wyoming County, Virginia, was one of the six sons of Joseph McDonald of Augusta, now Montgomery County, Virginia, who saw service in the Revolution. He held the rank of captain. He had three sons—Joseph, William, and Stephen; and four daughters, who married Captain Thomas Shannon; Captain Thomas Pearis; Augustus Pack; and William Chapman, respectively.

McELROY (McELRAY), THOMAS
Born in Ireland in 1751 and came to America in 1773. Enlisted in 1776 in the Revolutionary Army from Chester County, Pennsylvania. Later moved into Virginia where he applied for pension, but his claim was rejected.

McEVER (McKEEVER or McIVER), ANGUS
Service—Pennsylvania   No. 9012   No. W. 5355 and B.L.Wt. 299

Enlisted in Pennsylvania in 1777 as a private under Captain Beatty of the Third Pennsylvania Regiment, commanded by Majors Bowman and Butler. He took part in a number of battles. He was first assigned to the Twelfth Pennsylvania Regiment, commanded by Colonel William

WEST VIRGINIANS IN THE REVOLUTION

Cook. In the year 1778, he was transferred to the Third Pennsylvania Regiment commanded by Colonel Thomas Craig. He had one of his thumbs shot off and apparently received other wounds. He received pension in Berkeley County, Virginia, where he died August 15, 1837. He was married prior to 1794. His wife, Catherine, secured widow's pension, aged 86 in 1844, and died December 10, 1846.

McFARLAND, DANIEL (Colonel)

Born, 1731; died, 1817. Served as a colonel commanding the body of rangers of Ohio and Monongalia counties from April 22 to July 20, 1778, and also took active part at other times during the Revolutionary War period.

McFARLAND, JOHN

John McFarland, who had served as a soldier in the Revolutionary Army, died in 1839 and is buried in the Forks of Cheat Baptist Graveyard in Monongalia County.

McFITRICK, DUNCAN

Enlisted under Captain Stephenson in 1775.

McGEE, THOMAS

Service—New Jersey   Va. No. 13145   No. S. 5752

Born, Cumberland County, New Jersey, March 11, 1757. Substituted for Elihu Seeley and enlisted for guard duty in Cumberland County, under Captains Ewing and Foster; in New Jersey Regiment commanded by Colonels D. Potter, Ellis, Ogden, and General Washington. Secured pension in Preston County, Virginia, 1833. Supporting data filed by Colonel John Fairfax and David Trowbridge.

McGILL, CHARLES (Major)

Commanded part of the Berkeley County soldiers at the battle of Guilford Courthouse. Lived in Berkeley County and was a member of the Order of the Cincinnati.

McGUIRE (MAGUIRE), JAMES

Enlisted in the Revolutionary Army in Berkeley County.

McINTIRE, JOHN (Captain)

Served in the Revolutionary War and lived in Shepherdstown after its close.

McINTIRE, ROBERT

Service—Virginia   Va. No. 3389 and 3532   No. S. 5743

Born, June 17, 1761, in Frederick County, Maryland. Enlisted in what was then Youghiogheny County, Pennsylvania, now Fayette County, Pennsylvania, from Redstone Old Fort, now Brownsville, in company under Colonel John Gibson and Captain Josiah Springer. Guarded stores that had been brought over the mountains by pack horses for the Clark expedition.

Served against the Shawnee Indians under General George Rogers Clark and Colonel Zackquill Morgan. Other officers were Colonel John Harden, Colonel Lamphrey, Major Cracraft, Captain Stewart, Robert Terrel, Captain George Jackson, Benjamin Whaley, Michael Brice, Lieutenant James Paull, father of Colonel George Paull, and Adjutant John Mahan. Major George Wall also was with Clark's troops. Bazaleel Prather was brigade major and Major Crittendon aide-de-camp. Went from Chartiers Creek, some troops by water and some by land, to Fort Henry at Wheeling, where they were joined by other troops to a strength of 2000 men. Took to the boats at Wheeling, went down the Ohio River, remained two months, and returned January 9, 1782.

Received pension in Brooke County, Virginia, in 1832, which was dropped in 1835 without evidence of its later restoration.

McINTIRE, THOMAS (Captain)

Ensign in Third Pennsylvania Battalion, January 8, 1776; second lieutenant, March 8, 1776; wounded and taken prisoner at Fort Washington, November 16, 1776; exchanged, August 7, 1776; lieutenant of an independent western Pennsylvania company, December 30, 1777; captain, March 8, 1779. Served to May, 1782.

McINTIRE, THOMAS (Captain)

Thomas McIntire, son of Andrew and brother of Charles, enlisted in January, 1776, as an ensign in the Continental Army and was made a lieutenant in March of the same year. He was wounded in November at Fort Washington, was captured, spent nine months in prison, and was then exchanged. He went to western Pennsylvania, where he became first lieutenant and later captain of an independent company and served until May, 1782. Later years of his life were spent in Harrison County, Virginia.

McINTIRE, WILLIAM

Was a son of Nicholas McIntire of Shepherdstown. Served with the Revolutionary forces in the West and was killed at Limestone, Kentucky.

McKAY, WILLIAM
Service—North Carolina   Va. No. 23878   No. W. 7429

Born in Scotland, October 23, 1759; died October 6, 1836. Parents came to North Carolina in 1772 or 1773 where William enlisted as a private under Captain McCrea and Sloan in the Sixth North Carolina Regiment, commanded by Colonel Hamright, and served in several enlistments between 1776 and 1781. He was married in North Carolina, probably in Blandon County, February, 1787, to Nancy McKay, who had a brother, Hugh McKay. One son, Neil, was born April 19, 1788. William and Nancy McKay had lived in Ohio and Tyler County, Virginia, for 40 years prior to 1833 when pension application was made. Supporting data was filed by the Rev. Thomas Jones and Robert Gorrell. Pension was issued in 1834.

McKEOWN (MACKSON), JOHN
Service—Pennsylvania Pa. No. 2334 No. S. 41823

Enlisted, Baltimore County, Maryland, in the spring of 1776, and served four years and ten months. Part of his service at least was under Captains Marshall and Ashman, Second Pennsylvania Regiment, commanded by Colonel Miles in General Wayne's brigade. Took part in the fighting at Long Island, White Plains, and Brandywine. Supporting data from Walter Dorsey. Pension application in 1818 refers both to Baltimore, Maryland, and Jackson County, Virginia.

McKINNEY, WILLIAM
William McKinney, one of the first settlers in Ritchie County, Virginia, was a soldier in the latter part of the Revolution. He was born, September 4, 1760, and died June 24, 1848. (The service record of William McKinney, Va. No. 5054 and No. S. 16470, may be that of the same man but the connection is uncertain. Another soldier of same name is No. 23744 and No. S. 9017, and whose correspondence with his home folks in North Carolina is sent from western Virginia.)

McKNIGHT, BENJAMIN
Enlisted in Captain Shepherd's company. Was killed or died, February 15, 1777.

McKNIGHT, MICHAEL
Service—Virginia Va. No. 17908 No. S. 38200

Born about 1750. Enlisted under Captain Abel Westfall. Served seven years under General Muhlenberg in the Continental Line. Fought at White Plains, Brandywine, Monmouth, Camden, Eutaw Springs, Hanging Rock. Siege of Ninety-Six, Savannah and Yorktown. Applied for pension, October 10, 1820, Hardy County, Virginia.

McMILLAN (McMILLIAN), JOSEPH
Service—Virginia Va. No. 23820 No. S. 18116 and B. L. Wt. 26772

Born, Fauquier County, Virginia, 1763, the son of John and Martha McMillan; died, July 9, 1853. Enlisted, Fauquier County, Virginia, February 24, 1781, under Captain T. Morehead in the Virginia militia commanded by Colonel Armstead Churchill in General Meadows' Brigade.

Soldier was married July 22, 1791. Wife's name Jane. Had moved from Fauquier to Greenbrier County in 1785. Pensions received there by both soldier and his widow, who was aged 82 in 1856. Supporting data submitted by Martha and Joseph McMillan, James Watts, and Susanna Hanna. Bounty land warrant for 160 acres was also issued.

McMILLEN (McMILLAN) ROBERT
Service—Pennsylvania Va. No. 12530 No. W. 7426

Born, York County, Pennsylvania. Enlisted in Chester County, Pennsylvania, under Captain Ramney and Cunningham in the First Pennsylvania Regiment, commanded by Colonel Harum or Herman, under General Porter, and served in several enlistment periods between

July 1777, and 1781. Married, August 22, 1785. Wife, named Mary, was aged 79 in 1845. Three or four children were born in Pennsylvania, according to Isaac Coburn. Supporting claims presented by the Rev. David Trowbridge, and Isaac Mathews. Pension granted to soldier in Preston County, in 1833. He died there, October 16, 1834, and his widow likewise received pension.

McNEEL, JOHN

Lived in Frederick County, Virginia, and in Maryland. Settled in Pocahontas County, Virginia, near the Levels about 1765. Fought in the battle of Point Pleasant in 1774, then returned to Frederick County, where he served in the Revolution.

McNEILL, DANIEL (Captain)

At Willow Hall, Hardy County, Virginia, lived Captain Daniel McNeill of the United States Navy in the Revolution. He also commanded the U. S. S. Boston in the war with the Barbary States.

McSWAYNE, JOHN

Enlisted under Captain Shepherd in Berkeley County. Was killed or died, February 15, 1777.

McVANY (McVANCY), CHRISTOPHER

Born in Pennsylvania in 1757. Enlisted, Frederick County, Virginia, in 1777, and served in the Virginia militia under Ensign Mitchell, Lieutenant Doren and Captain Morgan in Colonel Fansler's Regiment. Took part in the fighting at Cowpens.

He was married in Augusta County, Virginia, October, 1796. Name of wife, Mary. Received pension in Upshur County, Virginia, 1833 but seems to have been dropped in 1835. Supporting data submitted by Jacob Cozer, minister, James Brown, and Margaret Means.

McWHORTER, HENRY

Service—N. J., N. Y., and Pa.   Va. No. 12929   No. S. 7210

Born, New York, November 13, 1760; moved to Bucks County, Pennsylvania. Then to Hampshire County, Virginia, in 1786, and to Harrison, now Lewis County, Virginia, in 1791; and died there February 4, 1848. He enlisted in a company of New York Minute Men in Orange County, New York, in 1776, under Captain John Wisner and Colonel Livingston. In July, 1776, he was one of five men who were attached to the Flying Camp. Among his officers were Colonel Isaac Nichols, General George Clinton, and others. In November 1777, he enlisted in company of militia in New Jersey, under Colonel Sawyers. In the spring of 1778, he enlisted in Northumberland County, under Captain Thomas Champlain.

He married a Miss Fields. Supporting data in this case was submitted by John Neeley, Alexander West, William Powers, John Talbott, Daniel Stinger, and Samuel Jones. Had a furlough signed by Dr. Henry White. Pension granted in Lewis County, Virginia, in 1835. The amount appears later to have been reduced. The town of McWhorter, Lewis County, is named for this soldier.

MEADE (MEAD), WILLIAM
Service—North Carolina   No. 23946   No. S. 19394
Born, Frederick County, Virginia, August 22, 1762; died, February 1841. Enlisted, September 1778, and served until January 1781, from Wilkes County, North Carolina. Served under Captain George Baker, Colonel Howard and Cleveland. Took part in battle of Cowpens. Knew Colonel Daniel Morgan, Joseph McDowell, Charles McDowell, General Nathaniel Green, Major Charles Gray, Andrew Pickets, Colonel James Avery, General Sumpter and others. Was wounded several times and received pension in Logan County, Virginia. One son, Samuel, was named.

MEADOWS, FRANCIS
Born, 1754; died, December 20, 1836. Enlisted, Augusta County, Virginia, in February 1777, and served until 1781 under Captain Laird and Lamb, Tenth Virginia Regiment, Continental Establishment, commanded by Colonels Green, Wood, and Wheaton. He was married in the fall of 1790 or 1791 in the County of Rockingham to Frances Bush, who was born in 1772. They received pension in Monroe County, in 1819, at which time they had sixteen children, twelve of whom were sons. Six, under 14 years of age, remained at home. Supporting data in their case was filed by Jonathan Roach, Elizabeth Fisher, and Henry Maggart.

MEADOW, JOSIAH
Service—Pennsylvania   Va No. 2123   No. S. 7225
Enlisted, Bedford County, Virginia, in 1778 under Lieutenants Isaac Hyler and Hiddens, and Captain Joseph Renfroe largely in frontier service against the Indians. He saw service on Wolf Creek in Monroe County and at Fort Donnally near Lewisburg. He also marched through Tennessee to Chickamauga in Georgia, fighting back the Indians from the frontier which was then along the Blue Ridge and Cumberland mountains. After this expedition, he took part in George Rogers Clark's expedition into the Illinois country. In 1781, as a substitute for John Mitchell of Bedford County, he helped convey prisoners to Fredericksburg, Virginia.

After his military service, he returned to the Bluestone Valley where he married a daughter of Robert Lilly, who had settled there ten years earlier. He received pension in Summers or Mercer County, Virginia, in 1832. Supporting data was filed by John Neely and Bainster Meadow.

MEDCALF, JOHN
Private under Captain Stephenson. Died, December 1, 1775, and was buried at Roxbury Camp.

MEDLAR, BOSTON
Service—Maryland   Va. No. 2891   No. S. 38212
Born, 1763. Enlisted, 1777, although evidently but 14 years old, and

served as a drum major under Captain Daniel Stuls, Seventh Regiment, First Brigade, Maryland Line, under Colonel John Gunby. Took part in the fighting at Staten Island, Brandywine, Germantown, Monmouth, the two battles of Camden, Guilford Courthouse, Siege of Ninety-Six, Eutaw Springs, and Hunting Bluff on the Gumbee River when Colonel Lawrence of the Infantry was killed.

Affidavit is filed by George G. Brewer of the Maryland Land Office in 1849 that Medlar had served as a drum major from May, 1780, to November 15, 1783, after enlisting as a drummer in 1777. Letter from Alex Yearley, agent, December 13, 1849, indicates that as a drum major Medlar should have received a larger pension. There was also inquiry as to land bounty, which he apparently did not receive although he did receive pension as a private, while living in Jefferson County, Virginia, 1818. His wife was aged 43 in 1820 at which time they had four children. Supporting data was filed by Daniel Briant.

MERRITT, LAROSE (ROSEY)

Larose S. Merritt was born in 1738 and died, July 30, 1831. He was a private in the Virginia Line during the Revolution. He probably lived on Merritt's Branch of Guyan River, Cabell County, west of Salt Rock, where he settled after moving west from Greenbrier County.

MESSENGER, ABNER
Service—Connecticut   Va. No. 23338   No. S. 9022

Born, Hartford, Connecticut, 1760; died, Preston County, Virginia, 1845. Enlisted, Hartford County, Connecticut, 1778 and served until 1783, under Captain A. Mills, Captain James Stoddard, Captain Mathew Smith, Colonel Enoch Meads, Generals Waterbury, Putnam, and Preston. Took part in the campaign about West Point, Horseneck, White Plains, and Bradford, after joining Washington at Philipsburg. His unit was composed of drafts from the militia, comprising a brigade of two battalions.

He applied for pension in Preston County, 1832. When his application was rejected or refused on account of want of proof, so conscious was he of his rights that despite his 75 years of age, he mounted on an old horse and went all the way to New York to secure proof of his service. His old horse died on the way. He then continued on foot until he found his captain, James Stoddard, who gave him his supporting affidavit, with which he returned on foot to his home in Preston County. Other supporters of his claim were William Brice and Benjamin Jeffers. Certificate was issued in 1834.

MIDDLETON (MIDLETON) JOHN
Service—Virginia   Va. No. 535   No. W. 7464 and B. L. Wt. 28594

Born, Louden County, Virginia, November 20, 1761; died, Harrison County, Virginia, January 31, 1837. Enlisted in Louden County, and served from September 1780, until April, 1781, as a private under Captan Dan Figgins and Berry, First Lieutenant Mathew Rust, Second Lieutenant John Russel, Ensign Sam Oliphant, in Virginia Line regiment commanded by Colonel Elias Edmonds. Other officers were Generals Lafayette, Muhlenberg, and Baron Von Steuben, who addressed his group when they received their discharge.

The soldier married Eleanor Hardy in Frederick County, Virginia, March 28, 1797. In 1832, they were living in Harrison County, where application was made for pension which was granted in 1833. Supporting data was submitted by Robert Parks, Zachariah Hickman, Sam B. Davis, John Romine, and Abraham Batten. The widow also received pension and bounty land warrant for 160 acres.

MILLAM (MILAN), RUSH
Service—Virginia   Va. No. 12740   No. S. 7943

Born, Culpepper County, Virginia, 1759; moved to Bedford County 1761; to Botetourt, 1786; and to Kanawha in 1812. Enlisted in Culpepper County January 15, 1781, and served in the Virginia Line under Captain Cummins, Colonel Merriweather, Calloway, Baron Von Steuben, and Colman.

Pension certificate issued in 1833 in Kanawha County, but length of service was later questioned. Important papers were submitted by A. W. Quarrier of Kanawha County, 1835. Other supporting data by Calhoun Walker and Walter Williams. Records of June 1, 1840, indicate that full service had been established.

MILLER, DAVID
Served in the Revolutionary Army under Captain Stephenson in 1775.

MILLER, JACOB
Jacob Miller, a soldier in the Revolution, died in Monongalia County, in 1778, and is buried at the site of Kern's Fort, Arch Street, Morgantown.

MILLER, JOHN
Service—Virginia   Va. No. 16587   No. S. 9026

Born, Berkeley County, Virginia, February 1, 1759. At Hanging Rocks, Hampshire County, enlisted in the Virginia Line under Captain Foreman and Lieutenant Miller, and served six months at Fort Pitt, Wheeling, and at Yorktown. Received pension in Morgan County, in 1833. Supporting data submitted by the Rev. M. Rizer and Richard Cell.

MILLER, PETER
Service—New Jersey-New York   Va. No. 12053   No. W. 7456

Born, Woodbridge, New Jersey, May 15, 1759; died April 14, 1838, in what is now Marion County. Enlisted 1776, in Orange County, New York, and served under Captains Blauvelt, Parsons, and Martin in New York and New Jersey Lines under Colonel Drake, General Scott, and James Clinton. Took part in battle of Long Island and on guard duties. Married, February 5, 1785, Goshen, New York. Name of wife, Mary. She was aged 82 in 1845. Pension granted in Monongalia County in 1833 to the soldier, and also to his widow. Supporting data filed by M. Fleming, Ann Carpenter, sister of Mary Miller, and John Miller.

MILLER, PHILIP
Service—Continental Va.   Va. No. 19247   No. W. 3707 and B. L. Wt. 40691

Enlisted at Warm Springs, Virginia, in the spring of 1776, and served as a private under Captain W. Brady in the regiment commanded by Colonel Stevenson, Rollins, and General Washington. He took part in several campaigns during which he was taken prisoner at Hoboken Ferry after the capture of New York by the British and held prisoner for two years.

Soldier was married to Lois Benjamin by John Loneberry, September 13, 1785. While living in Washington County, Pennsylvania, in 1823, application was made for pension, which was granted following year. Soldier was aged 63 in 1823 and his wife 54. Among other persons mentioned in this case are the following, of whom several are evidently their children: Jonathan Miller, Jacob Miller, J. Barker, Christopher Miller, Peter McMahan, William Catlett, F. Delong, Mathias Ambrose, Hannah (Miller) McAnaspy, and Joshua Russell.

MILLER, SAMUEL
Service—Maryland   Va. No. 23505   No. S. 15940

Born in Kent County, Maryland, January 6, 1755, and was living in Brooke County, Virginia, in 1797. Enlisted, March 1, 1776, in the Kent County Minute Men under Captains William Ringold, Page, and Williamson, which were assigned to guarding the Chesapeake Shore. Pension certificate was issued to him in Brooke County in 1834. Supporting affidavits were filed in this case by the Rev. Lewis Browning, Edward Worrel, Rebecca Peck, and William Wilson.

MILLIGAN, HUGH
Service—Pennsylvania   Va. No. 17864   No. S. 38232

Enlisted in Pennsylvania, February 13, 1776, and served three years as private in company of Captain Abraham Smith and William Wilson in the Pennsylvania Line Regiment, commanded by Colonels William Irvine and Chambers. Took part in the battles of Three Rivers, White Plains, Brandywine, Monmouth, and Germantown. Was discharged at Trenton, New Jersey. Pension was granted while residing in Hardy County, Virginia, in 1820.

MILLIGAN (MULLIKEN), JOHN
Service—Pennsylvania-Virginia   Va. No. 16653   No. S. 13939

Born in County Down, Ireland, 1751; emigrated to America and was living in Berkeley County, Virginia, in 1793, and in Ohio County in 1833. Died, February 5, 1838. Served nineteen months as a private between 1775 and 1781 under Captain Stevenson, Frazier, and Evans in the Virginia Line under Colonel Swope and General Freeding. Also mentions Captain Stinson, Morgan, Price, Smouzer, First Lieutenant Henshaw, Second Lieutenant George Scott, Ensign Abraham Shepherd. Also names Robert White, Joseph Swearington, William McCue, and William Chorters. Received pension in Berkeley County 1833. Supporting data was filed by Robert and William Stewart, and Adam and John Farris.

WEST VIRGINIANS IN THE REVOLUTION

MILLS, JOHN (Lieutenant)
Service—Virginia   Va. No. 1936   No. W. 5378 and B. L. Wt. 1512

Private, Thirteenth Virginia, February 2, 1778; regiment designated Ninth Virginia, September 14, 1778; ensign, August 6, 1779; transferred to Seventh Virginia, February 12, 1781; second lieutenant, May 26, 1781. Served to January 1, 1783.

September 13, 1785, Ohio County, Virginia, was married to Ruth Shepherd, daughter of Colonel David Shepherd. Among those witnessing the ceremony were General Benjamin Biggs, James Mitchell, John McIntire, William Boggs, David Shepherd, father; and Moses Shepherd, brother of the bride; Mary McCulloch, Elizabeth McIntire, Rachel Crawford, the Rev. Richard Yates, who performed the marriage ceremony, and his wife. Much information given in statement by Mrs. Lydia S. Croger, wife of Moses Shepherd.

Supporting data filed by John White, Solomon King, and Archibald Woods. Soldier received five years full pay under act of March 22, 1783. Bounty land warrant was received for 200 acres. Soldier died, September 13, 1833, and is buried in Stone Church Cemetery, Elm Grove, Wheeling. His widow received pension certificates in 1839 and 1844.

MILLS, THOMAS
Service—Virginia   Va. No. 16808   No. S. 16200

Born in 1765 on Elk River, Maryland; moved to Ohio County, Virginia, resided in Tyler County, Virginia, in 1833; moved to Monroe County, Ohio, in 1834. Volunteered in 1781 with Captain Silas Zane's company and served from May until October when it was disbanded. In May, 1782, again volunteered with Captain Zane and was wounded four miles from Wheeling by Indians by eight bullets. After his recovery, he volunteered against the Indians in 1791 under Joseph Biggs, commander of the Kirkwood Blockhouse, and was out again in 1793 under Captain McMahon.

Received pension in 1833 in Ohio or Tyler County. Supporting data filed by Noah Zane, George Dully, and Abraham McColloch.

MILOY (MILEY or MELEY), JOHN R.
Service—Massachusetts   Va. No. 12585   No. S. 38224

Enlisted in New Jersey, according to statement, and served three years under Captain Flowers of the Third Massachusetts Regiment, commanded by Colonel Graten. Took part in the Battle of Stillwater. Served from 1776 to 1779 and received discharge at Peekskill Hollow, New York. Received pension, Harrison County, Virginia, 1819.

MINEAR (MANIER), DAVID
Service—Virginia   Va. No. 23565   No. S. 15932

Born, Bucks County, Pennsylvania, 1755; died, October 20, 1834, Tucker County, Virginia (then Randolph County). Also lived for a time in Hardy County, Virginia. Enlisted in the spring of 1779 in Monongalia County. Served under Captain Salathiel Goff in 1781, probably at Minear's Fort which stood upon the land of his father on Cheat River, and at Wilson's Fort in the Tygart Valley. As an Indian spy ranged as far as Morgantown and Dunkard Creek. Was also under Colonel Lyons, Major William Haymond, and General Clark.

In 1781, three men were killed during an Indian attack on the settlements along Cheat River. David Minear's father, Frederick Cooper, and Daniel Cannon saw Kentucky service under General Clark. Their company was fired upon by Indians, nine men were killed and wounded, four of whom were buried in the sand on the river bank three days journey from the Falls of the Ohio. At the Indian village of Piqua, fifteen men were killed. April 16, 1783, Indians killed and scalped his brother, Jonathan.

Pension certificate was issued in 1834. The soldier died the same year so payment was made to his children: Enoch, Elizabeth (Minear) Bonnifield; and Mary (Minear) Miller. Supporting affidavits were filed by Thomas Parsons and Aaron Langtry.

MITCHELL (MITCHEL), JOHN (Sergeant)
Service—Continental, Va.   Va. No. 16387   No. S. 5761

Born, May, 1763, Dawston, Lancashire County, England. Emigrated to America, 1774, landed at Yorktown, Virginia, and settled in Hampshire County, Virginia. There enlisted as a soldier in August, 1780, under Captain Pendleton in the Virginia Line, Continental Establishment, in regiment commanded by Colonel Harrison. He served as a cavalryman in the State Line, then as an infantryman in the Continental Line, and finally as a sergeant of cavalry in the Continental Establishment. Mentions among officers Colonel Charles Harrison, Colonel Robert Harrison, Major Lewis Booker, Lieutenant Daniel Richardson, Captain James Culbertson, Captain Frederick, Lieutenant Michael Freeman, and Ensign Sissler.

Received pension, Lewis County, Virginia, in 1833. Soldier died, April 29, 1840. Supporting data submitted by Jacob Teter and John Wagoner.

MITCHELL, THOMAS

In Captain Shepherd's company. Drafted, January 1, 1777, into another unit. Probably taken prisoner, November 16, 1776, and exchanged.

MOORE, CATO, 1st (Lieutenant)

Cato Moore, 1st, was born in 1752 on the Eastern Shore of Maryland. He was a resident of Shepherdstown during the Revolution. He married Margaret Cooke in 1780 and one son, Cato Moore, 2nd, was born in 1783.

He served in the Revolution as a first lieutenant of Grayson's Conditional Regiment February 3, 1777, and was wounded in the battle of Brandywine September 11, 1777. He resigned February 3, 1778. He was called "King Moore" because of land grants which he received from the King.

MOORE, ELIJAH (Lieutenant)
Service—New Jersey   Va. No. 12362   No. S. 38344
Resided at Deerfield, Cumberland County, New Jersey at the outbreak of the Revolution. There enlisted, February 1776, as a private under Captain Joseph Bloomfield in the Third Regiment of the New Jersey line, commanded by Colonel Dayton, and took part in the expedition against Canada. Marched to Elizabethtown, then to Albany up the Mohawk at which time a treaty was made with the Indians by General Schuyler. From Fort Schuyler, marched to Oswego where there was a skirmish with the Indians and to other points until Fort Independence was reached. There he became ill and was discharged. He had another short period of service, after which he served as lieutenant of militia until the end of the war. He took part in the engagements at States Island, Monmouth, Red Bank, and Cooper Creek. He received pension at Steubenville, Ohio, but was removed to western Virginia in 1827.

MOORE, ENOCH
Service—Maryland   Va. No. 1908   No. S. 5785
Born, New Jersey, June 18, 1758. While he was a child his parents moved to Allegheny County, Maryland, where he lived until 1791 or 1792 when he moved to Harrison County, Virginia. While living in Maryland, he enlisted in the spring of 1778 and served six months as an Indian spy along the Ohio River under Captain Henry Enock of a Maryland Regiment. He was at Enock's Fort and also at Jackson's Fort. Supporting data was filed in his case by Colonel Daniel Morris and James Bartlett.
The soldier received pension in Harrison County in 1832, but was dropped from the rolls in 1835 on the grounds that he was one of the early settlers who was styled an Indian fighter, but whose service was not covered by the provisions of the Revolutionary pension laws.

MOREDECK, WILLIAM
Served as a private under Captain Shepherd. Died February 15, 1777, on a prison ship.

MORGAN, ABEL (Surgeon)
Surgeon in Eleventh Pennsylvania, February 14, 1777; transferred to Eighth Pennsylvania, July 1, 1778. For a time during the Revolution, Dr. Morgan was held prisoner in the Ship Jersey in Walabou Bay. He resigned February 1779, and a few years after his return home to Shepherdstown, Jefferson County, Virginia, died from the effects of his long and terrible confinement.
He was born in New Jersey in 1755, a son of Captain Richard Morgan. He died in Jefferson County, in 1785 or 1788. He was survived by his widow, Elizabeth Bedinger Morgan, and five children: Joseph, Jacob, Daniel, Olivia, and Elizabeth.

MORGAN, ABRAHAM (Colonel)

Grandson of the pioneer Richard Morgan. Served in the Revolution and was known as Colonel Morgan. Married Mary Bedinger in 1787 and after her death moved to Kentucky.

MORGAN, ADAM

Before the Harrison County court, April 20, 1785, Adam Morgan proved that he had served nine months as an Indian spy.

MORGAN, BENJAMIN
Service—Virginia   Va. No. 2972   No. W. 3854

Born in Philadelphia, Pennsylvania, December 25, 1760; moved to Berkeley County, Virginia, while a boy, and died there, February 24, 1836.

Enlisted in 1778 or 1779 under Captain David Kennedy for the pack train service to Fort McIntosh, commanded by Colonel Murray and General McIntosh. Took part in the building of Fort Lawrence on the Tuscaroras River. Witnessed the killing of Lieutenant Parks by the Indians. Was discharged by Captain John Lyles. In 1781, enlisted under Captain Edward Davis under Colonel Darke and General Lincoln, and in a clash with British cavalry was wounded by a sword cut in the shoulder. He was discharged, and then re-enlisted under Captain John Hart, and again was under Colonel Darke. He took part in the siege and capture of Yorktown. Pension was granted him in Monroe County, Virginia, in 1832. Supporting data was filed by William Vass, Samuel Clark, and Henry Alexander.

In Hagerstown, Maryland, July 18, 1783, Morgan was married to Ann Ellis, who was born January 14, 1766. She also received a widow's pension. Their children were: John, 1784; Phoebe, 1786; Moses, 1788; Aaron, 1790; Jesse, 1792; Ellis, 1798; Nancy, 1801; Eleanor, 1804; Benjamin, 1805; James R., 1809; Hannah, 1811.

MORGAN, DANIEL (Major-General)

Born in New Jersey in 1737; came to what is now Berkeley County, West Virginia in 1755, and that year shared the perils of Braddock's expedition against the British at Fort Duquesne. Was wounded in the neck and chest. Engaged in agricultural pursuits near Martinsburg until near the beginning of the Revolution when he purchased land in Frederick County, near Winchester. He organized a company of Virginia riflemen and entered the Revolutionary service as captain, July, 1775; took part in the expedition against Quebec; was taken prisoner, December 31, 1775; appointed colonel of the Eleventh Virginia, November 12, 1776. This regiment, largely filled with men from the Eastern Panhandle counties of what is now West Virginia, was designated as the Seventh Virginia, September 14, 1778. He was made a brigadier general of the Continental Army, October 13, 1780, and served to the end of the war.

For his brilliant exploits with his riflemen on various fields, particularly at Cowpens, he received the thanks of Congress. He was appointed in 1794 to command the Virginia troops which were called out to suppress the Whisky Rebellion in Pennsylvania. He died, July 6, 1802, and is buried at Winchester, Frederick County, Virginia.

MORGAN, DAVID

Born, Christiana, Delaware, May 13, 1721; died in Monongalia County, May 9, 1813. He was a son of Morgan Morgan and Catherine Garrettson or Garrison. With his father, he removed to near Winchester and later established a home in Berkeley County. Then with his brother, Zackquill, he came to the Monongahela Valley about 1766-68 and settled on the Monongahela between Fairmont and Morgantown. He married Sarah Stevenson, a Quakeress, of Pennsylvania, and to them were born the following children: Stephen, Sarah (Burriss), Zackquill, Morgan, James, Jacob, Elizabeth, David, Catherine, and Evan T. Morgan.

At the outbreak of the Revolution, Morgan Morgan, a son, was in command of a company of Virginia militia. When Captain William Haymond's company was formed in Monongalia County, during the Revolution, Morgan Morgan became a lieutenant of it, and his father, David, and three other Morgans, David, Evan, and James, joined the company as privates.

David was an engineer and aided the commission named by the Governor of Virginia to survey the Mason and Dixon line. He was with George Washington on some of his expeditions in the Monongahela region. He is buried near the Morgan Mines, Marion County.

His most celebrated exploit was the hand-to-hand fight in 1779 near his home along the Monongahela River in which he killed two Indians who had attempted to kidnap or kill two of his children.

West Virginians in the American Revolution

Assembled and Edited by ROSS B. JOHNSTON

The sources of this material are from the files of the Pension Office at Washington from various county records, from notes of patriotic societies, principally the Daughters of the American Revolution, Sons of the American Revolution, Sons of the Revolution, and from a large miscellaneous group of published and private sources. Corrections and additions to this list will receive the careful attention of the editor.

MOORE, SAMUEL
Service—Virginia   Indiana-Va. 7027   No. S. 17983

Born, Staunton, Augusta County, Virginia, July 14, 1761. At the outbreak of the Revolution lived in Greenbrier County. Enlisted under Captain J. Armstrong in the Virginia Militia commanded by Major Hamilton, and served from February, 1781, to September, 1781. He applied for and received pension, October 25, 1832, Putnam County, Indiana. Supporting data submitted by the Rev. George Piercy and William Robertson.

MORGAN, EVANS (Ensign)
Service—Pennsylvania-Virginia   Va. No. 23401   No. S. 11098

Born, Town Creek, Alleghany County, Maryland, March 1, 1754; removed to Frederick County, Virginia while an infant, and in 1773 came with his father to Monongalia County, Virginia. Reference is made to his being a son of Daniel Morgan and a brother to Captain Morgan Morgan, but his father was probably David.

He enlisted, March, 1776, under Captain Nelson in the First Pennsylvania Regiment, Continental Line, commanded by Colonel DeHose or DeHouse. He served as a private until 1780 when he received a commission as ensign from the Governor of Virginia. His statement mentions many officers: General Hand; Colonels Brodhead, Housaker, Oldham, Harley, Wine, Johnson, Angus McDaniel; Major Huffnagel; Captains Zadock Springer, Biggs, Butler, McCullough and others.

He received pension in 1834 which was increased in 1836. Supporting data was filed by Colonel Dudley Evans, Mathew Gray, and David P. Morgan. The soldier died in 1850 and is buried in the Fairview Cemetery, Monongalia County.

MORGAN, JAMES

James Morgan, who was one of the five Morgans serving in Captain William Haymond's company of Monongalia County militia during the Revolution, is buried in the Cramer Cemetery, Winfield, Marion County.

WEST VIRGINIANS IN THE REVOLUTION

MORGAN, MORGAN (Lieutenant)
Born, Winchester, Virginia, in 1746; came with his father, David, to the Monongahela Valley, and died in Monongalia County, in 1820. He was the commander of a company of militia at the outbreak of the Revolution. When Captain William Haymond organized his company of Monongalia County militia in 1777, Morgan Morgan became its first lieutenant. With him into the service of this company went no fewer than four other members of the Morgan family as privates.

MORGAN, WILLIAM (Colonel)
Colonel William Morgan was one of the hundred men who assembled at Morgan's Spring near Shepherdstown in 1775 and from thence marched with Hugh Stephenson to join Washington at Boston. After the war, William married Agnes Vail, daughter of Isaac and Elizabeth (Jennings) Vail of Orange, New Jersey. They left one son, Jephtha, who lived in Berkeley County.
Colonel Morgan was the son of Isaac Morgan and the grandson of Richard Morgan, who built one of the first houses in the Shenandoah Valley near Shepherdstown.

MORGAN, WILLIAM, JR.
Son of George Morgan. Enlisted in Berkeley County and was known as Captain Morgan. Served in Captain William Morgan's company in the skirmish at Piscatawa.

MORGAN, WILLIAM, SR. (Captain)
Served in the French and Indian War under his father, Richard Morgan. Married Drusilla Swearingen, daughter of Thomas Swearingen. In 1776-77, raised a company near Shepherdstown and led them to Washington. His men took part in the action at Piscatawa. In 1779, he led a party to Kentucky. He died in 1788, leaving three daughters and five sons, who were Abraham, George, Ralph, Raleigh, and Zaccheus.

MORGAN, ZACKQUILL (Colonel)
Born in 1735 and came from the Eastern Panhandle in 1766-68 with his brother, David, to settle in the Monongahela Valley. His stout log cabin became Fort Morgan and the nucleus around which grew up Morgan's Town, now Morgantown. He died January 1, 1795.
He was made county lieutenant of Monongalia County, February 17, 1777, and was the military and civil leader of the community. After the Revolution he laid out the town of Morgantown which was established by act of the Virginia Legislature in 1785. He maintained an inn. His home on University Avenue, north of Fayette Street, stood until torn down a few years ago to make way for a filling station. In this house his granddaughter, Drusilla Morgan, born in 1814, died in 1904.
Colonel Morgan was married twice; first to Nancy Paxton, to whom three children were born: Ann Nancy, who married John Pierpont, and who was grandmother of Francis H. Pierpont, one of the leading spirits in the organization of West Virginia and who was the war-time governor

of the Restored State of Virginia; Temperance, who married James Cochran; Catherine, who married Jacob Scott. Morgan's second wife was Drusilla Springer, and they had eleven children: Levi, Uriah, James, Zodac, Morgan ("Mod"), Zackquill, Hannah, Sally, Rachel, Drusilla, and Horatio.

MORGAN, ZACKQUILL (Sergeant)
Service—Pennsylvania-Virginia   Va. No. 12360   No. W. 1912

Born, Frederick County, Virginia, September 18, 1758; died, February 27, 1834-35. Came to Monongalia County, while a young man, and there in 1778 enlisted under Captains James Brinton, Samuel Mason, Campbell, and Evans and served as a private and sergeant in the Eighth and Thirteenth Pennsylvania Regiments commanded by Colonels Morgan, Brodhead, and General McIntosh. Many other officers are named.

Pension was applied for and secured in Monongalia County, in 1833, but it was later suspended without full explanation shown. Supporting data was filed by Joseph Heartley, James Morgan, a nephew, Evans Morgan, brother, and Stephen Morgan. The soldier married Sina or Cina West in Monongalia County, September 19, 1794. To them were born the following children: Stephen, 1797; Sally, 1800; Mary, 1802; Malinda, 1805; Katherine, 1807; Rebecca, 1810; John Parimont, 1812; David James, 1815; Samuel, 1817; Elizabeth, 1820. The widow of the soldier received pension in 1849 while living in Marion County.

MORGAN, ZEDEKIAH

Born, Norwich, Connecticut, March 8, 1754; died, French Creek, Upshur County, Virginia, October 12, 1822. He was twice married; first to Ruth Dart, of Connecticut, and then to Rebecca Watson of Boston.

He served in the Revolutionary War as a teamster (or conductor) from 1779 to 1781. In regard to the transportation of supplies to the army, Assistant Quartermaster Ralph Pomeroy at Hartford writes to Quartermaster General Pickering in the field, July 15, 1781: "There are three brigades of teams with conductors and another brigade with the provisions, with orders to unload and lend wheels as occasion may be. The pieces of artillery are drawn with 68 yoke of oxen each, one by seven and one by six. These teams will have to return for their carts which came from the North River. Carts loaded with tents, haversacks, etc., at Rocky Hill."

MORRIS, AMOS
Service—Virginia   Va. No. 12930   No. S. 7244

Born, August 25, 1758, Apple Pie Ridge, Berkeley County, Virginia. Moved to Youghiogheny County, Virginia, now Greene County, Pennsylvania, and resided in Monongalia County, Virginia, when the Revolution broke out. There enlisted, May, 1778, and served two years while protecting and guarding the western frontiers. His officers were Lieutenant Springer, Captains Cross, Clark, Whetsel, Clark, Brady; Colonels Evans, and Gibson.

He applied for pension in Monongalia County in 1832, which was granted in 1833. Supporting data was submitted by George Wade, James Troy, Henry Yoho, Sam Minor, and William Stiles.

MORRIS, HENRY

Born in Virginia, 1747, son of William and Elizabeth Stipps Morris; died, 1824, Nicholas County, Virginia. Married Mary Byrd (Bird), daughter of John Byrd of Jackson River, Bath County, Virginia, who was born about 1747 and died after 1820. Morris took part in the battle of Point Pleasant in 1774 and was active in other events of frontier life in the Kanawha Valley.

The children of Henry and Mary Byrd Morris were: Sarah, married Charles Young, March 29, 1793; Betsy, born, 1778, and Margaret, born, 1780, both killed by Indians in 1792 in Nicholas County; Polly, born, October 10, 1783, married Jesse James of Bath County; John, born, 1783 and died September, 1855, married Jane Brown, March 13, 1807; Catherine, born, 1787, died December 1853, married William Byrd or Bird of Bath County, who may have been a cousin; Lean, married Archy Price; (there may also have been still another daughter).

The Byrd family on Jackson River was one of those visited by tragedy during the Indian raids of 1756. John Byrd, the head of the family, was killed; Sarah, born, 1743, had a narrow escape from the Indians but a sister was captured and apparently spent the rest of her life with the Indians. Besides Mary, who married Henry Morris, there was also Thomas and John, who married a sister of Andrew Hamilton, and a sixth child, name unknown.

MORRIS, JOHN

Served in George Rogers Clark's expedition into the Illinois country in 1778 and 1779. He was captain of Kanawha County militia and served with the Virginia troops in the Whisky Rebellion in Pennsylvania. He was the father of Bishop Thomas A. Morris, and of Edmund Morris, first clerk of Cabell County. He had moved from near the mouth of Campbell's Creek, Kanawha County, to near Bethesda Church, Cabell County, and died near there in 1818.

MORRIS, WILLIAM

Born in England and emigrated to Philadelphia. He later moved to Orange County, Virginia, where he married Elizabeth Stipps. To them were born eight sons and two daughters. The Morris family was living in the Kanawha Valley at Fort Morris, at the mouth of Kelly's Creek, when Dunmore's War broke out. Six of William Morris' sons, William, Jr.; Henry, Leonard, Joshua, Levi, and John, joined the army of General Andrew Lewis in 1774 and took part in the Battle of Point Pleasant. William, Jr., was wounded.

Following are the members of the family: William Morris, Jr., born, 1746, married Catherine Carroll, 1768; Henry, born, 1747, married Mary Byrd; Leonard, born, 1748, first married Margaret Price and then Margaret Lykins; Joshua, born, 1752, married Francis Simms; Levi, born, 1753, first married Margaret Stark and then Margaret Jarrett; John, born, 1755, married Margaret Droddy; Achilles (Carroll) Morris, born, 1760, married Elizabeth Jarrett; Benjamin, born, 1770, married Nancy Jarrett; Elizabeth, born, 1772, married Michael See; Frances, born, 1773, married John Jones.

MORRIS (MORRISS), ZADOC (ZADOCK)
Service—Delaware   Va. No. 9058   No. S. 38247

He enlisted as a private in Captain Thomas Holland's company, Colonel David Hall's Delaware Regiment, in June, 1777. On August 16, 1780, he was reported missing in action, but for what reason is unknown.

He received pension in Monongalia County, in 1819, at which time he was 60 years old and his wife, 50. They had sons, aged 14 and 13, and a son and daughter, twins, aged 11. Supporting data was submitted by Joseph Lapp. His pension was suspended in 1821 but was restored in 1829.

MORROW, CHARLES (Captain)
Lived both in Martinsburg and Shepherdstown and served three years in the southern campaigns during the Revolution. Was a brother-in-law of James Rumsey, inventor of the steamboat.

MORROW, JOHN (Colonel)
Was a resident of Shepherdstown. Near the close of the Revolution, he may have been colonel or lieutenant-colonel of Berkeley County militia. He accompanied some of the militia to the West in 1779. He married the widow of Major Henry Peyton, formerly Mary Rutherford, daughter of Robert Rutherford.

MORROW, RALPH
Ralph Morrow, who spent his latter years in Taylor County, Virginia, was a soldier in the Revolutionary Army.

MORROW, THOMAS (Captain)
Taken prisoner in battle of Long Island; exchanged in ill health and died in 1778. Was made captain during his imprisonment.

MORTON, EDWARD
Service—Virginia   Va. No. 4980   No. S. 5778

Born, 1764; died, February 20, 1852. Enlisted Augusta County, Virginia, in September 1780 and served under Captains Bell, Hicklin, Buchanan in the Virginia Line under General Morgan at Cowpens, Clover Lick, and the siege and capture of Yorktown. Received pension in Pendleton County, Virginia, 1833, for six months service. Supporting data filed by Edward Stewart and William McCoy.

MOUNTS, HUMPHREY
Before the Harrison County court, July 20, 1818, Humphrey Mounts made affidavit that he had enlisted in the Legion commanded by General Pulaski for one year, and that he was on furlough owing to ill health

at the time General Pulaski was killed at Short Hills. He later rejoined the army at Wilmington and continued under the command of Captain Bodkin in the same legion of horse until discharged at Ringwood Furnaces by Lord Sterling.

MOUNTSFIELD, THOMAS
Private in Captain Shepherd's company. Taken prisoner and died, February 5, 1777.

MOUSER, JACOB
Born in Germany and served in the German Regiment in the Virginia Line during the Revolution. He probably lived in Hampshire County, during the Revolution, and later moved to Rowlesburg, Preston County, Virginia, where he kept a tavern. His children were: Rebecca, William, Mary Ann, Elizabeth, Benjamin. Rebecca, born, November 17, 1803, married Abraham Wilson, son of William and Rebecca Ferguson Wilson, December 28, 1820, according to Monongalia County marriage bonds. Resided in Taylor County, where she died in 1880 and is buried in the Haymond Cemetery.

MUCHLEVAINE (MUCKLEWAINE), (TUNIS)
Service—Virginia   Va. No. 23337   No. S. 9043
Born, August 19, 1759, Rockingham County, Virginia, and later lived in Pendleton, Randolph, Nicholas, Lewis, and Kanawha counties, Virginia. While living in Pendleton County enlisted in August 1776, for Revolutioary War service, and served under Captains Davis, Trimble, Stewart, Hutton, Nelson, Bogard, Duvall, Dyer; Colonels Gregg, Hutton, McCoy, and Westford. Pension was issued to the soldier in Kanawha or Lewis County in 1834 but was suspended two years later in letter which also mentions as suspended the cases of Alex Thompson, Isaac Mace, and Zephaniah Nicholas. Supporting data had been filed by D. Hardway and Jacob Mucklewaine.

MURPHY, PATRICK
Private under Captain Shepherd. Died on prison ship, February 15, 1777.

MYERS, CASPER
Private in Captain Shepherd's company of riflemen. Died in prison, February 16, 1777.

MYERS, HENRY
Born, March 15, 1736, Berkeley County, Virginia. He enlisted in 1776 in York Town, Pennsylvania, to which place he had gone to learn his trade, in a company commanded by Captain Christian Stakes in a regiment commanded by Colonel Swope. He served in this company until Colonel Swope, Captain Stake, Lieutenant Holsinger, and Ensign Barnett were captured at the surrender of Fort Washington on York Island, November 16, 1776. The regiment being nearly destroyed, he was trans-

ferred to a corps under General Putnam and took part in the capture of the Hessians at Trenton, December 26, 1776, and was one of the guards sent with the prisoners to Philadelphia. He was discharged, returned to Berkeley County, and there engaged in militia service under Captain Duncan and later under Captain Linder, and took part in the siege of Yorktown.

Pension was applied for in Berkeley County, August 15, 1832. Supporting statement submitted by Major Henry Bedinger, who knew him in service. He also mentions Teter Myers, his brother, Archibald Scherer, and John Kisinger as persons familiar with his military activities.

MYERS, LUDWIG (Captain)
Lived near Shepherdstown. Served as a captain of infantry during the Revolution.

NAY, JACOB
Before the Harrison County court, Jacob Nay testified that he was drafted for eighteen months service in Culpepper County, Virginia, and served in the company of Captain Lamb in Colonel Gaston's Regiment under the immediate command of Baron Von Steuben. Soon afterwards, he was transferred to the corps of cavalry commanded by Captain Gunn under Colonel White and continued in this corps for twenty months. He was then permitted to rejoin his old regiment under Major Findley and continued with him until his discharge by General Scott. He was in the skirmish at Jones Island where Colonel Lawrence was killed.

NAY, JOHN
Born, Culpepper County, Virginia, 1750; died, October 9, 1838. There enlisted in 1778 as a private and served in various periods of enlistment until 1781 under Captain Reed, Generals Washington and Lafayette. Took part in the siege and capture of Yorktown. He mentions Colonel Benjamin Reed, Joseph Campbell, Benjamin Brice, and William Nay, a brother. He received pension in Harrison County, Virginia, in 1833. It was reduced in amount in 1835.

NEAL, JAMES (Captain)
Service—Virginia   Va. No. 17443   No. S. 38257

Served three years or more in the Continental Line as a captain in the Seventh, Ninth, and Thirteenth Virginia Regiments in the Division of Generals Green and Muhlenberg. Took part in the battles of Brandywine and Germantown. Resigned, January 3, 1779. After the Revolution, he brought a party of colonists to Wood County, Virginia, on the south side of the Little Kanawha River at what is now Parkersburg. Here he established a blockhouse and stockade, known as Neal's Station, which became an important frontier outpost.

He applied for pension in Wood County, in 1818, which was issued in 1821. His claims were supported by Colonel Hugh Phelps, Majors James G. Laidley, David Steel, Jacob Springer, and Captain Uriah Springer. One child, Mary Neal Foley, is mentioned.

NEELY, JOHN
Service—New York   Va. No. 12107   No. W. 5408 and B. L. Wt. 38524

Born in New York City, 1758, and there enlisted in the Revolutionary Army in 1776; after the Revolution, moved to Uniontown, Pennsylvania, and later settled near the Lewis and Harrison County boundary line, where he died June 22, 1835. He is buried at the Broad Run Baptist Cemetery, Lewis County.

He served under Captains Telford, Fellner, Major Dennison, Colonel McClaugherty and General George Clinton, and also knew Major General James Clinton, brother of General George Clinton. Helped build Fort Montgomery and was there until November. Then from March, 1777, until October, 1777, was at Fort Clinton at which time it was captured. Was discharged, then re-enlisted and returned to New York. Helped build the fort at West Point in March, 1778, after which he was engaged in service on the frontier against the Indians, Tories, and British. Captured forty horses and many supplies. Was discharged in 1779. (He seems to have had a brother-in-law of the same name who may have served in 1780.)

Pension was granted in 1833, suspended, but apparently later resumed. Bounty land warrant was received for 160 acres. (A notation under B. L. Wt. 38956 indicates some uncertainty in the records.) Supporting data by Isaac and Philip Cox, James and John Brown, and Catherine Williams.

The soldier was married, March, 1787, in Fayette County, Pennsylvania, by James Neal. Wife's name Margaret. Their children were as follows: William, 1787; Mary, 1790; Matthew, 1791; Thomas, 1794; Lloyd, date missing; Filburn, 1796; John Hopkins, 1798; George, date missing.

NEIL, RICHARD
Born, 1756. Enlisted for three years at Williamsburg in 1778. Was wounded at Gates Depot. Made new pension application in Monroe County, in 1832, which was rejected.

NEILSON, JAMES
Enlisted, June 20, 1775, under Captain Stephenson.

NELSON, THOMAS
Served under Captain Stephenson in the Revolution. Was taken prisoner.

NETTLES, ABRAHAM
In the Greenbrier County Court in 1786 it was ordered certified that Abraham Nettles, a disabled soldier of the Continental Army, was unable to make a living owing to wounds received in service, and it was ordered that he be continued as a pensioner.

NEVILL, JOHN
Service—Virginia   Va. No. 12451   No. S. 5827

Born, Hampshire, now Hardy County, Virginia, November 30, 1765.

Enlisted in March or April, 1781, and served six months as a private under Captains Stump and Anderson, Lieutenants Hornback and Sommerville in the Virginia Line under Major Higgins, Colonel Edmonds, Generals Lafayette, Wayne, and Muhlenberg. Also mentions Ensign James Duncan. Pension was granted in Hardy County, in 1833. Supporting data was filed by Martin Hawk and Jacob Yoakum. Apparently Nevill had substituted for Thomas Talbott and Isaac McNeill.

There is also a bounty land warrant from the Colony of Virginia but without explanatory papers.

NEVILLE, JOSEPH (General)

He was born in Fauquier County, Virginia, in 1740, and died at Moorefield, Virginia, now West Virginia, March 4, 1819. He served as a member of the House of Burgesses from Hampshire County, in 1773 and again in 1776.

He was also a member of the conventions of December 1, 1775, and May 6, 1776, the last of which declared for independence. He served gallantly through the Revolutionary War and was commissioned brigadier general. He was county surveyor of Hampshire County in 1784 and as such was one of the surveyors who helped to complete the Mason and Dixon Line.

He was often an associate of General George Washington in surveying lands in Hampshire County. As a justice of the peace he had arraigned before his court at Moorefield the first murder case in that part of what was then Hampshire County.

NICHOLAS, LEAVEN
Service—Pennsylvania-Virginia   Va. No. 23027   No. S. 9440

Born in Kent County, Maryland, 1756. Lived in Fayette County, Pennsylvania, at the outbreak of the Revolution, and enlisted there in 1776, but moved to Greenbrier County, Virginia, in April, 1777. He served two years as an Indian spy under Captain Haglin in the Pennsylvania and Virginia Line under Colonels Lynn and Crawford. Received pension while living in Lewis County, Virginia, in 1833, and died there. Supporting data was filed in his case by David Cox and Benjamin Reynolds.

NICHOLS, RICHARDS
Service—Pennsylvania   Va. No. 12088   No. S. 7271

Born, Prince William County, Virginia, 1759. While living in Washington County, Pennsylvania, in 1775, was drafted into the militia; substituted for his brother in 1776; volunteered in 1777; in 1778, substituted for his brother under Captain James Wright. Served as a private nineteen months under Captains Rickets, Crooks, Cisna, Wright, Ross, Crawford, in Campbell's Regiment of the Pennsylvania Line under Brodhead and McIntosh. Was in the engagement at Smoky Island.

Received pension in Wood County, Virginia, in 1833, which was dropped in 1834 without anything to show reinstatement. Supporting data submitted by Reece Wolf, A. Samuels, D. B. Spencer, and James Henderson.

WEST VIRGINIANS IN THE REVOLUTION

NICHOLS, WILLIAM
The grave of William Nichols, a veteran of the Revolutionary War, is in Marion County, near Fairmont.

NICHOLS, ZEPHANIAH
Service—Virginia.   Va. No. 23004   No. S. 9439
Born in Maryland in 1763 or 1764. Made application for pension, August 20, 1934, in Lewis and Kanawha counties, Virginia, and apparently proved two years service as an Indian spy. Pension was issued in 1833 but was dropped in 1836.

NICKLE (NICKELL), ISAAC
Service—Virginia   No. R. 7646
Born in Augusta County, Virginia, 1761. Took part in the Indian campaign of 1774 under Captain John Lewis, fought in the battle of Point Pleasant of that year in a company with Captain John Henderson. In 1777, he was drafted in Greenbrier County, under Captain Arbuckle and Colonel Lewis, Marched to Elk River, and from there to Point Pleasant where he served out his enlistment. He was drafted in 1781 out of Captain Andrew Nickle's company of militia to take part in expedition against the Indians along the Great Lakes, but hired a substitute in his stead. The soldier applied for pension in Monroe County, Virginia, in 1833, but his claim was rejected. Supporting data was filed by Samuel Clark, Robert Coalter, Henry Alexander, and John Dowell.

NIPPER, (NIPPERS), GEORGE
Service—Virginia   Va. No. 13857   No. S. 38265
Enlisted in Hampshire County, Virginia, and served from 1778 to 1781 as a private in the company of Captain Wallace in the Sixth Virginia Regiment, commanded by Colonel Richard Campbell. Took part in the campaigns at Waxhaw where he was taken prisoner, and at Yorktown. Received pension in Hardy County, Virginia, in 1819, at which time the soldier was 66 years old. His family consisted of the following: Reuben, 19; Delilah, 21; Milly, 18; Betsy, 15; Polly, 12; Nancy, 9. Supporting data was filed in this case by John Smith, and Colonel Joseph Van Meter.

NIXON, JOHN
Enlisted as a private under Captain Shepherd. Reported absent after February 15, 1777.

NORRIS, JOHN (Sergeant)
Service—Virginia.   Va. No. 16713   No. W. 19930
Born, Fauquier County, Virginia, July 4, 1760; died, February 12, 1835, and is buried in the Mays Cemetery near Jackson's Mill, Lewis County. Enlisted, February 1777, in Fauquier County, served five months as private and three months as sergeant under Captain Scott in the Virginia militia. He mentions among other officers First Lieutenant John Kincheloe,, Second Lieutenant J. Hathaway, Ensign James Hathaway,

Captains Thurston, Morgan, Morehead, Holmes, and Colonels Stricker and Hollingsworth.

Soldier was married to Mary Jones, March 25, 1782, Fauquier County, by the Rev. James Craig of the Episcopal Protestant Church. Soldier received pension in Lewis County, in 1833, and widow also received pension after his death. Supporting data was filed by John Bailey, Mrs. Frances Bailey, a sister, and others.

NUTTER, CHRISTOPHER
Service—Virginia   Va. No. 6538   No. W. 5434 and B. L. Wt. 26388

Born, Sussex County, Delaware, January 21, 1760; died February 21, 1845. Enlisted at Nutter's Fort, Harrison County, Virginia, and served from 1780 to 1783 as a private under Captain William Lowther with the Virginia troops under George Rogers Clark and Jackson in activities on the Ohio River and in the Nutter's Fort vicinity. Mentions Captain Thomas Nutter.

Married Rebecca Morehead, June 28, 1785, Harrison County, Virginia, with Isaac Edwards as minister. Soldier received pension in 1833 and his widow got pension after his death. Bounty land warrant was received for 160 acres. The widow, born 1767, died October 10, 1861.

NUTTER, THOMAS (Captain)

Came to Harrison County, Virginia, in 1770, and built Nutter's Fort about 1772 which became an important border post. He was a captain of Virginia militia during the Revolution and took an active part in the suppression of Indian raids. He died shortly before an inventory of his personal estate was made, August 6, 1802, for his son and administrator, Christopher Nutter, and was buried in the Nutter Cemetery near his former home.

OBART (OBERT), JOHN
Service—New Jersey   Va. No. 4629   No. W. 4752 and B. L. Wt. 25381

Enlisted in 1775 in New Brunswick, New Jersey, in the company of Captain John Conaway, First New Jersey Regiment, Continental Line, and took part in the battle of Monmouth. He was married in Cortland County, New York, to Mary or Polly Stone, but the date is uncertain. Soldier applied for pension in Washington, D. C., in 1818, which was later transferred to Harrison County, Virginia.

Soldier died, June 17, 1832, at age of 80. Widow applied for pension in Cortland County, New York. Bounty land warrant issued for 160 acres. Supporting data submitted by Moses Scott, George Miller, and Amanda McKeel.

ODELL, JEREMIAH
Service—Virginia   Va. No. 16635   No. S. 6905

Born, Powell Fort, Shenandoah County, Virginia, November 1, 1761; died 1842 or 1843. Enlisted in the summer of 1779 or 1780 in Shenandoah County and served in the company of Captains Denton and Sharp in the Virginia Line commanded by Colonel Edwards and General Stephens.

In his home county, the soldier was married to Rachel Watters by James Ireland, August 6, 1782. Their children are as follows: Jacob, Christine (Nutter), Miriam (Hughes), Jeremiah, and John. In Nicholas County, Virginia, in 1833, pension was granted the soldier but it was suspended two years later. Supporting data was submitted by Elverton Walker, John Campbell, John Smith, William Eagle, Rachel Odell, Jacob Dodson, Margaret Foster, and James Allen McArany.

OGDEN, SAMUEL
Service—New Jersey   Va. No. 19585 and 19305   No. S. 33273
Enlisted in New Jersey and served from May 10, 1780, to June 5, 1783, under Captain Jonathan Phillips, in the New Jersey Light Infantry. Continental Establishment, commanded by Colonel Shreve. Took part in the military activities at Springfield and was at the siege and capture of Yorktown. In the closing days of the war, he was transferred to Captain Bowman's company, which was later under Captain Weyman.

The soldier was 61 years old in 1824, at which time his wife, Elizabeth, was 55, a son, John, 15, and a daughter, Mary, 14, years of age. Soldier received pension in Washington County, Pennsylvania, and his wife in Brooke County, Virginia.

OLDHAM, CONAWAY (Lieutenant)
Enlisted as a private under Captain Stephenson. Later commissioned lieutenant.

OLDHAM, WILLIAM (Colonel)
Son of Samuel Oldham, Berkeley County, Virginia. Enlisted under Captain Daniel Morgan, June, 1775. Went with him to Quebec. Apparently escaped capture. Moved to Kentucky. Noted as an Indian fighter. He was colonel of Kentucky militia, and served at St. Claire's defeat in 1791 where he was killed.

O'NEAL, JOHN
Service—Pennsylvania.   Va. No. 16626   No. S. 38272
Enlisted, Ohio County, Virginia, in the fall of 1776 in company commanded by Captain Van Swearingen, marched to Hannahstown, now Greensburg, thence to Philadelphia where his company was attached to the Eighth Pennsylvania Regiment under Colonel McCoy, a part of General Anthony Wayne's division. In April, 1777, he was taken prisoner by the British and held until May, 1778, when exchanged, rejoined his company, and served until the capture of Cornwallis. During the fighting about Yorktown, he was wounded in both shoulders and discharged by Lieutenant Colonel Stephen Bayard. He then enlisted with Captain Francis Revellie of Maryland in the Fourth Maryland Regiment, commanded by General Smallwood which was also under General Wayne, and was wounded again at Little Rock and discharged.

He applied for pension in Ohio County, in 1818, which was granted in 1820. He had two children at that time; Bennett and John. Two brothers of the soldier, Bennett and Johnson, are also mentioned. Supporting data was submitted by James Bonar and William Durno.

O'NEALE (O'NEAL or O'NEIL), CONSTANTIA (CONSTANTINE)
Service—Pennsylvania. (12756)   Va. No. 16554   No. W. 5446

Enlisted, August 9, 1776, Kittanning, Pennsylvania, under Captain Van Swearingen of the Eighth Pennsylvania Regiment commanded by Colonel McCoy. His discharge, showing service from August 9, 1776, to October 19, 1779, under Van Swearingen, and signed by Lieutenant Colonel Stephen Bayard is filed in the War Department offices.

Pension was issued to the soldier in Ohio County, Virginia, or Jackson County, Virginia, in 1833, apparently on application made in 1827. Soldier, born, 1753, died September 16, 1834. Wife, formerly Catherine Shepherd, died January 17, 1847. Their children were: Deborah, married Abel Van Sikock; Mary, married James Manning; Betsy, married John O'Neal (perhaps this name is wrong); Barnabas. Supporting data was filed by Obadiah Hardesty, John O'Neal, and Rachel Henry.

OLIVER, SAMUEL
Service—Virginia   No. S. 38270

Enlisted, Frederica, Delaware, February 12, 1776, and served as a private six years. Served under Captain Adams in Continental Regiment commanded by Colonel Hazlett and Lord Stirling, and fought at Long Island, White Plains, Trenton, and Princeton. Reference is made to the Delaware Blues with which he may have served.

Pension application was made in Lewis County, Virginia, which was granted in 1819. The widow, Lydia, died in 1839 before the pensioner. William Oliver, an heir, died in 1852.

ORNDORFF, CHRISTIAN (Captain)

Distinguished by service at Bennington and Skeenborough. Lived at Sharpsburg but moved to near Shepherdstown after the Revolution. His daughter married Jonathan Hagar who named his settlement Elizabeth Town in her honor, but it was later changed to Hagerstown.

ORR, JOHN
Service—Maryland and Pennsylvania   Va. No. 16180   No. R. 16849

Enlisted, 1777, Baltimore, Maryland, in company of Captain J. Baker. Marched to Kent and served on guard duty along the Delaware. Drafted again at Baltimore under Captain Clendenen, and Colonel Holland. His father took him to Redstone, Pennsylvania, in 1780, there volunteered under Captain John Ashcraft, marched against the Indians up the Allegheny, and later was with Colonel Crawford in the Sandusky campaign. He was wounded in the hip, was furnished with a horse by Colonel McClelland and sent to the fort on the Ohio at McMahan's Bottom until he recovered.

Received pension in Preston County, but it was dropped when Special Agent Singleton refused to give him credit for service which he called that of an Indian spy. Soldier married Elizabeth Johns, January 1792, in Fayette County, Pennsylvania. Their children were Catherine (Fortney), John, Hiram, Ruth (Menear), George, William. Soldier died, April 14, 1840; his widow died, February 7, 1851. Supporting data filed by James Collins and Rachel McClelland, a sister of the pensioner.

OUR, (OURS or OWER), SEARCHMAN
Service—Virginia   Va. No. 23668   No. R. 16873

Born in Hampshire County, Virginia, in 1775; died, September 15, 1844. There he enlisted in March, 1778, under Captain Robert Cunningham in the Virginia Line and was engaged in various marches and guard duty. Other officers were Lieutenant Park, Captain Morgan, Major Taylor and Colonel Gibson.

His wife, Mary Simon, was born in 1761. Their children were: Catherine, 1783; Ann Maria, 1784; Elizabeth, 1786; Eve, 1788; Sarah, 1791; Jacob, 1796; Solomon, 1801. Another son, born in 1780, was dead. Pension was granted both soldier and his widow in Hardy County, Virginia. Supporting data was filed by Jacob Barkdoll, Jacob Ketterman, and George Simon.

PAINE (PAYNE), GEORGE
Service—Virginia   Va. No. 20908   No. S. 38980

Enlisted, Fauquier County, Virginia, and served from 1780 to 1782 as a private under Captain Atwell and Armstead, Virginia Regiment of the Continental Line, commanded by Colonel John Green and Sam Howes, and Majors Smith and Sneed. Received honorable discharge, January 17, 1782, Salisbury, North Carolina. Applied for and received pension, Hampshire County, Virginia, 1829. Death probably in 1839.

PAITSELL, JACOB
Service—Virginia   Va. No. 35956   No. W. 3858 and B. L. Wt. 24982

Enlisted, Rees Tavern, Burks County, Virginia, in the fall of 1777 and served until 1790 under Captain Sam Moore of the Pennsylvania Line Regiment, commanded by Colonel Thomas Craig. Married December 8, 1790 in Martinsburg, Berkeley County, to Mary Cashman or Kershman. Soldier received pension in 1829. He died November 4, 1840, and his widow likewise received pension. Her pension application, made out by her uncle, Christian Black, is written in German. Bounty land warrant for 160 acres was issued in May, 1856.

PARKER, JAMES
Service—Virginia   Va. No. 16378   No. W. 6853

Born, 1759, Middletown, Maryland, and died April 15, 1838. Enlisted, Hampshire County, Virginia, in 1778 under Captain Abraham Johnson in the Virginia Regiment commanded by Colonel Riddle and Major Van Meter under General McIntosh. Took part in several campaigns in Virginia. Also mentions other officers. Married in Hampshire County, December 1782, to Rebecca Wolf. She was aged 86 in 1848. Their children's names are blurred but appear to be James, Thornton, Elizabeth, Daniel, and Ashford.

Soldier received pension in 1833 in Hampshire County, as did his widow. Their claims were supported by Thomas Carskaddon, Fred Sheetz, Henry Pursett, and Captain Ed McCarty.

PARROT, CHRISTOPHER (Sergeant)
(Name changed to Parriott in 1835 by petition of surviving sons)
   Born, March 25, 1755, Prince George County, Maryland, died, October 1, 1820, Romney, Hampshire County, Virginia. Believed to be of English descent. Enlisted at Annapolis, Maryland, August, 1777, and served until August, 1780, under Colonel J. E. Howard of the Second Maryland Regiment, and took part in battles of Trenton, Princeton, Brandywine, Germantown, Monmouth, Stony Point, and Yorktown. He apparently reenlisted and served until 1782 or 1783.
   Soldier was married, January 21, 1781, to Martha Clark in Marlborough, Prince Edward County, Maryland. She was the daughter of Abraham Clark, and died December 19, 1839, at Moundsville, Marshall County. In 1839, their children were named as John, Ann, Dennis, and Joseph.

PARSONS, JAMES
Service—Virginia   Pa. No. 16476 and Va.   No. S. 40239
   Enlisted at Accomack Courthouse, Virginia, in 1776 and served eighteen months as a fifer under Captains Palmer, Braxton, and Easthan in the Ninth Virginia Regiment, under Colonel Fleming, and Lieutenant Colonel Matthews. Took part in the battle of Germantown. In 1780, served an additional six months. Pension was granted in Cumberland County, Pennsylvania, in 1820. (Note Captain James Parsons following.)

PARSONS, JAMES (Captain)
   Captain James Parsons, second son of Thomas Parsons, Jr., was born in Virginia. He enlisted in the Revolutionary War and rose to the rank of captain. He and his brother, Thomas, were early explorers of Randolph County, and established claims in the Horseshoe of what is now Tucker County as early as 1770. (Note above James Parsons.)

PARSONS, JOSEPH
Service—Virginia   Va. No. 23321   No. S. 8942
   Born in Queen Anne County, Maryland, in 1755. Moved to Virginia in 1763-64 and lived in Rockingham or Augusta County. Was living in West Augusta, now Lewis County, West Virginia in 1776. After the Revolution lived in Wood and Jackson counties.
   Enlisted in the Revolutionary Army May 1, 1777, and served under Ensign Radcliffe and Captain James Booth at Buckhannon, West, Arnold and Nutter forts in the Upper Monongahela Valley. Mentions Captains Maxwell, Tremble, and Jackson; Lieutenants Freeman and Brake, and Ensign Timothy Dorman. Refers to the killing of Captain Booth by the Indians, June, 1778.
   Pension was granted in Lewis County, and Jackson County, 1833, but he was dropped from the rolls in 1835. Evidence in the case is submitted by Elias Parsons and Captain William Parsons, both nephews. His claim was supported by David Sleeth, Adam Flesher, and Alex West.

PARSONS, THOMAS
   Born in Virginia, November 11, 1731, and died in Hardy County, Vir-

ginia, in 1804. He was married to Mary Renick in 1758. He served in the Revolutionary War as a private, first in the Seventh Virginia Regiment, then in the Eleventh Virginia Regiment, and then in Company Nine under Captain George Rice of Colonel Daniel Morgan's Eleventh and Fifteenth consolidated regiments.

PARSONS, WILLIAM (Captain)
He was born in Hardy County, September 25, 1760, the first son of Thomas and Mary Rennick Parsons; died September 10, 1829, and his will is filed in Randolph County. Settled in Randolph (now Tucker) County, in pioneer days and built a home on Horseshoe Run. He is buried in Bethel Cemetery, Tucker County.

Cadet, Sixth Virginia, March 25, 1776; coronet, Third Continental Dragoons, February 6, 1777; taken prisoner at Tappan, September 27, 1778; lieutenant, January 1, 1778; captain, November 1779; retained in Baylor's Consolidated Regiment of Dragoons November 9, 1782, and served to end of war. Land bounty was received by Parsons for his military services.

(Compare with second William Parsons).

PARSONS, WILLIAM
Service—Virginia   Va. No. 13194   No. R. 7981
Born, October 15, 1760. Enlisted in Hampshire County under Captains Fisher and Cunningham in unit commanded by General McIntosh. He married Catherine Stoker, April 5, 1785, and their marriage is recorded in Hampshire County. A brother, James Parsons, is mentioned, and this brother offers a supporting affidavit in the Samuel Bonnifield case also. Pension claims seem to have been confused with that of another William Parsons who was rejected by Special Federal Agent Singleton in 1835. (See first William Parsons.)

PATTON, JOHN
Service—Pennsylvania   Va. No. 16452   No. S. 8931
Born, 1749. Enlisted, Chester County, Pennsylvania, and served periods in 1776, 1777, and 1778 under Captains J. McDowell and Hays in the Pennsylvania Line Regiment commanded by Colonel Montgomery. Fought at Staten Island and Princeton. Received pension in Harrison County, Virginia, 1833. Supporting data filed by John Waldo and Daniel Morris. (The suspension marked against this pensioner on the printed list of 1835 is in error and belongs to rejected File No. R. 8012 of John Patton of Greenbrier County.)

PATTON, JOHN
Service—Virginia   No. R. 8012
Applied for pension in Greenbrier County, August 22, 1835, which was refused on the grounds that the applicant had performed only civil duty for self preservation.

PATTON, TRISTRAM
Born, Tyrone County, Ireland, 1752; emigrated to America in 1777; died,

1843. He served in the Revolutionary Army and is believed to have been a member of Washington's body guard. He married Jean Nelson in 1808 and lived for many years in Monroe County, Virginia.

PATTON, WILLIAM

Born, April 21, 1761; settled in Coleran Township, Lancaster County, Pennsylvania; there was married in 1786. Came to Harrison County, Virginia, about 1800 and settled on a tract of 300 acres near West Milford. He died, July 28, 1826, and is buried in a private cemetery on the same land. He served as a soldier in the Revolution.

West Virginians in the American Revolution

Assembled and Edited by ROSS B. JOHNSTON

The sources of this material are from the files of the Pension Office at Washington from various county records, from notes of patriotic societies, principally the Daughters of the American Revolution, Sons of the American Revolution, Sons of the Revolution, and from a large miscellaneous group of published and private sources. Corrections and additions to this list will receive the careful attention of the editor.

PAUL, HUGH

Before the Cabell County Court, September 24, 1832, Hugh Paul made affidavit that he had served as a Revolutionary soldier and that he was entitled to a pension.

PAYTON, (PEYTON), HENRY
Service—Virginia   Va. No. 23336   No. S. 8943

Born in Culpepper County, Virginia, January 19, 1760. Enlisted 1777, in the Revolutionary Army from Amherst County, Virginia, in the company commanded by Captain Proctor under Colonel Skilton and was stationed at Point Pleasant in border defense for some time. Mentions the killing of Robert Gilmore which brought on the murder of Chief Cornstalk and other Indians at Fort Randolph, Point Pleasant. He was drafted in 1778 and also served in 1780. Among his officers were Captain James Dillard, Captain Preston, Colonels Lynch, Higginbottom, and Captain John Stewart from whom he received discharge in winter quarters after the surrender of Cornwallis at Yorktown.

Was pensioned in Cabell County, Virginia, in 1834, but was removed from the rolls in 1835. Supporting data was submitted by Elisha, Moses, and William McComas, Solomon Thornbridge, Roland Berry and Frederick Bughrin. Died in Cabell County, 1836.

PECK, PETER
Service—Virginia   Va. No. 23674   No. S. 18156

Born, Lancaster County, Pennsylvania, August 18, 1755; died June 23, 1837. Enlisted in Shenandoah County, Virginia, June 15, 1777, and served until 1871 in broken periods of enlistment under Captains Fenton and Cunningham in the Sixth Regiment of the Continental Line, commanded by Colonel Tipton, Mathew Boyer, and General Muhlenberg. Took part in the battles of Brandywine, Germantown, Guilford Courthouse, and the siege and capture of Yorktown. Married Margaret Green, but date and place are uncertain. Applied for pension in Mason County, Virginia, 1832.

PENCE, JACOB, SR.

Settled with his brother, Valentine, in Rockingham County, Virginia, prior to 1747. Served in the Augusta County, Virginia, militia under Captain William Nall from September 10, 1774, until the end of the Revolution. Was at the Battle of Point Pleasant, and his Revolutionary service is accepted under Nat. No. D. A. R. 175459. After the Revolution he moved to Bath County, then to Callaghan's Station, and to Monroe County. He was born, 1742, and died in 1819. He married Elizabeth Trust in 1762, and to them were born three sons, Henry, David, and Mose. Henry married Nancy Stodghill.

PENDLETON, NATHANIEL (Captain)

Joined Captain Stephenson's company in 1775 as a private. In 1776, enlisted as first lieutenant in Captain Gabriel Long's company of riflemen. At the battle at Fort Washington, he was captured. After his exchange, he became a captain in Colonel Rawling's Regiment. He moved to New York after the Revolution.

PENDELTON, PHILIP (Colonel)

Was the son of Nathaniel Pendleton of Culpepper County, Virginia. Removed to Berkeley County, Virginia, near Martinsburg, where he was admitted to the bar in 1772. From 1777 to 1781 he was an officer of the Berkeley County militia, and its representative in the state assembly of 1779.

PENINGER, CHRISTIAN

Was a private under Captain Stephenson. Lost his life as a prisoner, February 15, 1777.

PENINGER, HENRY
Service—Virginia   Va. No. 7004   No. S. 8946

Enlisted in the Virginia militia in Pendleton County, Virginia, and served two years as a private and Indian spy under Captains Stewart, Hamilton, and McCoy under Colonel Lewis. Pension was granted him in 1833 upon application from Lewis County, but he was stricken from the rolls in 1836.

PEPPER, WILLIAM
Service—Delaware   Va. No. 12531   No. S. 5901

Born, Sussex County, Delaware, August 23, 1761. There enlisted in the spring of 1776 and served eighteen months as private under Captains George Smith, Moore, and Herman Kirkwood in the Delaware Line, under Colonel Collit. He applied for pension in Harrison County, in 1833, which was granted. It was suspended in 1834, but resumed May 29, 1841. Supporting data was filed by James Radcliffe, Thomas C. Nutter, Samuel Hall, Hamilton Gass, and Isaac Johnson. In 1841, it is stated that Johnson Pepper is the only surviving child. In 1820, a son, Parker, aged 16, was living. The pensioner at that time was totally blind.

WEST VIRGINIANS IN THE REVOLUTION 221

PEPPER, WILLIAM
 Born in England, emigrated to America and settled in New Jersey. He is listed among the members of Captain Bond's company, Fourth Battalion, Second Establishment, of the New Jersey Line during the Revolutionary War, and later emigrated to western Virginia.

PERKINS, ELIAS
Service—Virginia   Va. No. 2555   No. S. 5908
 Enlisted in Botetourt County, Virginia, and served eighteen months under Captain Stribling and Major Sneed in the Second Virginia Regiment, commanded by Colonel Howe, from June, 1780, to January 17, 1782. Born, about 1759; died September 4, 1839. Received pension in Greenbrier County, in 1832.

PERRY, THOMAS
Service—Maryland   Va. No. 4717   No. W. 8505 and B. L. Wt. 52780
 Enlisted in Montgomery County, Maryland, in 1781, and served as a private under Captain Price in the Third Maryland Regiment, commanded by Colonel Adams. Took part in the siege of Yorktown and the capture of Cornwallis, and was discharged when his company was disbanded at Annapolis, Maryland.
 Soldier seems to have received pension while living in western Virginia in 1818. He was married to Mary Blake in Bath County, Virginia, July 1, 1817, by the Rev. Josiah Osburn. After the soldier's death, Mary Thomas received pension and also bounty land warrant for 160 acres.

PETERS, CHRISTIAN (Sergeant)
Service—Virginia   Va. No. 12957   No. S. 5898
 Born in Rockingham County, Virginia, October 16, 1760. There he enlisted, June 1, 1779, under Captain Robert Cravans and Jeremiah Beasley and served ten months as private, corporal, and sergeant in the Virginia Line under Major Jack Willis, Generals Green, Morgan, and Campbell, and took part in the battles at Cowpens, Hot Water, and Jamestown.
 His pension application, filed in Monroe County, Virginia, in 1832, describes in detail the campaigns with General Morgan and General Green in Virginia and in the Carolinas. He took part in the capture of a party of Tories in the Black Swamp in North Carolina. He was one of the riflemen, presumably an expert marksman, and says that he carried his own rifle, tomahawk, and butcher knife throughout his army service.
 He received pension in 1833 in Monroe County, where he had resided since 1789. Supporting data was filed in his case by James Dunlap, Samuel Clark, Henry Alexander, John Peters, a brother, and John Dunn. The town of Peterstown, Monroe County, West Virginia, bears his name.

PETERS, GODFREY
 The grave of Godfrey Peters, a soldier in the Revolutionary War, is on Booths Creek, Marion County, West Virginia.

PETERS, JOHN
Service—New Jersey and Virginia   Va. No. 12532   No. S. 5902

Enlisted, New Jersey in 1776 in the company commanded by Captain John Anderson in the New Jersey Flying Camp Regiment, commanded by Colonel Johnson, which took part in the battles of Long Island and White Plains. He also seems to have been a substitute in Louden County, Virginia, for Philip Unkafer, under command of Captain Thomas, Colonel West or Colonel Clapham. Received pension in Hampshire County, Virginia, 1833. Supporting data filed by John Arnold and John Myers.

PETERSON, THOMAS
Service—New Jersey   Va. No. 12956   No. S. 5899

Born, April 9, 1756, Somerset County, New Jersey, died July 14, 1836. Enlisted in February 1775 in New Jersey under Captain Conrad Turnick. Served most of a period of six months on Staten Island subduing Tories. In July, 1776 was drafted for a month in New York under Captain Joseph Caskeen and Colonel Quick; in August, was under Captain Babcock at Amboy; in October was under Captain Richard Compton and Colonel Peter Boone at Springfield fighting British and Tories; in November and December was with Captain Scott and Colonel Quick. His total service covered an eighteen months period. Received pension, Brooke County, Virginia, in 1833. Supporting data submitted by David Pugh and Mose Congleton.

PHILLIPS, ELIJAH
The grave of Elijah Phillips, a veteran of the Revolutionary War, is in the French Creek Cemetery, Upshur County.

PHILLIPS, THEOPHILUS (Lieutenant Colonel)
Born before 1750 and was living in Springhill Township, Monongalia County, Virginia, but later Fayette County, Pennsylvania, and in 1776 his house was used as the first meeting place of the Monongalia County Court. During the Revolution, he served in the militia, rising to the rank of lieutenant colonel in the Fifth Battalion in 1782. In 1784, Washington, while visiting in the Monongalia Valley, stopped over night with Colonel Phillips. He died in 1789 on his way from New Orleans to Philadelphia. His will probated October 10 of that year mentions a wife and ten children.

PHILLIPS, THOMAS
Before the Randolph County Court, November 25, 1811, Moses Phillips, one of the heirs of Thomas Phillips, made oath that he never knew his father to receive compensation for land for services under General Clark against the Indians.

PHILLIPS, W. B.
The grave of W. B. Phillips, a soldier in the Revolutionary Army, is in the French Creek Cemetery, Upshur County, West Virginia.

PIERCE, JOHN
Service—Maryland   Va. No. 16840   No. S. 38306

Enlisted at Winchester, Frederick County, Virginia, in June 1775, in the rifle company of Captains Daniel Morgan and Stephen and under General Montgomery took part in the storming of Quebec. The soldier applied for pension which was granted in Jefferson County in 1820. Supporting data was submitted by Ferdinand Shultz, Peter Lauck, Major Adam Heiskell, Captain Abraham Shepherd, and J. Swearingen.

PIERPONT (PIERPOINT), JOHN

John Pierpont served under Captain Zackquill Morgan in 1775 in the Virginia militia. He was born in 1714 and died in 1796. His home, built in Monongalia County, in 1769, became well known as a frontier outpost. Here George Washington was a guest in 1784. Here was born Francis H. Pierpont, who played an important part in the formation of West Virginia.

PIGMAN, JESSE (Captain)

Jesse Pigman, who later was a captain during the Revolutionary War, made a settlement in Monongalia County, in 1773, and was a member of the grand jury for Augusta County in 1775.

PILES, JAMES

In the Price Memorial Cemetery near Olive Church, Monongalia County, is buried James Piles, a soldier in the Revolutionary War, who died at his home near there in 1778.

PILES, ZACHARIAH
Service—Virginia   Va. No. 16.   No. W. 10896 and B. L. Wt. 50894

Born, July 15, 1758, Frederick County, Maryland; removed to Monongalia County, Virginia at age of 10, where he resided until his death, November 15, 1840. He was married in Green County, Pennsylvania, July 6, 1814, to Susannah Lazer, or Lezar, by Daniel Wooley, justice of the peace.

While in the South Branch Valley, he enlisted in the fall of 1776 under Captains Davy, Wiggins, and Scott, and served under Colonel Hite and Vanmetre, and General McIntosh. He was granted a pension in Monongalia County, in 1833, which seems to have been dropped in 1834. Suit was filed in this case which remained in court for many years until dismissed in 1852. Widow seems to have received pension in 1853 and also bounty land warrant for 160 acres. The widow was aged 70 in 1856.

Supporting data was submitted in this case by Peter Haught, Dudley Evans, Captain Scott, John Petty, General E. S. Pendall, William Price, John Walker, Samuel Miner, Captain J. Lantz, Hon. Edgar Wilson and W. G. Brown.

PINDALL, JACOB

In the Wiseman Graveyard near Lowesville, Monongalia County, is buried Jacob Pindall, a veteran of the Revolutionary War, who died near there in 1829.

PINDALL, PHILLIP (Captain)

Phillip Pindall, who served in the Revolutionary Army, died in Monongalia County, in 1804, and is buried in the Wiseman Graveyard near Lowesville. He was born in Maryland in 1731. Pindall was commissioned May 16, 1778, as a captain of a company in Colonel Lemuel Barrett's Battalion.

PITMAN, JOSEPH

In 1803, Joseph Pitman, who had been a soldier in the Revolutionary War, settled on Bill's Creek, Barbour County, and there spent the remainder of his life.

POLLOCK, THOMAS

Private in Captain Shepherd's company. He was drafted into another company January 1, 1777.

PORTERFIELD, CHARLES (Colonel)

Sergeant in Captain Daniel Morgan's company in 1775. Taken prisoner at Quebec. Commanded one of the rifle companies raised by Morgan, 1777-78. Killed at Camden, South Carolina, at head of his command as lieutenant colonel in the Virginia Line.

PORTERFIELD, GEORGE (Captain)

Sergeant in Morgan's riflemen. Promoted to captain. Served as sheriff of Berkeley County. Was born in 1740 and died in 1824.

PORTERFIELD, ROBERT

Was adjutant of Colonel Daniel Morgan's Regiment in 1777. According to Danske Dandridge, the Porterfields lived near Gerrardstown, now Berkeley County, West Virginia.

POWELL, GEORGE

Lived in Shepherdstown. Took part in the storming of Stony Point under General Anthony Wayne.

POWELL, ISAAC

The grave of Isaac Powell, veteran of the Revolutionary War, is found on the old Powell farm, Clinton District, Monongalia County, three miles from Opekiska. He died in 1818.

POWELSON, HENRY

Service—New Jersey   Va. No. 23196   No. W. 3864

Born, Somerset County, New Jersey, 1758; died, July 8, 1845. Enlisted in New Jersey in 1775 or 1776 and on different tours as a drafted militiaman served under Captains Stotts, Wheeler, Vauss, Flagg, Garrett, Vandiver, Low, Fulkinson, Carr, Moore, Babcock, and Denike, under Colonel Frederick Frelinghuysen. Received pension in Hampshire County, Virginia, 1833. Name of wife, Abigail Brewer. Supporting statements filed by

Cornelius and Rimer Powelson, brothers, Ephriam Dunn, John Brady, Christopher Heiskell, and John Stump.

POWERS, WILLIAM (Captain)
Service—Virginia　　Va. No. 16936　　No. S. 18164 and B. L. Wt. 26741

Born, Frederick County, Virginia, November 9, 1765, but early settled at Powers Fort, Bridgeport, Harrison County, Virginia. Enlisted as an Indian spy in 1781; served as an ensign of scouts under Colonel William Lowther in 1783; held a commission as captain of rifle company in the Fourth Battalion, Eleventh Regiment Virginia militia in 1796; as a justice of the peace was a member of the Harrison County Court in 1800, and continued a justice in Harrison and Lewis counties more than thirty years. After his marriage he settled on a Revolutionary war grant on what was later the farm of the late J. Goodloe Jackson near Jane Lew and once served as sheriff of Lewis County.

He was pensioned, April 1841, for Revolutionary services, but through error, was dropped from the pension rolls in August of that year. He was restored in 1850. He died June 6, 1856, and is buried with his wife in the Broad Run Cemetery of Lewis County. Supporting data in his case was submitted by John Brown, John Schoolcraft, Alexander West, and Adam Flesher.

PRENTISS, STANDARD (Sergeant)

Before the Wood County Court, July 6, 1818, Standard Prentiss made affidavit that he had enlisted as a sergeant in Connecticut under Captain Dyer in the Twentieth Regiment commanded by General Putnam, and that he was discharged from said service in New Jersey at the completion of his term of enlistment. His claim was approved by the court and forwarded to the War Department.

PREWITT, OBEDIAH

Before the Mason County Court, May 14, 1834, Obediah Prewitt, aged 79, stated that he enlisted in May, 1778, in Goochland County, Virginia, under Captain Miller Dillant, and marched to Richmond, Williamsburg and Yorktown. Was then granted permission by General Nelson in command of the Virginia militia to return home. In 1778, he was drafted under Captain Edward Duke and served another period of three months. In 1779, he was one of those called out under Colonel Morris and Ensign Lacy to attack a British vessel which had gone aground in the James River. In April, 1781, served another three month term under Lieutenant David Rutherford, Major McClum and Major Armistead and in the fall of that year was out again under Colonel Curd. Became ill and received his discharge. Most of the service was with the Fifth Regiment of Virginia militia. Soldier was born in Goochland County, Virginia, July 6, 1755. Later moved to North Carolina, and from thence to Mason County, Virginia.

PRICE, JACOB
Service—Virginia　　Va. No. 12090　　No. S. 3730

Enlisted at Fincastle, Botetourt County, Virginia, in 1776, and served as a private two years under Captain Thomas Posey in the Seventh Virginia Regiment, commanded by Colonel Lewis. Before the Greenbrier County Court in 1784 it was ordered that this soldier, who had been wounded in the Revolutionary War, be recommended to the Governor and Council as a pensioner. He appears to have been admitted to the Virginia pension rolls February 23, 1796. In Greenbrier County, Virginia, 1833, he was placed on the United States pension roll. Soldier died June 28, 1841.

PRICE, RICHARD
Service—Virginia   Va. No. 12067   No. W. 2435 and B. L. Wt. 10244

Born, Louden County, Virginia, February 18, 1757; died, July 18, 1834, and is buried in Lawson Cemetery, Marion County, West Virginia. Enlisted at Leesburg, Virginia, and served from January, 1777, one year as a private under Captain Payton Harrison and Colonel Spottswood; in 1780, was out two months under Captain Francis Russell; in May, 1781, served under Captain Cleveland and Colonel Matthews; and also served in 1781 guarding prisoners from Cornwallis' captured army. Was engaged in the battles of Brandywine, Germantown, and skirmish at Bacon's Branch.

Married Elizabeth Arnett in 1827. Received pension in Monongalia County in 1833, with supporting data from David Musgrave, James Price, Thomas and Daniel Arnett. Widow also received pension and bounty land warrant for 160 acres. She was aged 77 in 1853.

PRICE, THOMAS

Before the Randolph County court, March 23, 1790, Thomas Price, an old soldier, who had been wounded at the battle of the "Point" in the company of Captain John Lewis of Augusta, was recommended to the Executive as worthy of aid, and approval given a pension of fifteen pounds.

PRICE, THOMAS

It was ordered by the Greenbrier County Court in 1785 that Thomas Price be allowed four hundred acres of land by right of settlement, he having proved to the court he was entitled to the same by actual settlement made before the year, 1778, he being in Continental service, when the commissioners settled the claim to unpatented lands in this district.

PRICHARD, REES (Ensign)
Service—Virginia   Va. No. 12545   No. S. 38316

Enlisted as an ensign in the fall of 1775, 1776, 1777, in the company of Captain Abel Westfall in the Eighth Virginia Regiment Continental Establishment, commanded by Colonel McCarty, at which time the soldier was living at Sullivan Island. Soldier was granted pension while living in Hampshire County, Virginia, in 1819, but was stricken from the pension rolls in 1820, and there is no evidence to show reinstatement. Supporting data submitted in this case by James Monroe, Daniel Carmichael, John Hiett, John Candy (Gandy) and Colonel Edward McCarty. Died September 25, 1830.

PRICKETT, JACOB

Married Dorothy Springer near Winchester, Virginia, and came to the Monongalia Valley about 1772 and built Prickett's Fort, which became an important border outpost, and which was garrisoned by militia during the Revolution and Indian wars. Land was confirmed to Prickett in 1781, and Colonel William Crawford had reported that he visited Prickett's home there as early as 1766. Prickett is commonly accepted as having had military service in the Revolutionary War.

Following are the names of the children of Jacob and Dorothy Prickett: Josiah, married Charity Taylor; Nancy, married Reuben Bunner; Isaac, married Mary Campbell; Dorothy, married James Dunn; Mary, married Jacob Lucas; Martha, married Peter Parker; James, married Mary Springer; Isaiah, killed and scalped by the Indians in 1774; the names of two children are missing.

PRITCHARD, (PRICHART, PRICHARTT, PRICKETT), GEORGE
Service—Virginia   Va. No. 5976   No. W. 5594

Born, Culpepper County, Virginia, 1736; died, June 19, 1822. Enlisted in Culpepper County, in 1776 in company commanded by Captain John Thornton, Third Virginia Line Regiment for three years. He took part in the engagements at Trenton and Queens Island and was discharged at Philadelphia, March 15, 1777, owing to disability.

Soldier was married, October 1780. His wife, Elizabeth, was aged 60 in 1820 and their children were as follows: Polly, 26; Lydia, 21; Fanny; George, 15; and four grandchildren: Mary, 15; Betsy, 9; Amelia, 4; Joanna, 3. Pension was granted in Harrison County, Virginia, in 1819 to the soldier, and later to his widow. Supporting data was submitted by George Dakon.

West Virginians in the American Revolution

Assembled and Edited by ROSS B. JOHNSTON

The sources of this material are from the files of the Pension Office at Washington, from various county records, from notes of patriotic societies, principally the Daughters of the American Revolution, Sons of the American Revolution, Sons of the Revolution, and from a large miscellaneous group of published and private sources. Corrections and additions to this list will receive the careful attention of the editor.

PRINGLE, SAMUEL (Captain)

The grave of Captain Samuel Pringle, who was a member of the Virginia Militia during the Revolutionary War, is in the Philadelphia Cemetery at Hampton, Upshur County.

PRYOR, WILLIAM

The pension application of William Pryor goes into much detail about frontier service about Point Pleasant. Pryor was born in Albemarle County, later Amherst, about 1752, moved to the Great Kanawha in 1773 and planted corn the following spring. He was driven away by the Indians but was at Point Pleasant in 1775, where he saw Captain Isaac Shelby, who had been left there with the wounded after the battle there in October, 1774. Pryor enlisted under Captain Mathew Arbuckle, who commanded Fort Randolph at Point Pleasant. Among the officers were Lieutenants Andrew Wallace, James Gilmer, James Thompson, Ensigns Samuel Wood and James McNutt, and Captain William McKee. Pryor was out on frequent expeditions in the neighborhood of the fort.

In 1777, Colonels Skillern and Dickinson came out on an expedition against the Shawnee towns. They were joined by General Hand of the Continental Army from Pittsburgh, who ordered the expedition abandoned. Some of the men threatened to mutiny against orders of General Hand.

The murder in 1777 of Chief Cornstalk and other Indians, who were held at the fort as hostages, brought on an attack in force by Shawnees in the spring of 1778. The fort held off the savages but it was thought necessary to send messengers to the Greenbrier settlements to give the warning of the Indians. Philip Hammond and Pryor agreed to go, but Pryor gave way to his older brother, John, at the request of Hammond. These two men, disguised as Indians by Nonhelema, the Grenadier Squaw, sister of Chief Cornstalk, who was living with the whites at the fort, successfully passed through the Indians and got to Fort Donnally near Lewisburg in time to warn the settlers and enable them to make proper defense against the attack which followed a short time afterwards. While the Indians were still in the neighborhood General George Rogers

Clark stopped at the fort on his expedition against the Illinois country.

Pryor later served under Captain Samuel Higginbotham of Colonel Christian's Regiment. Among his comrades were Zedekiah Shumaker, William Brown, and Samuel Allen. He again was out under Captain Richard Ballinger with a brother, Nicholas, and Richard Tankersly.

PURDY, (PARDY), JONATHAN
Service—New York   Va. No. 16389   No. S. 5956

Born, Connecticut, August, 1759. Enlisted in Westchester County, New York, and during the period from 1776 to 1781 served a total of two years as a private in Captain Paulding's company with First Lieutenants Purdy and Lockett, Colonels Graham, Thomas DeBoyse, and General George Clinton.

Soldier moved to Ohio County, Virginia, about 1790, and was there granted a pension, August 5, 1833. Supporting affidavits were filed for him by Daniel de Lavan, Carl Lochman, and James Parrot.

PURGETT, HENRY
Service—Virginia   Va. No. 16977   No. S. 18170

Born in 1753, Franklin Town, Maryland. Enlisted in 1778 in the Revolutionary Army in Hampshire County, under Captain Abraham Johnson in Colonel Johnson's Virginia Regiment, and served a little over six months. Ended service in 1781. Mentions Colonels Riddle, Brodhead, Major VanMeter, and General McIntosh. Received pension in Hampshire County, October 21, 1833. Supporting data filed by James Parker, Fred High, and John Ludwick.

PYLE, (PILE) WILLIAM (Lieutenant)

Was ensign in Captain Stephenson's company. In 1776, was first lieutenant in Captain William Brady's company. Was on special duty at battle of King's Bridge and so escaped capture when Fort Washington surrendered, making prisoners many of his comrades.

PYLEATT, ROBERT
Service—Continental Pa.   Va. No. 23086   No. S. 8987

Born in Pith Valley, Franklin County, Pennsylvania, August 15, 1753; crossed the mountains in 1776, and was living in Ohio County in 1833. Enlisted in Somerset County, Pennsylvania and in Ohio County in 1776, and served two years under Captains Cluggage and Ogle in the Pennsylvania Line under Colonels Thompson and Hand. He had been badly wounded in the arm which was shattered so as to render him unfit for military service, and had a discharge from Hand.

Pension certificate was issued in Ohio County, November 5, 1833, but the amount seems to have been later reduced. Supporting claims were made by Abram Rodgers, Richard Hardesy, and Samuel W. Keenan.

QUEEN, JOHN
Service—Virginia   Va. No. 16380   No. S. 5962

Enlisted in Loudon County, Virginia, and served as a private fifteen months under Captain Daniel Fegins in the Fourteenth Virginia Regiment under Generals Green and Muhlenberg. Mentions Captain J. Harvey, Lieutenant Charles Binns and other officers. Received pension, August 3, 1833, while living in Hampshire County, Virginia. Soldier was born in 1755.

RADAR (RADER) MICHAEL (Captain or Major)
Service—Virginia   Va. No. 23130   No. S. 7349

Born in Rockingham County, Virginia, March, 1750; died June 18, 1839. Enlisted in Shenandoah County, Virginia, in 1777. Service included three months as private, three months as a captain, and six months as a major. His claim of a captaincy was sustained but the record does not show proof that he held the rank of a major. Radar claimed that records were destroyed but evidence shows that there was a company commanded by Captain Rader. His regiment was commanded by Colonel Gibson, with Colonel Steele, Colonel Zane, and General Hand as other officers.

Pension certificate was issued November 5, 1833, at which time soldier was living in Jackson or Lewis Counties. Also mentions Greenbrier and Marion Counties. Mentions his father, James Rader, and Michael Rader, Jr., presumably a son.

RADCLIFFE, WILLIAM
Service—Virginia   Va. No. 12665   No. S. 9049

Served two years as a private under Captain Cunningham in Colonel Neville's Regiment. Records are missing from the pension office file.

RAINS (RAMIS), JOHN
Service—Virginia   Va. No. 14300   No. W. 4058

Born, 1758, and died in Kanawha County, September 7, 1847. Enlisted, 1776-1779, and served three years as a private in company of Captain Lamb in the Tenth Virginia Regiment, Continental Establishment, commanded by Colonel Stevens and General Whealon.

Soldier married Margaret Dooley, daughter of Thomas Dooley, in Rockingham County, Virginia, January 14, 1785. They had nine children. The soldier received pension while living in Monroe County, Virginia, in 1819. The widow, aged 82, was granted a pension in 1847, at which time she was living in Fayette County, Virginia. Supporting data was filed by John Smith.

RAINS, JOHN
Service—Virginia   Va. No. 749   No. S. 5969

Born in Culpepper County, Virginia. Enlisted in 1777 or 1778 an served three years as a private in the company commanded by Captain Gillison of the Tenth Virginia Line under Colonel Green. Took part in the battles of Monmouth, West Point, White Plains and Yorktown.

Received pension while living in Lewis County, Virginia, in 1832. Supporting data submitted by Elizabeth Lacy, a sister, Adam Rouse, and

WEST VIRGINIANS IN THE REVOLUTION

Thomas Bland. Pension seems to have been temporarily suspended, but was resumed in 1836.

RANDALL, JACOB
Service—Virginia   Va. No. 23670   No. W. 5666

Born in Hampshire County, Virginia, 1759; died, December 14, 1840. Enlisted, March 10, 1778, and served six months as a private and three months as an ensign under Captain Moses Hutton, with Lieutenant Sylvester Ward, and Ensign J. Heath. In 1781, he was an ensign in the company of cavalry of which Captain Daniel Richardson and Lieutenant John Rennick were officers.

Court records of Hampshire County record the marriage of Randall to Milly, or Amelia, Yoakum, November 6, 1782, by the Rev. Valentine Powers. Their children were as follows: Elizabeth, October 3, 1784; Catherine, October 12, 1786; Ruth, October 1, 1788; Margaret, September 15, 1790; Rebeckah, November 7, 1792; Amelia, July 23, 1795; Jemima, March 11, 1798; Asenith, January 27, 1801; Abel, October 1, 1803; Ruth Claypool, September 4, 1804; Silas, May 10, 1806; Tabitha, February 19, 1808; Mary, June 3, 1811.

Soldier received pension in Hardy County, Virginia, 1834. Widow applied for pension in 1841 which was granted. Supporting data was filed by Jacob Rorabaugh, John Davis, Jacob Fisher, and Jonas Green.

RANDALL, JAMES
Service—Maryland   Va. No. 2930 and 2130   No. W. 26354

Born, Kent County, Maryland, 1761; died, Harrison County, Virginia, March 20, 1853. Enlisted in Kent County April 1777, and served eight months as a private under Lieutenant Reed and Captain Perkins in a Maryland regiment, stationed at Bay Shore and Chestertown on guard duty.

Received pension, November 9, 1832, while residing in Harrison County, Virginia. Widow, Elizabeth, received pension in 1854 at which time she was 74 years old. Among persons supporting their claims were James W. Jones, a relative, H. Gass, James Winter, and M. Hall.

RANKIN, JAMES
Service—New Jersey   W. 3867

James Rankin applied for pension, August 27, 1836, while living in Lewis, or Monongalia Counties. His wife's name was Rebecca. No other records are in the file.

RAUSCH, (ROUSH) JOHN (Captain)

Born 1742, in Shenandoah County, Virginia, the son of John Adam Rausch; died at Point Pleasant, Mason County, Virginia, in 1816. He served in the Revolutionary War as a captain in the Shenandoah County militia.

RAVENSCROFT, FRANCIS
Service—Virginia   Va. No. 7402   No. S. 38325

Enlisted, April 30, 1777, Berkeley County, Virginia, and served three years under Captain Trs. Willis in the Sixteenth Virginia Regiment, commanded by Colonel Neville. Took part in the engagements at Monmouth, Powell's (Paulus) Hook, and Stony Point.

Received pension, aged 59, in 1819, while living in Hampshire County. Pension was dropped in 1820 but was reinstated in 1821. In 1820, his wife, Joanna, was aged 16, and they had a daughter, Mary, aged 16.

READ, JOHN
Service—Virginia   Va. No. 23450   No. S. 15961

Born in Prince Edward County, Virginia, in 1745, and enlisted in 1777 in West Augusta, (now Harrison County, Virginia) in 1777. Served as a private under Captain Lowther in the Virginia regiment commanded by Colonel Duvall. Engaged in the Indian wars and as a frontier guard. Received pension in Harrison County, in 1834. Supporting data was submitted by John Davis, John Summerville, Sotha Hickman, and Christopher Nutter.

REAL, DAVID
Service—Virginia   Va. No. 23556   No. S. 15611

Born in Hampshire County, Virginia, in 1765 and enlisted, August 4, 1779 and served six months under Captains James Parsons and Stinson in the Virginia and Continental regiments, commanded by Colonel James Williams. Received pension in Hardy County, Virginia, February 28, 1834. Supporting data was submitted by Joshua Orrahead and Jonas Dunlap.

RECE, (RICE), ALLEN
Service—Pennsylvania   Va. No. 16715 and 25859   No. W. 5697 and B. L. Wt. 26732

Born in Bucks Valley, Pennsylvania, October 7, 1759; came to Cabell County, Virginia in 1803, and settled on Mud River north of Blue Sulphur; died, November 29, 1837. Enlisted in the Pennsylvania Line in 1777 under Captain Singers in unit commanded by Colonel Irwin, Colonel Robertson, and General Lacy. Substituted for James Faris; reenlisted under Captain Furgeman for nine months; served three months under Captain Thomas in regiment commanded by Colonel Robertson in brigade under General Lacy, and was discharged in New Jersey. In 1781-82, served as a militiaman substituting for John Hawkins. Was discharged at Newton, Bucks County, Pennsylvania. Worked as wagon driver for a time. Guarded British soldiers at Tanney Town, Maryland and was on camp service at Trenton.

Soldier was married to Mary Clymer, February, 1785, by the Rev. Robert Mitchel of the Presbyterian Church. She was born September 9, 1763. They had a son, Joseph. Soldier received pension, September 16,

WEST VIRGINIANS IN THE REVOLUTION

1833, in Cabell County. Widow likewise received pension and also bounty land warrant for 160 acres. Supporting affidavits were filed by Ebenezer Webster, John Everett, John Merrett, Albie Rece, and John Hannon.

REDMAN, JOHN
Service—Virginia   Va. No. 19017   No. W. 5691
Born in Hampshire County, Virginia, 1763; died October 8, 1836. Enlisted in 1778 and remained in service until 1783 under Lieutenant Vincent Howell in the First Virginia Regiment commanded by Colonel Lee and Colonel White, stationed in the west on the Ohio River. Soldier's marriage to Sarah Day in 1785 is recorded in Hampshire County. He received pension in 1823 and his widow, who was aged 80 in 1844, likewise received pension in Hardy County. Mention is made of Richard and Nimrod Rachel Redman, presumably near relatives.

REDMAN, RICHARD
Service—Virginia   Va. No. 20867   No. S. 38327
Born in 1759, and enlisted in Hampshire County, Virginia, as a private in the company of Captain Atwell, Second Virginia Regiment, Continental Establishment, commanded by Colonel Hawes. Served eighteen months, and was honorably discharged at Salsbury, North Carolina. Pension granted in Hardy County, Virginia, in 1829. Wife at that time was aged 65. Mention is also made of John Redman, probably a brother. Supporting data was filed by George Payne.

REDGWAY, NOAH
Claim for pension was rejected, No. R. 8641, in report of W. G. Singleton, November 30, 1834.

REED, ARTEMUS
Service—Massachusetts   Va. No. 6223   No. S. 38326
Enlisted, May, 1775, in the company of Captain William Smith in the regiment of Colonel John Nixon. Re-enlisted with Captain Gilman in the same regiment, was then with Colonel John Grayton's command, and later with Nay Smith's unit. He was discharged at West Point, New York, June 2, 1784, after six year's service. Soldier was aged 72 in 1818 and his wife 69. Pension was granted in Brooke County, Virginia, February 1, 1819.

REED, GILES, (JILES OR SILAS)
Service—New Jersey   Va. No. 9286   No. S. 39033
Enlisted at Princeton, New Jersey, in 1776 in the Third Jersey Regiment, Captain Patterson's company, commanded by Colonel Dayton, New Jersey Line. Took part in the fighting at Short Hills, Brandywine, Germantown, and Monmouth. He applied for pension in Fayette County, Pennsylvania, in 1818, and later moved to Monongalia and to Harrison County. He was granted pension, April 15, 1819, but was dropped from the rolls in 1820. Supporting data was filed by Mathias Chips, Samuel Sutton, and George Reed.

REED, ISAAC
Service—New Jersey   Va. No. 13147   No. W. 5868
Born in Hunterdon County, New Jersey, in 1757; lived in Fayette County, Pennsylvania, for a time, and then moved to Monongalia County, Virginia. He enlisted in 1776 in Trenton, New Jersey, and served seven months as a private under Captain Mott in regiment commanded by Colonel Philips, Major Anderson, and General Washington. Was in the battles of Trenton and Monmouth. Married Rebecca Titus, who was born in 1763. Pension was granted to the soldier in 1833 and also to his widow in 1846 and 1848. Supporting data filed by Benjamin Titus and Nathaniel Reed. Mentions Colonel Haymond, Colonel Dudley Evans, and Major J. Carothers.

REGER, ANTHONY (Ensign)
Anthony Reger, son of Jacob Reger, first lived in Hampshire County and later in Barbour County. He enlisted in the Revolutionary Army, April 16, 1777, and was commissioned an ensign in Captain Silas Zane's company under Colonel William Russell in the 13th or 15th Virginia Regiment.

REGER, JACOB, JR.
Served in the Revolutionary War. On his return from the war, he was employed with John Schoolcraft at Bush's Fort, Nutter's Fort and Beech's Fort in the upper Monongahela Valley as scouts to guard these forts from Indians. They ranged the regions along the Seneca Trail which led from the Tygarts Valley settlements to the Ohio River.

REGER, LEONARD (Sergeant)
Leonard Reger, son of Jacob Reger of Hampshire County, served in the Revolution as a sergeant in Captain William Darke's Company, Eighth Virginia Regiment.

REGER, PHILIP
Born in Hampshire County about 1767 and in 1782, at the age of 15, enlisted as a volunteer private in Captain James Summerall's company of Virginia troops. He served six months until the close of the war, being stationed at Winchester to guard British prisoners from Cornwallis' army. He was living in Lewis County when granted a pension in 1832. Supporting data is filed in this case by John Talbott, David Sleeth, William Camp, William Radcliffe, and John Reger, a brother.

REXRODE, ZACHARIAH
Service—Virginia   Va. No. 4124   No. S. 5983
Enlisted, December 1779, and November 1781, Rockingham County, Virginia. Served as a private for six months under Captains Braxter and Cowgar in the Virginia Militia Regiment under Colonel Bowser, Major Hamilton, and Generals Muhlenberg and Von Steuben. Took part in the siege and capture of Yorktown. Applied for pension while living in

Pendleton County, Virginia, and it was granted, January 11, 1833. Supporting data filed by James Keister and William McCoy, Sr.

REYNOLDS, BENJAMIN
Made application for pension as a Revolutionary soldier while living in Jackson County. No records on file. Wife was Barbara Harpold.

REYNOLDS, GEORGE
Lived near Shepherdstown and there enlisted in the Revolutionary Army.

RHODES, THOMAS
Service—Virginia   Va. No. 16227   No. S. 17045
Born, Loudoun County, Virginia, July 4, 1756. Enlisted at Leesburg, Virginia, February 8, 1777, and served two years under Captain Brown in the First Regiment of the Virginia Line, under Major Allison, Colonel Gibson, General Muhlenberg, and General Washington. Was in the battles of Monmouth, White Marsh Hill, and Stony Point. Pension was granted in Tyler County, Virginia, July 18, 1833. Supporting data submitted by the Rev. Rezin Davis, Asa Harris, and Elizabeth Harris.

RICE, BAILEY
Service—Virginia   Va. No. 15908   No. S. 39044
Born, 1747. Enlisted in August or September 1780, and served as a private eighteen months under Captain John Marshall and Bentley in the Second Virginia Regiment, commanded by Colonel Hawes, John Green, and Major S. Sneed. Took part in the battles at Camden, Guilford Courthouse, Ninety-Six, and Eutaw Springs. His discharge was signed by Francis Gray, lieutenant of the Third Detachment. Soldier received pension, November 27, 1819, while living in Wood County, Virginia. Wife, Elizabeth, was aged 55, in 1821. Their children at that time were Lucinda, aged 22, and Malinda, aged 13.

RICHARDS, GEORGE
Service—Virginia   Va. No. 16934   No. S. 18572
Born in Rockingham County, Virginia, 1759. Enlisted in Monongalia County, Virginia, March 2, 1780, as an Indian spy and served two years under Captains Joseph Gregory and Lowther, and Colonel Wilson. Certificate of pension was issued in Lewis County in 1833, but was dropped two years later. Supporting data was filed by William Mitchell and John Cain. The case seems to have been kept alive, however, as it is entered on a new record, June 27, 1872, and records filed by Captains Booth, Trimble, J. P. Kegemus, and on July 5, 1872, by Colonel Benjamin Wilson.

RICHARDS, ISAAC
Service—Virginia   Va. No. 12737   No. S. 9056
Born in Rockingham County, Virginia, in 1759, and died in Harrison

County, Virginia, prior to May 17, 1833, at which time pension certificate for services in the Revolution was granted. Enlisted in Harrison County in the spring of 1781 under Captain George Jackson and served six months in the Virginia Regiment commanded by Colonel Crockett, Major Lowther and General Clark. Supporting data was filed by Josiah Dawson, William Richard, Edward Goodwin, and Henry Flesher.

RICHCREEK, (RICKCRICK), PHILIP
Service—Virginia   Va. No. 3320   No. W. 4571 and B. L. Wt. 592

Enlisted, in Lancaster County, Pennsylvania, April 1, 1781, and served until June 28, 1783, as a private under Captain Pearson in the Second Regiment of the Pennsylvania Line, commanded by Colonel Stewart and General Wayne. Took part in the fighting at James Town or Green Spring, and the siege and capture of Yorktown.

Marriage bond of Philip Rickcrick (Richcreek), and Sarah Rogers, signed by Richcrick and Henry Armstrong, October 13, 1787, is filed in Loudon County, Virginia. Soldier was born about 1763 and died, August 27, 1842. He received pension in 1818 and also bounty land warrant for 100 acres, at which time he was living in Jefferson County, Virginia. Widow applied for pension in 1844 which seems to have been granted to her while living at Cincinnati in 1845 and 1848.

RICHMOND, WILLIAM
Service—Virginia   Va. No. 16535   No. S. 9088

Born in Pennsylvania, 1752, and moved to Botetourt County, Virginia, in 1775, where he enlisted in October of the same year in Lieutenant Wood's company in the Third Virginia Regiment commanded by Colonel Neville. Marched from Botetourt County to Savannah Fort, now Lewisburg, where the company wintered. In the spring, marched to Point Pleasant. Then under Colonel Neville went with Captain Andrew Hamilton against the Indians and served two years and one month. Mentions Lieutenant Andrew Wallace, and Captain M. Arbuckle. Received pension in Greenbrier County in 1833. Supporting data filed by Captain Charles Arbuckle, son of Captain M. Arbuckle, and Francis Welch, who was 90 years old.

RIDER, ADAM
Enlisted in 1775 under Captain Stephenson. Again enlisted in his company in 1776. Was drafted into another company, January 1, 1777.

RIFFEE, JACOB
Service—Virginia   Va. No. 23053   No. S. 9066

Born in Culpepper County, Virginia, June 3, 1861. Enlisted, July, 1777, in Culpepper or Rockingham County in company commanded by Captain Ferguson in the regiment under Colonels Hoock, Clark, and Alcock. Received pension in Harrison County, Virginia, October 29, 1833, which was suspended in 1835 and not resumed. Supporting data was filed by Eli and William Martin.

West Virginians in the American Revolution

Assembled and Edited by ROSS B. JOHNSTON

The sources of this material are from the files of the Pension Office at Washington from various county records, from notes of patriotic societies, principally the Daughters of the American Revolution, Sons of the American Revolution, Sons of the Revolution, and from a large miscellaneous group of published and private sources. Corrections and additions to this list will receive the careful attention of the editor.

RIGHT (WRIGHT), BAZZELL (BAZZLE)
Service—Penn. Md.   Va. No. 23580   No. S. 15966

Born in Prince George County, Maryland, 1764. Enlisted, September 3, 1779, Hagerstown, Washington County, Maryland, and again at Fort Pitt, Pennsylvania, in May 1780. Served six months at Hagerstown under Captain William Lewis and Lieutenant Lane, followed by service at Fort Pitt in 1780 and also under Colonel Ebenezer Zane, chiefly serving as an Indian spy. Received pension in Lewis County, Virginia, in 1834, which was suspended the following year, with no evidence of reinstatement. Supporting data was filed by Jesse Tanner and Sam Hines.

RINEHART, THOMAS
Service—Maryland   Va. No. 16212   No. S. 5986 and 16211
                                        (Agency Book)

Born in Reading County, Pennsylvania, July, 1741; died, March 13, 1833, Preston County, Virginia. Enlisted, September 1776, in Washington County, Maryland, and served under Captains Klapsadler and Lynne in the Maryland militia under Colonel Shrycock on guard duty at Fort Washington, Fort Lee, and Fort Frederick. After the Revolution, Rinehart came to Monongalia County, in 1798, in the region later included in Preston County. He received pension in 1833, but was dropped from the rolls in 1835. Supporting data was submitted by Adam Shaffer and Jacob Startzeman.

ROACH, JONATHAN
Service—Virginia   Va. No. 12149 and 11059   No. W. 3870

Born, Rockingham County, Virginia, 1761; died, June 14, 1832, Monroe County, Virginia. Enlisted in Orange County, Virginia, February, 1779, under Lieutenant John Goodall, and served as guard for the prisoners captured with General Burgoyne at Saratoga. Served two years and nearly four months under Captain Madison, Major John Roberts and Colonel Taylor, and was discharged by Colonel Taylor in May, 1781. Gave his discharge to Nathaniel Mills with his claim to any bounty land. Later in 1781, substituted for James Craig in the Rockingham County militia under Captain Smith, Major Long, and Colonel Samuel Lewis. Marched through Charlottesville, Richmond, Williamsburg, to Yorktown where he was discharged eight days before Cornwallis surrendered.

Christian Peters, Jacob Meadows and Mathew Meadows certified that each of them had seen Roach in service during the Revolutionary War. Other data was filed in his behalf by Benjamin Holstead and Matt Maddy. The soldier married Ruth Meadows in October, 1782, and to them were born twelve children, but names are not given. Roach received pension, April 1, 1833, in Monroe County, Virginia, and his widow was granted pension in 1848.

ROBARDS (ROBERTS), ARCHIBALD
Service—Maryland   Va. No. 16555   No. W. 5737 and B. L. Wt. 11395

Born, Frederick County, Maryland, 1763; died, Hardy County, Virginia, April 18, 1836. The record of his marriage, July 24, 1787, to Mary Ann Basley, is filed in Frederick County.

Enlisted in Maryland, December 1776, and served nearly twelve months under Captains Boyer, Gaithers, Hoff, and Masters in a Maryland regiment commanded by Colonel Bruce and General Smallwood. First substituted for Jacob Kerns for six months, after which he served several short terms as guard and at barracks. Mentions Lieutenant Jeffrey Magruder, and Captain Boyd. He received pension in Hardy County, Virginia, in 1832. His widow also received pension. Supporting affidavits were filed by Charles Turley, Joseph Walker, and Thomas Borgess.

ROBERTS, ISAAC
Service—Virginia   Va. No. 23912   No. S. 19453

Born, Mecklenburg County, Virginia, December 2, 1760, son of Thomas Roberts. Served several periods of enlistment between 1780 and 1783 as a private in the company commanded by Captain Binns Jones in the Fourth Virginia Militia under Colonel Lucas and General Gates. Took part in the battle of Camden, South Carolina. A discharge was given Roberts by Major Anderson at Boyds Ferry, where he appears to have been a munition stores' guard.

Among the officers mentioned in his pension application are Colonel Thomas McCallister, Major Davis Hudson, Captain Elijah Graves, John Morris, Joseph Hudson, W. H. Morris, Stephen Spurlock, and Andrew Barrett. Pension granted soldier in Cabell County, Virginia, in 1834. Name of wife, Rebecca. A brother, Thomas Roberts, is mentioned.

ROBERTS, JAMES

Enlisted in Captain Stephenson's company as a private in 1775. Enlisted under Captain Shepherd in 1776. He was an armorer and after the battle of Fort Washington, which almost wiped out this company, he was discharged, December 6, 1777. His home was near Shepherdstown.

ROBERTS, RICHARD
Service—Virginia   Va. No. 15053   No. S. 39052

Born in Virginia in 1756; died, January 30, 1830, in Brooke County, Virginia. Enlisted January 26, 1776, Culpepper County, Virginia, as a private with Lieutenant Henry Field under Captain George Slaughter in the Eighth Virginia Regiment, commanded by Colonel Bowman and Colonel Muhlenberg. His regiment marched to join the northern army and provided reinforcements for its troops. Largely occupied with camp and guard duty. Received honorable discharge, February 4, 1778, from General Scott at Valley Forge.

Pension was granted in Brooke County, Virginia, upon application of April 27, 1818. At this time his wife was 65 years old, and their children given as a son, 27, a daughter 22, another daughter 31, and a granddaughter, 11 years old.

ROBERTS, THOMAS
Service—Virginia   Va. No. 23093   No. W. 5738

Born, December 22, 1762, in Mecklenburg County, Virginia, the son of Thomas Roberts; died, March 13, 1848. Married, December 23, 1788, in Charlotte County, Virginia by the Rev. Thomas Roberts to Nancy May. Enlisted in Mecklenburg County, in 1780, as a substitute for Jacob Watson and Thomas Roberts. Served as a private under Captain William Lucas in the Virginia militia under Colonel Mumford and General Green. Took part in the battle of Guilford Courthouse, and was on marches to the Roanoke and Dan Rivers.

Applied for pension in Cabell County, Virginia, which was granted in 1833. The widow received pension in 1849 and died, July 20, 1852. Among members of the family named, besides his father, are Isaac Roberts, a brother, and Oney Roberts, possibly a sister. Supporting data was filed by Thomas McCallister, Allen Rice, and James Brown.

ROBINSON, BENJAMIN (Colonel)

Born, July 7, 1758, in Virginia, a son of William Robinson, a pioneer settler on Robinson's Run, Eagle District, for whom that stream was named. While a resident of Carolina County, Virginia, he raised a company of Minute Men in the Revolutionary War and fought under Sergeant Boyle, Captains Jones and Harris, Colonel William Washington, and Colonel Alexander Spottswood. He was promoted to the rank of colonel in 1776 and was in the battles of Brandywine and Germantown. He applied for a pension, December 24, 1832, in Harrison County, Virginia, which was granted.

He settled on 400 acres of land near Lumberport, established mills and floated lumber down the streams to Pittsburgh markets. He continued to be active in border affairs and in 1785 led the chase after the Indians who had massacred Thomas Cunningham. He was sheriff of Harrison County in 1794 and died in 1833.

His first wife was Magdalene Webb; born May, 1781; died, August 20, 1784. She was the daughter of William Webb; born, June 11, 1700; died, February 1, 1778; and Mary Margaret Webb; born, November 25, 1712; died November 11, 1781. Their children were Elizabeth; born, August 10, 1782; died, August 20, 1855. She married Henry Coffman, son of Jacob Coffman. Felix, born March 31, 1784; died, September 9, 1853, who married Elizabeth Wood.

The second wife of Colonel Robinson was Mrs. Mary Assom Wilkinson, widow of J. Wilkinson. She was born, April 8, 1757; died October 29, 1823. Their children were: David, born, 1786; died, 1853; married Sarah, daughter of David Wamsley. Margaret, born, 1787, and married Colonel John Sommerville, 1805. Magdaline, born, 1788; died, 1814; married John Boggess, 1805. Mary Elizabeth, born, 1791; died, 1864; married Dr. Caleb Boggess, 1817. Benjamin, born, 1792; died, 1818; married Nancy Webb. John; born, 1794; married daughter of David Wamsley. Malinda, born, 1797; died, 1823; married George W. Boggess. Susannah, born, 1795; married Albertus Boggess. William Marshall, born, 1788; married Emaline Francis or Stringer, 1823.

ROBINSON, ISAAC (Sergeant)

Before the Mason County, Virginia, court, December 3, 1832, appeared Isaac Robinson, aged 78, who made the following statement: born, December, 1754, in Virginia near the North Carolina line; captured at age of five by Shawnee Indians with whom he remained seven or eight years. Bearing marks on ear and nose of Indian tortures, he was surrendered at Fort Duquesne and restored to his parents in Botetourt County in 1781.

The following January, he volunteered in a company of infantry commanded by Henry Paulding and Lieutenant Graham. Served as an orderly sergeant, marched to Bedford, joined General Greene at Guilford, and was with Lee's Light Horse on the day of the battle. Became ill and was discharged. Hired William Shelton as a substitute in the Yorktown campaign. Moved west after the Yorktown campaign and served as a spy until Wayne's treaty. Settled in Robinson District, Mason County, Virginia, and there built Fort Robinson, as defense against the Indians.

ROBINSON, JAMES
Service—Conn., Md., N. J. and Penna.   Va. No. 12742   No. S. 7432

Enlisted, Frederick County, Maryland, and New Jersey, spring of 1776, and July, 1778, and served fourteen months under Captains Cresap and Brady in the Twelfth Pennsylvania Regiment, commanded by Colonels Hall and Durkee. Received pension, aged 85, in 1833, while living in Harrison County. His claim was supported by Joshua Hawkins and William McCree.

ROBINSON, JOHN (Sergeant)
Service—Penna.   Va. No. 10841   No. S. 39055

Enlisted, December 1776, and remained in service until 1780. First service was under Captain Henry McKinley and Colonel William Cook in the Twelfth Pennsylvania Regiment, as sergeant and quartermaster; then in the Second Regiment under Brigadier General Conaway as conductor of military stores; and with the Third Regiment, under Captain William Craigs and Colonel Thomas Craig as quartermaster sergeant.

Pension was granted to the soldier, May 20, 1819, in Hampshire County. At that time he was 70 years old, his wife, Margaret, 62, and their children as follows: Catherine, 20; Nelson, 13; Elizabeth, 12.

ROBINSON (ROBESON), JOHN
Service—Virginia   Va. No. 12135   No. S. 6017

Born in Augusta County, Virginia, March 15, 1758; and was dead when his pension certificate was issued in 1833. He enlisted in Monroe or Greenbrier County, Virginia, and served in 1776 and in 1780 under Captains Thomas Wright and John Wood in Virginia regiments, commanded by Majors James Hamilton and Andrew Anderson, and Colonel Armstrong. His service was against the Indians on the Kanawha, New and Cumberland Rivers.

Among his comrades who are mentioned, James Alton, Swift Berry, and Edward Cornwell were dead; William Butcher had moved to Kentucky; James and John Shaver, and William McCarley had gone away. His claim was supported by the Rev. James Christy, John Hutchinson, and Robert Christy. Pension certificate was issued in Monroe County, April 1, 1833.

RODGERS, ABRAHAM
Service—Virginia   Va. No. 16171   No. S. 6026

Born, October 17, 1760, Queen Anne County, Maryland, but was living in Brooke County, Virginia, when drafted into service in October, 1776 at the age of 16 years. He was under Ensign George Cox and Captain Isaac Cox at Holliday's Cove while protecting the frontier against Indian depredations. In May, 1777, again volunteered and served more than fifteen months in the company of Captain Ogle under Colonel Shepherd, and under Captain Sam Brady, Captain Benjamin Bigg, Colonels Gibson, Brodhead, and other officers on the Ohio frontier.

Pension was granted for his military services, 1833, in Brooke County. His claims were supported by General Cox, Jeremiah Browning, W. McCluney, and William Baxter.

RODGERS, RHODAM
Service—Virginia   Va. No. 2132   No. S. 6021

Born, Fairfax County, Virginia, in 1756; died Harrison County, Virginia, 1861. In 1777, he volunteered in the Revolutionary service from Fairfax County, under Captain Dennis Ramsey, marched to Alexandria, where he was transferred to the regiment of Colonel William Renley (Ronney or Romney); marched to White Plains, New York, thence to Germantown, served three or four months, and was discharged by Brigadier General Charles Scott. In August, 1780, again volunteered under Captain William Mason, Lieutenant James Nesbitt, and under Colonel Comney Lucas marched to Fredricksburg, Richmond, Petersburg, Cheraw Hills, and to Pittsylvania Courthouse where he was again discharged. While at Cheraw Hills, he was engaged in a skirmish during which he was wounded in the face by a bayonet which broke the jaw bone, and was also wounded in the hand. The British party of thirty or forty was captured.

Received pension while living in Harrison County, Virginia, in 1832 which was amended in 1835.

ROE, JOHN

John Roe, aged 61, made affidavit before the Harrison County, Virginia, court that he had enlisted for service in the Revolutionary War in 1779 in the Third Jersey Regiment, Colonel Dayton, in company under Captain Richard Cox in the Jersey Line in Maxwell's Brigade. Pension was granted upon application dated May 18, 1818. Soldier and wife were both aged 55.

ROGERS, DAVID (Colonel)

The State of Virginia by executive order, February 6, 1851, allowed the heirs of David Rogers land bounty for his services as a colonel in the state line from June, 1778, to the end of the war. His will is filed in Hampshire County, West Virginia.

Rogers was a native of Ireland, who emigrated to America, first settled as a merchant at Old Town, Maryland, and in 1775 made a settlement five miles above Wheeling on the Ohio. In December, 1776, while a major of militia and a representative of West Augusta in the senate of Virginia, he was made a captain in a Virginia regiment, but did not qualify. In February, 1777, he was ordered to station fifty men at Wheeling and at the mouth of the Little Kanawha to guard these posts and neighboring settlements. When Ohio County, Virginia, was organized, he became county lieutenant, March 4, 1777. He later married the widow of Captain Michael Cresap and settled on the Potomac in Hampshire County, Virginia, opposite Old Town, and was succeeded as Ohio County's military officer by Colonel David Shepherd.

Early in 1778, he was chosen a special envoy from Governor Henry to Bernado de Galvaez, the Spanish governor of Louisiana. On his return from New Orleans, his party was attacked by the Indians above the mouth of the Licking, and all but thirteen were captured or killed. Simon Girty later boasted that he killed Rogers himself.

ROLLINS (RAWLINGS), MOSES
Service—Virginia Va. No. 5973 No. W. 10241 and B. L. Wt. 339 and 449

Enlisted, October 5, 1780, in Culpepper County, Virginia, under the command of Captain Smith and was attached to the regiment commanded by Colonel Buford in the Virginia Line. Served until the end of the war. In the battle of Guilford Courthouse, he received a wound and from other infirmities incident to his Revolutionary service, both legs were amputated below the knees.

Married Nancy Cave, of Ritchie County, Virginia, December 5, 1814. In 1820, the soldier was 57 years old, his wife 25. Their children were Henry, Jeremiah, Sally, Edward, and Rebecca. Soldier received pension in Harrison County, Virginia, 1819, and died February 4, 1856. His widow received pension in 1857. Apparently two bounty land warrants were issued, one for sixty acres and one for one hundred acres. Supporting data was filed by Sam Washington, J. B. Tyson, Benjamin Taylor, Richard Cross, M. McKenney, Zedidiah Goff, F. Bunnett, Abraham Smith, Thomas West, and Amos Culp.

ROMINE, JOHN
Service—Virginia   Va. No. 1247   No. S. 6008

Served as a private for six months under Captain T. Carson in unit commanded by Colonel Merriweather. Applied for pension in Harrison County, Virginia, which was issued in 1833, but apparently dropped in 1835 and not reinstated.

RONEMOUS, ANDREW, CONRAD, and LEWIS

These three brothers were members of the bodyguard of General Gates. Their family was one of the earliest to settle in that part of Berkeley County which is now included in Jefferson County, West Virginia.

West Virginians in the American Revolution

Assembled and Edited by ROSS B. JOHNSTON

The sources of this material are from the files of the Pension Office at Washington from various county records, from notes of patriotic societies, principally the Daughters of the American Revolution, Sons of the American Revolution, Sons of the Revolution, and from a large miscellaneous group of published and private sources. Corrections and additions to this list will receive the careful attention of the editor.

ROSE, ISAAC
Service—Virginia   Va. No. 16402   No. W. 5713

    Born, 1753; died February 17, 1829. Enlisted in Monongalia County in 1777 and served until 1780 under Captain Scott in the Thirteenth Virginia Regiment, Continental Establishment, under Colonel Gibson and General Hand. Pension was granted the soldier in Nicholas County in 1820. After his death his widow was granted pension, which was received until her death, November 30, 1843, in Braxton County. The other heirs, William, James, Hannah, Ezekiel, Charles, and Amelia, filed application for unpaid amounts in 1846. Among persons mentioned in this case are Margaret Johnson and David Johnson as supporting witnesses.

ROSEBROUGH, JOHN
Service—Penn.   Va. No. 16432   No. W. 11172 and B. L. Wt. 93085

    Enlisted in Cumberland County, Pennsylvania in 1775, in the company of Captain Ripley in the Sixth Pennsylvania Regiment, commanded by Colonel Irvin, Colonel Hartley, and General Thompson. Took part in the engagements at Saratoga, Three Rivers and at Ticonderoga, at which latter place he was wounded. Was also engaged on much guard duty. Thomas Dann, a British soldier of Burgoyne's army, who had been captured at Saratoga, made affidavit that John Rosebrough was one of the guards while he was a prisoner. Another supporting affiant was Jonathan Lukens.

    Soldier received pension in Hampshire County, in 1833, which was suspended, but later restored. He married Arsenath McGuire of Hardy County, Virginia, in 1836, and died, June 27, 1840. Bounty land warrant for 160 acres was later issued for Rosebrough as a private in Colonel Adam's regiment of the Pennsylvania line.

WEST VIRGINIANS IN THE REVOLUTION

ROUSH, (Rouch), JONAS
Service—Virginia   Va. No. 12720 (Transferred to Ohio)   No. S. 4785

Born, Holman Fort, Shenandoah County, Virginia, September 1763; moved to Mason County, Virginia, 1798, where he died in 1850. He enlisted in Shenandoah County as a substitute for his brother, Henry, and served three months in the company of Captain Al, Aul or Awl in Colonel Bird's or Burt's Regiment, and was transferred to Colonel Darke's Virginia Regiment. He was at the siege of Yorktown, and while on his way to Winchester, Virginia, with prisoners, was taken sick at Fredericksburg, and discharged.

He was granted pension in Mason County, Virginia, in 1833. His wife, having died in 1837, he removed to Meigs County, Ohio, to live with his daughter. Among supporting data is that filed by Michael Roush, George Roush, and Daniel Miller.

ROW (Rowe or Roe), JOHN
Service—New Jersey   Va. No. 1794   No. W. 5726

Enlisted in 1779 in Morris County, New Jersey, in the company of Captain Cox in the Third Jersey Regiment, commanded by Colonel Francis Barber, General Sullivan, and General Lafayette, and took part in the battles at Springfield, New Jersey, and Jamestown, Virginia. He remained in service until 1781.

Soldier was born in 1759 or 1761 and died September 29, 1829. He was married in Essex County, New Jersey March 27, 1779, and lived there until the spring of 1784. Then he moved to New York City in 1790, then to Fayette County, Pennsylvania, until 1796, at which time he moved to Harrison County, Virginia. His wife, Susannah, was 55 years old in 1820. The children of John and Susannah Rowe were: Clarissa, June 18, 1782; Lewis, August 23, 1784; Elizabeth, April 7, 1788; Edward, May 18, 1791; John, February 6, 1794; James, February 1, 1797. Soldier received pension in Harrison County, in 1818, which was suspended but later restored. His widow received pension in 1839. Supporting data was filed by D. Cane, John Long, and Humphrey Faires.

ROWAN, JOHN

The Rev. John Rowan was born in Maryland, April 12, 1749. He enlisted in the Revolutionary Army and was run down and trampled by British cavalry in the battle of Brandywine. He married Elizabeth Howard of Ann Arundel County, Maryland, moved to Randolph County, Virginia, April 12, 1809, and died at Beverley, December 29, 1833. His wife died February 19, 1844. Their children were: John, Thomas, Joseph, Francis, William, Nancy, Elizabeth, Bethany (Bathany), and Labbannah.

RUCKER, HENRY
Service—Virginia   Va. No. 5059   No. S. 6278

Born in Maryland in 1744. Service in the Revolutionary War under Captains Booth, Pindal and Gregory. Applied for a pension in Harrison County, Virginia, in 1832, which was issued in 1835 but was later dropped as not coming under the provisions of Act of June 7, 1832. Mentions a brother, John Rucker.

RUMSEY, JAMES

Rumsey, who won fame as the inventor of the steamboat, lived at "Bath," now Berkeley Springs, and later at Shepherdstown, Jefferson County, Virginia, and had seen service as a Revolutionary War soldier.

RUNION, ELIJAH
Service—Virginia   No. R. 9079

Born in Shenandoah County, Virginia, July 11, 1757. There he resided until 1781-82, when he removed to Ohio County, then to Harrison County, in 1815, and then to Mason and Jackson Counties. He enlisted May 17, 1778, and saw service under Captains J. Kar, Swearingen, Colonels Gibson, Zane, Shepherd, and General McIntosh. Under Captain Rader Milderbock he took part in the expedition against the Indians at Munsie Town. He applied for a pension while living in Jackson County, in 1833, which was rejected, apparently for failure to show sufficient service. Supporting data was filed by Sam Lenner and Jesse Carpenter.

RUSH, CONRAD

Enlisted under Captain Shepherd in 1776. Was taken prisoner and was killed or died in prison, February 15, 1777.

RUSSELL, JEFFREY

Before the Superior Court of Law in Cabell County, Virginia, October 9, 1811, Russell testified that he had enlisted for three years in 1776 in Mecklenberg County, Virginia, and had served as a private in the Fourteenth Virginia Regiment until December 28, 1779, when he was discharged at Philadelphia. He had failed to keep his discharge when applyng for compensation, and had received no land warrant. His claim was supported by Mark Russell. On October 31, 1811, he was issued land bounty Warrant No. 6068 for three years' service as a private.

RUSSELL, NICHOLAS

Was a private under Captain Shepherd. He was taken prisoner but was soon exchanged. He served out his enlistment, which ended October 1, 1778.

RUSSELL, THOMAS
Service—Virginia   Va. No. 1036   No. S. 38345

Enlisted early in 1777 as a private in the Twelfth Virginia Regiment, in the company of Captain Mitchell under Colonel James Wood. Served until the end of the war when he was discharged at Winchester, after taking part in the battles of Brandywine, Germantown, Monmouth, and Guilford Courthouse, and the siege and capture of Cornwallis' army at Yorktown.

Soldier applied for pension in Berkeley County, Virginia, June 10, 1820, at which time he was 64 years old. On file is the affidavit of Captain Joseph Swearington, late captain in the Virginia Continental Line, which states that Russell was a brave and valuable soldier. Pension was granted.

RUTHERFORD, ROBERT
Service—Virginia   Ohio—9735   No. S. 38341

Resided in Shenandoah County, Virginia, at the outbreak of the Revolution. Enlisted as a private and wagoner under Captain James Wallace in the Virginia Line in regiment commanded by Colonel Benford and took part in the campaign in North and South Carolina.

Applied for pension in Clark County, Ohio, in 1818, which was granted in 1819. Pension was discontinued in 1822, but in 1825, at which time the soldier was living in Cabell County, Virginia, pension was restored. At that time, the soldier was 63 years old and his wife 67.

RYAN, JOHN
Service—Virginia   Va. No. 16889   No. S. 18584

Born in Hampshire County, 1759, and while living on Patterson's Creek enlisted in the Revolutionary Army in August 1778 or 1779. Served twelve months under Captains Abraham Johnson, Josiah Swearingen, and Richardson under Colonels Harrison of Rockingham County, Morrow of Berkeley County, Gibson, and G. D. Camden, Generals McIntosh and Broadhead. He took part in the military activities at Fort McIntosh and Fort Lawrence. He received discharges from both Captain Swearingen and Captain Richardson. Soldier received pension in Randolph County, Virginia, in 1833. Supporting affidavits were filed by Adam See or Cee, The Rev. Thomas Collett, Thomas O. Williams, and Ely Butcher.

RYLAND, NICHOLAS N. (Captain)
Service—Pennsylvania   ,Va. No. 17930   No. S. 38346

A resident of Pennsylvania, but enlisted in Baltimore, Maryland, April, 1777, and served until November 15, 1783, as private, cornet of horse, lieutenant and captain under Captains Legur and Stake in the Third Pennsylvania Regiment, and in Pulaski's Legion, under Colonel Butler and Count Pulaski. He was in the engagements at Egg Harbor, Monmouth, Savannah, and at the siege and capture of Yorktown. He received pension while living in Lewis and Harrison Counties, Virginia. Supporting affidavits were filed in this case by Patrick and John Handline, and Paul Bentalon.

RYMER, GEORGE
Service—Virginia   Va. No. 27870   No. S. 9469

Born in England in 1755 and emigrated to America in 1772. While living in Augusta County, Virginia, he enlisted in 1780 and 1781 and served nine months as a private under Captains Gibbons, Bell and Buckhannon in the Virginia militia commanded by Colonels Moffett and Vance. Took part in various marches and guard duty.

Applied for and received pension while living in Pendleton County, 1834. Supporting evidence submitted by Jack Homer, Jacob Seybert, and Smith Thompson. Pensioner died November 30, 1845.

SALTER, JAMES
Service—Virginia   Va. No. 19803   No. S. 41125

Enlisted in 1776 in Ohio County, Virginia, in the company commanded by Captain Silas Zane in the Thirteenth Virginia Regiment under Colonel Russell. He was later transferred to the Ninth Regiment, under Colonel D. Campbell. Took part in the battles of Germantown and Brandywine, and remained in service until 1780.

In Ohio County in 1826 he applied for pension. Captain John Mills of Ohio County testified as to his services as did Captain Uriah Springer of Fayette County, Pennsylvania, and W. C. Chapping. Pension was granted in 1827 which was transferred to Scioto County, Ohio, in 1838. His pension application refers to his wife, aged 84 in 1826, at which time the soldier was 72. Reference is made to a nephew, William, living in Fayette County, Pennsylvania, to whom the soldier owed money.

West Virginians in the American Revolution

Assembled and Edited by ROSS B. JOHNSTON

The sources of this material are from the files of the Pension Office at Washington, from various county records, from notes of patriotic societies, principally the Daughters of the American Revolution, Sons of the American Revolution, Sons of the Revolution, and from a large miscellaneous group of published and private sources. Corrections and additions to this list will receive the careful attention of the editor.

SAMMONS, JOHN
Service—N. J. and N. Y.   Va. No. 16392   No. S. 6045

Born, Orange County, New York, 1758 or 1759. Residing in Essex County, New Jersey, or Orange County, New York at time of the Revolution. Enlisted and served seventeen months as a private under Captain Thomas Wolverton and Captain John Weizner of New Jersey and New York regiments, commanded by Colonel Martin, Colonel Nicholas and General Green and General Clinton. Took part in the Long Island campaigns. Names many other officers.

Received pension while living in Greenbrier County, Virginia, in 1833, which was later reduced. Supporting data filed by Richard Sammons, a nephew, and John Haptonstall.

SAMONS (Sammons, Simons, or Simmons), REUBEN
Service—New Jersey   Va. N. J. 15340   No. S. 41121

Enlisted in Essex County, New Jersey, May 1, 1781 as a private under Captain William Helm or Helms in the Second New Jersey Regiment, commanded by Colonel Dehart. Took part in the Yorktown campaign. Received his discharge at Newburg, New York, on June 1, 1783. Pension granted in New Jersey in 1819 and transferred to Greenbrier County, Virginia in 1821. Supporting data submitted by Benjamin Bidlock.

SAMPKINS, THOMAS

Before the Wood County, Virginia court, June 3, 1818, Thomas Sampkins, aged 75, made affidavit that he had served as a private in the Revolutionary War in the company of Captain Thomas Porter of the First Virginia Regiment. He was in the battle of Germantown and at the siege of Yorktown when Cornwallis and his army were captured. He was discharged at Winchester in 1781.

SAMS, JONATHAN
Service—Virginia   No. R. 9168

Born in Berkeley County, Virginia, November 19, 1762. While residing on the Monongahela River in Pennsylvania or Virginia, Sams volunteered and served one month as an Indian spy at Deckers' Fort under Lieutenant Jones, commander of the fort. He volunteered and marched later from the neighborhood of Beesontown in Captain John Beeson's company, was in Colonel Crawford's Indian campaign, and in the battle of Sandusky when Crawford was captured. He subsequently served at several frontier stations, a part of the time under Captain John Evans in Monongalia County, protecting the inhabitants against the Indians. Had about five months additional service.

His application for pension in Wood County in 1833 was rejected as having been engaged only against the Indians since 1783 and not having had six months' service in a regularly organized military corps during the Revolutionary War.

SAMS (Sands), SAMUEL
Service—Virginia   Va. No. 1911   No. S. 6049

In Augusta County, Virginia, substituted in the militia for six months for William Dickey in 1780, serving under Captain James Tate and Major Frank Triplett, Major Brooks, Colonel Howard and General Morgan. Marched to South Carolina and was in the battle of the Cowpens in 1781. He was with a company when Colonel Washington captured a hundred Tories at Rugleys' Mills. He was discharged at Salisbury, North Carolina, returned home, and was drafted in June for three months under Captain John Campbell, Major Long and Colonel Cameron. Took part in the siege and capture of Yorktown. He was in the battle of Jamestown where he was commanded by Captain John Dickey and Colonel Huggart, later under Colonel William Bowyer. In 1782, he substituted for three months for Hugh Brown under Lieutenant John McCarney against the Indians, serving most of this period at Clover Lick on the Greenbrier River.

He received pension in Monroe County, Virginia, 1832, at which time he was 74 years old. He was a comrade of Berryman Jones and Samuel Clark. Supporting data was submitted by the Rev. James Christy.

SANFORD, WILLIAM (Captain)

Official orders of the State of Virginia, September 25, 1807, stated that the representatives of William Sanford were entitled to land allowed a captain of the Virginia line, Continental Establishment, for seven years and ten months service. Warrants 5398 to 5404 were issued. He was second lieutenant, Second Virginia, September 21, 1775; lieutenant, February 1776; Captain, December 25, 1776.

His will, recorded in Hampshire County, May 10, 1801, mentions his wife, Penelope; son, Thornton, and seven daughters: Harriett (Gaither), a widow in Kentucky; Nancy, wife of William Taylor; Emma, who, since death of William Sanford, married Jacob Johnson; Theresa, wife of Samuel Slycer; Sydney, 21; Eliza, 6; Myrtle, 7; and an infant son, Thornton. His widow later married Abraham Hawk.

SAPP, JOSEPH
Service—Delaware   Va. No. 18448   No. S. 41122

Enlisted in the Revolutionary Army in Delaware in 1776 and was discharged owing to wounds, January 26, 1783. Served four years under Captains Caldwell, Holland, and Jacquets, and Colonels Patterson, Hall, and Vaughn. He was in the fighting at Creckolds Town, Staten Island, and Monmouth. In the surprise at Camden he was wounded in the arm by musket ball and buckshot. He was in the hospital at Charlotte three weeks. In the attack on Ninety-Six, he was again wounded. He was captured by the British and paroled by Colonel Croger, the British officer in charge of the prisoners. His final discharge was from Colonel Walter Stewart, inspector of the northern army.

He applied for a pension in Monongalia County, Virginia, in 1820, at which time the soldier was 60 years old, and his wife, Sara, 58. Their children were: Samuel, 21; Henry, 19; Elizabeth, 14. Pension was granted in 1822 and for a time Sapp drew one pension as an invalid and another only as a Revolutionary War soldier. He was dropped from the roll in 1824, but in 1826 the Secretary of War restored both pensions to him. Supporting data was filed for him by Colonel Ralph Berkshire, William Lazier, Thomas Wilson, and N. Evans.

SARGENT, JEREMIAH

The grave of Jeremiah Sargent, who served in the Revolutionary Army, is in a cemetery just above Lock No. 3 on the Little Kanawha River in Wirt County.

SAULSBURY, WILLIAM

Before the Pocahontas County court, September 5, 1832, William Saulsbury, aged 90, testified that he enlisted under Captain John Lewis, Lieutenant Samuel Vance, and Ensign Jacob Warwick in May, 1774, in Augusta County, now Bath, at the Warm Springs, and that he was in the battle of Point Pleasant in October of that year, and was discharged in November. He also served three months as a guard at Warwick's Fort, and had a total service of at least ten months. He names William Sharp as a possible supporting witness. The court declared that it believed Saulsbury to have had Revolutionary service and recommended a pension for him.

SAYRE, SEELEY

Born in Orange County, New York, May 7, 1751, and died in Hampshire County, Virginia, January 3, 1815. His place of residence during the Revolution was Florida, Orange County, New York. He entered service August 8, 1777, in the Fourth Regiment of Orange County Militia, commanded by Colonel John Hawthorne. His wife was Mary Thompson.

SCALES, NATHANIEL
Service—North Carolina   Va. No. 23828   No. S. 18201

Born, April 13, 1758, Smith River, Pittsylvania County, Virginia. Lived in Rockingham and Henry County, Virginia, during the Revolution.

Enlisted under Captain John Leake and Lieutenant John Davis in the Virginia militia under Colonel James Martin and General Ruther at Rocky Springs, North Carolina, and took part in the campaign against the Chickasaw Indians, and also against the Tories. Mentions Adjutant Robert Martin, Colonel James Martin, Peasly, Grimes, Alexander, and others.

Pension granted in Cabell County, Virginia, in 1834. Supporting data filed by John Laidley and the Rev. Edmund McGinnis. The soldier died in Cabell County in 1834.

SCHOOLCRAFT, JOHN
Service—Virginia　　　　　Va. No. 16590　　　No. S. 7468 and B. L. Wt. 307417

Born in Hampshire County, Virginia, February 13, 1757; resided in Ohio County, at the beginning of the Revolution; resided in Monongalia County, in 1782 and 1783; at termination of the war was in Lewis County.

Enlisted, February 1777, in Ohio County, and served under Captain Bilderbock as an Indian spy, and under Captains Mason, Van Swearingen, Christopher Carpenter, Colonels Zane, Shepherd, and General McIntosh. His pension application describes the attack on Fort Henry at Wheeling and on other frontier forts, including Fort Lawrence on the Tuscaroras River. He later joined the regular troops at Fort Pitt under Brodhead, and served in the Coshocton raid in 1780.

In Harrison County is recorded the marriage of Schoolcraft to Nancy Brown, July 18, 1805. Soldier applied for pension which was granted in Lewis County, Virginia, in 1833. Warrant for bounty land was also issued. Supporting data was filed by P. McCan, James Brown, Henry McWhorter, and Carr Bailey.

SCHREADER, JACOB
Service—Pennsylvania　　　　　Va. No. 16020　　　No. S. 42002

Enlisted, Berks County, Pennsylvania, 1777 or 1778, and served until March 9, 1781, as a private under Captains Bull, Mousers, and Vanhorn in the Sixth Pennsylvania Regiment, commanded by Colonels Harmer and Hampton. Took part in the battle of Monmouth and aided in the capture of the ship Shrewsbury. Received pension while residing in Pendleton County, Virginia, in 1819. Had eight children, four girls and four boys. The oldest boy, nine years old, was crippled. The oldest girl was 17 years of age.

SCOTT, DAVID (Captain)

Born on the South Branch of the Potomac, but in 1779 moved to the present site of Granville, Monongalia County, West Virginia, which town was established by his son, Felix. He built one or more mills in the vicinity and was prominent in that vicinity.

In 1779, Indians murdered his daughters, Fanny and Phebe, as they were taking dinner to men in the hayfield. Later, a son, James, barely escaped capture. Captain Scott himself had sustained an injury in military service which caused the entire loss of his right forearm, and which enabled him to draw a pension. An old house, said to have been built by Captain Scott in 1776, was standing recently on the farm of the Gapen family, who are descended from the youngest daughter of this pioneer settler.

SCOTT, JAMES
Service—Virginia   Va. No. 2492   No. S. 6067

He was the son of Captain David Scott under whom he served as a musician in the Thirteenth Virginia Regiment, Continental Establishment, under Colonel Gibson and General McIntosh from the fall of 1776 to November, 1778. His father hired a substitute in 1779. He received a pension in Monongalia County, Virginia, in 1832. Supporting data was filed by Captain John Dent. The soldier died in 1839 and is buried in the Granville Cemetery, Monongalia County, West Virginia.

SCOTT, GEORGE (Lieutenant)
Served as a second lieutenant in Captain Stephenson's company of riflemen.

SCOTT, JOHN
In the Monongalia County court, November 13, 1810, Jacob Scott made oath that David Scott was the heir-at-law of John Scott, who died while in service in the Thirteenth Virginia Regiment of the Continental Line, during the Revolutionary War. Sufficient evidence having been produced, Land Bounty Warrant No. 5900 was issued, January 7, 1811.

SCOTT, JOHN E. (Lieutenant)
The heirs of John E. Scott were allowed land bounty for service as a lieutenant in the Thirteenth Virginia Regiment of the Continental Line, during the Revolution, as of November 18, 1811. His will, dated October 25, 1805, is filed in Hancock County, West Virginia, and certified as of April 11, 1811.

SCOTT, WILLIAM
Service—Virginia   Va. No. 18884   No. 38356

Born, 1751. Enlisted in Berkeley County, Virginia, late in the summer of 1777 and served as a private in the Fourth Virginia Regiment, in the company of Captain James Lucas, commanded by Colonel Robert Lawson. Served two years in the Continental Establishment. Continued in service until April, 1779, when he hired a substitute. He was at Middlebrook in the Jerseys, in the battle of Monmouth, and in some small skirmishes while the British were in Philadelphia. No evidence of his servce is found other than the affidavit of Colonel David Hunter who swore that he knew him and had been informed by different Revolutionary officers that Scott had been in service and had acquitted himself with honor. Pension was granted him in Berkeley County, Virginia, in 1823. Mention is also made of Alexander Scott, but without indication of his family connection.

SEABURN, JOHN
Was a corporal in Captain Shepherd's company of riflemen. Died in prison, January 15, 1777.

SEAMAN, WILLIAM

Enlisted as a private in Captain Shepherd's company. He was captured at Fort Washington, November 16, 1776, but was released near summer on parole. He returned to his home and died near Darkesville.

SEASE, Sea, Sees, Cees, or Cease), MICHAEL
Service—Penna.　　　　Va. No. 23041　　　No. S. 9475 and B. L. Wt. 95257

Born, Lancaster County, Pennsylvania, 1764; resided in Westmoreland County, during the Revolution. Enlisted, April 1, 1782, under Ensign Gageby, and Captains Johnson and Wilkinson in Major Craig's Regiment., under Colonels Campbell, Martin, and Streets.

Married, February 24, 1808, in Westmoreland County to Rebecca Miller, with Christopher Barrier, Presbyterian minister, officiating. Pension was issued to soldier while living in Harrison County, in 1833, but was later dropped from the rolls. The widow, aged 84 in 1860, likewise seems to have been refused a pension, but bounty land warrant for 160 acres was issued in that year. Supporting data was submitted by H. Gass, William Martin, Jacob Lees, Sam Miller, and Adam Padabaugh Martin.

SEIBERT, WENDEL

The home of Wendel Seibert, who was a soldier in the Revolutionary War, was built in Berkeley County in 1791 and is still standing, and occupied by his descendants.

SELMAN, JOSEPH
Service—Virginia　　　　Va. No. 20177　　　　No. S. 38361

Enlisted in 1776 in Virginia in the company of Captain Lee or Leigh in the First Regiment of Virginia regulars under Colonel George Gibson, for a period of three years; marched to Valley Forge where he was put under Captain Hefler and attached to regiment of Colonel Feebecker, under General Washington. Was later transferred to Colonel Posey's Regiment, in General Wayne's army. After expiration of his term of enlistment, was discharged, and then re-enlisted for another year, most of which was spent in the South. Took part in the battle of Monmouth, the taking of Stony Point, and the battle of Cowpens. He was discharged at Philadelphia. Received pension in Harrison County, 1830, at which time he was 80 years of age.

SESSLEY, JOHN
Service—Penna.　　　　Va. No. 14298　　　　No. S. 38189

Enlisted in Bedford, Pennsylvania, in 1775 a few days after the battle of Bunker Hill and served as a private under Captain Cluggett in a Pennsylvania regiment. Was honorably discharged after a year at Graves End, New York. Enlisted in the Continental Army as a private in the spring of 1777 in Captain Archibald McAllister's company in the brigade of Colonel Hartley of Little York, under Brigadier General Anthony Wayne. Applied for pension which was granted in Berkeley County, Virginia, in 1819. His wife, Sarah, was 60 years old in 1820. The soldier died in Michigan about 1832.

SEXTON, NOAH
The grave of Noah Sexton, a veteran of the Revolutionary War, is in the French Creek Cemetery, Meade District, Upshur County.

SEYMOUR, FELIX
Born in England in 1725 and died in Hampshire County, Virginia, February 1798. During the Revolution his residence was Moorefield, Virginia. He was married to Margaret Renick in 1752. Soldier enlisted May 26, 1776, under Captain Casewell in the Fifth Company of North Carolina troops, and was discharged, February 8, 1780.

SHAFER, PETER
Service—Pennsylvania   No. R. 9411
Born in Lancaster, Pennsylvania, February 1760 and there enlisted in the Pennsylvania militia in 1776. Served three enlistment periods of three months each under Captains Petree, Rubley, and Groush, under Colonels Greenwald, Masteller, and Generals Washington, Wayne, and Muhlenberg as a convoy for ammunition and baggage wagons. Came to Martinsburg, Berkeley County, Virginia, in 1793, and there applied for pension in 1834. Supporting affidavits offered by Gregory Maxwell, Harrison Shover, the Rev. N. Young, and George Porterfield.

SHANER (Shaver), GEORGE
Service—Virginia   Va. No. 7130   No. S. 38370
Enlisted at Shepherdstown, Virginia, in 1781 and served until 1783 under Captains Bedinger and Kirkpatrick in the Fifth Virginia Regiment, commanded by Colonels Gaskins and Posey in Von Steuben's Brigade. After the surrender of Cornwallis, marched to Savannah, Georgia, under Colonel Posey, and joined the troops under General Wayne at Charleston, South Carolina. Received pension in Jefferson County, Virginia, in 1819, which was dropped in 1820, but was restored in 1825. Soldier was 71 years old in 1820 and his wife 54. Supporting data filed by Jacob Haynes and Captain Henry Bedinger.

SHANK (Schenck in German) CHRISTIAN
Service—Md. and N. J.   Va. No. 2360   No. W. 19344
Born, Germany, 1751, and died in Morgan County, Virginia, March 22, 1836. Enlisted in Sussex County, New Jersey, and in Middleton, Maryland, in 1776 and in 1781, and served as private and corporal under Captains Sowers, Troutman, and Shaeffer in the Flying Camp contingent under Colonel Maston or Martin, and Generals Sullivan, Putnam, and Lord Sterling. Took part in the campaigns on Long Island. Was discharged from Michael Troutman's company.
Married Juliana Schmitin, May 30, 1781, Middleton, Maryland. She was born June 4, 1762. Their children were: George, July, 1782; Christian, 1784; John, 1786; Anna Marie, 1788; Catherine, 1789; Jacob, 1792 (died in 1793); Elizabeth, 1794; Susanna, 1797; Anna, 1801; Sara, 1803. Pension was issued to soldier in Morgan County, 1832, and to his widow in 1837.

SHARP, JOHN
Service—Penna.　　　　Va. No. 8279　　　　No. S. 38367 and 25437

Enlisted in Lancaster County, Pennsylvania, in 1777 and served until 1781 in the company of Captain James Taylor in the Fifth Pennsylvania Regiment, under Colonels Carpenter and Ewell in Continental Establishment under General Wayne. Participated in the battles of Brandywine, Germantown, and Stony Point. Received honorable discharge from Captain Thomas Bund at Reading, Pennsylvania, in 1781, at which time he was too ill for service. Soldier received pension in Harrison County, Virginia, in 1819, at which time he was 64 years old and his wife 67. Supporting data submitted by Elizabeth Kennedy.

SHARP, SPENCER

Enlisted in western Virginia in 1781 under Captain Robert Warren. Applied for pension, December 27, 1849, at Marietta, Washington County, Ohio, but claim was rejected.

SHARP, WILLIAM

Before the Pocahontas County, Virginia, court, September 4, 1832, William Sharp, aged 92, testified that he was drafted into service in the Revolutionary War in January, 1781, while living in that part of West Augusta, now included in Pocahontas County. He served under Ensign James Tumbler and Captain William Kincaid in a company of Colonel Sampson Mathews' regiment, was marched to Portsmouth, engaged in skirmish with the British, and remained there until the following spring when he was discharged.

During the summer of 1774 he served with Captain Andrew Lockridge of Bath County, against the Indians. With William Mann, he was sent by Colonel Andrew Lewis with a message to Lord Dunmore who was then at Fort Pitt, Pittsburgh, and did not return until the day following the battle of Point Pleasant. He had also served under Captain Charles Lewis in 1764 and 1765 in the expedition against the Indians on the Muskingum River. He names John Bradshaw as a witness to his service.

SHAVER, PAUL

Born in Pendleton County, Virginia, in 1759, son of Paul Shaver, who died on the South Branch, 1772. Served as an Indian spy in Randolph County, in 1776 for six months under Captain Maxwell. In 1777, volunteered in the Virginia militia under Captain Stuart for the defense of the western waters. Marched from Randolph to West's Fort. He was detached for spy duty. Joined the troops under General George Rogers Clark in the expedition which captured Vincennes and the Illinois country. He remained there under Captain Kincaid or Kinkead until 1780. Received a wound in the right leg at Andersontown. Pension was granted in Lewis County, Virginia, in 1833, but was later suspended.

SHAVER, PETER

Served as an Indian ranger and spy in the Revolution. He was born in Pendleton County, Virginia, the son of Paul Shaver, whose other sons were George, John and Paul.

Peter married Sara Riggle; their sons were John, James, Jacob, and Francis. Francis married Phoebe Hall; their children were Susanna, Sara, John, James, Jacob, Hezekiah, Frances Riffle, George W., Mary, Eleanor, and Edward. James married Elizabeth Campbell; they had eight children, one of whom was John Riffle Shaver. John Riffle Shaver married Sara Cunningham and they were the parents of eight children, among them being Clem L. Shaver of Fairmont, West Virginia, and Washington, D. C.

West Virginians in the American Revolution

Assembled and Edited by ROSS B. JOHNSTON

The sources of this material are from the files of the Pension Office at Washington, from various county records, from notes of patriotic societies, principally the Daughters of the American Revolution, Sons of the American Revolution, Sons of the Revolution, and from a large miscellaneous group of published and private sources. Corrections and additions to this list will receive the careful attention of the editor.

SHAW, CHARLES
Service—Virginia   Va. No. 6175   No. S. 7484

Enlisted in Fauquier County, Virginia, in the spring of 1781 and served six months as a private under Captain Helms in the Virginia Line, Continental Establishment, in Colonel Edmonds Regiment, under Generals Washington and Lafayette. Took part in the siege and capture of Yorktown. Received pension in Harrison County, Virginia, in 1833, which was later dropped, but reinstated. Supporting data submitted by Hamilton Gass and Jacob Copen.

SHEETS, JOHN

Born in Lancaster County, Pennsylvania, 1750-53. Enlisted at Chamberstown (now Chambersburg, Pennsylvania) and served six months as a private under Lieutenant James Young and Captain Snyder of the Pennsylvania Line. Took part in the battle of Trenton. Removed to Patterson Creek, Hampshire County, Virginia, in 1803, then to Wood County, in 1811, where he was living when he received pension in 1833. This was suspended in 1835. Sheets was a German unable to speak or understand English well, and this case received extended consideration. In 1841, he was very infirm, his wife was blind, and both were dependent upon relatives. Pension was resumed in 1842-43. Supporting data was filed by John Sheets, son, Henry Sheets, nephew, Barnes Beckwith, Jonathan Prentiss, Thomas Maddox, and the Rev. Benjamin Mitchell.

SHEETZ, ADAM

Enlisted in Captain Stephenson's company and then in Captain Shepherd's company. He was captured but was soon exchanged. He was drafted out of Shepherd's company January 1, 1777, to another rifle company. In December, 1778, he joined the fourth company of Morgan's Riflemen under Captain Charles Porterfield. He came from York, Pennsylvania, to Shepherdstown about 1762. After the Revolution, he had a widely known gunshop at Shepherdstown.

SHELL, NICHOLAS (Surgeon)
Served as a surgeon during the Revolution for six years. After the Revolution he returned to Shepherdstown where he died in 1803. He had a son named John N. Shell.

SHEPHERD (SHEPARD) ABRAHAM (Captain)
Lieutenant of Stephenson's Virginia Rifle Company, July, 1775; Captain of Stephenson's Maryland and Virginia Rifle Regiment, July 9, 1776; taken prisoner at Fort Washington, November 16, 1776; exchanged August 26, 1778; appointed captain of the Eleventh Virginia to rank from July, 1776, but was retired September, 1778, being absent owing to illness. He was afterwards discharged and died in 1822.

He was born at Shepherdstown, November 10, 1754, being the youngest son of Captain Thomas Shepherd, the founder of Shepherdstown, and his wife, Elizabeth Van Meter. His wife was Eleanor Strode.

SHEPHERD, DAVID (Colonel)
Born in Berkeley County, Virginia, near Shepherdstown, where his father, Thomas, was one of the earliest settlers of the Shenandoah Valley, allied with the Hites and the Van Meters. In 1770, he removed to the West and settled at the forks of Wheeling Creek in what is now Ohio County, West Virginia. He acted as commissary for a time, and in January, 1777, was chosen county-lieutenant for the newly created Ohio County, and acted in that capacity until his death. He led a regiment in Brodhead's Cochocton expedition in 1781. During 1783 and 1785, Shepherd served in the Virginia legislature, and during the Indian wars was active in the protection of the border settlements.

SHEPHERD, JOHN
Born about 1749 and died at Red Oak, Ohio, in 1812. He was married in 1773 to Martha Nelson. He served under Captain William Cherry in the Fourth Virginia Regiment, from April, 1777, to March, 1778.

SHEPHERD, WILLIAM
Enlisted under Captain Stephenson in 1775. He was born in 1737 and married Mary Clarke. He later moved to Ohio County where he died in 1824.

SHEPPARD, JONATHAN
Service—Maryland   Va. No. 18487   No. S. 38565

Born at New Mecklenburg, now Shepherdstown, Jefferson County, West Virginia, 1759-1760. Enlisted July 1, 1775 while living at Old Town, Maryland, and again in 1776 for three years, and served under Captains Michael Cresap, Beale, and Davis, in Colonel Moses Rawlings' Regiment. Was in the battle at Fort Washington, was taken prisoner there and carried to England. After his release, he came to Pennsylvania, then to Harrison County, Virginia, and then to Reedy, where he died April 16-17, 1825, and is buried on the home farm. Pension was issued to him while in Lewis County, Virginia, in 1822. His service was certified by John Reed, Thomas Beale, and Nathan B. Magruder.

SHEPHERD, WILLIAM

He was the oldest son of Colonel David Shepherd, and served in the Revolutionary War. He married Rebecca McConnell by whom he left one child. In January, 1790, Rebecca Shepherd petitioned the state of Virginia for pension in recognition of her husband's military services.

SHERMAN, JOHN
Service—New York   Va. No. 25216   No. S. 7503

Born, 1756, and at the outbreak of the Revolution lived in Dutchess County, New York. There he enlisted, June 20, 1776, and continued in service until November 1, 1780, as a private under Captain John Darlin in New York troops under Adjutant Hamilton, Colonel Humphrey, and General James Clinton.

Soldier was living in Brooke County, Virginia, in 1833 when he received pension for his services. Supporting data was filed by the Rev. John Hale, Jacob Wiswerger, and Dr. James M. Dawson.

SHINGLETON, WILLIAM
Service—Virginia   Va. No. 14729   No. S. 38371

Born about 1754 and was living in Culpepper County, Virginia, during the Revolution. He enlisted in the spring of 1778 and served until 1780, was a private under Captain Roberts in the Virginia regiment commanded by Colonel Taylor. Served as guard at Albemarle and Winchester for prisoners from Burgoyne's army. Was honorably discharged at Harpers Ferry, Virginia. Received pension in Harrison County, Virginia, in 1819. Supportng data submitted by Jonathan Humphrey.

SHINN, ISAAC
Service—Virginia   Va. No. 23319   No. S. 7505

Born, Burlington County, New Jersey, October 9, 1760; in 1773, removed from New Jersey to Stafford County, Virginia, thence to Hampshire County and West Augusta, now Harrison County, Virginia. Married Agnes Drake in Harrison County, February 16, 1785. She died April 16, 1853. Their children were: George of Illinois; Isaac of Missouri; Rachel Wilkinson of Virginia; Mary Smith of Virginia; Debora Davidson of Ohio; Rebecca Carl of Ohio; Tibiatha, wife of Hiram Shinn of Illinois; Samuel, dead; Benjamin, dead; Hannah Shinn, wife of Edward Shinn of Ohio; Agnes Bartley of Missouri; Susanna Bartley of Missouri.

Shinn enlisted in 1778 and served six months under Captain William Robertson or Robinson at Jones Fort; in 1778, six months under Captain Andrew Davis or Davidson at Jones Fort as scout and spy; in 1780, six months as scout and spy under Captain James Gregory at the blockhouse at Clarksburg; in 1781, under Captain John P. Duvall at the same station; and in 1782 another six months service at Clarksburg under Captain Duvall. Soldier received pension in Harrison County in 1833, but between 1835 and 1838, continued efforts were made to bring about its suspension. This seems to have been done. On May 5, 1860, the fight was still being made for payment of pension arrearages, but it is not certain if this was successful.

SHOBER (SHOVER), JOHN
Service—Maryland—Navy   Va. No. 16810   No. W. 6041

Born, Frederick Town, Maryland, August 17, 1759; died, October 3, 1836, in Berkeley County, Virginia, where he had lived since 1785. Married Susannah Bowers in Berkeley County, December 22, 1785. She was born September 15, 1768, but date of death is not given. Their children were: Ann, April 21, 1788; Catherine, August 20, 1789; John, May 22, 1791, died; Susannah, March 6, 1793; Henry, January 12, 1795; Eliza, September 28, 1796, died; John B., September 28, 1798; Elizabeth, September 8, 1800, died; George, October 11, 1802, died; Mary Ann, March 27, 1806; Adain, January 24, 1810.

Shober enlisted in 1776 and re-enlisted in 1777. His first enlistment of three months was extended because he was wounded, taken to the Reading hospital, and suffered for six months more from his injuries. Was under Captain Nicholas White in the regiment of Colonel Charles Beatty, and was stationed at Lord Stirling's post near Bascom Ridge, New Jersey. In his next service, took part in skirmish at Quibble Town. In September, when the British landed at the head of Elk Valley, marched with a company under Captain Hoff in Virginia militia under Colonel Baker Johnson and General Smallwood. In an attack in a party of forty men, he received a ball through his thigh, and had four other balls passing through his clothes without inflicting another wound except a scrap of lead which entered under a rib and remained there for years.

In 1780, enlisted as marine and served as a sailor on the Frigate *Confederacy*, of 36 guns, under Captain Harden. Became ill and was placed in hospital on island of Hispanola, returning to Philadelphia in October, 1781, from which place he returned to Frederick Town, Maryland. Soldier received pension, as did his widow. Supporting data filed by Colonel John Strother, Philip Rhure, and Dr. John Baltzall.

SHORES, THOMAS
Service—Virginia   Va. No. 15312   No. S. 6083

Enlisted at Apple Pie Ridge, Frederick County, Virginia, in the spring of 1777 and in February, 1780, and served three years as private under Captain George Rice, Eleventh Virginia Regiment, Continental Establishment under Colonel Daniel Morgan. Fought at Brandywine and at Conchers Bridge.

While living in Hampshire County, Virginia, in 1819, pension was granted the soldier. At that time he had a son, Thomas, aged 39, and a daughter, Margaret, aged 30. Supporting data filed by Lander Shores,

Samuel Abernathy, and Lydia Abernathy. Pensioner was stricken from the rolls in 1822, but appears to have been reinstated in 1833.

SHRIEVES, (SHREAVES, or SHREEVES) WILLIAM
Service—Continental, Va.   Va. No. 6231   No. S. 38358 and B. L. Wt. 2074

At the age of 17, enlisted in 1780 in Louden County, Virginia, and served as a private three years under Captain Beakins or Bedkin in Armand's Legion of Dragoons. He was living in Randolph County, Virginia, in 1819, when he received pension. At that time his wife appears to have been dead, and there were two children, James and Katherine. Bounty land warrant for 100 acres was also received by the soldier. His death occurred in August, 1835.

SILMAN, JOSEPH

Joseph Silman, aged 60, declared before the Harrison County, Virginia court in 1818 that during the Revolution he had served one year in Major Posey's Battalion in General Hayner's Brigade after which he was transferred to Colonel Elliott's Regiment, from which unit he received his discharge. Soldier had two children, one aged 13 and one aged 14 years.

SIMONS, ASA
Service—Conn. Mass.   Va. No. 16522   N. S. 7519

Enlisted at Springfield, Massachusetts, in October, 1777, and served under Captain Granger, Adjutant Ball and Major Webb, and in Connecticut under Colonel Campfield, under General Gates, remaining in service until 1782. While living in Shenandoah County, Virginia, he received pension in 1833, which was suspended later that year but reinstated in 1835. Supporting data was submitted by Jacob Rudolph and Joseph Bond. Soldier was born in Springfield, Massachusetts in 1759 and died December 16, 1841.

SIMMON, JOHN
Service—Virginia   Va. No. 7053   No. S. 7512

Born in 1755, and enlisted in Augusta, now Pendleton County, West Virginia, in 1777 or 1778. Served as a private upwards of six months under Lieutenant Given and Captains Lockridge and McCoy in Lockridge's Regiment of the Virginia Line. Received pension in Pendleton County in 1833. Supporting data filed by Robert McCoy and Eli B. Wilson.

SIMPKINS, CHARLES
Service—New Jersey   Va. No. 12993   No. R. 9588

Born, Cumberland County, New Jersey, April 1, 1758; died, June 7, 1843, and is buried on the Marshall Garlow farm, Monongalia County, West Virginia. Enlisted in New Jersey in the summer of 1777 and remained in service until January 1, 1781, under Captains E. Loomis, Beasley, Davis, Daniels, Wescott, in Second Jersey Regiment, commanded by Colonel Hillman, Colonel Shrieve, and Lieutenant Colonel Dehart. He took part in the fighting about Mercer's Fort and was present at the execution of Major Andre, the British spy.

Soldier received pension in Monongalia County, Virginia, in 1834. His widow, Barbara, to whom he was married, January 2, 1782, apparently was receiving no pension at the time of her death, January 27, 1850. Mary Simpkins, probably a daughter, seems to have sought arrears in pension in 1858. Supporting data was filed by Richard Harrison, Jacob Cramer, Nancy Conaway, and Elizabeth Watt.

SIMS, JAMES (Sergeant)
Service—Virginia   Va. No. 23916   No. S. 19464

Enlisted in Culpepper County, Virginia, and served from June, 1777, until 1780 as a sergeant under Captains John Tutt and James Tutt in the Virginia militia under Colonel Slaughter. Soldier was born in Culpepper County, Virginia, in 1755 and resided there until 1800 when he removed to Nicholas County, Virginia. He was residing there in 1834.

SIMS, JOHN
Service—Virginia   Va. No. 23099   No. S. 7518

Born in Culpepper County, Virginia, February 12, 1755; resided in Augusta County, in 1769; and in Lewis County, Virginia, in 1819. He enlisted in Augusta County in June, 1777, and served two years as private under Captains Hopkins, Arbuckle and Bell in the Virginia Regiment of Colonel Dickinson under General Hand. A number of other officers were also named in his service record.

Pension was granted to the soldier in Lewis County in 1833 but after an investigation, the soldier was dropped from the rolls, March 16, 1835. Supporting data was submitted by William Bennett and Job Houghton.

SINNETT, (SINNAT, SENATE, or SENNATT), PATRICK
Service—Virginia   Va. No. 16534   No. W. 8296 and B. L. Wt. 26881

Born in Ireland, March 17, 1752; emigrated to America in 1773 and soon afterward went out in a company commanded by Captain John Skidmore under the King and was at the battle of Point Pleasant against Cornstalk and his Indians; settled in Rockingham County, Virginia (now Pendleton County) until about 1815, when he removed to Wood County, Virginia. He served fourteen months in the Revolutionary Army in 1781 and 1782 as a private under Captains Rush, McCoy, Huston, Smith and Coger in the Virginia Line under Majors Rucker, Darke, Generals Washington, Wayne and Lafayette. Was in the battles of Jamestown, Hot Water, and Yorktown.

Soldier married Catherine Hefner, May 1, 1783, in Pendleton County, Virginia. The soldier received pension in Wood County, where he died December 19, 1850. His widow received pension in Ritchie County, Virginia, in 1856 at which time she was 88 years old. Bounty land grant of 160 acres was issued in 1855. Supporting data filed in this case by Zachariah Rexrode, James Keister, Daniel Haymond, J. J. Jackson, H. L. Prentiss, Henry Rexrode, and Thomas Harris.

SKIDMORE, ANDREW

The grave of Andrew Skidmore, a soldier in the American Revolution, is in the Skidmore Cemetery, at Sutton, Braxton County.

SKIDMORE, JOHN (Captain)

Served as a captain in the battle of Point Pleasant in 1774 and was a captain of militia in 1777. James and Joseph Skidmore, early emigrants, appeared in Pendleton County, Virginia, before the French and Indian War. John Skidmore was the president of the first county court of Pendleton County in 1787, and Joseph was a member of the first grand jury.

James, John, Joseph, and Andrew were probably brothers, and likely the sons of Andrew Skidmore who emigrated from England to Norfolk, Virginia.

SKIDMORE, WILLIAM

Lived in Berkeley County and there enrolled as a private in the Revolution. He later drew a pension for his military services.

SLAVEN, JOHN
Service—Virginia   Va. No. 16866 and 2554   No. S. 6110

Enlisted in Augusta County, Virginia, in 1776 as a private and served under Captain Michael Bowyer, Twelfth Virginia Regiment commanded by Colonel James Wood in General Scott's Brigade, until 1778. He was in the battles of Germantown and Brandywine. Application for pension was filed in Randolph County, Virginia, 1819, and again in Pocahontas in 1832 owing to confusion in names and pension granted in both cases. Claim was proved by evidence of Major Henry Flesher, supported by William McCoy.

SLEETH, DAVID W.

Born in Frederick County, Virginia, May 18, 1769. Resided in Monongalia County, Virginia, (now Lewis County), in May, 1777, when he enlisted as a private under Captains Booth, Jackson and Davis. He applied for pension in Lewis County, Virginia, which was granted in 1833, but upon later investigation his name was stricken from the rolls.

SLEITH, JOHN

In Lewis County, in 1846, Anna Parsons, aged 85, testified that John Sleith had gone out from Pendleton, then Augusta County, Virginia, as a substitute for a man named Mouse, and enlisted in Armand's Legion of Dragoons. He was at the surrender of Cornwallis at Yorktown, wore trooper's clothes, had a troop horse, sword and pistols. The maiden name of Anna was Flesher; she had married Sleith in

1777-78, a Baptist preacher, Joseph Redding, officiating; Sleith died in 1793 or 1794; Anna married Charles Parsons in 1796, and he died November 4, 1823.

Adam Flesher of Lewis County, a brother of Anna, supported her claim, as also did George Butcher of the same county. Andrew Flesher of Jackson County, a younger brother, testified for her. Elizabeth Flesher, wife of Andrew, testified that she knew Ann Flesher and John Sleith, a soldier in the Revolution. She was married in 1793, and her daughter, Mary, was born January 12, 1795, after Sleith was dead.

SMELL, PHILIP

Born in Bucks County, Pennsylvania, April, 1758; resided there until 1790, when he moved to Berkeley County, Virginia, and from thence to Monongalia County, in 1794. There he died, April 20, 1835. Soldier enlisted in the Revolutionary Army in the spring of 1776 and served six months in the militia under Captain Ludwick and General Washington, taking part in the battles of Brandywine and Monmouth. He also claimed twelve months service as a teamster. Soldier applied for pension in Monongalia County, which was granted in 1834. His claim was supported by Samuel Hanway.

SMITH, CHARLES
Service—Continental Va.   Va. No. 23572   No. S. 15649

Born in Frederick County, Virginia, June 2, 1763. There enlisted, December, 1777, and served as a private under Lieutenants Calimese and Huskell under Captain Tunstons in the Virginia Line. Took part in the skirmish at Battle Town, Frederick County, Virginia. He was living in Jackson County, Virginia, in 1863, at which time he received a pension, which was reduced in amount the following year.

SMITH, DANIEL
Service—Penna. Va.   Va. No. 16890   No. S. 18396

Born in Reading, Berks County, Pennsylvania, 1755, where he resided until the winter of 1777-78 when he removed to Winchester, Virginia, and later to Harrison County, Virginia. He enlisted as a private in Reading, Pennsylvania, and later in Frederick County, Virginia, serving in the First Pennsylvania Regiment, and the Second Virginia Regiment, under Captains Lazier, Heiskill, and Gillinan, under Major Ross, Colonel Darke and General Morgan from March 1777 until the spring of 1783. He was granted a pension in Harrison County in 1833 which was apparently suspended in 1834.

SMITH, GEORGE P.
Service—Virginia   Va. No. 16891   No. S. 18595

Born in Berkeley County, Virginia, July 4, 1757, resided in Augusta County, Virginia in 1774. He enlisted May 8, 1777 and again January 10, 1778, and served two years under Captains Tate, Arbuckle, Long and Dickey in Virginia units commanded by Colonels Skillern, Dickinson, and General Hand. Substituted for Alfred Neal, April 11, 1779, to July 27, 1779; for James Harris, April 12 to July 18, 1781; and for George Richardson from July 28 to October 22, 1781.

Pension certificate issued to him in Lewis County, in 1833, which was dropped in 1835. Supporting data submitted by Abraham Whetsel and Jacob Wimer.

SMITH, JACOB
Service—Maryland   Va. No. 16718   No. W. 7186 and B. L. Wt. 39337

Born in 1758 and died July 26, 1834. Enlisted in 1781 at Sharpsburg, Maryland, and served as a private under Captain Chaplin in Colonel Rawling's Maryland militia on guard duty at Frederick Town and Fort.

Was married to Catherine French in 1814 at Sandy Creek Glades, fifteen miles from Morgantown, Monongalia County, Virginia, by the Rev. Kidwell Smith, Baptist minister. Soldier received pension in Morgan County, Virginia, in 1833. His widow received pension in 1853 and bounty land warrant for 160 acres was issued in 1856. Supporting data was filed by John Ellenburger, Michael Pentony, Stephen Pentony, Henry Spohr, Matthias Ambrose, and Phineas Ogden.

SMITH, JAMES
Service—Virginia   Va. No. 4718   No. S. 38385

Enlisted in 1776 in Augusta County, Virginia, in company of Captain David Lord in the Tenth Virginia Regiment under Colonel Stephens. Was in engagement at Stony Point. Resided in Greenbrier County, Virginia, in 1818, when he received pension certificate. Supportng data was filed by John Crookshanks.

SMITH, JAMES
Service—Penna. Dela.   Va. No. 8892   No. W. 6120

Enlisted, January, 1776, as a private in the company of Captain Henry Darby in the First Regiment, Delaware Line, under Colonel Haslet in Lord Stirling's Brigade. Took part in the fighting on Long Island, Buckwheat Fields, N. Y., White Plains, Brunswick, Princeton, and Trenton. In 1777, he served three tours in the Pennsylvania militia of two months each.

The soldier was married August 22, 1773, to Flora Erskine. Soldier, aged 75, received pension in 1819 while living in Monroe County. He died November 28, 1837, and his widow, received pension in 1837 at which time she was 92 years old. A daughter Betsy is mentioned. Supporting data was submitted by John Francis and James Boyd. (A revised pension certificate may have been issued to the widow in 1839 whose death was probably December 5, 1844.

SMITH, JOHN
Service—Maryland   Va. No. 16182   No. S. 6117

Born in Prince George County, Maryland, July 17, 1760; died in

Harrison County, Virginia, in 1840. Enlisted in Frederick County, Maryland, in 1776, as a private in the company of Captain Hillery in the Virginia Line Regiment commanded by Colonel Johnson. Soldier was issued pension in Harrison County, Virginia, July 16, 1833.

SMITH, JOHN
Service—Md. Va. Va. No. 23391 No. W. 6117

Enlisted in Frederick County, Maryland, and Shenandoah County, Virginia, June, July or August, 1776, and served a total of eight months until 1782, under Captain Price in the Virginia Line and Virginia Militia under Colonel Smallwood, General Washington and General Lafayette. Fought at Germantown and Yorktown. Was furloughed in the winter of 1778 with John Ritenour Valentine and Daniel Shyrock. In the spring of 1779 obtained Conrad Temple as a substitute. His father moved to Shenandoah County in 1779 or 1780, where John Smith served in the Shenandoah County militia under Captain Downey, Lieutenant S. Odell, Colonel Merryweather, Captain Noll, Lieutenant Rinker and Colonel Darke.

Was married to Susan Hawn, October 4, 1778, in Shenandoah County, Virginia, by Elder James Ireland. Soldier, aged 74, received pension in Pendleton County, Virginia, in 1834, and died there, May 4, 1839. His widow received pension in 1844, at which time she was 80 years old. Supporting evidence was submitted by William Eagle, Jeremiah Odell, A. W. Dyer, Adam Smith, Madaline Ridenour, and Jacob Smith.

SMITH, MARK
Service—Virginia Va. No. 16892 No. S. 18594

Born in Pendleton County, Virginia, in 1761, and there enlisted in Captain Robert Davis' company for three months and three weeks, and in the company of Captain Thomas Hickley, and was discharged in York County after eight or nine weeks service near the close of the Revolution. Also apparently had two years service as an Indian spy in Captain Wilson's company. Pension appears to have been issued in Lewis County, Virginia, in 1833, but later suspended. Grave of the soldier is on the Maxwell farm near the bridge crossing Stone Coal Creek near West Virginia Route 5 in Lewis County, West Virginia.

SMITH, THOMAS
Service—New Jersey Va. No. 23560 No. S. 15989

Born in Monmouth County, N. J., October 11, 1751, and was dead before November 21, 1834. He enlisted in 1775 in New Jersey under Captain William Emlee or Embley, in the Second or Fourth New Jersey Regiment, commanded by Colonel White. Other officers were Captains Pittman, Waycough, Conover, and Colonels Morgan, Ray, and Generals Wayne, Washington, Stirling and Charles Lee. He took part in the battle of Long Island and was discharged at Bergen Point, New Jersey. Pension granted in 1834 for two years service, while living in Harrison County. Supporting data submitted by Anthony Coon, Henry Boother, and Oliver Shurtcliffe.

SMITH, WILLIAM
Service—Virginia   Va. No. 4102   No. S. 6121

Born December 20, 1752, and resided in Augusta County, Virginia, when he enlisted March 20, 1782, under Captain Payne. He served twelve months and nine days in the regiment of Colonel Haws, commanded by General Muhlenberg. In his pension application, he says that he enlisted at the same time and place as Dennis Callihan. Soldier received pension while living in Pendleton County, Virginia, in 1833.

SMITH, WILLIAM
Service—Maryland   Va. No. 429   No. S. 38376

Enlisted, Frederick County, Maryland, in 1776, then re-enlisted in the spring of 1778 under Captain Roxberry of the First Maryland Regiment, commanded by General Smallwood. Served until 1780 and took part in the campaigns on Long Island, White Plains and Camden. Was discharged at Saulsbury, South Carolina. Soldier lived in Berkeley County, Virginia in 1819, when pension certificate was issued to him. He died September 29, 1830. Supporting data filed in this case by Peter Snowden.

SNIDER, JOHN

The grave of John Snider, who served as a soldier in the Revolutionary Army, is on the Marshall Garlow farm near Fort Martin in Monongalia County, West Virginia.

SOCKMAN JOHN
Service—Penna.   Va. No. 8860   No. W. 11513 and B. L. Wt. 26893

Enlisted, Philadelphia County, Pennsylvania, January 1, 1776, under Captains Church and Farmer in the Pennsylvania regiment, Continental Establishment, commanded by General Butler. Took part in the White Plains campaign, and was wounded in the battle of Cowpens.

He was married to Catherine Ichner, who was born in Wurttemberg, Germany, at Wheeling, April 9, 1821, by the Rev. John Armstrong of the Protestant Episcopal Church. He applied for pension in Muskingum County, which was granted in 1819, at which time he was 66 years old. He was transferred to Ohio County, Virginia, in 1820, where he died, December 12, 1827. His widow received pension also. Bounty land warrant for 160 acres was issued to a son, John Sockman. Supporting data was filed by George Dulty, William Holliday, Theodore Kraft, and William Erving.

SODOWSKY, JAMES

Born in 1748 in Hardy County, Virginia, and died in 1831 in Bourbon County, Kentucky. He served as private in 1779 in an expedition against the Indians in Kentucky. He married Mary Ball Brown. Their son, Jacob, who was born in 1790 and died in 1866, married Mourning Bowles.

West Virginians in the American Revolution

Assembled and Edited by ROSS B. JOHNSTON

The sources of this material are from the files of the Pension Office at Washington, from various county records, from notes of patriotic societies, principally the Daughters of the American Revolution, Sons of the American Revolution, Sons of the Revolution, and from a large miscellaneous group of published and private sources. Corrections and additions to this list will receive the careful attention of the editor.

SOMMERVILLE, WILLIAM (Captain)
Service—Continental Pa.   Va. No. 12185   No. S. 41178

Entered service, August 8, 1776, as first sergeant in Captain Wendel Oury's company in the Eighth Pennsylvania Regiment, and served for a month, then became ill but when sufficiently recovered served at Fort Pitt in the quartermasters' department under Colonel Arch Steel, D. Q. M. Gen. In October, 1778, was on expedition to Fort McIntosh and on the Tuscaroras.

He was appointed conductor of artillery in the Western Department, which together with commissionship of military stores, he held until his resignation in 1781. His accounts were settled with the Board of War in 1786 for the pay of a captain with subsistence, under Chevalier De Cambray. Pension certificate was issued in 1818, at which time Sommerville was living in Berkeley County, Virginia. His wife was aged 33 or 34 at that time. Their children were: Nancy Gibbs, November 3, 1809; Elizabeth A., February 23, 1812; Marguerite B., June 8, 1815; Robert A., March 11, 1817; William Lawrence, March 5, 1819.

SPANG (Spong), DAVID
Service—Virginia   Va. No. 12548   No. S. 39848

Enlisted at Shepherdstown early in 1781 as a private in the company of Captain Henry Bedinger in the Fifth Regiment of the Virginia Line. He was at the capture of Cornwallis' army at Yorktown and fought at the Widow Gibbons' against the Indians near Savannah, Georgia, under General Wayne. Was discharged at Charles Town, South Carolina.

Soldier applied for pension in Berkeley County, April 25, 1819, at which time he stated his family consisted of his wife, aged 50, daughter, aged 14; and his mother, Cary Keyser, aged 80. His claim was supported by his former commanding officer, Captain Bedinger. He was still living in 1797.

SPENCER, JOHN
Service—Virginia   Va. No. 16405   No. W. 3883

Enlisted in Albermarle County, Virginia, in February, 1781, in company commanded by Captain Thomas Morman in Colonel Thomas Posey's Regiment; was honorably discharged in December, 1782, after participating in the siege of York and several skirmishes with the Indians near Savannah town in Georgia.

On November 4, 1785, married Mary Humphrey, daughter of David Humphrey. They had a daughter, named Susan. Soldier born in 1763 and died on July 22, 1830, applied for pension in Greenbrier County, Virginia, in 1819. Widow applied for pension which was granted in 1843 and 1849.

SPRINGER, JACOB (Lieutenant)

Commander of the garrison of the frontier fort at Holliday's Cove, now Hancock County, Virginia. He was a descendant of the Springer family which emigrated from Sweden to Delaware early in the seventeenth century. One branch of this family removed to the Monongahela region, where Jacob enlisted. On October 31, 1778, he was commissioned ensign in the Ninth Virginia Regiment, became a lieutenant, August 8, 1779, was transferred to the Seventh Virginia February 12, 1781, and served to the end of the war. He died, June 16, 1823.

SPRINGER, URIAH (Captain)

First lieutenant, Thirteenth Virginia, December 19, 1776; captain, August 25, 1778. This regiment was designated the Ninth Virginia, September 14, 1778. Springer was transferred to the Seventh Virginia, February 12, 1781, and served to the end of the War. He was captain in the United States Army, March 7, 1792, assigned to Third Sub-Legion, Septempber 4, 1792, and was honorably discharged, November 1796.

STACKHOUSE, JOHN
Service—Virginia   Va. No. 6002   No. S. 38409

Enlisted in Harrison County, Virginia, February, 1777, and served until March 1, 1780, as a private in the company of Captain David Scott, Thirteenth Virginia Regiment, Continental Establishment, commanded by Colonel John Gibson. He applied for and received pension in Harrison County, January 29, 1819, at which time he was 69 years old. His wife was aged 45 and there were two children, a daughter, aged 15, and a son, aged 13.

STALEY, PETER
Service—Pennsylvania   Va. No. 23634   No. W. 6194

Born in Pennsylvania in 1754; died, July 16, 1837, Jefferson County, Virginia. Enlisted in York County, Pennsylvania, July 1776 as a private under Captain Veanary, Pennsylvania Line under Major John Finley; marched to Philadelphia, Brunswick, Princeton, Amboy, Elizabeth Town, Newark, Banion Point, Hurlgate, then through Jersey to Woodbridge, thence through Princeton to Philadelphia where he was discharged by Major Finley in February, 1777.

The marriage bond of the soldier, dated September 21, 1790, to Margaret. Mumson, signed by Peter Staley and Jacob Staley, is filed in

Berkeley County, West Virginia. Pension was granted the soldier in 1834 in Jefferson County, Virginia, and to his widow. She was 69 years old when she applied for pension in 1839. Peter Staley, father of the soldier, and Dan Staley, a brother, are mentioned.

STALNACKER (STALNAKER), SAMUEL
Service—Virginia   Va. No. 23121   No. S. 9487
Born in Hampshire County, Virginia, in 1763. Enlisted in April, 1780, in a part of Monongalia County, Virginia, now included in Randolph County, West Virginia, as an Indian spy under Captains Board and Cunningham, and Colonels Lowther and Wilson. He also mentions Captain Carpenter, Lieutenant Adam Stalnacker, Lieutenant Tanner, Ensign John White and Ensign John Brown. Applied for pension in Lewis County, Virginia, which was granted in 1833, but was suspended in 1835. Supporting data filed by Thomas Brown and Ezekiel Powers.

STALNAKER, VALENTINE
Applied for pension as a Revolutionary soldier while living in Randolph County, in 1834, at which time he was 95 years old. He had acted as a frontier spy about the time of the battle of Point Pleasant. His pension application was refused on the ground that his service was previous to the Revolution.

STEEL, HENRY
Before the Randolph County Court, November 25, 1811, Jeremiah Channel, one of the heirs of Henry Steel, testified that he never knew his father-in-law to receive compensation in land for his services as a Revolutionary War soldier.

STEEL, THOMAS
Service—Penna.   Va. No. R. 10100
Was drafted in the militia of Pennsylvania in Chester County, in 1776, for six months under Captain Marsh, Major Hammond, Colonel Moore and General Putnam. Before his enlistment had terminated, he secured a substitute to return to his wife who was sick. He was later drafted in Lancaster County, under Captain Boyd but was never called into actual service. His application for pension in Monroe County, Virginia, in 1836 was supported by the Rev. Jacob Cook and Hugh Caperton, but was refused because the applicant had not personally served at least six months.

STEEL, WILLIAM
Service—N. C.   N. C. No. 1654   No. W. 6196 and B. L. Wt. 8156
Enlisted at Hillsboro, North Carolina, in 1778 and served as a private and corporal under Captain Thomas Donah in the Fourth North Carolina Regiment, Continental Establishment, under Colonel Archibald Lyttle. Took part in the engagements at Bruin (Bonar) Creek and Stone Ore. Was wounded in the hand by a sword cut which deprived the soldier of the use of a thumb and finger. Was discharged at Salisbury after two years service.

Soldier was married on December 29, 1812, by the Rev. John Davis of the Baptist Church to Cerela or Cerlia Howard. Their marriage bond in Amherst County, Virginia, shows that Steel and wife had both been married before. Two children, Juanna, aged 7, and Molly, aged 5, are mentioned in 1820, at which time the soldier was aged 74 and his wife 45.

Pension was granted to Steel in 1820 and he was transferred from North Carolina to Virginia. He died, February 8 or 9, 1832. His widow received pension while living in Cabell County, Virginia, in 1854. Bounty land warrant for 160 acres was granted in 1855. Supporting data was filed in this case by Thomas Bane.

STEPHEN, ADAM (Major General)

Of Scotch descent. Educated as a physician, early removed to Virginia and settled in the lower valley. In 1754, he was the senior captain in Colonel Joshua Fry's regiment and when Washington took command, Stephen was made a major. He was with Washington at Great Meadows and the next year was severely wounded at Braddock's defeat. He recovered, served throughout the French and Indian War, and commanded the Virginia regiment raised in Pontiac's War (1763).

The following year, he was a magistrate of Frederick County, and when Berkeley was laid off in 1772, became its first high sheriff. In Lord Dunmore's War, he was second in command to the Governor, and at Fort Gower made a speech in favor of the colonial cause. He was in close touch with the Virginia leaders of the Revolution.

He was a member of the Convention of 1775. The next year he was made a brigadier general, fighting at Princeton, Trenton, and elsewhere in the Jerseys. In 1777, he was made a major general, serving with honor at the Brandywine. After the battle of Germantown, he retired to his home at Martinsburg, which he founded. He was several times sent to the Virginia Assembly.

In 1788, he was a member of the Virginia ratifying convention and strongly supported the Constitution. Three years later (1791), Stephen died at Martinsburg. He was noted for his great stature and unusual strength, and was particularly feared by the Indians. One of his daughters married Alexander Spottswood Dandridge.

STEPHENS, JOHN

In January, 1825, John Stephens, aged 67, of Greenbrier County, Virginia, but late of Fayette County, Kentucky, appeared before the Greenbrier County Court, produced a certificate, No. 9407, signed by J. C. Calhoun, Secretary of War, and asked to be restored to the pension list.

STEPHENS, JOHN

Before the Cabell County, Virginia, court, September 24, 1832, John Stephens made oath that he had served in the Revolutionary War and that he was entitled to a pension.

STEPHENSON, DAVID (Major)

Served as a major in Colonel Daniel Morgan's Rifle Corps. Before the Revolution lived on the Bullskin in Berkeley County.

STEPHENSON, HUGH (Colonel)
He was one of the five sons of Richard Stephenson, who settled on Bullskin Creek, Berkeley County, Virginia. He commanded a company of riflemen during the French and Indian War, and was recommended by Washington to command one of the rifle companies raised in the Shenandoah Valley in 1775. In 1776, he was raised from captain to colonel, and was employed in raising a rifle regiment, when he became ill and died at his home.

The heirs of Colonel Hugh Stephenson of the Revolutionary Army were allowed land bounty for two years, three months and three days service in addition to what had been previously received by an executive order of the State of Virginia, December 18, 1838. His will, proved in Berkeley County, Virginia, November 20, 1776, reads:

"To my wife, Ann, the plantation on which I now live, containing about 200 acres, during her natural life; to her one negro woman, named Nell; to my wife, all the residue of my estate, both real and personal, on this side of the Alleghenies, except the slaves hereafter disposed of, for and during her natural life; that she shall apply the benefits toward her support, and to the support and education of the following children, sons and daughters of myself and the said Ann, named William, John, Magnus, Hugh, Nancy, and Betty, until they shall arrive at lawful age." He gave a slave to each of the children. After the death of his wife, the plantation was to be sold and the returns divided among the children, and several large tracts of land were also left to his children.

STEPHENSON (Stephens), JOHN
Service—Virginia   Va. No. 23107   No. W. 6204 and B. L. Wt. 38562

Born in Amherst County, Virginia, March 28, 1761 and died March 3, 1841, Greenbrier County, Virginia. Enlisted in 1778, Henry County, Virginia, and served as a private under Captain W. Renfrow, Major Monroe Conaway, and Colonel Lynch in Virginia regiments as a substitute for George Griffith, William Griffith, and William Stephenson.

Soldier was married in Greenbrier County, April 28, 1791, by the Rev. McCue to Sally Morehead, the daughter of a Greenbrier County blacksmith. Pension was granted the soldier in 1833. He died in 1841 and his wife received pension and bounty land grant of 160 acres.

STEPHENSON, WILLIAM (Lieutenant)
Served as a lieutenant under General George Rogers Clark in his western campaign.

STEPLETON, ANDREW
Service—Virginia   Va. No. 6920   No. S. 36799

Enlisted at Romney, Hampshire County, and served six years and two months as a private in the company of Captain William Voss in the Twelfth Virginia Regiment, commanded by Colonels Wood and Neville under General Scott. Took part in the battles of Brandywine and Monmouth. He was wounded in the left arm at Brandywine and in the thigh during the battle of Monmouth. He was discharged at Winchester, Virginia, in 1783.

Soldier received pension in 1819 at which time he was living in Jefferson Township, Switzerland County, Indiana. In 1821 he gave his age as 99 and that of his wife, 59. They had two children, Betsy, aged 18, and John Cole, aged 9.

STEVENS, JOHN
Service—Md. Continental   Va. No. 16092   No. S. 6152

Enlisted in Prince George County, Maryland, August 15, 1777, and served until September 1778, as a private under Captain Thomas Ball in the Maryland regiment commanded by Colonel Rawlings, in Continental Establishment. Pension was granted to the soldier while living in Berkeley County, in 1833, at which time he was 75 years old. The certificate was sent to George Porterfield.

STEWART, RALPH (Captain)
Service—Virginia   Va. No. 23949   No. W. 6168

Born in Augusta County, Virginia, 1752, later removed to Giles and Montgomery County, and died in Logan County, November 17, 1835. About 1800, he had a cabin on Clear Creek in what is now Wyoming County, West Virginia. His wife, Mary Clay, was the daughter of Mitchell Clay, first settler of Mercer County, Virginia, and their marriage bond, dated June 25, 1788, is filed in Montgomery County, Virginia. They were married by the Rev. Edward Morgan.

Was commissioned captain in 1773 by Lord Dunmore, Governor of Virginia, and served as a ranger. Was at Point Pleasant under General Lewis in the battle in 1774. In 1778, his commission was renewed by Patrick Henry, then Governor of Virginia, was ordered with his company to South Carolina to join the army under General Green, and was attached to a regiment commanded by Colonel Robert McCleary and Major Smith. Fought at Guilford Courthouse, Hot Water, Ground Squirrel, Charlottesville, and Yorktown. He was wounded in the right arm by a sabre cut from one of "Butcher" Tarleton's men and was on the invalid roll for the state of Virginia. His commission and discharge, left with Colonel George Pearis for safe-keeping, were lost or stolen when the latter's home was plundered.

Soldier received pension in 1834 and his widow received pension in 1846 at which time she was 74 years old. Supporting data was submitted in this case by Edward Burgess, Patience Chapman, Mitchell Clay, Francis Hedrick, Charles L. Clay, and the Rev. Richard Brooks.

West Virginians in the American Revolution

Assembled and Edited by ROSS B. JOHNSTON

The sources of this material are from the files of the Pension Office at Washington, from various county records, from notes of patriotic societies, principally the Daughters of the American Revolution, Sons of the American Revolution, Sons of the Revolution, and from a large miscellaneous group of published and private sources. Corrections and additions to this list will receive the careful attention of the editor.

STONE, HENRY
Service—Virginia   Va. No. 13149   No. S. 6151
   Born in Frederick County, Maryland, in 1762; moved to Louden County, Virginia, and there enlisted in 1781 as a private in the company of Captain Lewis in the Virginia regiment among whose officers were Adjutant Harry Foot, Colonel Alexander, Colonel Dabney, under General Wayne. He moved to Green County, Pennsylvania, in 1804, and to Monongalia County, Virginia, in 1808 or 1809, where he was living in 1833 when he received pension. His claim was supported by Richard Harrison.

STONE—JOHN
Service—Penna.   Va. No. 12484   No. S. 6160
   Born in Lancaster County, Pennsylvania, in 1753, and there enlisted in 1775 or 1776 in company commanded by Captain Naggle. Took part in the engagements at Sechmore Point, Dorchester, and skirmishes on Long Island. After the Revolution, he resided in Maryland for a time, then in Botetourt County, Virginia, and received pension in Monongalia County, Virginia, in 1833. Supporting data was filed in this case by Jacob Lentz, James Cartmill, and John Moon. After the death of this soldier, his widow, Sarah Stone, according to Pension Office records, married John Dodd.

STONKARD, JOHN
Service—Penna.   Va. No. 19165   No. S. 41205
   Enlisted in Lancaster County, Pennsylvania, in January, 1775, in the Second Pennsylvania Regiment, in the company of Captains Reese and Watson under Colonel Woods and General Montgomery. Was wounded in the leg and arm in the battle of Quebec and was about fifteen steps from General Montgomery and his aide, McPherson, when they fell. When Colonel Campbell ordered a retreat, he was left with other wounded

men on the Plains of Abraham for some time in a kind of hospital. When he was able to march, he rejoined his command under Captains Reese, Watson, and Webster. He was on wagon guard the day of the battle of Brandywine, and his brother, James, was killed in the engagement. He was honorably discharged at Valley Forge, March, 1778.

While this soldier was in the service, his parents moved to Virginia, where he joined them after his discharge. He received pension in Pendleton County, Virginia, in 1824. Supporting data filed by Joseph Wright.

STOUT, CALEB
Service—New Jersey   Va. No. 2153   No. S. 7593

Enlisted in New Jersey in 1775 in the company of Captain Brady in the Second New Jersey Line Regiment, under Colonel Maxwell, and took part in Arnold's Quebec Expedition. In February, 1776, marched through Albany, Stillwater, Lake George, Ticonderoga, Crown Point, St. John, and Quebec. Taken ill with smallpox, and with 50 or 60 other sick, was left behind and taken prisoner. Sent to Halifax where he was in prison for two years.

Was pensioned in Harrison County, Virginia, where he made application, July 20, 1818. He was aged 73 and his wife 70 in 1821. He was dead before November 20, 1832.

STOUT, MOSES (Ensign)

Born in Hunterdon County, New Jersey, and died in Harrison County, Virginia. Married Abigail Hart, born 1754, daughter of John Hart, signer of the Declaration of Independence, and his wife, Deborah Scudder Hart, at Hopewell. He served in the Revolution as a member of the New Jersey militia as a sergeant and then as ensign in Captain Stout's company in the Third Jersey Regiment.

STOUT, THOMAS
Service—Virginia   Va. No. 23043   No. S. 7626

Born in Monmouth County, New Jersey, 1751. Resided in Augusta, now Harrison County, Virginia, at the outbreak of the Revolution, and in 1776 there enlisted as an Indian spy. He served under Captain Lowther at Nutter's Fort, Captain Springer at Prickett's Fort, Captain Carpenter at West's Fort, and under Captain Robinson and Captain Booth. He also mentions Isaac Beesley, John Cutright, Alexander West, and Joseph Parsons among other prominent frontier defenders. Supporting data was filed by Lovel Corbin and William Wilkinson.

Soldier received pension in 1833 while living in Harrison County, Virginia, but was dropped from the roll two years later because of insufficient proof of Revolutionary service.

STRADLER (STATLER), JACOB

The grave of Jacob Stradler or Statler, a soldier in the Revolution who died in 1778, is in the Price Memorial Cemetery near Olive Church, Monongalia County, West Virginia.

STRAIN, WILLIAM
William Strain, who served in the Revolutionary Army, is buried in Brooke County, Virginia, in the cemetery which he provided by will on his own farm. The Strain property has been in continuous possession of the family since 1782.

STRODE, JAMES (Captain)
Born, 1727; died, 1795. When the Revolution began, he was too old for field service but took part and was enthusiastic in the work of recruiting volunteers for enlistment in the army. As captain, commanded a company of militia in Berkeley County, Virginia. He was active in civil life as well as in military affairs before and after the Revolution. He was one of the first justices of the peace and justice of the county court at the organization of Berkeley County, May 1772.

STRODE, SAMUEL (Sergeant)
Enlisted from Berkeley County and saw service as a sergeant under General George Rogers Clark.

STRUPE, MELCHOR
Before the Cabell County, Virginia court in 1826, Melchor Strupe made application for a pension as a Revolutionary soldier, but died before his claim was approved. He lived near Barboursville on a farm west of the Horseshoe Bend on the north side of Mud River.

STUART (STEWART, STEUART, STEURT), EDWARD (Lieutenant)
Service—Virginia   Va. No. 12068   No. W. 6170 and B.L.Wt. 26039

Born on the Cowpasture River, Augusta County, Virginia, in February, 1759, and died at his home on Elk Creek, Barbour County, Virginia, April 7, 1844. He enlisted in Bath or Augusta County, in the Revolutionary Army, and served as follows: in 1778, two months as a private in Captain Andrew Lockridge's company against the Indians; in 1779, three months in Captain Robert McKery's or McCrory's company on the Augusta frontier; in 1780, two months under Captain John McCoy near Richmond; in 1781, three months in Captain Thomas Hicklin's company of the regiment commanded by Colonel Samuel Vance, and was at Yorktown when Cornwallis surrendered; in 1782, three months as ensign in Captain George Poage's company against the Indians. On October 19, 1790, he was recommended as lieutenant in Captain James Hicklin's company. He was known as captain when he lived on Elk Creek after the Revolution.

In Augusta County, April 4, 1786, Stuart was married to Mary Calaghan by the Rev. Samuel Shannon. Soldier received pension in Bath County, Virginia, in 1833, which was transferred to Harrison County, 1839. Soldier's widow received pension and 160 acres of bounty land. Supporting data was filed in this case by Adam Dickinson, George Hicklin, John Graham, James Nutter, and John, Hannah, Samuel, and Felix Stuart.

STUART, JOHN (Colonel)

Born near Staunton, Virginia; his father was David Stuart, a native of Scotland, who was county lieutenant of Augusta County; his mother was Mrs. Lynn Paul, the widow of John Paul, granddaughter of the Laird of Loch Lynn, Scotland, and the niece of Mrs. John Lewis, whose husband founded Staunton. Colonel Stuart settled in Greenbrier County, in 1769, at the age of 19, near Frankford but later settled near Fort Spring, Greenbrier County, and the fine old Stuart home which was built about 1789 is still standing.

In 1774 when General Andrew Lewis set about recruiting an army to march with Lord Dunmore against the Indians beyond the Ohio, Colonel Stuart organized a company of Greenbrier men and joined Lewis' army. In 1778, when the Indians attacked Fort Donnally, northwest of Lewisburg, he led reinforcements from Fort Union.

His wife was Mrs. Agatha Frogg, whose husband, William, was killed in the battle of Point Pleasant. They had four children: Charles A., who married Elizabeth Robinson; Lewis, who married Sarah Lewis; Jane, who married Robert Crockett; Margaret, who married Andrew Lewis. Colonel Stuart became county clerk of Greenbrier County in 1780 and held that office until 1807, when he resigned to be succeeded by his son, Lewis. He died August 18, 1823, and is buried on the old Stuart estate.

STUMP, MICHAEL
Service—Virginia   Va. No. 30557   No. R. 10285

Born in Culpepper County, Virginia, in 1764, and in the company of Thomas Martin saw military service in 1780, 1781, 1782, and 1783. He applied for pension in 1834 which was refused although his claim was supported by John Likens, W. G. W. Currin and others. His grave is probably on the right fork of Steer Creek, Gilmer County, West Virginia.

STURM, JACOB

The grave of Jacob Sturm, a soldier in the Revolutionary War, is in the McElfresh Cemetery on Teverbaugh in Marion County, West Virginia.

SULLIVAN, PATRICK

Born in 1751 and died in Clarksburg, Virginia, in 1841. He served in the Revolutionary War in Thompson's Battalion of the First Pennsylvania Regiment.

SULLIVAN, PETER
Service—Virginia   Kentucky No. 19466   No. W. 3736

Enlisted in the Revolutionary Army in Middlebrook, Georgia, and served in the Virginia Line under Captain Stokes in the regiment of Colonel Christian Febigen in General Welding's brigade. Fought at Middlebrook, Monmouth, and Eutaw Springs.

Married Katy Ayrehart prior to January 1, 1794 (probably 1782), in Lincoln County, North Carolina. Pension was issued in 1825 in Floyd County, Kentucky. Soldier died in 1840, aged 85. His widow died, 1848, aged 87, in Wayne County, Virginia. Their heirs were David and Polly Sullivan; Susan and Amy Sellards. Supporting data was submitted by James Rupell, Jeremiah Williams, Thomas Spalding, David Hogan, and Reuben Mathews.

SUMMERVILLE, WILLIAM (Captain)
Served as an officer under George Rogers Clark in the western country. He later became postmaster of Martinsburg. He died in 1826.

SUTTON, ELIJAH
Service—New Jersey   Va. No. 12959   No. S. 6174
Born in Somerset County, New Jersey, July 14, 1755. Enlisted at Brunswick, New Jersey, and served under Captains Jacob Dunn, Hatfield, King and Countryman in the New Jersey Line in the regiment of Colonel Ogden and Colonel Martin. Took part in the battle of Germantown. Soldier applied for pension in Morgan County, Virginia, which was granted in 1833. Supporting data was submitted by Sam Brown, Phineas Ogden, and John C. Gustin.

SWAN, CHARLES
Service—Continental Va.   Va. No. 1962   No. W. 19425
Enlisted in Frederick County, Virginia, in 1776, and served three years in the company of Captain Jones in the regiment of Light Dragoons under Colonel Baylor, Colonel Clough and General Washington. Took part in the battle of Monmouth and was on marches through Virginia, Maryland, Pennsylvania, New Jersey and Delaware. In December, 1779, Swan was married to Catherine Gayor by the Rev. Hannass of the Presbyterian Church, Frederick Town, Maryland.
Pension was granted the soldier in Tyler County, Virginia, in 1832, at which time he was 79 years old. He died August 4, 1841. His widow received pension in 1843 at which time she was 83 years old. Mention is made of Frederick Gayor or Gayoe, possibly a brother of the widow.

SWAN, JOHN
Served as a soldier in the Revolutionary Army from Berkeley County. His wife was given aid in 1777 by the court during the absence of her husband, possibly as a prisoner.

SWEARINGEN, BENONI
Lived at Shepherdstown, and was the youngest son of Thomas Swearingen who established a ferry there in 1775. He was married three times. His second wife was Sarah Bedinger, who died in 1792 at the ferry on the Virginia side. Their son, Henry, was in the war of 1812. Benoni then married a third time but his wife died soon after their marriage. He volunteered with George M. Bedinger and

was in the battle of Germantown. He went to Boonesborough, Kentucky, in 1779.

SWEARINGEN, HEZEKIAH
Son of Colonel Van Swearingen, born in 1747, and married Rebecca Turner. He served in the Revolutionary Army. He died January 3, 1817.

SWEARINGEN, JOSEPH (Captain)
First lieutenant, Twelfth Virginia, March 1, 1777; regiment designated Eighth Virginia, September 14, 1778; captain-lieutenant, April 14, 1779; taken prisoner at Charleston, May 12, 1780; captain, February 18, 1781; remained a prisoner to the end of the war. He then returned to his home at Shepherdstown, where he died in August, 1821.

He was born, July 10, 1754, at Shepherdstown, the son of Thomas Swearingen. He married Hannah Rutherford, who was born in 1752. They had one son, Thomas, who was born, February 5, 1784, but there may have been other children. According to certificate signed by General Muhlenberg, he had eight years service in the Revolution. Bounty land warrants were issued to him.

SWEARINGEN, JOSIAH (Captain)
Son of Colonel Van Swearingen. Born near Shepherdstown, March 28, 1744; died August 9, 1795. Enlisted as a private in Captain Stephenson's company in 1755. Later served under General Hand and General McIntosh in the western service, where he became a captain. He married, January 5, 1777, to Phoebe Strode, the daughter of James Strode of Berkeley County.

SWEARINGEN, THOMAS, (Major)
Son of the Thomas Swearingen who established the ferry at Shepherdstown. He was a brother of Benoni and Joseph and was born in 1752. He served as a soldier in the Revolution and went to Kentucky in 1779. Two of his daughters, Lydia and Drusilla, married Morgans. His son, Van, was killed at St. Clair's defeat.

SWEARINGEN, VAN (Captain)
Son of Thomas Swearingen. Native of Berkeley County. About 1774, he moved to the west, settling on the Monongahela River in what is now Fayette County, Pennsylvania. At the outbreak of the Revolution, he raised an independent company of riflemen which, on August 9, 1776, was attached to the Eighth Pennsylvania Regiment. In the battle of Stillwater, (1777), he was wounded and taken prisoner.

Upon his release, he served with his regiment until August 10, 1779, when he resigned, settled in Washington County, Pennsylvania, and was its first sheriff (1781-1784.) In 1785, he removed to Brooke County, Virginia, near Wellsburg, where he was a scout during the Indian wars. He died, December 2, 1793, at the age of 51. His only daughter, Drusilla, married Captain Sam Brady, who, with his father-in-law, known on the frontiers as "Indian Van", ranks first in the defense of the western borders of Pennsylvania and Virginia. (Another account says that he was killed November 4, 1791 at St. Clair's defeat near Fort Recovery, Ohio, while serving as captain of a detachment of Kentucky militia.)

SWEARINGEN, VAN (Colonel)
Served as a colonel of militia. He succeeded Colonel Samuel Washington as county lieutenant of Berkeley County, Virginia, and was succeeded by Philip Pendleton as colonel of militia, April 3, 1777. He was born in 1719 and died in 1788. He married twice; first his cousin, Sarah Swearingen; and after her death, Priscilla Metcalf.

SWEGER, JOHN
Service-Pennsylvania   Va. No. 23508   No. S. 15998
Born in Louden County, Virginia, April 25, 1759. Enlisted in Fayette County, Pennsylvania, as an Indian spy in 1777, and served seventeen months under Captain Paradocks or Paddox, and Moon in the Pennsylvania militia. Pension was granted him while living in Harrison County, Virginia, in 1833, which was dropped in 1835. Supporting data was filed by Israel Shinn and John Allen.

SWIGER, CHRISTOPHER and JOHN
Christopher and John Swiger were both soldiers in the Revolution, receiving their discharge at Fort Pitt.
In his pension application, made in 1833 while living on Coon's Run, Harrison County, John Swiger stated that he had lived in Fayette County, Pennsylvania, from the age of 18 until the end of the Revolution. He was granted a pension as an Indian spy in Pennsylvania, but his claim was later disputed and he was dropped from the roll.
Christopher Swiger was not a pensioner. He married Eleanor Bacchus, February 2, 1798, and settled in Sardis District, Harrison County, on land granted him as bounty for his Revolutionary service. He later moved to Doddridge County, Virginia, where he died and is buried on Sycamore Creek.

SWINGLER, SAMUEL (Lieutenant)
Served as a lieutenant in Green County, Pennsylvania, then in Virginia, in 1776 in the militia for two months. In the month of June, 1777, volunteered for service in the Virginia militia under Lieutenant William Cross of Captain John Minors' company in the march from Jarretts Fort to Whitely Creek and to Fort Pitt.

SWISHER, JACOB
Service-Pennsylvania   Va. No. 12574   No. S. 6179
Born in Berks County, Pennsylvania, March 13, 1752, and there enlisted in the Revolutionary Army, in 1775. Served as a private thirteen

months under Captains Lesher or Leazure and Folk in the Pennsylvania line. Applied for and received a pension in Harrison County, Virginia, March 10, 1833, which was suspended two years later. The letter to Hon. Nathan Goff, Clarksburg, Virginia, which announces this suspension, also gives notice that Arthur Trader has been dropped from the rolls, and that the pension of William Cunningham has been resumed, who is understood to have been wounded in the back at the battle of Brandywine.

SYDNOR, FORTUNATUS
Service-Continental Va. Va. No. 18747 No. S. 38160 and B. L. Wt. 12558
Enlisted in Bedford County, Virginia, in 1775 or 1776 and served thirteen months under Captains Dabney, Eddens, and Baham under Colonel Harrison, General Wayne and others. Took part in engagements at Hampton and Portsmouth. Received pension in Bedford County, Virginia, in 1822. (Supposed to have lived in Randolph County, Virginia, but proof is not found in pension records.)

TANNER, SAMUEL
Born in Augusta County (now Rockbridge), Virginia, May 15, 1759, moved to Greenbrier, then to Monongalia and spent his last years in Jackson County, Virginia. Elijah Runnion and Jesse Carpenter of Jackson County, testified for him in connection with pension application, but it was refused, No. R. 10389.
Tanner enlisted in the Rockbridge County, Virginia, militia in April, 1777, under Captain Hall, and marched to Lexington; joined Colonel George Skillern at Lewisburg, and remained there several weeks; lay at the falls of the Kanawha some time on account of sickness, then marched to Point Pleasant under Captain Matthew Arbuckle; was at Fort Randolph when Chief Cornstalk was killed. Marched back to Rockbridge, arriving there in January, 1778; in 1779, served in the frontier forts in Greenbrier County; in 1780, was an Indian spy under Lieutenant John McClung at Colonel Andrew Donnally's fort, on Greenbrier, Kanawha, Meadow, Gauley, Cole and Guyandotte rivers; the next year performed the same service under Ensign George Hannelon; in 1783, was under Ensign James Graham.

TABB, GEORGE and WILLIAM
Enlisted in Captain Stephenson's company in 1775. Received their discharge in October 1775, and returned to their home in Berkeley County when they learned of the death of another brother.

West Virginians in the American Revolution

Assembled and Edited by ROSS B. JOHNSTON

The sources of this material are from the files of the Pension Office at Washington, from various county records, from notes of patriotic societies, principally the Daughters of the American Revolution, Sons of the American Revolution, Sons of the Revolution, and from a large miscellaneous group of published and private sources. Corrections and additions to this list will receive the careful attention of the editor.

TASKER, JAMES
Service—Virginia   No. 17658   No. R. 10396

Enlisted in Fairfax County, Virginia, September 18, 1777, and served six years as private under Captain West in his company in the Tenth Virginia Regiment, Continental Establishment, commanded by Colonel Stephens and General Weeden. Took part in the battles of Stony Point, and Blueford's Defeat. He was wounded and captured in the latter engagement.

Married Mary Harper in 1794. In 1818, the soldier was aged 62, his wife, 40, and their children were: Minty, aged 16; Elizabeth, 14; Richard, 12; Delilah, 10; and Fanny, 7. Soldier received pension in Hampshire County, in 1820, and died March 4, 1832. His widow was refused pension. Supporting data was filed by Sampson Henderson, Richard Tasker, Douglas Smith, Patrick McCarty, Reuben Davis, William Janny, William Duling, Jacob Knabenshue, George Tasker, John Ward, and Peter Smith.

TAYLOR, DANIEL (Sergeant)
Service—New Jersey   Va. No. 12008   No. S. 6201

Born in New Jersey in 1758 and enlisted, June, 1776, from Sussex County, in company of Captain Winters in the New Jersey Regiment, commanded by Colonel Taylor and Frelinghausen. Was engaged on various marches through Perth Amboy, Brunswick, Elizabeth Town, Wood Bridge and elsewhere.

Pension certificate was issued in Hampshire County, in 1833. Supporting data was filed by Jesse Monroe, Thomas Carskadon, and Thomas Taylor. Soldier was married to Margaret Thatcher, December 27, 1778, and died in Hampshire County, May 3, 1844. Land bounty warrant was issued to his heirs for his war services.

TAYLOR, EDWARD

In Hampshire County, the beautiful old home of Edward Taylor, a soldier in the Revolutionary War, is still standing. It is believed to have been purchased by him in 1806.

TAYLOR, JOHN

Before the Harrison County court, June 15, 1818, John Taylor testified that he enlisted in the regular army of the United States in a company commanded by Captain William Riley of the Fourth Maryland Regiment, and that he served a part of his time under Colonel Samuel Smith, at that time a representative of Congress from Maryland. He enlisted in the year of the battle of Monmouth and fought in that battle and also at Camden where he was captured and held a prisoner for sixteen months. He at length escaped from the prison ship on which he had been confined and continued in the service of his country until the conclusion of the war.

TAYLOR, PAUL

Service—Continental Pennsylvania   No. S. 18238

Enlisted at Paxton near Harrisburg, Pennsylvania, in 1775 and served until 1777 as a private under Lieutenant John Robinson and Captain Potts, in the Fifth Pennsylvania Battalion, commanded by Colonel Hartley. He fought at White Plains and at Brandywine. He applied for pension in 1832 and his claim was supported by Jacob Anderson and John Shober. He may have later lived in western Virginia.

TAYLOR, THOMAS

Service—New Jersey and Pennsylvania   Va. No. 12587   No. S. 7686

Born in Hunterdon County, New Jersey, in 1760, and there in the fall of 1776 enlisted as a private under Captain Gunandyke in a New Jersey regiment commanded by Colonel Taylor. Fought at Brandywine and White House. Stood guard over an uncle who was a Tory at Trenton, and the uncle tried to get his gun. Was in General Washington's retreat through Jersey. Colonel Taylor, his commander, brought off four field pieces. Mentions Major Bush, who was shot through the hip, and other officers. Was granted pension in Hampshire County, in 1833. Supporting data filed by Isaac Kuykendall, Isaac Pancake, and John Sloan.

TENNANT, RICHARD

Emigrated from Glasgow, Scotland, about 1760 at the age of 16. His father, Richard Tennant, was killed at the Storming of Quebec by General Wolfe in 1763. In 1769, he married Elizabeth Haught at Moorefield where he had settled a short time before. He served as a drummer in Lord Dunmore's War in 1774. He served with Peter Haught, a brother of his wife, in the Revolution, according to Jacob Haught, son of Peter.

During his Revolutionary service he had passed through the Monongahela Valley. Therefore, after the war he came with his family and that of his brother-in-law, Peter Haught, and settled on Jake's Run, Monongalia County. Tennant died in 1820 and is buried in the Tennant graveyard, three miles from Mooresville.

TENNEY, JAMES
Service—Massachusetts   Va. No. 4197   No. W. 3888

Born, December 21, 1766, the son of Josiah Tenney; died in Randolph County, Virginia, December 24, 1841. Enlisted at Shelburn, Massachusetts, December, 1780, in the First Massachusetts Regiment, under Lieutenants Shepherd, Green, Kilham, and Colonel Voss, and General Knox. Took part in actions from West Point along the Hudson, and at Philadelphia. His honorable discharge, dated, October 28, 1783, was signed by Major-General Knox.

At Charlemont, Berkshire, now Franklin County, Massachusetts, is the record of his marriage on April 14, 1785, to Thankful Shippee, with Samuel Taylor, clergyman of Buckland, officiating. The soldier received pension in Randolph County, Virginia, 1833. After his death his widow also received a pension in 1847 while living in Lewis County, at the age of 81. There was a large family but the names are not available.

THAYER, ABEL (Captain)

Served as a lieutenant and captain during the Revolution. Marched with a body of Minute Men to Lexington from Williamsburg, Massachusetts, as a lieutenant, April 27, 1775. His name appears as an officer with the rank of captain in Colonel John Fellows Regiment, at Roxbury Camp, May 31, 1777. His place of residence during the Revolution is given as what is now West Virginia. He was born in Braintree, Massachusetts, July 28, 1741; married Dorothy Curtis in 1761; died in Williamsburg, Massachusetts, May 24, 1805.

THOMAS, JOSEPH
Service—Virginia   Va. No. 23160   No. W. 6277

Born in Buckingham County, Virginia, August 3, 1759; removed to Kanawha County, Virginia, in 1796-98, where he died, August 1, 1839. He was married to Rebecca Thomas by the Rev. David Patterson, near Providence Meeting House, Buckingham County, Virginia, about 1786. Their children were Lewis, Polly, Washington, Henry, and Mathews.

Enlisted in 1777 under Lieutenant Clouth Shelton, and Captain James Franklin as a private in the Sixth Virginia Regiment, under Colonel Edward Stephens with forces under General Washington. Marched to White Marshes or Chestnut Hill, and took part in engagement there, after which the British occupied Philadelphia, and the American army went into camp at Valley Forge. The battle of Monmouth had just ended when he reached that point with American forces under Colonel John Green of Culpeper. Pursued British across North River to White Plains and Stony Point, but was not in detachment which reduced it. Was discharged in November 1778.

Received pension in Kanawha County, Virginia, in 1833. Supporting data submitted by the Rev. David Barbour, Marshall Bowman, Moses Wright, Captain John Thomas (a brother), Samuel and Nancy Hudson, Charles Brown, Thomas Mathew, and John Thomas, (a cousin). His widow likewise received pension.

THOMPSON, ALEXANDER
Service—Virginia   Va. No. 16720   No. S. 14691

Born in Augusta County, Virginia, March 29, 1763, where he lived until 1819 at which time he moved to Kanawha County, Virginia. In 1781, he was drafted into the Virginia militia under Captain Cunningham and Colonel Sampson Mathews, and his record gives some interesting information concerning Arnold's invasion of Virginia.

The soldier was marched from Augusta to Fredericksburg, thence to Cahill Point, on the James River between Richmond and Norfolk, then to Smithfield observing the movements of the British fleet; thence to Suffolk, which had been burned by the British. Remained at Camp Carson two months watching the British at Portsmouth. Several skirmishes took place in one of which Captain Cunningham was wounded. Was discharged at Richmond. In 1783, served under Captain John McKitlinch against the Indians about Fort Warnick or Warwick.

Soldier received pension in 1833, which was later suspended. Supporting data given by Daniel Ruffner, James Bell, and Captain Styles.

THOMPSON, JACOB
Service—Virginia   Va. No. 5979   No. S. 41240

Enlisted in the First Regiment of Virginia Dragoons under Captain Morrow or Morris, and served as a private. Took part in skirmish near Dorchester, South Carolina. Applied for pension in Harrison County, Virginia, which was issued in 1819. At that time soldier was aged 59, his wife, 59, a daughter, Polly, 26, and a granddaughter, Elizabeth, 10. Soldier died April 11, 1841, and his widow, April 24, 1842.

THOMPSON, STEPHEN

Before the Greenbrier County court, 1781, Elizabeth, the widow of Stephen Thompson, who died in service in the Revolutionary War, together with one child, was certified as entitled to aid.

THORNBURGH, THOMAS (Lieutenant)

Born, September 9, 1752, Shepherdstown, Virginia, the son of Sarah Shepherd and Thomas Thornburgh; died, May 5, 1793. Served as a lieutenant in the Revolutionary War, and after the war settled near Wheeling. Married twice; first wife named Ruth; second wife was Prudence Bentley Collins, daughter of William and Margaret Bentley. His children were Ephraim, Elizabeth, Prudence, Solomon, and Thomas.

THRALLS, RICHARD
Service—Virginia　　　　　Va. No. 16396　　　　　No. S. 6240

Enlisted at Hancock, Maryland, and served as a private two years under Captain Thomas Cabel, under Colonel Gibson, and General Brodhead at Fort Pitt, Fort Lawrence, and Fort McIntosh on the western frontiers. Received pension while living in Monongalia County, in 1833, at the age of 80. Supporting data filed by James Troy, S. Miner, William Brick, Alva Shriver, Neal Lougher, D. V. McHenry, J. Long, and Amos Morris.

TICHINAL, DAVID
Service—Virginia　　　　　Va. No. 6812　　　　　No. S. 7727

Born in Morris Township, New Jersey, October 16, 1764; resided in New Jersey until 1780; resided in Hampshire County, Virginia, for two or three years; then in Harrison County, Virginia, and died in Allegheny County, Maryland, in 1854.

Soldier enlisted in New Jersey in 1780 and served nine months under Captain Richardson and McCarty in the army of General Green on guard duty. His certificate of service in the militia as a substitute for his father, Moses Tichinal, dated March 12, 1782, and signed by Captain Isaac Parsons, is filed at the War Department. Pension was granted in Harrison County, in 1833. Supporting data was filed by J. Copin, R. Moore, H. Gross, and John Smith.

TINGLE, GEORGE
Lived near Shepherdstown at the outbreak of the Revolution. In 1776, enlisted in Captain John Nelson's company of riflemen from Maryland and Virginia, and joined Stephenson's company at Staten Island.

TOWNSEND, JOHN
Enlisted in the regular army in the State of New Jersey in the company of Captain Piatt, First Regiment of New Jersey regulars, in the year 1775, and for the war. He continued in this corps, took part in the battle of Germantown, and of Springfield, where he was wounded and sent to the hospital. He was later captured by the Indians and held a prisoner until the end of the war.

TRADER, ARTHUR
Service—Virginia　　　　　Va. No. 23390　　　　　No. S. 30169

Born in Augusta County, Virginia, in 1747. Enlisted in June, 1776, and served nine days less than two years as a private under Captains Morgan and Neel. Received pension in Harrison County, Virginia, in 1834, but was later stricken from the rolls.

TROTIER, PAUL
Land Bounty Warrant No. 664 was issued in lieu of Warrant 9719 in name of Paul Trotier, April 9, 1856, as a soldier of the Illinois Regiment of Virginia, State line in the Revolution. In Berkeley County,

Virginia, the records show that M. C. Nadenbousch was appointed administrator of the estate of Ann McKnight, who was an heir of Trotier.

TROY, JAMES (Sergeant)
Service—Virginia   Va. No. 12806   No. S. 7747

Born, Winchester, Virginia, 1759; died, January 15, 1841, Monongalia County, Virginia. Enlisted in 1774 as a sergeant under Lieutenant Phil Pierce, Lieutenant Sam Swindler, Captain Robert Fenole, Captain Lewis Rogers, Colonel William McCleery at Statler or Stradler's Fort, Monongalia County.

Pension was granted in 1833 but was suspended along with that of Haught, Piles, George Wade and others. The arrears were paid to heirs when his service was accepted in 1859. Supporting data was submitted by Amos Morris, George Wade, Henry Yoho, R. Berkshire, John Keck, Abram Richard, and Joseph Tennant.

TRUBY, JOHN

Before the Randolph County, Virginia, court, November 25, 1811, Valentine Stalnaker, one of the heirs, made oath that he heard John Truby, deceased, say that he had never received any compensation for his services rendered (during the Revolutionary War).

TUCKER, GEORGE
Service—Maryland   Va. No. 12586   No. S. 7763

Enlisted in Kent County, Maryland, and served six months as a private under Captain Crane in the Maryland line. Pension was granted the soldier aged 71, while living in Monongalia County, Virginia, in 1833. George Smith filed supporting data. Papers filed in this note the fact that Philip Reed, one of his regimental officers, was severely reprimanded by General Washington for carrying into camp on a pole the head of a deserter.

West Virginians in the American Revolution

Assembled and Edited by ROSS B. JOHNSTON

The sources of this material are from the files of the Pension Office at Washington, from various county records, from notes of patriotic societies, principally the Daughters of the American Revolution, Sons of the American Revolution, Sons of the Revolution, and from a large miscellaneous group of published and private sources. Corrections and additions to this list will receive the careful attention of the editor.

TUCKER, JOHN
Service—Virginia   Va. No. 5058   No. S. 6274
   Enlisted in Monongalia County, Virginia, in the spring of 1777, as a private under Captain Booth in a regiment of the Virginia Line, commanded by Colonel John Evans, and was engaged on duties at forts and outposts between the Ohio and Monongahela Rivers. Found the body of Mrs. Grigsby, a victim of the Indians, along Ten Mile Creek. Saw Miss Coon killed by the Indians at Coon's Fort in what is now Marion County, West Virginia. Was present when Mr. Woodfield and Mr. Miller were killed by the savages a short distance from Fort Kerns, at what is now Morgantown. Was granted a pension in Harrison County, Virginia, in 1833.

TUCKER, THOMAS
Service—Virginia   Va. No. 12588   No. S. 7762
   Born in Pocahontas, then Cumberland County, Virginia, in 1755. There enlisted in 1781 and served nine months as a private under Captains Hughes, Patterson, Crump, Holcomb, and Goods, and Major Tucker, Colonel Beverly Randolph, and General Lawson. Fought at Guilford Courthouse.
   Soldier received pension in 1833 in Pocahontas County, Virginia. His widow, Frances, applied for pension in Cartersville, Cumberland County, Virginia, in 1845. Supporting data was filed in this case by Wade and Hezekiah Mosby, Edward Watkins, the Rev. Francis Lowry, and Joseph Mathews.

TUNISIN, GARRET (Surgeon)
   Practiced medicine in Shepherdstown in 1773, and there enlisted in Captain Stephenson's company of riflemen as a surgeon in June, 1775. Marched to Boston and also served the companies of Morgan, Cresap and Price. Escaped capture at Fort Washington and served to the end of the war. He later returned to his early home in New Jersey.

TURLEY, JAMES
Service—Virginia   Va. No. 15372 and 23987   No. S. 11585

Born in Pennsylvania. Enlisted as a private in the company of Captain Cummins in Colonel Joseph Crockett's Virginia Regiment, while living in Bedford County, near Lynchburg, Virginia, and was under Captain John Chapman in Clark's Illinois Expedition. Received pension in Cabell County, Virginia, in 1834, at the age of 80. He died in 1838 near Ona, Cabell County.

TURNER, JOSEPH
Enlisted in the Revolutionary Army from Shepherdstown.

TURNER, THOMAS (Captain)
First volunteered in Captain William Morgan's company. In 1776-77, was promoted to captain. Married Sallie Swearingen, sister of Colonel Joseph Swearingen. He was still living in Berkeley County in 1797.

UNSELD, HENRY
Enlisted in the Revolutionary Army at Shepherdstown as a private soldier.

VANANSDELL, CORNELIUS
Service—New Jersey and Virginia   Va. No. 16801   No. S. 15691

Born in Somerset County, New Jersey, December 3, 1758. Entered service in New Jersey in 1776; spent two weeks at Staten Island under Captain Cornelius Lott; one month on the River Raritan under Captain Easty; one month at Amboy under Peter Travers; one month at Elizabethtown under David S. Comp. Enlisted for Hugh Bathin of Augusta County, to which place he had moved in 1780, and served under Captain John McCoy, Captain Peter Hull and Commander Samuel Mathews.

Received pension in Greenbrier County, Virginia, 1832. Supporting data filed by Thomas Blake, James Gregory, and James Acheson. Died in Lawrence County, Ohio, April 28, 1841.

VANASDAL, JOHN
Service—New Jersey   Va. No. 23403   No. S. 11611

Born, September 25, 1763, Somerset County, New Jersey, where he enlisted in 1776 as a musician under Captain Vanbright in New Jersey regiment under Colonel Nelson. Was in the battle of Monmouth.

Received pension in Brooke County, Virginia, in 1834. Supporting data filed by Edward Smith, Mose Congleton, and Thomas Peterson.

VANDEL, ABRAHAM
Service—New York   Va. No. 23256   No. S. 9496

Born, October 18, 1758, Duchess County, New York. Enlisted as a private in Orange County, New York, March 1, 1776, and served two years as a private under Captains Wiezner and W. Blaine in New York and Virginia regiments under Isaac Nichols and General Clinton. In 1783, moved to Rockingham County, Virginia. Helped build Fort Constitution on Hudson River; marched to New York and joined General Washington's army. Was engaged in battles of Long Island and White Plains. His division under Major General Heath marched to Peekskill after the battle of White Plains and his company was discharged as it was greatly reduced in numbers. He reenlisted, January 10, 1777, under Captain John Woods in Colonel McLaughlin's Regiment. In May he was a militiaman under Captains McCauley and Sheppard under Colonel Haythorne. Was stationed at Fort Montgomery when it was captured, but was absent from the fort so escaped capture. Helped construct fort at West Point. In 1779 was in Lord Sterling's army and in 1780 and 1781 was on guard duty.

Applied for pension at Gauley Bridge, Fayette County, Virginia, in 1833. Supporting data filed by William Morris, James Skaggs, Hiram Hill, and John Sammons.

VANDIVER (VANDEVER), WILLIAM
Service—Virginia   Va. No. 12567   No. S. 6308
Born on the Shenandoah River in Frederick County, Virginia, March 18, 1762; married Mary J. Vandiver; died in Hampshire County, Virginia, July 17, 1833. Enlisted in Hampshire County, May 1, 1781, under Captain Thomas Anderson and served six months as a private under Major John Higgins and Colonel Joseph Neville. Soldier was granted pension in 1833 in Hampshire County. Supporting data submitted by John Vance, John Parsons, Thomas Welsh, Samuel Vandiver, and Jesse Monroe.

VANGILDER, JACOB
The grave of Jacob Vangilder, a Revolutionary War soldier, is in Mount Zion Cemetery, Marion County, West Virginia.

VAN.METER, HANCE (or Johannes) (Captain)
Commanded a company of Berkeley County militia during the Revolution.

VANMETER, JACOB (Ensign)
Sergeant in the Twelfth Virginia, January 14, 1777; regiment designated the Eighth Virginia, September 14, 1778; ensign, September 8, 1779. Retired January 1, 1781.

VANMETER, JOHN (Captain)
Born about 1738, the son of Henry Vanmeter, one of the first settlers west of the mountains. In 1771, he owned land at the site of Waynesburg, Greene County, Pennsylvania. Early in the Revolution, he commanded a company of rangers from Westmoreland. Later he settled in Brooke County, Virginia, where he died about 1803. During the Indian wars, his home was attacked by Indians, his wife and daughter killed, and one son, John, carried into captivity. He never returned to civilization. The elder John afterwards married Mrs. Jemima Bukey, mother of the celebrated spy, Hezekiah Bukey. They lived on Short Creek.

VAN METER, JOHN (Major)

Served in the Revolution as a captain in command of a company of militia. On October 10, 1780, he was sworn in as major of the militia from Berkeley County, Virginia.

VANMETER, JOSEPH (Ensign)

Service—Virginia   Va. No. 23457   No. S. 16010

Enlisted in Hampshire County, Virginia, in 1776 and served two years as sergeant and ensign under Lieutenants Hite and Williams and Captain William Vause in the Twelfth Virginia Regiment, commanded by Major Lyon, and Colonels Woods and Neville. Took part in the battles of Brandywine, Germantown, Monmouth, and Bluefield. Pension was granted the soldier in Hardy County, in 1834.

VANMETRE, GARRETT (Colonel)

Served as a colonel of Virginia militia in 1775 and 1776, and died in 1788.

VAUSE, (VOSS), WILLIAM (Captain)

Captain, Twelfth Virginia, January 8, 1777; regiment designated the Eighth Virginia, September 14, 1778; retired February 12, 1781.

Before the Hampshire County Court, in 1833, William Inskeep testified that Captain William Vause had served to the end of the Revolution. He had died several years previously, leaving the following children: William, Thomas, Solmon, and Jemimah Fox, and Theodosia Vause, widow. Jemimah Fox died, leaving Absalom, Vause, George, William G., Gabriel and Amos, Elizae (wife of Joseph Williams), Ann (wife of Isaac Inskeep), Rebecca, who died leaving an infant, William Fox Temple, Julian Fox, Rachel Fox, and Sarah (wife of Ebenezer McCullough). The affidavits of several heirs were received at the same time. Before the executive department of the State of Virginia, the heirs of William Vause were allowed land bounty for one year's additional service as a captain in the Continental line, December 14, 1833, B. L. Wt. No. 7413.

WOODELL (WADDLE), THOMAS (Sergeant)

Service—Virginia   Va. No. 16654   No. S. 11697

In Mason County, Virginia, December 3, 1832, Thomas Woodell, or Waddle, aged 73, testified that he was born in Augusta County, Virginia, in 1759. In December, 1780, he was drafted into the militia and marched under Captain Patterson to join General McIntosh, but before joining the main army, his father followed the company and provided a substitute for him. He was again drafted under Captain Patterson and marched to Richmond, Fredericksburg, to Sandy Point, Portsmouth, and Camp Carson where he spent the winter. He was under Colonel Mathews, Colonel Bowyer, and General Muhlenberg. He was discharged and was again drafted, and served as a sergeant under Captain Dickey in the army of General Campbell. Supporting evidence in this case was submitted by Peter Peck, William Hawkins, and Isaac Robinson.

WADE, JOSEPH
The grave of Joseph Wade, a veteran of the Revolutionary War, who died in 1778, is in Price Memorial Cemetery near Olive Church, Monongalia County, West Virginia.

WADE, GEORGE
Service—Pennsylvania and Virginia   Va. No. 129   No. S. 7829

Applied for pension which was granted in Monongalia County, Virginia, in 1833. It was suspended in 1835, but arrears were paid to his heirs in 1859. The soldier died, October 30, 1842. Supporting data was filed by Joseph Denune and Thomas Wade.

WADE, HEZEKIAH
Service—Pennsylvania and Virginia   Va. No. 23034   No. W. 6387

Born in Frederick County, Maryland, April 6, 1754, the son of Joseph Wade; died, November 23, 1834, in Tyler County, Virginia. Enlisted as an Indian spy in April, 1776, and served in Pennsylvania and Virginia militia. Among officers mentioned by him in application papers are Colonel McClain of Uniontown, Williamson of Boston, Zane of Wheeling, Brodhead of Fort Pitt, and Captains Davy, Lucas, Minor, Cochran, Williamson, Mason and J. Ramsey.

In 1778, Joseph Wade, his father, Jacob Stradler, Michael Kiddingler, James Piles, John McDaniels and others to a total of 18 were killed by Indians near Fort Stradler or Statler. Soldier was married in Tyler County, Virginia, June 15, 1785 to Rebecca Joseph, who was born October 11, 1770. Proof of marriage is by family record and Mrs. Temperance Cochran and Mrs. Bolton, daughter of James Hamilin, and Nathan Joseph, aged seven, present at the marriage at his father's home. The children were: William Joseph, George, Hezekiah, Joseph, John Joseph, (one son had died); Ruth Wade Young. Both soldier and his widow received pension. Supporting data was filed by Peter Bartrug, Jacob Bowman, and Nathan Joseph.

WAGGONER, ANDREW, SR. (Major)
Served in the Revolution and is buried at Christ Church, Bunker Hill, Berkeley County.

WAGGONER, JOHN M.
Service—Virginia   Va. No. 12659   No. 7824

Born at White Marsh, Pennsylvania, in 1752; married Hannay Keyles at Moorefield in 1793; died at Romney in 1843. Enlisted in 1778 and served as a ranger under Captain Owens Davy and Colonel Charles Martin; was drafted and served under Captain John Harness and Colonel Riddle in General McIntosh's campaign, was at the siege and capture of Cornwallis, and also served as an Indian spy under Edward Freeman. His pension application states that his family and home were destroyed by Indians in 1792. Soldier received pension in 1833, in Lewis County, Virginia. Supporting data was filed by John Mitchell and others.

WAGNER, JACOB
Service—Pennsylvania   Va. No. 12559   No. S. 6320

Enlisted in Lancaster County, Pennsylvania, in 1778 and served two years under Captain Babskey in regiment commanded by Colonel Koovort, and served until 1781 in Pennsylvania, Virginia and South Carolina. Received pension in Preston County, Virginia, in 1833 aged 83.

WAGNER, PHILIP
Enlisted under Captain Stephenson. He was probably captured in the surrender of Fort Washington.

WALDO, JOHN J.
Service—New York   Va. No. 5057   No. S. 6321

Enlisted in Albany County, New York, in May, 1778, and served nearly nine months under Captains Thomas Brown and Haddock, under Major Abbott, Colonel Vanrensaaler, and General Williams. Received pension while living in Harrison County, Virginia, in 1832, at the age of 70.

WALKER, JOSEPH
Service—Pennsylvania   Va. No. 16724   No. S. 11657

Born in County Antrim, Ireland, 1753. Enlisted in Chester County, Pennsylvania, in March, 1776, and served under Lieutenant Finley, Captains Stewart and Elton in the Third Pennsylvania Regiment, commanded by Colonels McGaw and Penrose. Took part in the battle of Brandywine.

Received pension while living in Hardy County, in 1833. Soldier died, June 17, 1834. Supporting data was filed by William Heath, Charles Turler, and Major Joseph Neville.

Service—Virginia   Va. No. 23787   No. S. 18260

Enlisted in New London, Bedford County, Virginia, July, 1776, and served under Captain William Campbell in regiment of Colonel William Christie. Discharged at Williamsburg, August 28, 1777. Drafted and served in Botetourt County, and spent six months under General McIntosh on the western front. Was again drafted, and marched to Jamestown with General Lafayette's army; marched to the Carolinas under Captain David May, joined the forces of William Preston, fought at the battle of Reedy Fork, under Major Joseph Cloyd and Colonel Williams.

Received pension in 1834 in Logan County, Virginia, and died December 1835. Supporting data filed by Julius Webb, Catherine Anderson, John Lowery, and the Rev. Sheldon Parker.

WALKER, THOMAS
Service—Virginia   Va. No. 12394   No. S. 6339

Born in Orange County, Virginia, December 18, 1763. Was drafted in Rockingham County, in 1779 at the age of sixteen under Captain Michael Conger, joined the army of General Muhlenberg, engaged in a skirmish at Great Bridge, then marched into North Carolina, but shortly afterwards returned to Virginia; was again drafted under Captain Richard Riggin and served under General Stephens; was discharged on account

of illness three days before the surrender of Cornwallis at Yorktown.
Received pension in Monroe County, in 1833, and was paid to September 4, 1839. Supporting data filed by Christian Peters, James A. Dunlap, Jacob Meadows, and John Peters.

WALL, CHARLES
Before the Greenbrier County, Virginia, Court, August 25, 1818, Charles Wall, aged 70, declared that he enlisted in Augusta County, Virginia, in 1778, in company commanded by Captain John Lewis in the Second Virginia Regiment, commanded by Colonel Brant and Lieutenant-Colonel Charles Dabney. Served three years and was discharged at Philadelphia after taking part in the battle of Monmouth, Stony Point, Jamestown, and the taking of Cornwallis at Yorktown.

WALLS, GEORGE (Major)
Commanded force of Berkeley County riflemen. In 1781, he wrote Thomas Jefferson that all of his company might reenlist for the duration of the war.

WAMSLEY, DAVID
Service—Virginia   Va. No. 23024   No. S. 18669
Born in Augusta County, Virginia, November 19, 1775. Enlisted as an Indian spy in Hampshire County, and served two years. Applied for pension in 1834 which was granted, but was suspended the following year.

WAMSLEY, JAMES
Service—Virginia   Va. No. 16244   No. S. 6323
Born in Augusta County, Virginia, March, 1764. Enlisted in Rockingham County, Virginia, (later Pendleton County), March 1, 1781, and served two years as an Indian spy under Captains Hamilton and Hull, Colonels Gamble and Mathews, and Generals Wayne and Nelson. Applied for pension in Lewis County, Virginia, in 1833 which was suspended in 1836 as it was held that he had not had sufficient military service in the Revolution to entitle him to pension under the act of June 7, 1832.

WAMSLEY, WILLIAM
Service—Virginia   Va. No. 12879   No. S. 7806 and B.L.Wt. 7159
Born in Maryland in 1759. Enlisted in 1778 or 1779 in Virginia and served two years as a private under Lieutenant Robert Gamble and Captain Stephen Young in the Virginia regiment under Major George Wailes or Wattes and Colonel J. Crockett under General George Rogers Clark. Pension was granted the soldier in Harrison County, Virginia, in 1833. Bounty land warrant for 200 acres was also issued to him.

WANLESS, RALPH
Before the Pocahontas County, Virginia, Court, August 7, 1832, Ralph Wanless, aged 75, testified that he was born in England and lived on

the Calf Pasture River in Augusta County, Virginia, when drafted for service in the Revolutionary War. Served under Captain McCoy; then served as an Indian spy under Captain George Poage at Clover Lick; now in Pocahontas County, West Virginia, and also served a time at Norfolk, Virginia. Names Jacob Lightner, George Gay, and Martin Dilley as persons who could testify for him. Supporting data is filed by Gay and Dilley.

WARDSWORTH, (WADSWORTH) ROBERT
Service—Continental Virginia   Va. No. 5981   No. S. 41296

Enlisted on the South Branch of the Potomac in March, 1776, and served as a private and guard to General Washington almost four years under Captain Westfall in the Eighth Virginia Regiment. Took part in the engagements at Charlestown, Brandywine, and Germantown.

Received pension in Harrison County, Virginia, in 1819, at which time he was 68 years old. His children were Robert, 16; Mary, 15; Jesse, 14; Rachel, 12; and Nancy, 10. Pension was discontinued in 1820 as having too much property but was resumed in 1821.

WARE, MOSES

Before the Randolph County, Virginia, Court, Robert Maxwell testified that he saw in the possession of Jonathan Buffington, a military land warrant of 400 acres granted to Moses Ware for his military services (Revolution). With the said warrant was a bill of sale transferring land to Buffington and that the said warrant was lost when Buffington was "captivated" by the Indians. A new copy was ordered made and approved by the court.

WARWICK, JACOB (Lieutenant)

Jacob Warwick was born in 1743 in Augusta County, Virginia, and probably died on Jackson's River near Warm Springs, Bath County, Virginia, in January, 1826. He lived for some years at Dunmore and Clover Lick, Pocahontas County, Virginia. He took part in the battle of Point Pleasant, and was a lieutenant in the Revolutionary Army under Captain Samuel Vance.

WASHINGTON, SAMUEL (Colonel)

Born November 16, 1734, in Westmoreland County, Virginia. He was living in Jefferson County, Virginia, during the Revolution, and died there in 1781. He was married to Anne Steptoe, who was born in 1737. One son, George Steptoe Washington, was born in 1773, and there may have been other children. He was a colonel of Virginia militia, 1775-1776, and served as aide-de-camp to his brother, General George Washington.

WATKINS, STEPHEN
Service—Maryland   Va. No. 17705   No. W. 25852 and B.L.Wt.31735

Enlisted in Maryland, May, 1776, and served until May, 1780, as a private under Captain Sellman in the Fourth Regiment, Maryland Line, commanded by Colonels Smith and Hall, under General Gish. Took part in the battles of Long Island, White Plains and Monmouth.

Married Sarah Miller, June 26, 1804, with the Rev. Robert Manley as minister. In 1820, the soldier's age was 67, that of his wife 43, and their children: James, 16; Frances, 15; Arthur, 13; Thomas, 10; Stephen, 8; Gasway, 6; Hannah, 3. Pension was granted the soldier in Monongalia County, Virginia, in 1820. There he died, February 12, 1839. His widow likewise received pension, and also bounty land warrant for 160 acres. She died, August 13 1855. Supporting data was filed by David Kinkaid, Isaac McDonald, William Oberfield, and William A. Freeze.

WEBB, JOHN
Service—Virginia   Va. No. 6395   No. S. 41320

Enlisted in Bath County, Virginia, in 1780 or 1781 and served as a private eighteen months under Captain Lansdale in the Second Virginia Regiment, commanded by Major Snead. Took part in the engagements at Camden, South Carolina, Siege of Ninety-Six, and Eutaw Springs. Received pension while living in Pocahontas County, Virginia, in 1819.

WEEKLEY, THOMAS
Service—Maryland   Va. No. 12525   No. S. 6343

Born, Frederick County, Maryland, 1754; died in Tyler County, Virginia, November 27, 1843. Enlisted in Maryland, June 1, 1776, and served as a private twelve months under Captain Campbell in Maryland's Flying Camp contingent under Major Mantz, Colonels Griffin and Shryhock. Took part in the battle of York Island and White Plains. In January, 1777, substituted for John Thrasher under Captain Frazure, Major Sol Simpson, Colonel B. Johnson, and Lieutenant-Colonel Luckett. in 1778, served three months under Captain Sly and Colonel William Beattie. Received pension in Tyler County, Virginia, in 1833. Supporting data submitted by Sam Wheeler, Thomas Wells, and Duckett Wells.

WELLS, DUCKETT
Service—Maryland   Va. No. 12522   No. W. 4380

Born, Frederick County, Maryland, March 22, 1752; resided there at the beginning of the Revolution; moved to Greene County, Pennsylvania, in 1778-79; and to Ohio County, Virginia, now Tyler County, Virginia, in 1800. His records make interesting comment on the weather; Dry Year, 1806; Wet Year, 1807; Hail, August 20, 1807; Locust Year, 1812; Great Drought, 1819; Sleet, March, 1820.

Enlisted in Maryland in 1776 under Captain Frazure White in Maryland regiment commanded by Colonel Johnson. Received pension in Tyler County, in 1833, and died there, April 13, 1833. Supporting data filed by Thomas Jones, William Wells, and Thomas Weekley.

Married Sarah Lakin or Leakin, January 20, 1774, Frederick County, Maryland. She was born April 28, 1755, and after her husband's death likewise received a pension. She died, February 17, 1843, at the age of 88. Their children were as follows: Nancy, October 23, 1774; William, July 15, 1776; Abraham, July 20, 1778; Daniel, May 8, 1780; Thomas Duckett, April 11, 1782; Sarah, April 22, 1784; Deborah, July 23, 1786;

Richard Duckett, October 16, 1788; Otha, July 18, 1790; Mary, September 22, 1792; Elizabeth, May 29, 1797; Eli, December 8, 1799, died, June 23, 1826.

WELLS, JOHN
Service—Maryland   Va. No. 13154   No. S. 6351

Born in Queen Anne County, Maryland, in 1757, and there enlisted in August, 1776, under Captains Dean and Roberts as a private in the Flying Camp force under Colonel B. Richardson. In 1807, he removed to Monongalia County, Virginia, where he received a pension in 1833. Mention is made of Colonel Dudley Evans, who supported his claim, Colonel Samuel Hanway and Captain John Dent of Monongalia County.

WELCH (WELSH), JOHN
Service—Virginia   Va. No. 6807   No. S. 7847

Served six months as a private under Captain Figgan and Colonel Gibson. Received pension in Virginia in 1833, but it was suspended in 1835 and not reinstated.

WELSH, ISAAC
Service—Virginia   Va. No. 15315   No. S. 38461

Enlisted in Fauquier County, Virginia, January 27, 1776, and served three years as a private under Lieutenant Alexander White and Captain Thomas Blackwell in the Sixth and Tenth Virginia Regiments under Colonel Edward Stephens and Major-General Flebeeker. Took part in the battles of Brandywine, Germantown, Monmouth, and Stony Point, and received honorable discharge at Trenton, February, 1779.

Soldier received pension in Hampshire County, Virginia, in 1819, aged 65. He was later dropped from the rolls as having too much property, but the pension was restored. Soldier died, December 10, 1836. His widow was 58 years old in 1820, and their children as follows: Sylvester, 29; Dempsey, 23; James, 20; Lurena, 22; Mary, 17; Nancy, 15; Charity, 13. Supporting data was filed by James Parker, William Vance, and John Cundiff.

WEST, ALEXANDER
Service—Virginia   Va. No. 16231   No. W. 6450

Born in Accomac County, Virginia, August 11, 1760. The Harrison County, Virginia, courts record his marriage to Mary Straley, January 24, 1796, by the Rev. Joseph Cheworant, of the Methodist Episcopal Church.

Enlisted as a ranger and spy, May, 1777, in Monongalia County, now Lewis County, Virginia, and served twenty months as a private under Captains James Booth and George Jackson, and also served with General George Rogers Clark. Records of service were destroyed by Indians in 1787, when his father, his brother, and his brother's wife were killed and their home destroyed. Received pension in 1833, which was suspended two years later. His widow received a pension in 1851. Supporting data was filed by D. Stenger, Joseph Straley, Nicholas Alkire, Jacob Bush, and David Sleeth.

WEST, JAMES

On the list of Revolutionary soldiers, the name of James West is given as having had service in the Navy. In the Wetzel County, Virginia, Court, May, 1848, James G. West testified that on his way home from Richmond, Virginia, where he had just received land bounty warrant, he lost it and discovered his loss only when he arrived at his home. Connection between these cases has not been made.

WESTFALL, JOHN

Service—Virginia   Va. No. 12550   No. S. 41319

Enlisted in Hampshire County, Virginia, in 1780, for the duration of the war, and served under Captain Wallace in the Seventh Virginia Regiment, commanded by Major Riddle and General Green. Received pension in Harrison County, Virginia, in 1819. Soldier was born in 1753 and died, December 12, 1824. His wife gave her age as 54 in 1820.

West Virginians in the American Revolution

Assembled and Edited by ROSS B. JOHNSTON

The sources of this material are from the files of the Pension Office at Washington, from various county records, from notes of patriotic societies, principally the Daughters of the American Revolution, Sons of the American Revolution, Sons of the Revolution, and from a large miscellaneous group of published and private sources. Corrections and additions to this list will receive the careful attention of the editor.

WETZEL, JOHN (Captain)

Born in Switzerland about 1733. Emigrated to America with his parents at age of seven and settled in Rockingham County, Virginia. Here were born his famous sons: Martin, Lewis, Jacob, George, and John. About 1769, he moved to the West and settled on Wheeling Creek, nearly fourteen miles above its mouth. He removed his family to the Monongahela Valley, perhaps during the Indian outbreak of 1774, while he was acting as a scout for Lord Dunmore.

At the close of the French and Indian War, he returned to his home on Wheeling Creek, and for some time was captain of a ranger company. In 1777, his sons, Lewis and Jacob, were captured by Indians but escaped. Martin was taken in April, 1778, and remained with the Shawnees two years and four months. Captain Wetzel was killed in 1786 or 1787 while trapping on Captina Creek.

WETZEL, LEWIS

Born in August, 1763, on the South Branch of the Potomac, the son of Captain John Wetzel. He accompanied his father's family to the Ohio Valley, and in 1777 or 1778, was captured with his younger brother, Jacob, by Wyandot Indians and taken into Ohio. During the night they escaped and made their way back home, crossing the Ohio on bits of driftwood.

In 1782, his brother, George, was killed while hunting. The same summer, Lewis saw his companion, Joseph Mills, shot and killed, while he only escaped like fate by his fleetness of foot, and his ability to load his rifle while running. The next year, Lewis was with John Madison when the latter was waylaid and slain by Indians.

From the time of his captivity, Lewis was a bitter enemy of every Indian. Without warning, he killed an Indian near Fort Henry who was imitating a turkey's call. In 1784, he killed an Indian and rescued a captive girl. At the treaty of Fort McIntosh in 1785, Wetzel wounded a peaceful Indian, and after a similar deed at Marietta in 1789, was arrested, but no frontier jury would convict him. He continued to hunt Indians at every opportunity and remained a border hero for his daring, and his prowess with the rifle and his rare woodcraft. He visited New Orleans late in life and died in 1808 near Natchez.

WETZEL, MARTIN

Born, December, 1757, in Rockingham County, Virginia, the eldest son of Captain John Wetzel. In 1769, he came west with his father's family, and in 1774 served in Dunmore's War. In 1777, he was at the siege of Fort Henry at Wheeling, and aided in burying the dead after Captain Forman's defeat.

He was captured in April, 1778 or 1779, and adopted into the family of Chief Cornstalk. He escaped from a band of Indians on a pretext that he was going into Kentucky to steal horses. In 1781, he returned over the Wilderness Road to his home near Wheeling. There he married Mary Coffle. During the remainder of his life, he was almost constantly engaged in scouting and took part in twenty-two skirmishes, according to border annals, without receiving a wound.

WHALEY, JAMES

Before the Wood County, Virginia, court, July 6, 1818, James Whaley, aged 68, testified that he had enlisted in Virginia as a private in company commanded by Captain Bill of the Thirteenth Virginia Regiment, commanded by General G. Davison. He continued in service for three years until 1779 when he was discharged at Pittsburgh, Pennsylvania, but left his discharge in the hands of the paymaster. Took part in the battles of Germantown and Brandywine.

WHARTON, ZACHARIAH
Service—Virginia   Va. No. 16586   No. W. 6487

Born, Orange County, Virginia, March 27, 1760; died in Morgan County, Virginia, March 15, 1835. Married to Sarah Young at Orange Courthouse, January 8, 1788, by the Rev. Saunders of the Baptist Church. To them were born the following children: Nancy, Elizabeth, John, James, Samuel, Benjamin, Robert, Nelson, Joseph, William, and three others.

Wharton enlisted in Spottsylvania County, Virginia, in June, 1781, and served as a private under Captain Coleman, Major Hardman, Colonel Merriweather, and General Weeden. Took part in campaigns in Virginia. He attended his brother, Samuel, who was in a hospital receiving treatment for wounds.

Soldier received pension in Morgan County, Virginia, in 1833. His widow also sought pension and payment appears to have been made to the administrator of her estate after her death, February 14, 1848. Supporting data was filed in this case by John Young, brother of Sarah Wharton, Michael Widmyer, Michael Pentony, Thomas Ogden, and Jacob Betholl.

WHEELER, SAMUEL (Sergeant)
Service—Md. and Va.   Va. No. 12526   No. S. 6364

Born on the Eastern Shore near Cambridge, Maryland, March 4, 1760; moved to Louden County, Virginia, in 1780; then to Brooke County, Virginia, in 1792; then to Ohio County Virginia, in what is now Tyler County. Enlisted, June 1, 1776, and served as a private and sergeant under Captains Burgess and Trammel in the Flying Camp Regiment of the Maryland line, under Colonel Griffin and General Bell. Took part in the battles of York Island, and White Plains. Received pension in Tyler County, in 1834. Supporting data was filed by the Rev. John Ripley, Thomas Inghram, and Thomas Weekley.

WHITE, ALEXANDER (Captain)
Born in New Jersey in 1746; died in 1814. Enlisted in New Jersey and served from 1776 to 1779 as a captain in the Wagonmaster-General's Department of the Quartermaster General in the regiment commanded by Colonel Jacob West. Married Mary Clifford in New Jersey, January 25, 1768, and to them were born the following children: William, John, Henry, James, George, Nancy, Prudence, Margaret, Joseph, and Robert. The family resided in Hardy County, Virginia, for a time and then moved to near Jackson's Mill, Lewis County, Virginia, Samuel A., a brother of Alexander, moved to Ohio in 1797 at the time Alexander moved to Lewis County.

WHITE, JAMES
Service—Virginia   Va. No. 6832   No. S. 38468
Enlisted in Fauquier County, Virginia, in 1775, and served five years as a private in the company of Captain John Ashby in the Third Virginia Regiment, commanded by Colonels Mercer and Weedon. Took part in the battles of Brandywine, Germantown, Monmouth, and the siege and capture of Yorktown.
Pension was granted in Hampshire County, Virginia, in 1819, at which time the soldier was 72 years old. He died, July 22, 1832. His wife's name was Elizabeth. In 1820, the family included Nancy, aged 28, Margaret, 22, Mary, 20, and Parthena, 16.

WHITE, JOHN (Lieutenant)
John and William White were among the early settlers of Randolph County, Virginia, their settlement dating from 1772 to 1774. They were active in early Indian hostilities. John, who held the rank of lieutenant, was killed by Indians from ambush in 1778.

WHITE, JOSEPH
Service—Virginia   Va. No. 11317   No. S. 38469
Enlisted in Maryland in 1780, and was discharged after three years as a private under Captains Revelie, and Thomas Price in the Maryland Line under Colonel Adams and General Green. Participated in the siege and capture of Yorktown. Granted pension in Harrison County, in 1819, at which time he was 64 years old, and his wife, 55. Joseph White, a nephew, was 19, and Katy Lee, (no relation) aged 10.

WHITE, ROBERT (Captain)
Enlisted as a private in Captain Hugh Stephenson's company in 1775. Made second lieutenant of the Twelfth Virginia, commanded by Colonel

James Wood, March 1, 1777; was badly wounded at Short Hills, June 26, 1777; promoted to first lieutenant, September 1, 1777; regiment was designated the Eighth Virginia, September 14, 1778. He was again wounded in 1778; was promoted captain in 1781, and served until the close of the war.

He married Arabella Baker, daughter of John Baker and Judith Howard Wood Baker, of Shepherdstown. From 1793 to 1826 he was known as a distinguished jurist. (Check Lieutenant Robert White.)

WHITE, ROBERT (Lieutenant)

Born, 1759; died, 1831. Enlisted as a private in Captain Hugh Stephenson's Company, June 20, 1775, and marched from Morgan's Spring, Berkeley County, Virginia, to Boston, Massachusetts, to join General Washington's army. Made an ensign the following summer and later on October 4, 1777, fought as a lieutenant in the Twelfth Virginia Regiment, under Major William Darke of Berkeley County. Was wounded in 1778, taken prisoner the same year, and exchanged. Later engaged in drilling troops near Philadelphia. Owing to bodily infirmities retired from military service and was pensioned by Act of Congress of May 15, 1828. (Check Captain Robert White.)

WHITE, SAMUEL
Service—Virginia   Va. No. 16448   No. S. 7871

Born at Havre de Grace, Maryland, December 5, 1756. Resided in Chester County, Pennsylvania, in 1777, and there enlisted under Captain I. Taylor in the Virginia Line under Major Bell and Colonel Gibbons. Served as a private at Brandywine, Germantown, and Trenton. Received pension in Ohio County, Virginia, in 1833. Supporting data filed by John Church and John Parriott. Soldier died, July 4, 1835.

WHITE, WILLIAM (Captain)

First mentioned in Kercheval's *History of the Valley of Virginia* when in 1734 he left Maryland and settled in Shenandoah County. As early as 1768, he was known as "Captain" White, and was led into Upshur County, by Samuel Pringle, where he became a guardian of the Buckhannon colony. With Colonels William Lowther, Jesse Hughes, and John Cutright, he was active at Bush's Fort on the Buckhannon River, West's Fort on Hacker's Creek, and Nutter's Fort at Clarksburg. He was captured by the Indians in 1778 but escaped. On March 15, 1782, he was killed by an Indian just across the river from the fort at Buckhannon and is buried in Heavner Cemetery, Upshur County. He is said to have been killed by a Delaware chief whose son White had killed some years before.

WHITEMAN (WHITMAN), HENRY
Service—Penn. and Va.   Va. No. 6604   No. S. 7881

Born at Philadelphia, Pennsylvania, 1759, and there enlisted in the Revolutionary Army; later he resided in Augusta, Pendleton, and Randolph Counties, Virginia.

First service was in the Pennsylvania militia and later in the Virginia militia. Mentions Captains Lester, Ewell, Anderson, and Colonels Smith, Boyd, Dabney, and Generals Ervin, Bull, and Cowatts. Was hired by Colonel Andrew Boyd as a substitute for Philip Heckart, a Quaker of Augusta County, in 1780. Served three months in the company of Captain Thomas Hicklin in 1781. Later substituted for Henry Swadley of Rockingham County, and was under Captain Houston in Colonel Harrison's Regiment at Jamestown; and in the fall of 1781, substituted for George Puffinburg of Augusta County. Was present at Cornwallis' surrender, and fought at Brandywine and Germantown.

Received pension in Randolph County, Virginia, in 1833. Supporting data submitted by Thomas O. Williams, Ely Butcher, and George Keller.

WHITEMAN, MATTHEW
Service—Virginia   Va. No. 16901   No. S. 18654

Born in Augusta County, Virginia, in 1759 or 1762; died in Randolph County, Virginia, June 28, 1836. Enlisted in Rockbridge County, Virginia, in the spring of 1778, and served upwards of six months under Captains Gray and Cunningham, under Major Murray, and General Washington. Soldier received pension in Randolph County, Virginia, in 1833. His claim was supported by the Rev. Thomas Collett, John Stalnaker, Simeon Harris, John Bradshaw, and Adam See.

WHITING, FRANCIS

Before the Berkeley County, Virginia, court, February 20, 1788, Francis Whiting, a wounded officer, presented proof that he had been on the list of pensions and that his wounds still justify his retention on the pension roll.

WHITT (WHITE), ROBERT
Service—Virginia   Va. No. 23157   No. S. 7880

Born in Amelia County, Virginia, 1755, and there enlisted as a private under Captain J. Shelby in the regiment of Colonel Montgomery under General Clark. He was granted a pension while living in Logan County, Virginia, in 1833.

WICOFF, JOACHIM
Service—New Jersey   Va. No. 2873   No. W. 4401

Born, November 18, 1749; died, May 18, 1841. Enlisted at White House, Huntington County, New Jersey, and served as a private eighteen months under Captain Stillwell in the New Jersey militia between 1776 and 1779. In the spring of 1780, removed from Huntington to Somerset County, New Jersey. Married to Hannah Yerks, February 26, 1772, at Six Mile Run, New Brunswick, New Jersey. She was born March 15, 1755: died October 23, 1844.

Soldier received pension in Brooke County, Virginia, in 1832. His widow was granted pension in 1854 which was sent to Thomas Bambrick, Fairview, Hancock County, Virginia. Supporting data was submitted by Thomas Peterson, John Pittenger, Thomas Bambuck (Bambrick), William Flanagan, and Hugh Pugh. Nancy Moore was mentioned as a relative.

WEST VIRGINIANS IN THE REVOLUTION 305

WIDMYER, MICHAEL
Service—Virginia   Va. No. 12350   No. S. 11857

Born in Hartford County, Maryland, May 23, 1761. Enlisted in Berkeley County, Virginia, in September, 1780, and served six months as a private under Captains Ambrose and Anderson, under Majors Stubblefield, Swerington, Lucas and Glenn in the Virginia Line under General Stephens. Took part in the campaigns in Virginia and in the Carolinas. Received pension in Morgan County, Virginia, in 1833. Supporting data submitted by the Rev. M. Rizer, and Mathias Ambrose, a son of Captain Ambrose.

WILLIAMS, DANIEL

Born in 1753 in Wales, emigrated to America before the Revolution, and settled on the western Virginia frontier. There he enlisted in the Revolutionary Army. In 1777, he served in Captain West's company of riflemen; in 1778, he was in the Eleventh and Fifteenth Virginia regiments, and later served in the Seventh Virginia Regiment and in Clark's Expedition. His wife, Mary Ann Bolton (Aldridge) was born in London. She had one child, Chloe, who died in 1841, leaving no children.

WILLIAMS, GABRIEL (Sergeant)
Service—Maryland   Va. No. 5220   No. W. 9896

Served in 1776 in the Flying Camp. Enlisted February 6, 1780, in the Seventh Maryland Regiment, under Captain Mason, Colonel Gumley, and General Smallwood and served three years as a sergeant. Took part in the battle of Long Island, Monmouth, Camden, Eutaw Springs and Cowpens. Sold his pay and discharge to Major Bailey for fifteen pounds in gold.

Married June 22, 1784 by the Rev. M. Powell to Margaret (Williams). Their children were: Clark, December 3, 1784; Abigail, December 10, 1786; Elizabeth, September 9, 1788; Ruth, December 15, 1790; John, December 6, 1792; Gabriel, December 21, 1795; Mark, January 18, 1797; Syntha, March 9, 1799; Margaret, November 10, 1801; Otha, November 4, 1803; and an unnamed child, July 8, 1808. Soldier received pension in Monongalia County, Virginia, 1819, aged 63; died November 20, 1827. His widow, aged 59 in 1820, received pension in 1840 or 1846, either in Monongalia County, Virginia, or in Indiana.

WILLIAMS, HENRY
Service—Continental N. J.   Va. No. 12783   No. W. 18353

Born, Essex County, New Jersey, February 14, 1762. Enlisted in February 1776, under Captains Britton and Holmes in the Second Jersey Regiment, commanded by Colonels Spencer and Summins and General Conway. Took part in the battles of Flatbush, Brandywine, Germantown, and Monmouth. His original discharge, signed by General Washington, was given to Dr. Isaac Smith, Inspector of Invalids, at Trenton, New Jersey, in 1785, who issued following statement: "I have inspected Henry Williams, who has service in the Second Jersey Regiment, as a private, and was disabled by a wound. He is allowed the sum of five dollars per month from May 3, 1785."

Soldier was married, December 26, 1786, to Sarah Fairchild. She was born March 17, 1768; died, October 15, 1839. Their children were as follows: Samuel, December 14, 1787; Joseph, February 2, 1790; Lewis, July 26, 1792; Sarah (Culp), September 14, 1796; Mary (Bennett), September 14, 1796; Foster, December 14, 1800; Phoebe (Summers), June 25, 1803; Rhoda, (Kioner), February 11, 1807.

Soldier received increase in invalid's pension in 1831 in Monongalia County, Virginia, and in 1833. His widow was also allowed pension which was paid to her heirs who were represented by Lewis Williams, a son.

WILLIAMS, ISAAC

Isaac Williams was born at Chester, Pennsylvania in 1737. At eighteen, he enlisted in the Braddock campaign as a ranger and spy. In 1758 and to 1767 he hunted on the Missouri River. In 1768, he led his parents from Winchester to Buffalo Creek, now Brooke County, near West Liberty. He accompanied the Zanes in explorations around Wheeling, Zanesville, and elsewhere. In 1774, he accompanied Lord Dunmore on the expedition against the Shawnees and was present at the treaty negotiations in Ohio. He is accepted as having had Revolutionary War service also. In 1787, he settled at Williamstown, Wood County, on land preempted in 1770 by Joseph Tomlinson and his children, Joseph, Samuel, and Rebecca, who had married Williams. Williams died, September 25, 1820.

WILLIAMS, JEREMIAH
Service—Pennsylvania   Va. No. 12525   No. W. 2710 and B. L. Wt. 29020

Born in Cumberland County, Pennsylvania, February 14, 1761; died February 6, 1845 in Tyler, now Marshall County, Virginia, and is buried in the Williams Cemetery near New Martinsville. He was the son of Lewis Williams and his mother was probably Eleanor Shelby.

He enlisted in June, 1778, under Captain John McFarland in the Pennsylvania Line under Major Springer, Colonel John Evans, and General McIntosh and took a leading part in the defense of the western settlements. He took part in General McIntosh's expedition against the Indians and helped build Fort McIntosh. He also served under General George Rogers Clark. In March, 1780 or 1781, he served as an Indian spy under Lieutenant James Marshall. In the spring of 1782, he served as a private under Captain John Huston. In later years, he served under David Shepherd, lieutenant of Ohio County, as a spy between Fort Henry, Wheeling, and Fort Harmar, Marietta, Ohio.

He was one of the first permanent settlers in what is now Wetzel County, West Virginia, in 1791 purchasing the farm of Adam Rowe, who was driven out by Indians. On June 7, 1798, he was married to Mary Ewart by the Rev. Joseph Doddridge. Soldier received pension in 1844. His widow received pension and also received bounty land warrant for 160 acres. Supporting data is filed in this case by the Rev. J. Ripley; William Wells; Ann Ankrom (nee Ewart), sister to Mary Williams; Francis Collins; Sampson Thistle. Their children were Lewis, Frances, Mary Jeremiah, Jr., Elizabeth, Francis, Eleanor, Harrison, Shelby, Ann, Evan, May, and Rachel.

WILLIAMS, ROBERT
Service—Virginia   Va. No. 1040   No. S. 41355

Enlisted in Hampshire County, Virginia, in the spring of 1779, and served as a private under Captain Andrew Wallace in the Third Virginia Regiment. Continental Establishment, under Colonels Hite and Blueford. Was wounded in the battle of Blueford's Defeat. Received pension while living in Hampshire County, Virginia, in 1818.

West Virginians in the American Revolution

Assembled and Edited by ROSS B. JOHNSTON

The sources of this material are from the files of the Pension Office at Washington, from various county records, from notes of patriotic societies, principally the Daughters of the American Revolution, Sons of the American Revolution, Sons of the Revolution, and from a large miscellaneous group of published and private sources. Corrections and additions to this list will receive the careful attention of the editor.

WILLIS, ROBERT CARTER (Colonel)
In 1777, was lieutenant colonel of Berkeley County militia. Was a large land owner in Berkeley County.

WILLIS, WILLIAM
Service—Mass., Sea Service-Pa.   Va. No. 12746   No. S. 7900
Enlisted in New Bedford, Bristol County, Massachusetts, July 28, 1775, and served until 1778, as a private under Captains Earl, Crandon, and Soper in sea service and under Colonel Marshall.

Was living in Monroe County, Virginia, in 1833, where pension was granted, which was increased later by special acts of Congress. Interesting descriptions in the files in this case, including passports and testimony of Thomas de Grasaf, governor of Corsica. Soldier was born in 1760 and died June 28, 1853. Supporting data was filed by Elnathan West, Stephen West, E. D. Banks, secretary of Massachusetts, and Captain Francis Young.

WILSON, ASA
Service—New Jersey   Va., and Pa. 29638   No. S. 17203
Enlisted in New Jersey as a fifer in May, 1776, when he was only fourteen or fifteen years old, in the company of Captain Webster in the Flying Camp Regiment under Colonel Turman. Was engaged in the campaigns on Long Island. Was taken prisoner and held for six years. Soldier was born near New Brunswick, New Jersey, and resided there at time of enlistment; resided in Green County, Pennsylvania, in 1834; and in Preston County, Virginia, in 1840. Pension was granted in Pennsylvania, which was later transferred to Virginia. Supporting data was filed by Elijah Hardesty.

WILSON, BENJAMIN (Colonel)
Born, November 30, 1747, Shenandoah County, Virginia; moved to Hardy County, Virginia, when young; died December 2, 1827, in Harrison County, Virginia of Scottish descent. Was a lieutenant under Lord Dunmore, a member of his staff, in the expedition against the western

Indians in 1774. Was present at the treaty with the Indians at Camp Charlotte on the Scioto River, following the defeat of Cornstalk at Point Pleasant, October 10, 1774. Said to have heard the speech of Chief Logan.

Settled in the Tygart Valley and became a captain of militia, active in Indian affairs, and was in charge of several frontier blockhouses. Took a leading part in recruiting men for the Revolutionary Army and ranked as a colonel. Was clerk of the first Harrison County court, served as a delegate to the Virginia Assembly, and was a member of the Constitutional Convention of the United States in 1788. Remained clerk of Harrison County for thirty years—until 1814.

Married Ann Ruddell of Hampshire County, September 4, 1770; and after her death, Phoebe Davisson of Harrison County, December 15, 1795. There were thirteen children by the first wife and seventeen by the second. Those named in his will were: William B.; Stephen R.; Benjamin; John; Cornelius R.; Thomas W.; Josiah; Mary; Sarah; Ann; Edith; Elizabeth; Deborah; Archibald B.; Philip D.; Noah L.; Margaret; Phoebe; Martha; Juliann; Harriett; David B.; and James Pindall.

WILSON, ELI B.
Service—Virginia　　　　　Va. No. 3973　　　　　No. S. 6401

Born in Augusta, now Pendleton County, Virginia, in 1755; died, November 11, 1845. Enlisted in 1776 as a private under Captains J. McCoy, Hicklin, and Lieutenant Quinn in the Virginia line under Colonels Vance and Mathews. Served at Colonel Donley's Fort on guard duty and at Colonel Vance's Fort on Back Creek, Virginia chiefly engaged in expeditions against the Indians and on outpost duty.

Married, October 29, 1788. Received pension in 1833. His widow, Hannah, does not seem to have ever made formal application for pension but requested arrears of her husband's pension. Supporting data is filed by James Hicklin and William McCoy, Sr.

WILSON, GEORGE
Service—N. C. and Va.　　　　Va. No. 16246　　　　　No. S. 6391

Born in Anson County, North Carolina, in 1760. There enlisted in October, 1779, and served as a private under Captains Legett, Blinker, and Knowles in the Third North Carolina Regiment. Took part in the battle of Cowpens. In the battle of Camden in August, 1780, was taken prisoner. He served as a militiaman in 1779 and as an Indian spy in 1782 and 1783, probably under Captain Benjamin Wilson in the Tygart Valley.

Soldier received pension in Lewis County, Virginia, in 1833, which was later suspended. Supporting data was filed by Nicholas Gibson and Francis Riffles.

WILSON, JAMES
Service—Virginia　　　　　Va. No. 6803　　　　　No. S. 41352

Enlisted in Berkeley County, Virginia, in August, 1776, as a private under Captain Samuel Gabriel Long in the Eleventh Virginia Regiment,

Continental Establishment, commanded by Colonel Morgan. Took part in the battle at Freeman's Farm. Continued in service after October 1779, and was discharged at Kaikiak, New York.

Received pension in Berkeley County, Virginia, in 1819. Soldier was aged 70 in 1820, and his wife, Elizabeth, between 60 and 70. A granddaughter, Elizabeth, is mentioned. Supporting data is submitted by George and Abraham Robinson.

WILSON, JOHN
Service—Pennsylvania   Va. No. 26429   No. R. 19029

Enlisted in Lancaster County, Pennsylvania, and served twenty months as a private under Captain Dehuff in the Thirteenth Pennsylvania Regiment, commanded by Colonels Walter Stewart and Atlee. Was engaged in the campaigns on Long Island. Served from 1776 to February 17, 1778. His discharge, signed by Colonel Stewart, indicates that he was wounded on Long Island. Soldier applied for pension in Preston County, Virginia, but died, August 12, 1832, aged 88, before receipt of his pension certificate.

He was married to Elizabeth Wilds, February 3, 1828, at Bruceton Mills, Preston County, by the Rev. George Hagans. His widow married John Biggs and died September 27, 1864. She received arrears due up to death of her husband, but there is no evidence that she received a pension.

WILSON, JOHN (Lieutenant)

Ensign in the Fourth Virginia, December 28, 1776; second lieutenant, March 12, 1777; first lieutenant, April 1, 1778. Killed at Eutaw Springs, September 8, 1781. (Heitman) Letter from Adjutant General's Office, August 29, 1935, says: "John Wilson, ensign in Captain Isaac Beall's company, also designated Captain John Stith's company, Fourth Virginia Regiment, also designated Third and Fourth Virginia Regiment, commanded by Colonel Thomas Elliott, Colonel Robert Lawson, Major Isaac Beall, and Colonel John Neville. Commissioned ensign, September 28, 1776; second lieutenant, July 17 or August 12, 1777; transferred to Captain George Wall's company, same regiment. Commissioned lieutenant, April 1, 1778; transferred May, 1779, to Captain John Steed's company, same regiment. Name last appears on muster roll, November, 1779, dated at camp near Morristown, December 9, 1779."

WILSON, JOHN (Lieutenant)
Service—Virginia   Va. No. 1912   No. W. 6533

The record of Lieutenant John Wilson of Mason County, differs widely from that of Heitman's Historical Register of Officers of the Continental Army, which shows that Lieutenant Wilson was killed at Eutaw Springs in 1781, but the pension application of his widow is so complete that it is given in detail.

Soldier said to have been at Yorktown at the siege and capture of Cornwallis' army. Married Anna B. Tidwell, May 21, 1785. She applied for pension in 1839 as the widow of Lieutenant John Wilson who had

WEST VIRGINIANS IN THE REVOLUTION 311

established nineteen months' service in the Revolution, and certificate was issued in 1845. Soldier died, August 31, 1823, and will is probated in Mason County, West Virginia. Their children were: Spencer, February 25, 1786; John, Jr., June 10, 1789; Gustavus, September 20, 1791; Elizabeth, September 22, 1793; Hanna, April 25, 1796; James Henry, February 10, 1799. Land bounty to the extent of 2,664 acres is divided among the heirs. Supporting data is filed by Richard Dozier and Penelope Laine.

WILSON, JOSEPH
Service—Virginia   Va. No. 17116   No. S. 38475
Enlisted in Rockingham County, Virginia, in June, 1780, and served under Captain Wallace in Virginia Line regiment, commanded by Colonel Campbell. Took part in the battle of Guilford Courthouse. Applied for pension in Lewis County, Virginia, which was granted in 1820, for eighteen months' service as a private. Wife was aged 40 in 1825 and their children as follows: Daulphin, 12; William, 9; John, 7; David, 3; and Hanable Thomas, an infant.

WILSON, ROBERT
Service—Virginia   Va. No. 13184   No. S. 6433
Enlisted in Botetourt County, Virginia, in November, 1780, and served until April, 1781, under Lieutenant Grimes and Captain Robertson, Major Campbell, and General Morgan. Took part in skirmishes along the Yadkin River. Applied for pension in Monroe County, Virginia, in 1833, which was granted, but later suspended, as showing insufficient service.

WILSON, WILLIAM
Service—Virginia   Va. No. 16629   No. S. 7907
Born in Montgomery County, Maryland, August 24, 1760; moved to Monongalia County, Virginia, at age of 13; there enlisted in Virginia line commands and served upwards of seven months. Among his officers were Captain George Jackson, Zackquill Morgan, Evans Morgan, John Evans, Dudley Evans, Samuel Hanway, Richard Hatte, Robert Ferrel, Matthew Gray, John Brady, Lieutenant Caleb Patterson, and Generals Clark and Brodhead. Soldier received pension at Morgantown, Monongalia County, Virginia, in 1833.

WINCKLEBACK, HENRY (alias SQUIRES, HENRY)
Service—Virginia   Va. No. 12353   No. S. 6389
Before the Monroe County, Virginia, court, June 7, 1832, Henry Winckleback or Winckleblack (known in the Revolutionary Army as Henry Squires), aged 77, testified that he entered the military service as a substitute in 1778 or 1779 and served nine months at Fort St. Lawrence under Captain Uriah Springer whose company was in the regiment of Colonel John Gibson; served at Fort Pitt under Captain Springer, Fort Henry at Wheeling under Captain Beck, and at Fort Pitt again under Captain Clark, and then to Fort McIntosh. While at the latter station, he was out with a party under Lieutenant Harris

which badly defeated a band of forty Indians. While at Fort Pitt, went out with Gibson and Crawford on their Indian campaign, defeated the Indians, killed ten, and dispersed the remainder.

He was born in Lancaster County, Pennsylvania, September 15, 1756. Before the Revolution, he lived in Greenbrier, later Monroe County, and was employed by James Byrnside to carry supplies to Fort St. Lawrence. It was on such an expedition that he enlisted. Pension was granted in Monroe County, Virginia, in 1832.

WINGROVE, JOHN
Service—Virginia   Va. No. 12968   No. S. 11856

Born in England about 1749; emigrated to America and settled in Louden County, Virginia, in 1773. Served in the Revolution under Lieutenants Butcher and Turrent, Captain Noland, and Colonel Alexander in General Wayne's Brigade. Was wounded in the knee in the battle of Jamestown. Was granted pension in Lewis County, Virginia, in 1833, which was later suspended. Although his wound and other facts proved that he had seen service, there is nothing to show that he was restored to the pension rolls.

WISEMAN, CALEB
Service—Penn.   Va. No. 20188   No. S. 41353

Enlisted in Lancaster County, Pennsylvania, in the spring of 1776 and served two years under Captain Dehoof in Pennsylvania Line regiment, Continental Establishment, under Colonel Atlee. Took part in the campaigns about Philadelphia and on Long Island. Soldier received pension in Wood County, Virginia, in 1830, at which time he was 74 years old. Supporting data was filed by John Wilson and Lewis Ott.

WISEMAN, JOSEPH
Service—N.C. and Pa.   Va. No. 2973   No. S. 11741

Born in Berks County, Pennsylvania, March 29, 1759; died December 27, 1836. His mother, Elizabeth Davis Wiseman, daughter of Samuel Davis, was born August 26, 1738, and died July 19, 1807. The soldier married Elizabeth Bateman before 1783. She was born July 10, 1762, the daughter of Henry and Elizabeth Bateman, and died September 3, 1842. Their children were: James, November 30, 1783; Isaac, November 24, 1785; Elizabeth, July 10, 1788; Samuel, July 18, 1792; Owen, July 21, 1794; Rachel, April 25, 1796; Sarah, January 15, 1799; Edith, October 11, 1800; Margaret, April 20, 1803; Joseph, June 4, 1805; Thomas, December 23, 1808.

Soldier enlisted in Berks County, Pennsylvania, and in Rowan County, N.C., and served as a private under Captain Perry Mitchell, Captain Thomas Berry, Major John Jones, Colonel Lock, and Colonel Mark Bird. Resided in Pennsylvania, North Carolina, Maryland, and in Rockingham County, Virginia, from which he moved to Greenbrier, now Monroe County, Virginia, in 1794. Took part in military activities from 1776 to 1779 in Pennsylvania, New Jersey, Maryland, the Carolinas. Received pension in Monroe County, in 1832. Supporting data filed by the Rev. James Christy, Henry Alexander, and Charles Keenan.

WITHERS, ALEXANDER SCOTT

In Old Hill Cemetery, just south of Main Avenue, Weston, Lewis County, and on U. S. Highway 19, is the grave of Alexander Scott Withers, a soldier of the American Revolution. He was a young lawyer who was brought from Alexandria, Virginia, to write a history, and out of it grew *Border Warfare,* the best known story of frontier life and Indian warfare.

WOLFORD, JOHN

Service—New Jersey   Va. No. 16722   No. S. 11898

Born in Montgomery County, Pennsylvania, in 1754; enlisted in the Revolutionary Army from Essex County, New Jersey; later resided in Hampshire and Randolph Counties, Virginia. Served six months under Captains Pipenger and Potty in New Jersey militia commanded by Colonel West, and was largely engaged on guard duty. Received pension in Randolph County, in 1833. Supporting data was filed by Sol Wyatt and D. Holden.

WOODELL (WADDLE or WOODELL), JOSEPH (Lieutenant)

Service—Virginia   Va. No. 23389   No. S. 11883

Enlisted in Augusta County, Virginia, and served fifteen months as a private and three months as a lieutenant. Woodell entered service in 1774 under Captain George Moffett at Clover Lick to guard frontiers against the Indians; was again drafted in 1777 under the same commander; accompanied the expedition of Colonel J. Dickinson to Point Pleasant against the Indians. In 1778, served under Captain Cooper, in Colonel Neville's regiment of General Woodford's brigade in Pennsylvania, New York, and New Jersey, and was discharged at Middlebrook, February, 1779. Was again drafted in 1781 and served as first lieutenant under Captain John Given (or Dickey), under Colonel William Bowyer, General Campbell, and General Lafayette, in the Virginia campaigns about Williamsburg. Soldier received pension in Pocahontas County, in 1834, aged 82, and died in 1835. Supporting data was filed by the Rev. John S. Blaine, Benjamin Tallman, James McCue, and William Slavens.

WOODFORD, WILLIAM

Served in the Eighth Virginia; drew pay from April to August, 1777, in Captain Richard Campbell's company, commanded by Colonel Abram Bowman; and from April to July, 1778, in the company of Captain Kirkpatrick in the Fourth Virginia, under Colonel James Wood.

Soldier married Hannah Moss. Their son, John Howe Woodford, born, 1796, and died, 1880, married Nancy Minear, the daughter of Adam Minear, the pioneer. The family believes that he was the son of Brigadier General William Woodford of Alexandria, Virginia. General Woodford married the daughter of Sir William Howe, had a son, named William, and it is noted that the name "Howe" is carried in the name of this soldier's son.

West Virginians in the American Revolution
(Woodfin to Young)

Assembled and Edited by ROSS B. JOHNSTON

The sources of this material are from the files of the Pension Office at Washington, from various county records, from notes of patriotic societies, principally the Daughters of the American Revolution, Sons of the American Revolution, Sons of the Revolution, and from a large miscellaneous group of published and private sources. Corrections and additions to this list will receive the careful attention of the editor.

WOODFIN, JOHN

The grave of John Woodfin, a soldier in the Revolutionary War, who died in 1774, is on the site of Kern's Fort, Arch Street, Morgantown, Monongalia County, West Virginia.

WOODROE (WOODROW), SIMEON

Service—Penn.   No. 6034   No. W. 3910

Born in West Nottingham, Chester County, Pennsylvania, in 1756; died in 1841 in Brooke County, Virginia. Enlisted in July, 1776, under Captain Kirk in Pennsylvania troops commanded by Colonel Bell and Colonel Comeroys, and served as private eight months.

Married, December 15, 1785, to Elizabeth Wright by Philip Scott, Esq., of Chester County, Pennsylvania. Soldier received pension in 1833 in Brooke County. There his widow applied for pension in 1843, and died either in the same year, or in 1844. Nancy Moore, a daughter, applied for pension unpaid to her father and mother. Supporting data is filed by the Rev. John Hale, Thomas Hambrick, William Melvin, William Langblitt, John and Jean Witherspoon.

WOODY, MARTIN

Service—Virginia   Va. No. 16721   No. W. 3912

Born in Goochland County, Virginia, April 30, 1758. Enlisted in Bedford County, Virginia, in 1777, or 1778, and served seven months as private under Captains Dawson and Trigg in Virginia and Maryland troops under Colonel Tucker, Colonel Merryweather, and General Muhlenberg. Applied for pension, which was granted in 1833, in Franklin County, Virginia. Lived in western Virginia, definite place of residence uncertain.

WOHLFARTH, JOHAN MARTIN
Was a member of Captain Stephenson's company in 1775 and 1776 when it was at Roxbury Camp and Staten Island.

WORK, DAVID
Service—Penn.   Va. No. 23049   No. S. 7961

Born in County Derry, Ireland, in 1743; emigrated to America, and enlisted in the Revolutionary Army, July 1, 1776, from Chambersburg, Franklin County, Pennsylvania. Served under Captain Conrad Snyder in Pennsylvania troops commanded by Colonel McGaw. Mentions Lieutenants Crawford and Young, Ensign Edward Crawford, Major Gabbrath, and Generals Ewing and Mercer. Received pension in Brooke County, Virginia, in 1833. Supporting data filed by the Rev. John Hale and Thomas Hambrick.

WORMSLEY, WILLIAM
The executive department of the State of Virginia certified, May 1, 1832, that William Wormsley was entitled to land bounty as private in the State line during the Revolution, and Warrant 7159 was issued in his behalf. The case was presented by Jonathan Wormsley of Lewis County, Virginia.

WRIGHT, JOHN
Service—Continental Va.   Va. No. 9849   No.S.41384 and B.L.Wt.1499

Enlisted in Botetourt County, Virginia, as a private of Armand's Legion, Virginia Line, and served under Captain Wallace, Twelfth Virginia Regiment, under Colonels Wood, Henry Lee, and Armand. Received pension in Botetourt County, Virginia, lived in Rockbridge County, in 1828, and in Allegheny County, in 1829. Received 100 acres as land bounty. Whether he ever lived in Monroe County is not determined.

WRIGHT, JOHN
Service—Virginia   Va. No. 4310   No. S. 6449

Born in Fairfax County, Virginia, in 1748; resided in Bedford County, at outbreak of the Revolution, and there enlisted in 1778. Served nine months as a private under Captains Moses and Green under Colonel Calloway of the Virginia Line, in Lawson's Brigade. Took part in campaigns against the Tories in the Carolinas. Received pension in Franklin County, in 1833. Believed to have resided in Monroe County, Virginia.

WYMER, HENRY
Service—Penn.   Va. No. 13157   No. S. 41388

Enlisted in Pennsylvania under Captains Craig, Christie and Reese, and served in the Third Pennsylvania Regiment, Continental Establishment, commanded by Generals Conway and Wayne. His discharge, signed by General Anthony Wayne, January 15, 1781, was presented to the court with his application for pension. He was later transferred to a command under Captain Marcus, a French officer. Soldier received pension in Pendleton County, in 1819.

YATES, WILLIAM P.

The grave of William P. Yates, supposed to have been a Revolutionary War soldier who died at an advanced age, is on the Burdette Farm, Ona, Cabell County, West Virginia, on the Prichard School Road.

YEASLEY, MICHAEL

Born in Pennsylvania, May 12, 1730; later became a citizen of Virginia, and died at Shepherdstown, Jefferson County, Virginia, September 1, 1808. He enlisted, August 9, 1776, and served as a private in Captain Benjamin Weiser's company of the German Battalion, Continental Troops; was discharged March 7, 1778. Married Catherine Welsh Nofesinger Entler, in Jefferson County, May 6, 1752. Their children were: Elizabeth, Catherine, Barbara, Polly, Eva, Sarah, and Magdaline.

YOAKUM (YOAKHUM, YOAHUM, YOCUM, AND YOKUM), JACOB

Service—Virginia   Va. No. 16925   No. R. 11939

Born, Hardy County, Virginia, December, 1753; died, May, 1838. The marriage of Yoakum and Mary Magdalene Welton, October 8, 1782, is recorded in Hampshire County, West Virginia. Enlisted in Hardy County, and served nine months as a private under Lieutenants M. and S. Hornback, Captains Stump and Harness in Virginia regiments, commanded by Major Garrett Vanmeter, and Colonel Benjamin Harrison, under Generals McIntosh and Muhlenberg.

Soldier received pension in Hardy County, in 1833. His widow received pension, November, 1840, aged 88, while living in Bourbon County, Kentucky, and died in 1841. Supporting data was filed by William Heath and Anthony Baker.

YOHO, HENRY

Service—Virginia   Va. No. 12222   No. S. 7996

Enlisted in Green County, Pennsylvania, in 1776, and served until 1778 as a private under Lieutenants Swingler and Cross, Captains Minor and Wetzel, Colonel John Evans, Colonel Laughlin and General Clark, while guarding the western frontier settlements. "No man, except possibly Lewis Wetzel, encountered so many hardships and risks of life," said Thomas P. Ray of Morgantown, West Virginia, September 25, 1832, in seeking adjustment of this man's case. Yoho received pension while living in Monongalia County, Virginia, in 1833. His claim was supported by Peter Haut and Stephen Gapen.

YOUNG, CHARLES

Service—Continental Pa.   No. 30587   No. S. 19896

Born in Germany, April, 1757. Emigrated to America, and settled in Philadelphia, Pennsylvania. Was bound out to serve seven years to pay his passage. Enlisted at Philadelphia, and after the war came with his parents to Berkeley County, Virginia, where his parents died.

Young enlisted in 1777 as a drummer, under Captain Pat Duffy in the Pennsylvania Artillery, Continental Establishment, under Colonel Thomas Proctor, but when a cannoneer was killed during the battle of Brandywine, he was then assigned as a gunner and matross. Was discharged at Trenton, New Jersey, by Brigadier General Anthony Wayne. Fought at Brandywine, Germantown, White Marsh, Barnhill Church, North River, and the Wilderness. Went with General Sullivan against the Indians. Also served in a rowing galley on the Delaware and took part in many skirmishes of less important character.

Soldier received pension certificate in Berkeley County, Virginia, in 1834. Supporting data was submitted by John Strother and John Shober.

YOUNG, CHRISLEY

Lived near Shepherdstown during the Revolution, and served as a private with Revolutionary forces in the South.

YOUNG, JOHN

Service—Virginia   Va. No. 16726   No. W. 7377 and B. L. Wt. 39499

Born in Lancaster County, Pennsylvania, August, 1760; moved to Augusta County, Virginia, in 1764; and to Kanawha County, Virginia, in March, 1783; died, May 16, 1833, in Kanawha County, Virginia. One record in his pension filed shows marriage to Keziah Townsend, January or February, 1796, in Montgomery County, Virginia, but court records show their marriage, May 20, 1789, as of Kanawha County.

Soldier served periods of enlistment from 1775 to 1778, and again in 1784 and 1793, a total of fourteen months. Mentions Captain All or Ault, Captain William Clendennin, Colonel George Clendennin, Colonel Benjamin Harrison, Lieutenant Jacob Pense, William Morris and others. Soldier applied for pension in 1833 in Kanawha County. His widow received pension in 1855 and also land bounty warrant for 160 acres. Supporting data was filed by Fleming Cobb, Andrew Donnally, Archibald Price, Nancy Slack, John B. and John D. Young, and the Rev. Nathan Calhoun.

YOUNG, JOHN

Born in Madison County, Virginia, February 18, 1761; settled on Anthony Creek, Greenbrier County, Virginia, about 1803 or 1804; died July 6, 1806. Supposed to have served in the Revolutionary Army. Married twice. His children were James, Elizabeth, Jane, John, Samuel, and William.

West Virginians in the American Revolution

Assembled and Edited by ROSS B. JOHNSTON

The sources of this material are from the files of the Pension Office at Washington from various county records, from notes of patriotic societies, principally the Daughters of the American Revolution, Sons of the American Revolution, Sons of the Revolution, and from a large miscellaneous group of published and private sources. Corrections and additions to this list will receive the careful attention of the editor.

In this issue Mr. Johnston completes the alphabetical check list of Revolutionary soldiers who at one time or other lived in West Virginia. The list, of more than thirteen hundred sketches, began with the October issue, 1939.

This issue contains a complete index of the check list.

YOUNG, JOHN

Service—Virginia   Va. No. 12150   No. W. 1975 and B. L. Wt. 92042

Born in Culpeper County, Virginia, in 1761; resided in Orange County, Virginia, at the outbreak of the Revolution; died in Pocahontas County, Virginia, July 5, 1843. Married Margaret Rogers, September 2, 1805, at the home of John McNeel, Little Levels, Bath County, now Pocahontas County, West Virginia, with the Rev. John Pinnal as minister. Young enlisted in Orange County, in 1779, and served as a private with Captain Ambrose Maddison in regiment commanded by Major John Roberts and Lieutenant Colonel Francis Taylor. Captain Garland was another officer in this command. He was later stationed at Albermarle Barracks as guard to prisoners, and took them across the Blue Ridge and down the Shenandoah Valley to Winchester. He was then discharged. He had previously served two "towers" in the militia, the first under Captain John Scott and the second under Captain Coursey.

Soldier applied for pension which was granted in Pocahontas County in 1833. Widow likewise received pension; she died December 11, 1862, aged 77. Bounty land certificates for 160 acres were issued also. Final adjustment seems to have been arranged by Colonel Samuel Young of pension arrearages in this case. Supporting data was filed by Isaac and Martha Adkinson, David Burgess, and David Kinnison.

ZANE, ANDREW

One of the brothers who were the founders and first settlers of Wheeling. He narrowly escaped capture while out scouting during the Indian raids of 1777. He was badly hurt when he jumped over a 70-foot cliff to escape pursuing Indians, but eventually made his way to safety at Fort Shepherd at what is now Elm Grove, Ohio County. He was later killed by Indians while on another scouting expedition.

ZANE, EBENEZER (COLONEL)

Born in 1747 and died in 1812. As colonel of Virginia militia participated in the defense of Fort Henry at Wheeling, September 1, 1777, against a large force of Indians and others which was the first serious attempt of the British and their savage allies against the western border settlements after the outbreak of the Revolution. He was in command at Fort Henry, September 11, 1782, when a company of British regulars, under Captain Pratt, and a large body of Indians, laid siege to the fort. He was a member of the Virginia Convention of 1788 which adopted the Constitution of the United States. He made the first settlement at Wheeling in 1769.

ZANE, ISAAC

Born on the South Branch of the Potomac about 1754, the youngest of the brothers who afterwards founded Wheeling. When nine years of age, Isaac was captured by the Indians and grew up among them, marrying into the Wyandot, and living like the red men. He often warned the border settlers of their dangers from Indian raids, and acted as guide and interpreter. About 1795, he bought a tract of 1800 acres in Logan County, Ohio, settled near Zanesfield, and died there in 1816.

ZANE, JONATHAN

Born in 1749 and died in 1824. Was a soldier and guide in General Daniel Broadhead's expedition up the Allegheny River against the Munsie and Seneca Indians in 1779, in which campaign he was wounded. He was a guide in the campaign of Colonel William Crawford to the Upper Sandusky, Ohio, in 1782. Participated in the defense of Fort Henry, Wheeling, both on September 1, 1777, and on September 11, 1782.

ZANE, SILAS (CAPTAIN)

One of the first settlers at Wheeling. He served in the Revolution as a first lieutenant of the Thirteenth or Fifteenth Virginia Regiment, from December 28, 1776, until he was made a captain in February, 1777. He served as captain until February 12, 1778, but was not present in the Ohio River settlements during the Indian attacks of 1777 as he was on service in the eastern states.

He returned to the Ohio, however, before the close of the Revolution and was at Fort Henry during the siege of 1782. At the close of the Revolution, he went with George Green to the Indian country with goods for a trader from Maryland. On their return, about 1785, the two traders were waylaid and killed on the Scioto. Silas Zane left an infant son bearing his name.

ZANE, WILLIAM

Probably the father of the celebrated Zane brothers, first settlers of Wheeling. William was a descendant of Robert Zane, who emigrated to America in 1763 and settled at Newton, New Jersey. It is supposed that the latter's first wife, grandmother of William, was of Indian origin. William was born in 1712.

His ancestors had been Quaker, but William left them, and removed to the South Branch of the Potomac, possibly within Berkeley County, Virginia. His son, Isaac, was captured there, and in the Draper Manuscripts is found a letter in which he mentions his own captivity. This letter was dated at Fort Henry, Wheeling, where he was living in 1777.

www.ingramcontent.com/pod-product-compliance
Lightning Source LLC
Chambersburg PA
CBHW020056020526
44112CB00031B/193